Der Säulenheilige: Früher haben sich immer [illegible]

haben einen Spass an den [illegible]

die Säulenheiligen kümmern!

Die junge Frau: Hier, lieber Alter! (Reicht [illegible]

(Nach einem Monat:) → | . . . . .

Die junge Frau & der junge Herr: Säulenheiliger, lieber [illegible]

(Nach einem [illegible]

Die junge Frau: Säulenheiliger, lieber Säulenheiliger [illegible]

ich komme noch mal vorbei!

(Nach acht [illegible]

Die junge Frau: Hier, lieber Alter! Jetzt mich [illegible]

~~[illegible]~~, aber ich ~~[illegible]~~ [illegible]

Der Säulenheilige: Genug, genug! Ich [illegible]

[illegible] [illegible]!

(Nach [illegible]

Die junge Frau: Ob ich morgen wieder [illegible]

[illegible] einmal in ~~[illegible]~~ [illegible] [illegible]

([illegible], [illegible] [illegible]

Facsimile of Musil's draft for the play fragment, *The Stylite*,
from the *Klagenfurter Ausgabe*

Theater Symptoms:

PLAYS & WRITINGS ON DRAMA

Robert Musil

Translated with an introduction by

GENESE GRILL

Contra Mundum Press   New York · London · Melbourne

Translation of *Theater Symptoms*
© 2020 Genese Grill.

All texts translated from Robert Musil, *Klagenfurter Ausgabe* (Klagenfurt: Robert-Musil-Institut, 2009) except for *The Double-I*, which comes from Robert Musil, *Tagebücher II* (Reinbeck bei Hamburg: Rowohlt, 1983), and *Tempora Maier*, which comes from *Tagebücher I* (Reinbeck bei Hamburg: Rowohlt, 1983).

First Contra Mundum Press edition 2020.

All Rights Reserved under International *&* Pan-American Copyright Conventions.
No part of this book may be reproduced in any form or by any electronic means, including information storage and retrieval systems, without permission in writing from the publisher, except by a reviewer who may quote brief passages in a review.

Library of Congress Cataloguing-in-Publication Data

Musil, Robert, 1880–1942
[Symptomen-Theater I *&* II; Der 'Untergang' des Theaters; Noch Einmal Theaterkrisis und Genesung; selections from Theater-kritiken; Dramen; selections from Dramatische Fragmente. English.]

Theater Symptoms / Robert Musil; translated from the original German by Genese Grill

—1ˢᵗ Contra Mundum Press Edition
622 pp., 5×8 in.

ISBN 9781940625416

    I. Musil, Robert
    II. Title.
    III. Grill, Genese.
    IV. Translator, Preface, Introduction.

2020942309

CONTRA MUNDUM PRESS gratefully acknowledges the financial support received for this translation from the AUSTRIAN MINISTRY OF EDUCATION, ARTS, *&* CULTURE.

TABLE OF CONTENTS

- o **Preface**
- viii **Introduction**

THEATER SYMPTOMS

- 2 Theater Symptoms I
- 20 Theater Symptoms II
- 35 Once Again Theater Crisis and Renewal
- 45 The "Decline" of the Theater (Theater Symptoms III)

SELECTED REVIEWS

- 76 Viennese Theater Events
- 80 Correspondences?
- 86 Moscow Art Theater
- 94 An Evening at the Theater
- 98 *The Death of Danton*
- 107 *Arms and the Man*
- 111 Moissi Epilogue
- 115 Moissi Guest Appearance
- 123 Austrian Supplement
- 127 Currency Speculation: or from Molière to Sternheim to Kaiser
- 131 Afterword to Moscow Art Theater
- 138 Jessner and *Brand*
- 146 Viennese Theater I

- 150   *Goat Song* by Franz Werfel
- 158   *Le Paquebot Tenacity*
- 162   Viennese Theater II
- 164   Viennese Theater III
- 168   *The Light*
- 175   The Reinhardt Guest Appearance in Vienna
- 178   The Vilna Troupe in Vienna
- 181   The Russian Cabaret
- 185   Yvette Guilbert
- 189   Ernst Toller's *Lame Man*
- 195   *Doctor Knock* by Jules Romains
- 200   Viennese Theater IV
- 204   Arthur Schnitzler's *Comedy of Seduction*
- 211   *Saint Joan*
- 216   *The Utopians* Scandal

PLAYS

- 226   *The Utopians*
- 412   *Vinzenz and the Mistress of Important Men*

SELECTED PLAY FRAGMENTS

- 494   *Prelude to The Zodiac*
- 511   *The Double I*
- 526   *The Stylite*
- 528   *Tempora Maier*

550   Index

PREFACE

ONE OF THE MOST REFRESHING THINGS about this collection of Musil's plays and writings on drama is that it brings us closer to Musil, the man, living in his particular milieu and time. When he throws his hat into the ring of the Viennese theater world with his two extraordinary plays, *The Utopians* and *Vinzenz and the Mistress of Important Men*, he is participating in the melee in a way that seems almost uncharacteristic for our picture of the aloof, self-exiled, and eventually politically-exiled and serious author of *The Man Without Qualities*. When we read his witty and sardonic reviews of contemporary theater productions, we feel his excitement, his irritation, his frustration, and his competitive edge. We share his despair over the scarcity of meaningful and transformative art and are surprised by his utopian visions for a way forward.

The plays and critical writings in this volume were written between 1921 and 1929. Musil, whom we think of as quintessentially Viennese, was born in Klagenfurt, in what was then Austro-Hungary; he had grown up in Brno (now a city in the Czech Republic) and had studied (philosophy, psychology, mathematics, and physics) in Berlin. Although the Austrian empire had been dismantled at the end of World War I, creating separate

Bohemian states, their inter-relationships were still strong, as evidenced by the fact that Musil wrote theater reviews about Viennese productions (sometimes starring or directed by Hungarians or Czechs) for two newspapers in Prague.

Musil's successful 1906 debut, *The Confusions of Young Törleß*, had been followed by his more experimental collection, *Unions* (1911). In the same year, he married Martha Marcovaldi, a widow and divorcée and the mother of two children, beginning a relationship that would be a prime support and inspiration for his literary work for three decades. In 1914, before participating in World War I as a soldier and also editor of the army newspaper, Musil had been a reviewer for *Der Neue Rundschau* in Berlin, introducing the reading public to Franz Kafka and Robert Walser. Ideas for his novel, *The Man Without Qualities*, were already proliferating in notes and drafts and related fiction projects at the same time as he was writing *The Utopians* (from 1908–1921). Even after the publication of the first part of the novel in 1930, Musil considered the play his major work. In 1924, he published his collection of stories, *Three Women*.

But in 1921 he is 41 years old. He is a critic of the feuilleton writers — those witty, casual, elegant scribblers who fill the pages of the Viennese newspapers. And he is one of them himself. The first volume of his great novel would not appear for 9 more years. He is struggling to make a living, to prove himself as a writer, to find his place among or above the throng; he is both inside and outside his era.

In these pages, we see the innovations of the time through his own eyes, as if we were seeing them ourselves: Stanislavski's Moscow Art Theater, the Yiddish troupes, the Jessner staircase and other Expressionist innovations in stage design. We experience the stirring atmosphere of Weimar Berlin and the burgeoning Viennese café society, with its dilletantes, playwrights, positivists, sexologists, anthropologists, musicologists, con-artists, and nymphomaniacs. Its bohemians and its Bohemians. We sense the fallout of Russian revolutionary activity — exiled aristocracy and the foreshadowing of bloody, internecine party struggles; hear the grumbling agitation of the workers' movements and the rattling of militaristic sabers. We even glimpse the "young people of Christian-Aryan worldview" who break up a controversial production of Schnitzler's *La Ronde*, with "Nibelungen-brass-knuckle-rings in their pockets."[1]

We sense the still-echoing shocks of World War I — palpable in the wounded bodies of soldiers, in the shattered idealism of a generation. We take the temperature of the encroachment of advertising, the cinema, and the commodification of the "culture industry." Psychoanalysis, Relativity, the "New Woman," jazz music, "Primitivism," Cubism, Dada, and Cabaret are all here — some

---

1. *Theater Symptoms*, 83.

strands initiated before the war and some after — seen through Musil's exceptionally clear eyes.

And since this is a moment *in between*, when many of the personages, cultural artifacts, and ideas of the old world still linger, as relics and ghosts of the pre-war period, we see Musil looking backward too, trying to understand what happened to art, to education, to society, and why; trying to salvage what is vital and to re-evaluate those values that no longer seem meaningful.

This is a pregnant moment. About to give birth to horrors. All the people who animate the reviews will have their lives turned upside down in what seems like the blink of an eye. Many, who in Musil's reviews exhibit extraordinary verve and spirit, will perish in concentration camps in the next decade. Others, like Musil himself, will go into exile and find their creative and personal lives in shambles. Others still will collaborate with the Nazi party or with the totalitarian Communist state.

Musil is advocating in these pages for an intellectual and emotional aliveness, a freedom and openness — in artistic and ethical experimentation — which the coming era would brutally crush. Perhaps we are at the juncture of a similar moment even now. Hopefully not. May his words, in any case, written with such urgency and passion on the eve of catastrophe, remind us of the important role of art as irreducible æsthetic and ethical experience.

INTRODUCTION

THE PLANETS SPIN, the elements unite according to laws that are themselves connected to other laws; but in every law that we know, something exists, just as it does in ourselves — a law that is precisely just the way it is, some kind of constant, a fact, an irrational, once-in-a-world, reckless self-persisting something, and the irrationality of mimicry and of the world touch each other through this pantomime; adventure and *ignorabimus* meet in the moment of a felicitous gesture. (*Theater Symptoms II*, 31)

A CRITIC AS ARTIST and artist as critic, Robert Musil maintained that "there could be no such thing as significant criticism that would not be literature, and, aside from pure lyric poetry, no significant literature that would not be criticism."[1] In his 1929 response to attacks on a pirated and recklessly adapted premiere of his play, *The Utopians*, he addressed his own critics, simultaneously leveling an attack on the state of contemporary literary criticism.

---

1. Robert Musil, *Gesammelte Werke II*, ed. by Adolf Frisé, Vol. II: *Prosa und Stücke. Kleine Prosa und Aphorismen. Autobiographisches. Essays und Reden. Kritik* (Reinbeck bei Hamburg: Rowohlt, 1978) 1188. Hereafter *GW II*.

"I have been called an unraveller," he wrote, "but I struggle to achieve synthesis."[2] Elsewhere, he lamented "the breathtaking non-intellectual spirit that fills not only the atmosphere of the theater, but our literature as a whole."[3]

The years 1921 to 1924 constituted the height of Musil's participation in the world of theater as both critic and dramatist. He had plans to collect his writings on theater into a book, which he considered calling *Pathology of the Theater* or *Theater from the Outside*. In one notebook entry, he writes that "A pathologist would be able to diagnose a great deal about our time through the theater."[4] Marie-Louise Roth, whom we thank for reviving an interest in Musil's theater writings with her 1965 collection of the original German theater reviews, notes that criticism was central to Musil's character, and that, despite some admired models such as Alfred Kerr, Franz Blei, and Alfred Polgar, even as a critic he considered himself an outsider.[5] Comparing himself to Thomas Mann, he notes that he is Mann's extreme opposite in his critique against "almost everything," concluding:

2. *Theater Symptoms*, 222.
3. *Ibid.*, 69.
4. Robert Musil, *Tagebücher I* [Diaries], ed. by Adolf Frisé (Reinbeck bei Hamburg: Rowohlt, 1978) 631. Hereafter *TB I* (or *TB II* for Vol. 2, containing the notes, appendix, and index).
5. See Marie-Louise Roth, "Musil als Kritiker," in *Gedanken und Dichtung: Essays zu Robert Musil* (Saarbrücken: Saarbrücker Druckerei und Verlag, 1987) 59–74. Hereafter *Kritiker*.

"partially that signifies my untimeliness; partially a kind of naughtiness! It suggests: autism, negativity, fanaticism and its variants…."[6] In addition to these tendencies, the reader should further be warned that Musil is likely to critique writers, such as Karl Kraus and Thomas Mann — who had achieved the sort of popular success that eluded him — more harshly than seems justified.

But, as Oliver Pfohlmann writes, "Neither before Musil nor after him was there an author who demanded more than he from literary criticism as an institution of the literary world. Parallel to his praxis as reviewer, he developed his critical conception against the backdrop of a utopian understanding of literature, wherein literature was considered responsible for the ethical progression of humanity."[7]

Thus, even though Musil may have taken up his various assignments as a theater reviewer out of naughtiness or negativity, or for practical reasons, i.e., to earn much-needed cash, his commitment to the questions involved, including work on the plays and play fragments he wrote during the same period, was profound. In his "Author's Afterword" to the forthcoming volume 10 of his Robert Musil *Gesamtausgabe*, Walter Fanta directs

6. *GW II*, 569.
7. See Oliver Pfohlmann, "Literatur- und Theaterkritik," in *Robert Musil Handbuch*, ed. by Birgit Nübel and Norbert Christian Wolf (Berlin/Boston: De Gruyter, 2016) 414–429 (quote from p. 415). Hereafter *Handbuch*.

us to a contemporary assessment of Musil as critic in a theater magazine, under the headline, *Viennese Critics. The Younger Generation*. After noting that Musil's work as literary writer, mathematician, and engineer schooled him for criticism, the 1925 article concludes: "He is easily the most objective of the local writers and he writes a German which is no fluff and all core [...]. He always has something to say. Musil is not a born critic; he has a calling. That he currently has no steady position as critic in Vienna is lamentable, but is really more evidence of the exceptional quality of this brain."[8]

In the 1920s, Musil was on the staff of the *Prager Presse* for one year as theater and art reviewer, and worked for other papers in Czechoslovakia, as well as in Austria and Germany. He reported almost exclusively on Viennese theater, which included guest appearances from Berlin (Vienna's rival in the German-speaking theater world), from Eastern Europe (sometimes via troupes who had emigrated to the United States), and translations from European and British productions.

Pfohlmann tells us that Musil wrote 56 reviews for the *Prager Presse* between March 1921 and August 1922 (sometimes up to three a week). He wrote for the *Deutsche*

---

8. See Walter Fanta's "Author's Afterword" to the forthcoming Vol. 10 of the *Robert Musil Gesamtausgabe* (Salzburg: Jung und Jung, 2020), not paginated at the time of this printing. Hereafter *Gesamtausgabe*.

Zeitung Bohemia (also in Prague) from September to December 1922 and began to write more for Viennese papers beginning in 1923. Between November 1923 and January 1924, Musil wrote five theater reviews for the Viennese *Abend*; but the fact that reviews had to be written at night, immediately after the performances, was excessively tiring. Another short stint was at the Viennese paper, *Der Morgen*, where he was laid off due to complaints about the severity of his reviews; and he published his more extensive theater-critical essays, the series referred to as *Theater Symptoms*, in his friend Ephraim Frisch's *Der Neue Merkur*.[9]

As Roth notes, Musil's reviews, "are written in a lively, scintillating, sarcastic, intellectually-immaculate language, in a precise, bellicose style.... [R]eminiscent of [Alfred] Kerr, this language shatters in terse formulations the apparent shimmering of non-art, eviscerates in exacting analysis the scaffolding of simulated values, to clear a place for true art."[10] The writing style, although elegant, light, graceful, and often extremely humorous, may occasionally seem dense in its English form, since even in German Musil's writing — made up of complex intellectual puzzles, puns, subtle irony, and sheer brilliance — sometimes seems to burst the bounds of what language can do. His tendency to remain objective,

9. Pfohlmann, *Handbuch*, 418.
10. Roth, *Kritiker*, 70–71.

to resist closure where one might expect a conclusion, can sometimes leave readers (including seasoned Musil scholars) in the dark about his judgments. Musil is capable of holding multiple aspects of any question up in the air at once, even within one sentence. German helps a writer to do this sort of suspended idea-juggling; English not so much. Thus, I have had to break up many very long sentences into smaller ones. Some readers might wish that I had broken up even more — but to have done so more than I have deemed necessary would have sacrificed the sense of energetic urgency, the frustration, the ecstasy that erupts from the critical texts.

Of his many reviews, I have chosen less than half, according to the following criteria: the reviews that best articulate Musil's theoretical poetics; those that treat important milestones, actors, and directors of his time; and those that have the most significant connections to his other more well-known work. To the series *Theater Symptoms* I, II, and *The "Decline" of the Theater* (which Musil himself referred to as *Theater Symptoms* III), I have appended the related essay, *Once Again Theater Crisis and Renewal*. A planned fourth installment of the *Theater Symptoms*, providing practical recommendations, was never written.

According to his own avowal, Musil was spurred on to the writing of his two finished plays, *The Utopians* and *Vinzenz and the Mistress of Important Men*, by his negative assessment of the contemporary offerings.

The Utopians (1921) — which took him approximately ten years to write and which he considered one of his major works — was written, he explained, to "finally, for once, bring some spirit into the controversies surrounding the theater."[11] It was awarded the prestigious Kleist Prize almost immediately, but was only premiered in 1929, against Musil's wishes, under the directorship of Jo Lherman — a con-man who could almost have come right out of one of Musil's own plays. Of the second, *Vinzenz and the Mistress of Important Men* (1923) — a farce that was performed to enthusiastic audiences even before its publication in book form — he reported, "Because, for once, it just all finally got to be too stupid, I have written a play in 14 days."[12] Both were written in tandem with his close analysis of contemporary theater and as partial answers to the problems this analysis posed.

When our self-proclaimed *monsieur le vivesecteur* begins, in the theoretical essays and reviews, to take apart the nature of theater and to provisionally put it back together in a more utopian mode in his own plays, he does so via his own characteristic methodology, his signature combination of "precision and soul." Intellect was required, but also an acknowledgment of the realm of the

11. See Robert Musil, *Briefe* [Letters] *I 1901–1942*, two volumes, ed. by Adolf Frisé (Reinbeck bei Hamburg: Rowohlt, 1981) 202. Hereafter *B I* (or *B II*, for the 2nd volume, containing notes, appendix, and index).

12. *TB II*, 839.

ignorabimus, i.e. that which cannot be known. The theater, made of words, gestures, dramatic structures, ideas, allusions, and something "once-in-a-world, reckless," made up of thought, but also of the "irrationality of mimicry and of the world" itself, is the miraculous juncture of an intellectual "adventure and *ignorabimus*" — the enervating and irreducible boundary between knowledge and mystery.

But, Musil laments, this ravishing boundary experience is rarely attained in the works of his contemporaries. Mostly, the contemporary theatergoer experiences a mundane muddle of commercial entertainment: cheap thrills, banal scenarios, and hackneyed tricks anticipated by the audience beforehand. With the exception of Stanislavski's Moscow Art Theater, the Yiddish theater, and some other rare individual directors (Reinhardt, Jessner), actors (Moissi, Lina Lossen), and authors (Büchner, Shaw), the avant-garde does not usually satisfy him either. Despite his sometimes sweeping criticisms, in his investigation of the problems and possibilities he is nevertheless always able and even eager to find something good in even bad works, exceptions to the rule, surprising exceptions to generally dreadful productions. Some people, though, are practically above criticism.

He calls his experience watching the Moscow Art Theater one of "the strongest shocks and the deepest moments of happiness, which art, which life, is capable of providing" and "the perfection of theater," despite the fact that he "did not understand a word." Yet, in general, language — the poetic force and lyricism of a play's *words* — is of vital importance to his assessment of its worth. We see him calling attention to the centrality of words, over and over, as in his review of Büchner's *The Death of Danton*, wherein we read:

> Büchner's words are like an outbreak of fever, conjuring up colorful, beautiful, irregular spots that merge into each other now and then to form strange figments. In the beginning was the Word: that goes for the whole epoch. And before the Word, was Shakespeare.

Of Shakespeare's language, in the same review, Musil raves:

> [O]ne mustn't think now about *the thing*, but must enter in somewhere through *a word*; then one must let go of the word, the way one lets one's hand drag a pencil after it; yet in a peculiar way — and then Shakespeare's word-world appears, and along with the word, the world.[13]

This celebration of the word is a polemical stance against the increasingly visual and non-verbal techniques of dramatic Expressionism.[14] Although in his early years

13. *Theater Symptoms*, 99.
14. See Walter H. Sokel, who writes, "The projection of abstract ideas and psychic situations into symbolic images and happenings

(in 1914) as a literary reviewer for *Der Neue Rundschau*, he was supportive and enthusiastic about young writers, by the 1920s Expressionism is faulted with having no ideas, Impressionism with elevating emotion over thought, and political art with presenting ideas that are too ideologically one-sided. He wants ideas, but not just any ideas. He wants *spirit* — denoted by that untranslatable German term, *Geist*, which, along with *spirit*, can also mean *mind, intellectuality, cultural life* — but decidedly not the kind of pseudo-spirit to be found in mindless emotion, simulated passion, or empty-headed "idea-howling." The right conditions for a "spiritual" art (with a different accent than Kandinsky's) up to Musil's standard seem to include an almost miraculous synthesis of at least two complementary but opposing forces — a coincidence of opposites within the creator's own personality. In a review of Franz Werfel's play *Goat Song*, Musil elucidates these two requirements of creation. One is "vision," the other is a personal force, a will:

↵ is one of the basic features of Expressionist drama. Consequently, language loses the pre-eminent rank it held in traditional drama [... and] an immediate appeal is made to the audience's visual sense rather than to its conceptual thought. The memory of empirical reality, with its demands for causal logic and plausibility, is suspended." *Anthology of German Expressionist Drama: A Prelude to the Absurd* (New York: Cornell University Press, 1963) xviii. Hereafter *Anthology*.

> One element of writing is the vision, the sight, the waking dream, the passivity, being overwhelmed with lights, shadows, the shapes that life takes; the writer lays beneath the tree of life and suddenly he sees the existence of something that is not himself. [...] Because being able to immerse oneself in the not-self is the one half of writing; the other half is the opposite: to be able to immerse oneself in one's self — to be able to will, to impart meaning. The writer sees the existence of his Not-Self before him, in fragments, sounds, or echoes: what does he do with them? He begins to interpret them, to connect, to amplify.

The ability of the artist to see what is *not self* is reminiscent of Yeats' idea of the "anti-self"; but in opposition to an anti-formalist tendency in contemporary works, Musil seems to stress the need for the second quality — an artistic hand and eye, a guiding, distinguishing force. While a mediocre writer may have one of these capabilities (Werfel, in Musil's estimation, had only the former), only the great writer has both. Even if a writer had these and other requisite qualities, society and its institutions, due to their inherent resistance to the new or to "the independent" (as Musil calls it in his wonderful review of Shaw's *Saint Joan*), would inhibit creative development at every turn. To foster the personal, social, spiritual conditions wherein such miraculous synthesis might be possible would, Musil acknowledges, be a utopian feat.

But that is also, he asserts, no reason to avoid the attempt. Despite his well-known skepticism and his ironic ridicule of simple-minded schemes for socio-political or æsthetic reform, despite his devastating subsequent experiences in the 30s and 40s — caught between the *dystopias* of German Fascism on the one hand and Soviet Totalitarianism on the other — Musil never fully abandoned the preoccupation with utopian thought which runs through his theoretical and creative writing of the 1920s.

Thus, after much deliberation, I have chosen to translate the title of his first play (*Die Schwärmer*) as *The Utopians*. Early alternative titles considered by Musil include: *The Weak Strong Ones*, *The Friends*, *The Hypocrite*, *Loneliness*, *The Last Way*, and *The Anarchists*, all stressing different possible aspects of the play's significance.[15] An early translation by Andrea Simon chose the somewhat negatively-weighted title, *The Enthusiasts*, and other American Musil scholars, like Burton Pike, who wrote in 1961 that the play was possibly Musil's finest work, called it *The Visionaries*.[16] Christian Rogowski shares the entry

---

15. See Rogowski, *Dramaturgy*, 73, and Burton Pike, who noted the considered title, *The Anarchists*, in his *Robert Musil: An Introduction to his Work* (Ithaca: Cornell University Press, 1961) 96. Hereafter *Introduction*.

16. Burton Pike wrote that, "After the dust has settled around *The Man Without Qualities*, Musil's only serious play, *The Visionaries*, may one day be considered his finest work. It contains in distilled form, and with the greater strength of a distillation, most

for the German term, *Schwärmer*, from Grimm's dictionary, revealing that it comes from the verb "to swarm," is etymologically related to the erratic, irregular movement of bees, was an "emblem of deviant, erratic behavior," and "became a term used for religious dissenters in Luther's time." Georg Christian Lichtenberg, who is quoted in Grimm, may have been one influence on Musil's thinking: "There are *Schwärmer* without capabilities, and then they are really dangerous people." There are certainly echoes of this aphorism throughout the play, but what Rogowski misses is that these echoes include an exploration of what happens when *Schwärmer* do have "capabilities." Rogowski concludes that Musil uses the term throughout his writings in a "clearly derogatory fashion" and that it "simultaneously evokes rebellious non-conformism, ecstatic irrationalism, and erotic infatuation."[17] Yet, while the words "Schwärmer" and "utopian," like the word "mystic," can be used as terms of abuse, for Musil they both had other, very important, positive connotations

↵ of the important elements of the later novel as well as many of its subordinate concerns." *Introduction*, 71.

17. See Rogowski, *Dramaturgy*, 96. Rogowski also argues for a more negative interpretation of Musil's theatrical conception, stressing Musil's doubts about the viability of theater as a social medium in a fractured, heterogenous society. While his assessments are eminently reasonable — Musil did have such very justifiable doubts and they are an important aspect of his criticism — I maintain that he never abandoned his own species of utopian thinking.

as well. Norbert Christian Wolf, noting that "*Schwärmer*" are "devotees of an 'other,' a 'second' reality, formulated pointedly: mystics," summarizes a general critical assessment that this association is not to be taken negatively, "but primarily indicates a principled openness."[18] And, of course, the term *Schwärmer* can be traced back to Nietzsche's Dionysian revelers, whose ecstatic, disindividuated swarm-like dancing is a vital counterpoint to Apollonian form and reason. Those who like to think of their Nietzsche and Musil as rationalists may be comforted: the precise recommended measure of Dionysian to Apollonian is as indeterminate in Nietzsche as is the optimal proportion of rationality to mysticism in Musil's conception.

But we do know that late drafts for *The Man Without Qualities* are rife with a variety of utopias, which the author *in extremis* considered as possible endings for the unfinished (unfinishable) novel. None was more favored than his "utopia of the next step," a mode of life and thought prefigured in *The Utopians* and in *Vinzenz and the Mistress of Important Men*, whereby an action may only be judged by what it brings in its wake, *ad infinitum*. This utopian state constitutes a radical resistance to closure and final conclusion, manifest in a life of creative aliveness and presence that is represented by another of

---

18. See Norbert Christian Wolf, "Die Schwärmer (1921)," in *Handbuch*, 157–190, this quote from 161.

Musil's favored utopias: the "Utopia of the Motivated Life." As Albrecht Schöne pointed out in his brilliant essay on the use of the subjunctive in Musil's novel, this mode of thought (like the subjunctive case that expresses it) is anathema to rigid (and declarative) systems. The utopian thinker, the possibilitarian, would, thus, be the first person to be expelled from any established utopia.[19] An ossified utopia, in other words, is already dystopian. The utopia of the next step is not a place or a fixed system, but a resistance to deadly habit and dull conformity, a creative openness, the only state wherein art can be created and experienced — in effect, a utopia without delusive ideals. As Thomas in *The Utopians* says to an outraged Miss Mertens: "Ideals are dead idealism."[20] And Musil's serious engagement with utopian thought, from these early plays and critical writings through the last decade of his life and the last notes for his life's work, are also a measure of the central social role he assigned to art.

In his critical writings, the pathologist of culture gathers symptoms of a pandemic of cultural decline by dissecting the diseased body of the Viennese theater world of the 1920s, in order to come to an understanding, not only of the living organism of all of art, but also of the social and political conditions most conducive to its

---

19. See Albrecht Schöne, "Über den Gebrauch des Konjunktivs bei Robert Musil," in *Euphorion* 55 (1968) 196–220.
20. *Theater Symptoms*, 235.

thriving. Theater, because of its closer involvement with commerce and its more traditional social aspect, was more immediately touched by the general trend toward commodification and the vitiating effects of the evolving "culture industry" than the novel or the world of poetry, and thus provided a preview, so to speak, of the degradations to come. Monika Meister calls attention to Musil's precedence as an early diagnostician of this "culture industry, as later defined by the Frankfurt School." Before Adorno and Horkheimer, Musil analyzed "the forfeiture of valid ethical norms that might direct society within the context of a contemporary vacuum of values and the lack of a reciprocal æsthetic relationship between form and content."[21]

Additionally, before Bertolt Brecht[22] or Antonin Artaud, whose dramatic theories of disruption are more well-known, Musil saw in theater a conducive experimental realm for transformative social experience. Musil anticipated Brecht's *Verfremdungseffekt* (alienation effect) by employing radical techniques of surprise and disruption in his plays, breaking the illusion of the theater frame;

21. See Monika Meister, "Drama, Theater," in *Handbuch*, 657–662, these quotes, respectively, from 661 and 657–8.
22. Musil only mentions Brecht in passing, and usually derogatorily, in his notebooks and letters. Although he would have had the opportunity to see some of his early productions, there are no reviews or mentions of specific works.

but his vision of drama was different from Brecht's more didactically political "epic theater."[23] Brecht, like Musil, eventually came to criticize what they both deemed the anti-intellectual, primarily emotional appeal of Expressionism, but his favored intellectuality was of another sort.[24] The important difference is that while they both worked to destabilize the status quo, exposing the absurdities of modern life and the hypocrisies of capitalism and commodification, Brecht did so in service to a new ideology (Marxism), while Musil tore away the veil of assurance without providing a new solidity to replace the old discredited one. Musil's destabilized world is a fact of life; Brecht's is a stage on the way to a new artificial order. Musil divests us of our false security and leaves us with a radical existential uncertainty. Theater, instead of a temporary propaganda tool for destabilizing the state, becomes an eternally regenerative ritual space wherein the social body and each ultimately isolated individual must continually encounter a terrifying, but liberating, openness.

Theater also made manifest Musil's interest in the æsthetic tension between internality and externality, or thought and action. Consider the chapter in the novel entitled, "A Chapter That May Be Skipped By Anyone Not Particularly Impressed by Thinking as an Occupation," wherein we are suddenly introduced to the problem

23. See Rogowski, *Dramaturgy*, 194.
24. See Sokel, *Anthology*, x and xxi.

of narrating a man thinking. As should be clear by now: Musil's theoretical writings and reviews of plays are not only relevant to drama, but to all of art. Moreover, in Musil's definition of art, they are therefore relevant to all of life, including politics, physics, psychology, biology, history, sociology, mathematics, religion, economics, and love. In fact, one of his most pointed critiques of the theater of his day is that its theoreticians and practitioners treat it as something separated from a multifaceted — and irreducibly *real* — life and thought. It is at once too removed from life — too artificial — and too inartistic. It lacks both mind and heart, both form and incommensurability, the Apollonian and the Dionysian. Or it has only one and not the other necessary part of the mystical pairing. For, as Musil writes in a review of the Moscow Artists, theater is emphatically not — "an ersatz life for those who want to be told about life or need to be entertained, nor is it a society amusement; it is, rather, meaning-making, interpretation of life, a ministering to humanity."[25]

One of the ways Musil explains theater's failure to fulfil this "meaning-making" role is by his differentiation between what he calls "illustrative" and "creative" theater. The former, the most common, is caught in the rut of mimesis, copying not even life but merely theatrical tropes. The latter grows from out of the individual complex character of the artist in each particular work of art, is consis-

25. *Theater Symptoms*, 135.

tent unto itself alone, and brings something utterly new and previously unimagined — not in a forced, provocative, or cheaply sensational fashion, but simply by being true to its own inner artistic necessity:

> [T]he illustrative is compared to the challenge of a creative theater, one that reflects the fact that we are actually made of spirit. Do not fear, we can still eat lobsters, conduct politics, and do everything else that is human (we should do this!); and as far as I am concerned, one can conceive of the spirit as materialistically as one wants. But we do not want to deny that the most meaningful moments are those wherein we are enlivened by some mysterious thought that carries us beyond ourselves and into the vastness of the universal. I admit that I don't know how to express this; since all of these words, *thoughts, spirit, idea,* have been abused and have earned, thereby, a bad name. Nevertheless, we know how to differentiate quite clearly between whether we are doing something in our lives in response to an internal spur or not. We know quite well that we can be vehement, and nevertheless remain hollow inside. We know quite well that we can have the most noble feelings and can express the grandest convictions, but that in the next moment nothing remains of them but the dregs. There is such a vast difference between our growth and our ossification, a difference that opposes all of the worthy distinctions we flaunt —

a difference that resists all of these exclamations mightily. And, briefly said, one must create a growing, evolving theater.[26]

In answer to the problem of a theater degraded by the priorities of actors and directors (stardom, cult of personality, financial and popular success), Musil postulated not only the "creative theater," but also "the writers' theater," an intellectually and spiritually-challenging theater activated neither by the market nor by the actors' desire to shine, but by the words, ideas, and images of poets who were vitally engaged in the creation of new art forms commensurate with the multi-dimensional nature of the modern experience. But Musil's advocacy of an evolving, living theater is paradoxically just as likely — in fact, more likely — to put forward classical playwrights, like Shakespeare or Goethe, as exemplars than one of his contemporaries. His critiques, thus, sometimes read as more reactionary than modernist, even though he excoriated his contemporary critics for their resistance to new work, even though he rallied with incomparable fervor for the necessity of fostering new playwrights. His belief in the primacy of the role and task of the individual creative artist as genius was traditional, with roots in the Enlightenment and in Romanticism, heavily influenced by Goethe as model and by Schiller's *Æsthetic Education of Mankind*. But his conception of the world with which that genius had to grapple was a very modern one:

26. *Ibid.*, 221.

> [T]he tragic conflict between the individual and the law must now be replaced by an avowed conflict with the laws of earthly existence — a conflict that is often unresolvable, but always bearable. Therein lies the difference between the time of the Enlightenment, which believed in the autonomy of the moral laws and reason, and the time of empiricism, which recognizes an infinite task with only partial progresses.[27]

This fundamentally modern shift from a world of moral laws and reliable truth to one of unresolvable — but bearable — conflict and uncertainty is threaded through every line and every formal move in Musil's works. This is not, as should be clear from the discussion about utopias, a nihilism, but a brave and radical *amor fati*.

Thus it should be no surprise, and is no contradiction, that although Musil's analysis of the conditions of theater is undertaken with painstaking accuracy, although it does arrive at a handful of theoretical principles, any particular proffered law may ultimately be obviated in the face of something more compelling than itself: a measure of unfathomable aliveness. He takes the pulse of a work of art, a play, a novel, a work of criticism, to test whether it throbs, whether it is made of the most palpable tension possible between the norms and the

---

27. *Ibid.*, 65.

deviations, the rationality and the irrationality that make up a "motivated" lived life — or he declares it dead: nothing but a conglomeration of ossified techniques, formulæ, and clichés.

So much — too much — of the art and criticism of his time was, he found, caught in a cycle of repetitive iterations of the *self-same* — that "seinesgleichen" that would make up part of the title for Part II of *The Man Without Qualities*.[28] Part III of the great novel ("Into the Millennium: The Criminals") breaks out of this deadening cycle through radical deviation, not only in the realm of morals and conduct of life, but also in its formal æsthetic experimentations.

The "other condition" of the sibling lovers' mystical criminality is the realm of utopian creative experimentation, the timeless 'second' reality of æsthetic experience central to Musil's critical theatrical principles and to the form and content of his dramatic writing. The play, the meaningful work of art, should be an ethical and an æsthetic experience, it should be *erschütterend* (shattering, explosive, convulsive); it should, to use another image from Musil's novel, "tear the paper" of normal reality, revealing other more vividly-seen realities.

28. Eithne Wilkins and Ernst Kaiser translated the title, "Seinesgleichen Geschieht," more literally as "The Like of It Now Happens," while Sophie Wilkins, under Burton Pike's editorship, arrived at the philosophically justified "Pseudoreality Prevails."

Musil sometimes seems to be defending and sometimes attacking Naturalism in his theoretical writings. He constantly objects to plots and motivations that do not make sense, are inconsistent, or not life-like. Yet this is not exclusively an attack on the level of abstraction or the symbolic nature of a work. Insofar as Musil well knew that metaphor could be even more expressive of the real complexity of life than a supposed mimetic depiction, his critical arrow is aimed at any artistic formulations (whether allegedly Naturalistic or abstract) that are haphazard, that do not seem to have grown out of an inner necessity or truth, at hastily thrown-together hack work, posing as profound.

"Naturalism," he wrote, "gave reality without spirit; Expressionism gave spirit without reality; both are non-spirit."[29] His tendency to lean toward rather than away from Naturalism might, however, seem clear in his preference for the work of Stanislavski's Moscow troupe over the anti-Naturalistic productions and theories of Expressionism, except that he argues that it would be a mistake to call what the Moscow Artists do Naturalistic: for they elevate the natural beyond the quotidian banal. This is what Musil aims for. Neither otherworldly fantasy, nor dull and pedestrian stories about dreary people, but real life at its highest and most spiritual pitch. This enlivening crisis or crux is often to be found in the tension between habitual conformity and creative interruption to patterns.

29. *GW II*, 1058f.

Musil's two finished plays anticipate the novel's æsthetic and ethical tension between the self-same and the criminal, creative variations that interrupt its habitual circling. In *The Utopians*, we find a powerful early metaphor for the tension between patterns and creative alternatives, presented later in the novel as the "two dozen cake pans" into which life is too-often poured and thus limited. In the 1921 play, Regina and Thomas talk about the way they used to walk along the patterns in a carpet (now in the house inherited by Thomas and Maria) as children. Thomas laments:

> *(Pointing to the patterns Regina has been walking on)* One never escapes from what has been predetermined. Sometimes I feel as though everything was already decided in childhood. Climbing, one always comes back to the same place, circling over the emptiness around a predetermined outline. It's like a spiral staircase.

And yet, like Ulrich and Agathe in *The Man Without Qualities*, and Alpha and Vinzenz in Musil's second play, their entire protest against the *self-same*, their resistance to normal life and its dissatisfying requirements, demands precisely that they do step out of the pre-determined lines in an imaginative act of ethical aliveness. To do so is terrifying and catapults one beyond the pale of normal, conformist social life. The "tragic conflict" between an isolated human being and the vast and terrifying world of unlimited possibilities is described by Thomas in *The Utopians* as the state of a man alone on his own plank amid infinity; and this image is central enough to Musil's thinking about theater's higher aims that he quotes this passage (as the words of "another writer"), in a review of Ernst Toller's *The Lame Man*, to illustrate what he deems "the suffering of Everyman, when he notices his loneliness among his fellows in that moment when it is a matter of the deepest things."[30]

Although Musil's "farce," *Vinzenz and the Mistress of Important Men* is, on its surface, lighter and less challenging than *The Utopians*, the "feeling of not being at home in the world," writes Burton Pike, "is not merely a comic pose"[31] for Alpha, the "mistress of important men," who calls herself an "anarchist." Nor is it a pose for Vinzenz, her childhood friend, who returns after an unexplained absence of 11 years to play a role similar to that of Anselm in *The Utopians*: the role of confidence man, but also classic fool, of the actor who reveals that all the other more serious-seeming characters are also living a sort of farce. Neither Anselm nor Vinzenz nor Alpha, on the one hand, nor Thomas and Regina, nor Ulrich nor Agathe in their own way on the other, can commit themselves to easy answers or a solid sense of reality. Thus, the theatrical tricks played by Musil on the audience in his "farce"

---

30. *Theater Symptoms*, 240.
31. Burton Pike, *op. cit.*, 98.

parody not only the theatrical conventions of his time, but also the conventions and trappings of any semblance of a stable, certain position in real life. Behind what Pike calls Vinzenz's "sophistic detachment ... lurks a refusal to commit himself or accept the world .... [M]ore exactly than any character in Musil's earlier works, except Anselm and possibly Thomas ... Vinzenz prefigures Musil's ultimate man of possibility, Ulrich."[32]

The same concerns and themes run through all of Musil's works and are found, in scintillating form, in many fragments of fiction, plays, essays, and aphorisms. I have only included a few of the many dramatic fragments from Musil's *Nachlass*, partially due to a question of space and time, but also because many may be too sketchy and disjointed for the general reader's enjoyment or illumination. I have left out the lengthy unfinished fragment entitled *The Little Napoleon* (or *Panama*), which is a farce inspired by Musil's experience of corruption as a soldier in WWI. I have also not included the lengthy notes for a work called *The Tortoise*. Many smaller sketches (1 to 2 pages) have also been left out.

In addition to the prelude, *The Zodiac*, probably a parody of Expressionism's excesses, which was published in Musil's lifetime, but never continued, I have included three unfinished fragments: *The Double I, The Stylite*, and *Tempora Maier*, in part because of their charm and their

---

32. *Ibid.*, 100.

interest to me personally, and in part because of what I deemed their relevance to the other material in this volume. *Tempora Maier*, especially, as a depiction of a dystopian society that exiles its authors and represses nuanced, intellectual thought, is a delicious satire of our own contemporary scene. The reader will hopefully find that, despite — or, why not? — perhaps *because* of Musil's serious commitment to art's ethical and social role, these and the other works in this book are a good deal of fun.

This is, of course, in keeping with Musil's main criterion that art, as in Novalis' definition of *philosophieren* quoted in Pater's "Conclusion" to *Studies in the History of the Renaissance*, is "*dephlegmatisieren, vivifizieren.*" Maria, in *The Utopians*, speaks the Nietzschean phrase, in opposition to her husband Thomas' relentless rationality: "I think that the only proof for or against a person is whether one rises or sinks in his presence." And even Thomas, who resists such anti-logical[33] pronouncements, proclaims in the last scene that he, too, is a dreamer, who, like his alter-ego, his creator Robert Musil, is so rational that he must indeed include the realms of dream, of mystery, of uncertainty in his ultimate honest picture of the world. He, like Vinzenz, is another prototype of Musil's

---

33. It has been suggested by Rogowski and others that the names Thomas and Anselm in the play are references, respectively, to Thomas Aquinas and Anselm of Canterbury, "whose dictum *credo ut intelligam* Musil cites on several occasions" (Rogowski, *Dramaturgy*, 102).

man without qualities, who is simultaneously necessarily a man of possibility, an eternal utopian, whose radical openness is a window on the abyss at the edge of "adventure and *ignorabimus*." To another character, Regina, Thomas avows their common ailment and talent in some of the play's last lines:

> I am ... a dreamer. And you are a dreamer. People like us just appear to be unfeeling. We wander, watch what the people who feel at home in the world do. And carry something inside ourselves that we do not sense. A sinking down through everything into bottomlessness at every moment. Without going under. The condition of creation.

And this sometimes uncomfortable, difficult, lonely, radically honest "condition of creation" is not only a cosmological moment, but is, at once, and just as importantly, a "creative condition" — the condition in which life-changing art may be born and experienced.

THANKS

This book could not have been completed without the toil of countless scholars before me who have prepared editions, scrupulously compiled annotations, and carefully read the primary texts and illuminating secondary sources. I am in debt to Burton Pike, translator, scholar, teacher, and my scholarly mentor, whose 1961 book introduced the English-speaking world to Robert Musil. I am also grateful to Walter Fanta for his painstaking editorial work on the *Klagenfurter Ausgabe* and for his generosity in providing me with the manuscripts of the relevant forthcoming volumes of his gargantuan *Gesamtausgabe* of Musil's works. The *Robert Musil Handbuch*, edited by Birgit Nübel and Norbert Christian Wolf, has been an invaluable resource. Birgit Nübel, who has long been a help and an inspiration, further took the trouble of sending me voluminous and priceless secondary material in a time when resources were otherwise inaccessible. Thank you, as well, to Mark Mirsky, who, due to his hunger for all things Musil, encouraged me two decades ago to embark on an earlier translation of *Vinzenz and the Mistress of Important Men*, which he published in two parts — as the first English-language version of this play — in *Fiction* magazine in 1999 and 2000. I also thank the Austrian Ministry of Education, Arts, and Culture for providing some financial support for this work. It remains to be said that a book such as this could never come to print without the quixotic vision and hard work of Rainer J. Hanshe, editor of Contra Mundum Press, along with the artistry of Alessandro Segalini, typographer. Last but not least, I thank you, readers, for sharing my love and respect for Musil's work.

Plainfield, Vermont, July 9, 2020

THEATER SYMPTOMS

THEATER SYMPTOMS I
[*Der Neue Merkur* (June 1922)]

Motto: when things regress, the last ones are first. This is the only way it can make sense today to call Vienna a theater city within intellectual Germany.

A respected Viennese critic, whom I believe must be an elderly gentleman — since, when I first opened my eyes, he was already writing clever remarks about good and bad plays alike, for the same newspaper as today — a friendly gentleman, in other words, always ready to discover the good and overlook the evil, always ready with comely anecdotes from literary history in his pockets, not without quality as a writer.... All in all, as should be clearly emphasized, an amenable personage amid all those others who stir the pot of public opinion.... A few days before I put these comments to paper, this critic wrote the following about a play by Sudermann:[1] "Sudermann, this wholly unique mixture of Schiller and

---

1. Hermann Sudermann (1857–1928), popular German novelist and playwright, who, despite liberal sentiments and modernist tendencies, is often accused of triviality and the sort of conventional dramatic resolutions that cater to, rather than challenge, what Musil would call theater's worst tendencies.

Sardou,[2] with his own touch of Lithuanian authenticity, is still the freshest, rarest theater blood that pulses in German lands. He has more temperament than taste, so that his dialogues are exceedingly glitzy on account of the falsest word-diamonds. But nevertheless: the way he suspends the arc of an act, yes, even a scene — in this he is a master. A theater master, who, in the moment of the creative act, when the fury of the stage has him in its grip, forgets everything else: taste, learning, criticism — he only wants to have an effect, and he certainly does. Because, in defiance of all intellectual windbags, he possesses these two things that cannot be learned: temperament and theater." — This was said about the three one-Act plays called *Morituri*.

I don't believe that a German critic would have been able to write that, but I do give the Viennese critic credit; as a man of taste and member of a "respected old culture," he has allowed himself to shift from his stance — from the state of affairs that obtained between 1880 and today — only as much as was unavoidable. And now that

2. Victorien Sardou (1831–1908), French playwright known for his concept of "the well-made play." George Bernard Shaw called Sardou's 1887 play *La Tosca* "a clumsily-constructed, shiftless, empty-headed turnip ghost of a shocker" — words that sound like some of Musil's own critiques of contemporary plays. See Julian Budden's "The Two Toscas" in *Tosca's Prism: Three Moments in Western Cultural History*, ed. Deborah Burton et al. (Boston: North Eastern University Press, 2004) 114.

he has regressed without noticing, he may well congratulate himself that his eyes have always seen the world just the way it was during the time of Heyse.[3] "Temperament and Theater" are, even today, driving the German theater downhill — no differently than they were at the time of Sudermann's success; and it is only a historical accident that one criticizes it in his work, while not even noticing it in other writers where it has an even more deleterious effect. The occasionally indecent feeling of honest people is a much more serious affair than the pomposity of an old conjurer. Now and again one holds temperament and theater against Sudermann, while "temperament" is a great part of Unruh's success, and "theater" of Hauptmann's. This question of dosage is very muddy.

That which one calls dramatic temperament in actresses today is always a hollow void in real life. The way that actresses "take the reins" (see how passionate I am!) when they are supposed to depict passion about events that they do not take seriously in private life, events like passion itself, probably owes much more to the general race-horse nerves of the star, to the excitement that really is only connected with the director and colleagues, than to the writer's words, whose meaning and dynamic

---

3. Paul Heyse (1830–1914) was a German writer of stories, novels, poetry, and plays, celebrated in his lifetime as the "Prince of Literature."

do not even come into consideration (I have seen it myself in a very significant actress playing Hedda Gabler); and the rages, jealousies, sorrows, and gruesome acts of their masculine colleagues are often the result of occasions that, if looked at soberly, are (not only in Sudermann) really so ridiculous, that they could easily be compared to the spontaneous combustion of orators — a condition characterized less by the readily available possibility of "make-up removal" than by its banality. At its core, this is the same sleight of hand that we see with bad writers or fervent enthusiasts, with a routinely sentimental Courths-Mahler,[4] the same sort of sentimental epidemic once pervasive in pastoral poetry, and the same kind that we find in all squared feelings, artificial feeling-feelings, those that are not activated by experience, but that are spread by contact with other feelings generally associated with an experience.

The talent to shape an experience so that a large part of the excitement communicated to writers and listeners does not come from the experience itself, but rather from the general emotional atmosphere that has been generated about it for the audience is the specific talent

---

4. Hedwig Courths-Mahler (1867–1950) was a popular German writer of formulaic romantic fiction, wherein socially-disadvantaged characters achieve romantic and economic success after overcoming the usual obstacles. She is a symbol for Musil of trivial, inartistic, shallow writing.

of the playwright who is successful in our theaters today. He rules over the life and death of his figures, not with the deep conscientiousness with which he would probably consider his own death, but rather with the fleeting feelings that one expresses when reading about death tolls in newspapers. He finds himself, so to speak, not at all in an individual psychological state, but rather in an excitation that is similar to a mass-psychological one. Everything that turns into the progress of an act, the arc of a scene, or the explosion of an ending is forged in the same flash in the pan fire that creates that stinking situation of mass suggestion, which makes, out of more or less reasonable people, an "audience." An audience that accepts the most enormous foolishness as funny or lofty and that either ignores the limitations that allow the author to take his work seriously or justifies these limitations as professional deformations of the dramatic writer. This theater is nothing but the brother of the trashy novel, a brother who has studied under a higher sort of master builder.[5] More important than the case of the experienced hack is that of the genuine writer who doesn't allow himself to be led, but only *misled* in his métier. He works from the inside out, but soon, the entire way in which his interior is arranged is determined by the frame in which it should fit. Just try to extract the spiritually significant part out of our most well-known

---

5. Most likely a reference to Ibsen's 1892 play *The Master Builder*.

playwrights — contemporary playwrights — and one will see how terrifyingly little of the pith of literature they contain.

Nowadays one can hardly speak the word "spirit" without thinking of Expressionism, which ruined it. Always, if art is spoken of, truth stands on a narrow bridge, and I seize, from memory, the sentence of a spirited, often excessively-spiritual writer, who maintained that the essence of the great playwright (whom he one day declared Georg Kaiser to be)[6] consists in the ability "to translate spirit into movement." For, this "dynamic" mass, this dimension of movement inserted into spirit, was precisely the decisive mistake dramatic Expressionism made about itself. To transform spirit into movement presupposes the existence of that which is to be transformed; it does not increase the spirit, but merely moves it around. Spiritually, this principle means, as one can easily see, nothing more than a stagnation that is stirred about in place. Expressionism was, in this regard, only enriched in its form, while it remained banal in its spiritual content, without, besides, getting beyond the evocation of already known ideas. What Expressionism loves to do is a kind of "idea howling." For, indeed, the

---

6. Musil's judgments of the Expressionist playwright Georg Kaiser were ambivalent. In one review, *Plays of the Time*, from March 26, 1924, not included in this collection, he calls him at once "perhaps the first dramatist in Europe" and a "genius of the superficial."

calling out of great human ideas — followed by two exclamation points instead of a question mark — ideas like Suffering, Love, Eternity, Goodness, Greed, Virgin, Blood, Chaos, etc. — is no more valuable than the lyrical activity of a dog howling at the moon, while Feeling answers him in the round. One can also not ignore that Impressionism, too, invented a theory of art, one which demanded that the writer should not think, but feel. And that the writer must speak, by avoiding analysis of spiritual facts, directly to feelings of "common sense." The genius dines upon the common spirit and the common spirit dines upon what comes out of the genius — a rather obscure process of administering a nutritional enema!

In truth, setting ideas in motion, when it is not a vain regurgitation, is nothing other than *having new ideas*. If I were forced to choose between Impressionism and Expressionism, I would choose the deceased Dilthey, whom contemporary Germans find so quaint — Dilthey, who saw the calling of the great writer as comparable to that of the prophets, thinkers, wise men, founders of religion and other great creators of the human spirit. If one tries to measure German artists of today by this spiritual criterion, one will understand why most people — whether from one or another faction — maintain that literature is just literature and that it is a thing that will be harmed by too much intellectuality.[7] With all due respect to the differences between the factions; but when one of their leaders — and not just any one! — decides to become a writer, this in itself is questionable. But, beyond this, a whole bundle of related questions is raised: why, in one or the other of his internal scenarios, he reaches for this or that "form," to what extent do these choices communicate social or formal conventions, et cetera? But if one simply accepts the common opinion — and that is more a question of pride than of truth — it follows that this writer will always be faced with the task of limiting and exploiting the conventions of expressive methods and forms, which even he cannot do without, to their greatest elasticity.

7. [Musil's note.] Here it is a matter of spirit, ideas, intellectuality. One uses such terms in an extremely patchy way in discussions about art — and this also inhibits progress. One ought to understand by intellectuality, the ability to reason, in both the bourgeois and scholarly sense. By spirit, that mixture, as much of experience as of the arrangement of experiences, a relationship, in other words, of as much reason as emotion, which has almost always distinguished the seeker upon internal paths; and by ideas, I mean those conceptions, never fully crystallized within the mother lode of feelings, which are formed therein. Neither Impressionism nor Expressionism produced ideas. The former, insofar as it preferred to follow the clues provided by facts, sometimes created the raw material of ideas, but its technique of only allowing facts and feelings to be expressed, had too little intellectual convergence.

That is approximately the precise opposite of what nowadays is considered expert practice. One repeats to us over and over that if only there were a proper playwright, one anointed with all the salves of theatrical training, who ideally had been fed on mother's milk from childhood, and if he were then a *pure* writer too, yes, then we would have our own Shakespeare. This may practically be on a level with the Christian miracles, but it is also a view with some value; one need not deny that there is some grain of truth in it, too. But one asks too rarely why the novel in the last hundred years has developed from formless gossip to the level of high art, into which we put everything spiritual we have, while on the other hand, the theater atrophies. And the answer would simply be, that along with countless stupid people, also a number of significant people devote themselves to the novel, while in the theater, the overestimation of the

↩ The latter did not create one single new idea, and instead of becoming the art of ideas it strove to be, became an art devoid of ideas. It was left hanging on a remarkable excess and lack of both reason and emotion. The attempt to arouse emotions or even ideas by declaiming their abstract nouns is a form of rationalism. On the other hand, it indicates nothing but a lack of reason in the most conventional sense when one tries to indicate "the gathering place of Communists by a red-lit window between dark curtains" as was attempted by H.v.Wedderkop in his excellent essay "Expressionist Stage" in the May issue of this journal. One should not, however, implicate the term "idea art" by these examples.

vulgar works against it. The circumstances are reversed there, so that the theatrical methods come first, and human sense only second.

That which is lasting in this "season," as it comes to an end amid the summer heat, tells us all we need to know about this problem. Literary pieces, small in number and staying power, struggle on amid a glut of theatrical works; some charming, some well-meaning among them; nothing stays with us.

Excepting Georg Kaiser's *Court Clerk Krehler*. The sketchy contours of this piece alone make it stand out boldly from the rest. But even in this case, the idea is announced as if on a placard and then hangs there shrilly and rigidly, despite the fact that it is paraded about. Franz Werfel's two new plays, *Goat Song* and *The Mirror Man*, also distinguish themselves; but, by virtue of an extremely noticeable resistance to literary fashion, they land, unfortunately, too far on the side of the theatrical Charybdis. Despite their artistically charming framing, there is disappointingly too little built in. Notes — precisely because unconscious! — of Fontane, Byron, Ibsen, Goethe, Maeterlinck, yes even — I need not say anything more about this — of other theatrical masters, reveal the meager inter-personal tension, which is really something different than nervous tension. The beautiful obscurity of the basic idea quickly runs out, leaving nothing but an illuminated event that follows the path of least resistance, transforming an "it could happen" immediately into an "it happens." In this way, merely fleetingly, allegorical relationships are added to already well-known ideas, which the critics, if they do not reject the work because of its occasional scattered beauties, interpret with astonishment as, perhaps, the battle of the Communist Party and the Bourgeoisie or of the psychological subconscious with its super-ego. Werfel himself offered explanations. They culminated in the belief that a playwright must be engaged and that everything else is "Yes-Man nonsense." Still, nevertheless, since it is well-known that a writer seldom does have an influence — least of all, anyway, if he takes himself seriously — Werfel experiences the theater like a child, as a great peep show, whose darkness and aroma and red velvet impel the heart to beat faster, providing something of the sweet operatic mood of existence. — I take this to be a reasonable stance; but Werfel misses something: that feelings want to be taken seriously; namely, they want to be felt; even playful feelings; they demand that one really plays, not plays at playing; the magic of childhood, of playing, of fairground highjinks, of suggestion, of magicianship, rests upon its being believed. If it is not taken seriously, it will not be merry. So, one can say that Werfel thought he was playing with a few deep ideas, but they played with him. So that, despite the will to uniqueness and the expectations which the writer may have had of these works, it is the face of the times that can be seen peering out of them.

One gets the clearest image of our path through Wildgans.[8] I don't want to waste too many words on his piece *Cain*. This biblical play is as empty as a watering can played like a pipe by a Beethoven. But as its creator is heralded as the Austrian successor to Gerhart Hauptmann, to discuss it would be to perform a critique of the times — as skull trepanation. I will begin with a verse from Wildgans' poetry book, *Mid-day*, which is not at all an early work: "The spirit can find deeper fulfilment / Manufacturing shoes, more contentment / Than in thoughts' highest production." In fact, nine-tenth of Wildgans' essence can be read in these three lines, without bothering to look further into his life's work.

8. Anton Wildgans (1881–1932) was one of the most popular playwrights and poets of Austria, and twice director of the Viennese Burg Theater. Wildgans was one of Musil's greatest literary and cultural nemeses. His name occurs again and again in Musil's notebooks and writings, as summarized by Walter Fanta: "For example, one reads of 'Austria as a Wildgans society' (Folder II/8, p. 158) and of the 'as-if author of the arrival of the absolute reign of the average men' (Folder 3/V, p. 24) …. The high point of the biting commentaries comes with the statement, 'I left Austria in 1931, because red and black were in agreement that they had lost, with Wildgans, a great Austrian writer' (Notebook 33, p. 43)." Walter Fanta, "Author's Afterword" to Volume 10 of the forthcoming *Robert Musil-Gesamtausgabe* (Salzburg: Jung und Jung, 2020). This is Fanta's summary of the commentaries in the *Klagenfurter Ausgabe*, which were written by Nicole Streitler. Streitler's book *Musil als Kritiker* (Bern: Peter Lang, 2006) provides more detailed commentary of the reviews.

One can ascertain a certain simple poetic inflection, in which the whole thing sounds as if it were being uttered by "no one less important than ..." and one must struggle earnestly to get to the bottom of it, so to speak. And of course, one notices that the "manufacturing" and the "production," even the "contentment," used together in this context, all come from the jargon of officialese. And naturally this discovery is not sufficiently or satisfactorily explained merely by the fact that a few bad expressions skidded under the poet's pen, but rather, also, lead one to ask: what kind of a person has officialese coming out of his mouth at the moment of highest emotion (poetry!)? One understands this man in just three lines, and knows practically everything else that can be expected from him.

The German public calls such an ability to recognize a person from three lines an æsthetic or a literary sensibility, and stresses, while generously overlooking its perhaps not quite pure form, the eternal essence of its content. It should, thus, be the content that is considered. But in fact, this content usually amounts to a so-called eternal truth that just happens to be expressed by Wildgans. In this case, it is a thought that has made its way today into elementary school pedantry, where it offers itself up as the soul's work ethic. Except — except that this same thought, already expressed in a hundred-thousand different ways, was always correct — *except* in this one variety, which the poet has given to it. For even the humblest Christian work ethic has never maintained that devotion to a shoe provides more contentment than devotion to God, only that devotion to work in service to God should take the place of the highest thoughts. Leave it to this poet to give an almost eternal truth a form — of an exceptional case — that would render it false. There is something about this writer — the examples are legion. A certain lack of something that I don't have to name: on the other hand, a surfeit of rhymes.

This something that is not there even makes itself felt in his directorial notes. Imagine, for example, that a woman is asked how long she had been married and she may answer: nine years today! A hundred different people might deliver this answer in about ten different moods, but the one who answers that today it has been precisely X-years with the emotional accent on "profound," answers like a human being who tunes herself to an emotional calendar, to a New Year's Eve reflection, and those other "profound" hours experienced by the bourgeois animal. Again, for example, as when a man, admitting that it is difficult to be satisfied, year in, year out, with just one woman, peers into the "most profound manly sorrow." In any case, these are minor issues, but one can learn from them what this writer means by profundity.

Thirdly, the characteristic mark of a well-behaved man is a lack of exceptional thought. Someone will be described as a "modern metropolitan type with an intellectual career"; a thoroughly normal woman speaks occasionally "somewhat hysterically"; and a man kisses her hand, "with a certain fervor." This certain uncertainty when it comes to the observation of life and this general connection of observations with already-existing ways of speaking is the well-known psychology of whatever is already generally thought and — what is generally gladly exchanged for eternal truths. But it is simultaneously the only thing in the world that can be rendered false.

A deprivation on the level of taste accompanies these intellectual shortcomings. It is naturally more difficult to make this clear to someone who does not feel it. But perhaps such a one can sense it without any explanation from sentences like: "Yes, where then are you hiding, merciful human being?!" or (at a reunion), "Human, friend, brother! After fifteen years!" Aside from poets, the only people who talk like this are, namely, people who have not learned their expressions from life, perhaps aging high school students or clerks writing society skits. On the other hand, compare this to when a husband speaks to his wife in an hour of soul-searching: "I am, nevertheless, happily at your service; let us chat a bit." Something overly didactic mixes in with the *grandezza*. (This didacticism is utterly rich in a poem, "Wantons": "You, also, are so ill-equipped with charm / That the brutal drive alone would harm / Your body, that is cold and banal.") The range of feelings is not, however, exhausted yet: "In the fullest swing of clever haughtiness," one expresses one's self like this: "I just said — or did I not say? — that the European women seem like cows, who would rather chew painted flowers out of golden frames than fresh, sweet clover on a green, open meadow! Metaphorically meant. But you, Madonna, seem to me to be an admirable exception from this."[9] Whereupon Madonna, "amused," answers: "Very dear sir, I am certainly not a cow." A blaze of anger, if it breaks out of a deep mood, looks something like this: "Anna: No one hinders you from doing that. Martin: What do you mean by hinder?! We have not yet arrived at an impasse where you could hinder me from leaving the house by physical force. But whatsoever you can achieve with words, facial expressions, intonations, to cripple my freedom of movement — that you do." This is how anger looks; love; power; this is how clever haughtiness looks. This sort of thing always existed in Germany, to be sure, but now it is returning to literature. These are vignettes from Th. Heine's *German Family Life*.[10] Not, however, devised as a caricature, but as an altar idol.

Nevertheless, Wildgans has the "touch" of a playwright. This can be judged without administering a smear test. Judging by what we have already seen of him,

9. Reminiscent of the way Anselm in Musil's drama, *The Utopians*, speaks to Maria.
10. Thomas Theodor Heine (1867–1948) was a German painter, illustrator, and caricaturist, who often published in the Munich journal, *Simplicissimus*.

Wildgans could perhaps be — still be — a strong, albeit raw talent; indeed, precisely what the public imagines could save them from literature by virtue of his fervent literary activity. I think of scenes, for example, like the first false step of a married man in love; torment, suffered by a virtuous girl, when the seducer is too slow in *Dies irae*. But this "touch" is more effective in familiar than in strange scenes. I had fun conflating the scenic directions from *Dies irae* and *Love* together: moonshine, evening sun, pink lantern light, full-moon night, moon-night, July night, starry night, deep stormy dusk, etc.; one sees that the writer leaves nothing to the imagination. Everywhere there are lamps aglow, with green, emerald-green, and red silk or paper shades; on the writing desks there are bronze writing sets and monumental ink wells. In such an atmosphere, the solid touch is softened by tendencies, a few of which, since they repeat themselves in his complete works in rather the same stereotypical manner, I offer as example: "Take your violin, Lady Past"; "Sometimes it would be good for there to be flowers, flowers surrounding books, red like sins"; "venal putrid pomp of prostitutes"; "She is the red orgy and the prayer"; "Poppy-quaff of forgetting, greed in blood, idolatry, fool's laughter, fool's song, dead frippery" are all phrases characterized by a combination of a complete lack of ideas with the highest emotional power, and at the emotional climax: "A violin has driven me mad!" or: "I kissed a whore!," followed by a profound silence or even the striking of a musical chord from out of the

immeasurable cosmic space. I conclude with the beautiful poem, "Harlequinade," the mysterious melody in one of the most effective scenes in *Dies irae*: "Wrapped in rags and tatters, behind the curtains, a poor thing swooned at my hopes almost ruined; that is my fool's soul — forgive her if she sometimes surpasses the ghoul."
— A hand with a certain touch can belong to a famous surgeon, but also a good barber.

It should not be concealed that there is a good deal of mating and inseminating in Wildgans' work; strumpets glisten, the Foehn blows without ceasing, skirts fly open, and there is even sodomy in one instance. This streak of audacity would be missed, were it not there. Together with the unending use of the most fraught agitations of the soul, such as secret dread or intense excitement, along with the permanent conflict between "Spirit" and the "Senses," by a Faustian preference for living amid walls of books, at every turn, the accompanying diction of humanistic denunciation rounds out this time-honored tendency to sometimes dare to resort to the kind of strong language used by the type who has climbed up out of the family daily into literature to show Godfather Parliamentarian and Professor that they are dealing here with a man's writer. It goes without saying that the bourgeois writer must ceaselessly fulminate against the bourgeoisie.

Even those people who "go along with the developments of the times" do not reject him; and, thus, we are already well on our way.

THEATER SYMPTOMS II

[*Der Neue Merkur* (December 1922 / February 1923)]

Vienna likes to hear itself called a theater city: its feuilletonists repeat it to her often, in the way that only a feuilletonist can. In truth, she is a city of actors. When one listens to the stories told about the glamour of times gone by, one hears the names of actors, never theater directors (excepting Laube,[11] for special reasons), and never the names of writers. Herein lies a symptom that is relevant not only for Vienna. Namely, this cult of actors ultimately leads to a theater without actors!

If I wanted to recount performances that have stuck with me over a long period, there would be almost no Viennese actors among them. Only guest performers. But the essential point here is also: it is not the actor, but the performance that comes from Berlin. I could name a large number of players in Vienna, too: but if they lack either the strength or the luck to flee, they will eventually

---

11. Heinrich Rudolf Konstanz Laube (1806–1884) was a German writer, dramatist, theater manager, and artistic director of the Viennese Burg Theater. Probably the special reasons have to do with Laube's part in the popularization of the liberal *Junges Deutschland* (young Germany) movement.

become well-behaved, well-groomed theater functionaries. Just the same, twice as much is written and spoken about actors in Vienna as is in Berlin. But to the wrong tune. When Mr. Z., a young actor, who is sometimes excellent and sometimes a complete flop, depicted S. Just in Büchner's *The Death of Danton* and made more of an impression than Moissie's Danton, then I am certain — without having to check — that the majority of critics either didn't notice or only half-noticed, and wrote: "… depicted a splendid S. Just," instead of saying that he depicted a feminine, perverted murderer, with oily, womanly tendencies. Another time, Mr. K., who is a versatile and always respectable actor, performed Iago as a well-behaved average fellow, so that the measure of infamy of that type perfectly sufficed for an Iago; but the majority of critics didn't notice that K. had created something new, at least for Vienna, nor that he had also raised a moral question. Indeed, Herr K. was criticized, while Ferdinand Bonn, who had smeared Iago in another production with the oldest of salves, was almost praised — by those same critics — more highly than they praised Moissi — who, in this case, was wonderful as Othello. I could provide many similar examples. How, then, shall a young actor not grow weary? In brief: it is a matter of the difference between two principles. According to one, the theater should be treated as a part of intellectual-spiritual life, principally connected, via literature, with all of life's forces, including quantum theory, religion, or politics; while the other sees in theater something special, namely — theater. In accord with this latter principle, highly evolved in Vienna, the achievements of the theater persist in having relevance only for the achievements of the theater: X's performance is always reminiscent of Y's or is equal to it or worse. And be it ever so dressed up in the choicest literary veneer (which it rarely is), this eternal self-referentiality of the actor to the actor, a feature of a particular culture, precisely the culture which considers itself a theater city, this reliance on the most inexact actorly measurements to ensure that anything new or unique — anything that would be worthy of being remembered in any performance — is not noticed by public opinion as long as it modestly refrains from leaping out, amid the familiar, well-known goings on, from the general monotonous background. Thus, the arc of a city, in which the actors do not attain to their highest performances, culminates in a literary atmosphere that is subsidiary to the actor. The social formula for this is, more or less: a third or fourth generation of genuine theater lovers, who destroy the theater because they overvalue it in isolation; the actor is more a symptom than the essence of this tendency.

And it is, indeed, in itself, a platitude if I say that the development of the art of action is dependent upon literature; but why, for God's sake, is this active art considered — not only in Vienna, but elsewhere, too — as literature's opposite? Why does one say that our writers write plays that do not suit our actors, and never asks whether our actors perhaps are insufficiently suitable for our writers? Why does one demand that the writer assimilate to the "requirements" of the actor, without mentioning that there, too, it is a matter of limitations? Why do our best actors, even if they do appear in new plays, prefer, ultimately, to perform in plays like those written by Hans Müller, Anton Wildgans, Sudermann, or the mediocre French writers?

I do not presume to be able to do more than touch on this problem, nor can I even adumbrate its entire outline; but it would be sufficient for now if we even merely were able to finally recognize the problematics of theater in this context.

*

It was Maeterlinck who, many years ago, in his book, *Wisdom and Fate*, expressed the idea that it is a hackneyed convention to call things tragic in theater that no longer affect us. Murder, manslaughter, extermination, these tragic endings; jealousy, fury, despair, and the other pathetic affects no longer play an important role in an elevated, true, and spiritually awake life, but rather belong more in the shady arena of unstable life — the kind that ends either in the cold water cure or, at worst, in no less miserable cases, in the "Court of Law" column in the paper. Doubtless, the most important decisions between two people are resolved more frequently in silence than in a word or a scream or the visible action of their bodies, and even when it comes to great and deep passions it is not characteristic to immediately burst out with ejaculations; rather, such experiences touch a person internally; there, where the roots of one's activity in the world and one's vision of the world color them. Great passions are never only personal, but always contain something objective; and this is what makes Dante's love greater than that of an unhappy serving maid who drowns herself, although, on the face of it, one would have to say that both loves would be immeasurable. Granted such thoughts, our theater seems to be an anachronism; granted such an anachronism, such a persistent exercise with an apparatus as large as the theater seems to be a truly remarkable socio-pathological fact. The majority of our tragic dramatic work depicts nothing but the attempt to arrange things in such a way that death comes at the end of them. Naturally, one cannot ignore the fact that death, this limit of existence, one of the most pregnant metaphysical experiences, has given birth to this desire to creep up on the abyss and blink down into it. Wherefrom, to be sure, the tragic theater acquired its exceptional position among the arts, as particularly lofty, which it by no means still deserves; but one must also not ignore the fact that death and passion have ossified into formal conventions in the contemporary theater, seemingly as necessary as having three or four acts. One must not ignore the fact that they are deeply felt almost as little as the street signs telling us to go right or left, which themselves once had their own relationship with heaven and earth. They are thoughtlessly spun-out commonplaces, and the most dangerous ally of any thusly-implicated literature is the actor himself.

In the theater, two spheres are in tension; one is literature, the other theater, and this results in a mixture of fear and a prejudicial favoring of the requirements that the actor is supposedly entitled to. Far be it for me to begrudge the actors the fulfilment of these requirements, for drama as a whole must pay them its respects; but how often are they strangers to human experience, when they express passion in a "role"?! The actor will use a role to invent a vehement simulacrum of life on the stage. He will make such gestures, sob, scream, careen about, find himself able to turn into strange characters and turn away from his own normal human one. He will be good, evil, sad, wild, heroic, envious, cruel, noble — all to a degree that his private life does not avail him. He wants to be able to be effective, or, as one says in short, be in his element. But in life, we are precisely not good, but good-intentioned. Not evil, but crafty. We are not sad, but in a bad mood. Not wild, but just nervous or imbalanced. The element of the actor is fabricated, thus, out of elements that do not exist. These elemental expressions do not really grip the emotions; instead, they merely grasp expectations of emotions that have already been pre-established in the audience, and these emotions come from the person of the actor just as little.

He plays neither himself nor anything that he has ever seen running about in real life, but rather *roles*, that is to say, something that a writer has written, because countless other actors have played something like them, actors who have played them, because other writers have written them, writers who have written them, because other actors had played them. One plays chains of concepts and effect traditions, not passions; actors merely act out passions; not people, but mirror-people;[12] and on the whole, they act out some kind of sluggishly circling, traditional status quo.

*

I once saw Wegener play old Raschhoff in Sudermann's play, *The Raschhoffs*, and it was like this: he made a damned familiar country squire out of the role, thick of tongue, thick across the belly, who can become damned disagreeable and can well stomach a glass of wine once in a while or a woman, without getting a buzz. He was a winning old chap — and one really needs to see merely one hair from such a type to already know the whole fellow; one has already seen him a hundred times; but that is the only reason why he gives one the creeps — yet one would have to lie, if one did not admit that, despite Sudermann, he was a perfect little genre piece in himself. It would, thus, be foolish to ignore that actors often create their best performances in bad plays, almost

12. A reference to Franz Werfel's 1920 play, *Spiegelmensch* (Mirror-man).

as if they were operating independently of literature. But how do they manage this?

This problem of the actor is the most difficult one for we few writers who want to realize new content in the medium of theater; we don't find it easy to properly take an adversary into consideration, when he is not only our obstacle but also our impetus. One always forgets, when one writes seriously about the theater, that it includes farce, operetta, and even cabaret. Just imagine what sort of a spectrum stretches out between bordello and madhouse! Should we assume that there is something going on inside an actor who creates the role of one or another "Mucki"[13] in one of those thyroid plays that still has something to do with the art of theater? We not only should assume it, but assume that whatever is going on is important. By this we recognize not only the essence of a role, but simultaneously its lower limit. This "Mucki" operetta has certain human features, precisely as much as are needed for the viewer to recognize it as a familiar type, and, what's more, it uses the opportunity as a theme for an infinite variety of prankish pantomimes with face, body, and soul. This giving and receiving of blows, this climbing over tables and sneaking into cabinets and creeping under beds is, doubtless,

---

13. Reference to "Mucki von Rodenstein," a character in Karl Michael Ziehrer's operetta, *Der Landstreicher* (first performed in 1899), a production well-known for its "Viennese spirit."

the source of our dramatic arts. We find it even when the classics are performed. Elements like jealousy, pride, the lack of resistance of an upright person against a crooked one. Regret of one who has been betrayed by fury, out of which, for example, the figure of Othello is constructed, youthful rashness in Romeo; Harpagon's miserliness; the depth of Hamlet; the suffering tenderness of Ophelia; the childlike nature of Desdemona; the sensuality of Salome; all of these elements have long grown independent of their characters; they move on their own, almost as if they were travelling mimetic requirements, depicting a kind of pathos-filled repertoire, out of which the average actor creates the every-evening pleasure of his self — exactly as an average writer creates his books.

And if Wegener, who is a significant actor, plays the economic councilor Raschhoff, it is nothing other than when, at a higher level, he uses the type suggested by the writer as a frame for an improvisation. Such a fellow, an old philanderer and country squire, who, even without Sudermann, runs around in Berlin and in literature and lets himself be found. The writer only needs to suggest the key; Wegener himself makes the sounds and even if one is no Wegener, one copies him, and since an old, playful, leaping buck is not that foreign from the life of any man, everyone will feel a little bit of his self even in the most unoriginal copy. This is why such roles are beloved by actors. It is no different than with

Mucki, but that here the pleasure in the actor's "creative" agility, that is to say, the creation of the motif of an observed type or of the actor's imagined character, is more rigidly subsumed. Now, it would be easy to believe that this is wrong in a few particulars, namely there, where the "role" does or says something that is completely ridiculous, sentimental, or impossible, something which occurs often enough, and not only in the dramas of Sudermann. But the actor understands how to depict such parts without arousing attention; they do not appear to be interruptions; they appear rather as lifeless spots, as a stagnation that then loosens itself up as the play proceeds — that is, the stagnation is not even noticed at all. When it comes to significant actors, something can even be produced in this way — something completely made up of elements of everyday life, an achievement possessing, after a fashion, all the attributes of perfection.

But at bottom, it doesn't even add the smallest thing to that which already exists, indeed, to what is usually already banal, because it is only a type. The actor does not possess a mystical extra-human superpower; instead, he merely concocts a general impression or intention about the character he plays — in essence no different than that of the writer's. This concoction comes primarily from out of his life experiences and reflections; and out of these, he — apparently half-consciously or, as one says these days, intuitively — develops his treatment. No matter how many fine or deep observations and intentions are involved, nothing more can come of it than the rendition of a type and its *mise en scène*, depicted with all manner of "strokes," unless the actor himself becomes his own writer. For, excluding the meaning of words, only that which is more or less typical, that which can be understood "by a sign," is accessible through the symbol language of the actor, i.e., the true mimicry, including the mimicry of the sound of language; only this can be seen from the outside and only this can be made understandable by means of mimicry. And since the actor cannot improve, but only amplify the writer, breathing the appearance of life into the thing, the more commonplaces he pours his art into, the more terrible is the marriage of life and death experienced by sensitive ears and eyes. The cheerful genre is, by contrast, much more impervious than the tragic, but I believe that the ephemeral nature of the art of acting stems in both cases from this same cause, and not from the fact that each performance only happens once. For the great impressions of life, too, come only once.

*

I am not ignoring the fact that there is something else at play here as well. The actor, who embodies the type that has been suggested by the writer, substitutes himself therein and supplants him, until he is the one looking out from the surface; result: a slice of life, how it moves and stands still; a little generic life but with a mysterious second face; an internal face that sees through the surface;

the actor's face. Something mask-like hovers above the charm of this artistic performance. If one tries to give one's self up entirely to this charm, one stumbles upon the pantomimic element of life itself. There comes a point in occurrences and passions when one can only free one's self through a shrug of the shoulders, a departure, through acting, a physical gesture. Entangled, precisely in the way that the strongest, the least simpleminded intellects among us are, in five-thousand-years of never-ending considerations, at the mercy of countless consequences, the immediate or distant effects of every possible position, sometimes nothing is more redemptive than to bid the intellect be silent and to remember that one, as body, as thing, is as unaccountable, unique, and absolute as a wandering cloud or the arc that has been drawn in the air by a hawk. While we shrug our shoulders instead of thinking, we feel ourselves retreat behind an internal circle of defense. The planets spin, the elements unite according to laws that are themselves connected to other laws; but in every law that we know, something exists, just as it does in ourselves — a law that is precisely just the way it is, some kind of constant, a fact, an irrational, once-in-a-world, reckless self-persisting something, and the irrationality of mimicry and of the world touch each other through this pantomime; adventure and *ignorabimus* meet in the moment of a felicitous gesture.

This summary of actors must seem somewhat far-fetched, somewhat unworldly and untheatrical-worldly. But I believe that no great person could dedicate his life to something less fundamental, and this must also be true for the great actor, except that the exemplary, the commendable aspects of his character, that personal charm, the actor's persona — which we hear so much about — are nothing more than a social expression of the phenomenon that was just discussed. In this, the actor is actually independent of the writer and surpasses him; the writer means something, and the actor is what he means; whence comes a certain justification of the actor's sense of himself as a gentleman who just happens to be served by the writer. But even in those cases where the actor surpasses even the greatest writer in his own imagination, his performance, compared to the achievement of the writer, is at least as much reactive as it is active; for, just as a person sometimes expresses that he will no longer walk with someone by following behind at a stubborn distance, whatever is unspoken in this gesture is transformed into content by the attempts, rushing on ahead, of whatever *is* given voice.

It is the binding opposition of the writer to the actor, to have to catch the mimetic absolute again and again in the relativity of the greatest possible spiritual connection, so that it can be set free again in its fully-fraught irrationality. And one must not overlook that this is, in a certain sense, a fatal opposition. For the actor, more than any other artist, must create from out of a sudden inspiration, and the performance falls to ashes if one demands of him the exegesis of a literary mosaic of ideas. He can, thus, only act impulsively and still poetically within a literary atmosphere of the finest kind, and since our theater lacks this (that it *can* exist at the highest level in theater has been proven by Stanislavski), the arts of acting and of writing stand today in a thoroughly unhappy relationship to one another. We have many more significant actors than significant playwrights, and the way things are, the actor rules the theater not without right. The other side of the matter is, however, that he not only overshadows the writer, but also literature itself; he prohibits those plays that could give the theater a new impetus, while consuming others, which — as when one abuses the consumption of alcohol — initially incite an intoxicated rush, but end in intellectual devastation.

It is a little ridiculous, I well know, to approach the living theater with such rigidly penitential requirements; all that is alive is a mixture and shall remain a mixture; there is nothing more terrifying than the solemn cultural bores on the stage. And nine-tenths of our playwrights, the intellectual artists at the helm, would probably die on stage, if the actor did not lend them some of his excess health. One follows up, then, if one will, a second line, the line where things are "the way they are in reality," that is to say, where intellect and anti-intellect have lain down together, more or less comfortably, and one assumes that the truth is somewhere in the middle. On the other hand, one should have unlearned long ago the irrational habit of "it's fine by me." But Nietzsche, in his dislike of Wagner, already prophesied the age of the actor, the one we approach today:

> ... in declining cultures, wherever the decision falls into the hands of the masses, authenticity becomes superfluous, disadvantageous, a liability. Only the actor still arouses great enthusiasm. Thus, the golden age dawns for the actor.

This prophecy need not be true, but it *is* dangerous. He was alluding to those people who express feelings that are not their own, but that belong to the fathers, the original fathers, or that are feelings belonging to all the world. These are, to be sure, the same feelings with which the popular favorites usually earn their admiration; morality is made of them but — something of which I will have occasion to speak — it is precisely at the point where everything seems new that we will find literature and criticism. May our actor remain better protected from this actor than he is protected from his own nature.

ONCE AGAIN THEATER CRISIS AND THEATER RENEWAL[14]

[*Der Tag* (April 20, 1924)]

Personally, I admit to having little interest in the question of whether the Viennese theater or even the German one is "declining" or being "renewed." I suspect that the one condition could scarcely be distinguished from the other. In recent times, when so much has declined, it has been proven that corpses have a rather tenacious hold on life, and we have developed a careful dexterity in not disturbing them with intellectual excitement during their convalescence. I am convinced, therefore, that even if it came to a world collapse and the creation of a new world, all the directors would affirm, in light of the unlimited possibilities, how wonderful it "would" be, if one "were" finally able, once again, to work creatively. But Director Bernau would be kept from it by the "housing shortage"; it would, after all, presumably be

14. This essay was published with the following note: "In last Sunday's edition we presented the perspective of the leaders of Vienna's theaters on this topic and believe it is important to supplement them by a judgment from the circle of writers. Robert Musil, whom we have turned to, provides the following response." Murray G. Hall saw it as "complementary" and as "journalistic preparation" for The 'Decline' of the Theater. See Fanta, *Gesamtausgabe*.

even worse on a new planet than it was on the old one. Director Beer would look around to see what was keeping Director Bach and Director Herterich — but more on this later. I don't even mean to blame anyone for it. The passion for creative work is so rare these days, is so little valued, and its requirements so ill-understood, that it would be frivolous to look for it in theater directors, who must — let us just say — have a highly developed feeling for financial responsibility.

It is, therefore, a good, if a surprising idea of the newspaper (since, when it comes to the survival of the theater *we* tend to rank below the costumers) to turn to a writer with the problem. I can even tell you for a fact what illness the theater suffers from: it is superfluous and is sick and tired of itself.

If this were not the case, could it really be thrown into decline merely by a passing lull in sales or an unexpected fluctuation of the franc, which does no damage whatsoever to soccer — and certainly none at all to Carpentier?[15] That something is superfluous is not contradicted by the fact that it lives in palaces, that thousands of people are economically dependent upon it, and that it is publicly bruited about to be so very, very important. It would be easy to point to many highly-esteemed

---

15. Presumably Georges Carpentier (1894–1975), French boxer, actor, and W.W. I pilot; Heavy Weight Champion from 1913 to 1920, who was just, at about this time, losing his preeminent status.

institutions in precisely this situation; the shells of life always remain intact longer than the life that lives in them. Society people, directors, actors, producers, theater personnel, critics, feuilletonists, reporters, photographers, designers, illustrated weeklies, and God knows who else, have an interest in speaking about the theater with a never-flagging eagerness, as if it were a matter of general importance.

And there would be frantic embarrassments if this were not a lie. Imagine if the masses, after one had educated them and altered the repertoire, had the same kind of interest in theater that they do in soccer or the movies. One would have to simply tear our theaters down and build new ones where one could get a cheap seat without having to crane one's neck or be forced to see the stage as if it were in miniature. One would have to change the showtimes so that even a person without a car would neither have to sit in the theater with a hungry stomach nor go to work in the morning without having had enough sleep. Not to mention the necessary adjustment of the theater to vital, general interests and of the general interest itself to the swift progress of art. Naturally, there is no one who would not deem something that demands so many and such thoroughgoing alterations to be a utopia. In that case, the reawakening of the theater to life is a utopia as well. But it is not, therefore, impossible.

To speak seriously: our theater originated in courtly times; later, in imitation of the court, it became a solemnized institution of bourgeois "society." Further, it was in service to "cultural education." Today, courtliness has disappeared; and the bourgeois liberal education ideal is fading. This is why the social basis of theater has become uncertain; and that is its crisis. But this is a partial symptom of a much larger problem. It goes without saying that the theater could, independently, mean something very grand and even sometimes succeeds in this today. But it owes its material existence, not to its intellectual, but, rather, to its social value, inclusive of the prejudice that insists that one must go to the theater. Along with bourgeois capitalism came the development of so-called higher pleasure — that muck wherein operettas and tragedies swim — which still has a certain elevating effect, but has acquired a certain sour after-taste. There is no doubt anywhere that the directors who today prophesy the collapse of theater's cultural mission do so only because they are doing bad business at the moment; they will do better once again. Even the niveau of theater can elevate itself — to the relatively high level that it attained between 1900 and 1914 in Germany — and then theater will have to make itself at home again amid its usual enduring decline. For it is an uncommonly expensive apparatus and must fulfill its goal if it is to remain lucrative. It would be much too awkward to adapt itself to changes in entertainment requirements; all that remains to the theater is the inverse option: it must increasingly and repeatedly bend those requirements in its own direction and be uncommonly culturally active — or it will become more and more passive.

Let us return once again to utopia. Contemporary questions could blaze up in the theater. Young people could find illumination in their souls. They could, at least, find in actors models for how to live, like they do today in the movies. The theater could inspire a powerful spiritual and intellectual stream in life. It would then truly be a moral institution, not in the somewhat pious, policeman-like way that Schiller implied, but rather as a creative zone and as one of the most important nuclei of an eternally necessary social renewal. What is lacking for this to happen today is almost everything. I would like to just point to criticism here. Of course, we do have some excellent critics with personal perspectives about this problem, but if you analyze the average gold standard of criticism, it is nothing but instructions about how to keep people awake who are threatening to fall asleep. This is called suspense, action, authenticity, composition, virtuosity and the like, but at bottom these are only recipes for making a conventional enjoyment — by which one would otherwise easily be bored — bearable. After approximately two years of critical activity I was just beginning to be able to ascertain that I understood the German dramaturgical laws, when it began to be unbearable for me to spend a few evenings a week at the theater. Very rarely will you find in our criticisms the airing of the intellectual significance of a play, a discussion of its ideas or passions. By contrast, you will find strongly emphasized the conception that dramatic literature is written for theater and culminates in theater. This is how dramatic literature slips naturally into the ghostly arena of an æsthetic that lacks an existential basis. You will also always find the mediocre critic *remembering*. He is a backward-looking man, whose memory saves up many characters and plays, and — lacking any interest in intellectual organization — he uses the next best obvious pretext to organize these remembered bits. His criticism is, thus, always directed toward externalities and this is what is called the theater experience. With critics like these, Shakespeare would never have escaped being deemed a plagiarist of Italian fabulists, and the dramatic literature of our times would have to lay it on pretty thick to come off as something new.

Alone, an interest in theatrical virtuosity (it has, by the way, waned considerably in Vienna) can never carry the theater in the long run. I have great respect for the art of acting, but without fertilization from literature, and particularly from contemporary literature, it must eventually arrive at a kind of torpor amounting to nothing but platitudinizing with expressive gestures. The great ability of today's actors hinders us from noticing that we are already very close to this condition. But we see a vast amount of charming theater — even some that is, momentarily perhaps, existentially convulsive,[16] but a general emptiness still prevails, a shallow feeling on the whole, an internal hollowness.

The actors would happily blame the writers for not giving them anything to perform, partially with good reason! But why doesn't the theater have more or better writers? The career of writing, with all its obstacles and its minor celebrity, is not attractive for ambitious young people, and talented people are usually ambitious. If one can avoid being a writer these days, it is cleverer to become a banker or a journalist; it is thus no wonder that almost the only ones left for art are the morons and subaltern knights of business, those who can't do anything else, because they can do nothing else. If a worthy person turns his attention to writing, he usually choses the novel and not the theater. It is one of our ridiculous lies that drama still deserves — officially, so to speak — the first place in literature, even though the focal point of European literature has, at least for the last hundred

---

16. This phrase, "existentially convulsive," is an alternative to Christian Rogowski's translation of Musil's central, positively-weighted terms, *erschütternd* and *Erschütterung* as "existentially devastating" or "existential devastation" in Rogowski, *Dramaturgy*, 54. The words literally mean *shattered/shattering*, but are imbued by Musil with existential dimensions. Whenever we see these words in Musil's reviews, it is a mark of high praise.

years or so, been the novel. In comparison to the psychological commotion aroused by the European novel, dramatic writing pales.

Thus, finally, I have no other option than, despite my own doubts, to defend the theater directors. It is a matter of a complicated cultural collapse phenomenon, a condition with many symptoms that all affect each other, and among which no single one is more primary than the other, because all of them together are only partial phenomena resulting in a social process. The theater is dying; perhaps. It has sinned greatly; but nevertheless, it is dying like a child inside its mother's womb, while its mother dies, too. In his time, Hermann Bahr translated his experiences with "Modernism" into an excellent truth. He said that a people does not acquire its writers until it has its writing. That is to say, first the atmosphere must be created, then something can flourish in it; and so it is with the theater as well. It is unfathomable what would have to happen — in elementary school and university, in private life and public — to make it live again. In the meantime, one struggles on, the best one can. Something or other will come of it sooner or later. And there is, indeed, much already there.

One more special word, said especially in response to the remarks of the director of the Burg Theater, our national theater. For if there is any stage that swims "in the stream of events" and cannot simply float, it is his theater. That is why I found his remarks so alienating.

His definition of the theater in times of crisis as a means of distraction and comfort is certainly a novelty in war-time history, but I cannot go along with his remark that, "the countless plays submitted to the Burg Theater present nothing of the noteworthy, new literary strength of Austria; we have nothing but the same old home-grown productions: Schnitzler, Schönherr, Hofmannsthal." What is disturbing about this, is that one does not know whether Herterich means that the newer, noteworthy plays have yet to be offered to the Burg Theater, or whether he means that these newer plays are not worth noticing. In any case, one would have to respond to both comments in the same way: that a director is someone who must be able to take note. That is one of his essential characteristics. That is the reason why he has at his disposal not only the large ceremonial stage where, as far as I am concerned, he can produce classical playwrights like Pierre Frondaie or Molnár, but also the smaller stages that he can reserve for better purposes. I could name a half dozen Austrian writers on the spot for Herterich, writers whose dramatic productions are more elevated than at least two thirds of the plays recently performed at the Burg Theater. Furthermore, it would be a doubly senseless homeland-protection policy to not only not produce the younger Austrians, but, on their behalf, to rule out the younger Germans as well. I hope that Mr. Herterich has merely not yet had the time to familiarize himself with the lofty literary responsibility that he bears as director of the Burg Theater, and that he truly stands by what he says; otherwise, using Hofmannsthal and Schnitzler as an excuse would be very nasty. Even these writers would not have found it so easy to achieve the "usual home-grown productions" (for which I would not, by the way, have congratulated them so heartily), had they grown up in a time that, after Herterich's fashion, had not felt "compelled" — to "take chances on new, young writers."

THE "DECLINE" OF THE THEATER
(Theater Symptoms III)
[*Der Neue Merkur* (July 1924)]

This essay[17] owes its existence to the theater directors. In Vienna — dependent upon the state of the market, the disastrous franc speculation, and the like — there is suddenly a new condition, which they call the decline of the theater. I don't believe in it. What is remarkable about this situation is not the continuing course of this crisis, but the circumstances surrounding its outbreak. The dependence of the "moral institution," of the "higher cultural assets" on the boom and slump experience of a relatively small social class, evidently repudiates a whole assortment of general cultural catch phrases and reveals that this luxury item depends upon a surfeit of the wealthy.

Naturally every child of our generation knew that even theaters are business ventures; but apparently this used to mean as little to the essence of theater as it means when one says about a body that one knows that it must possess extension in space. This was because our theaters did their business in the name of culture, or, more

17. [Musil's note.] See the essays *Theater Symptoms* in *Der Neue Merkur* 6, issues 3 (June 1922) & 10/12 (January/February, 1923).

properly expressed, because bourgeois society regarded the theater as a cultural institution and sponsored it with words and partial amenities (like the national and state theater), while leaving it, for the most part, as is its wont, to the whims of the free market. Alongside art, there are the two other traditional cultural assets, scholarship and religion. Religion lives off of the organization of power that it was able to construct in the middle ages, and, as for scholarship, the state has not taken it into its protection out of some sort of sense of obligation, but because it wanted to wrest this instrument of power out of the hands of the church. Certainly, intellectual movements played some role here too, but, without support from power politics, scholarship would never have been successful. The example of the theater demonstrates the way that society treats cultural assets when it has no ulterior interests: one may, without letting one's self be confused by acute instances of decline, assume that the illness or agony of the theater, this latent condition of enduring decline from which it has suffered since the beginning of human memory, is a symptom of a phenomenon endemic to our society.

Amusement Crisis

One must not, of course, expect exceptional revelations from this, but it is still valuable to look at the theater for once, not as we usually do, as something isolated, with its own special sufferings and causes, blaming literature, or the actors, their directors, the critics and all those factors that make up the circle of the theater and therefore cannot reach beyond it. If, instead, one wants to look at it, along with its processes, as a partial phenomenon of a larger process, it is beneficial to remember that it was designated as a so-called higher amusement, also called a culturally-enriching or an educational amusement. For this is the way it lives on in the consciousness or half-consciousness of our society. And this also explains why its emphasis rests more or less equally upon both components.

Our contemporary German theater originated in courtly times; later, in imitation of the court, it became a ceremonial institution of bourgeois society. What is important here is the dependent role assigned to art — be it a matter of writers or of actors — from the time of theater's inception. A courtly society, straining not to be bored, created these social events, along with hunts, balls, and other distractions — events wherein one saw one's self within a ceremonial frame. And that which was performed on the stage was not the content, but rather only a part of this frame. For the people, this theater was an opportunity to gawk at the splendid society and to participate in the shared space and, even more intensely, in the fleeting but shared pulse emanating from the stage. This character of a kind of ceremony with onlookers was also continued in capitalistic times and it is well known that up to contemporary times it has been one of its strongest economic supports, that going to the theater, that oft-mentioned seeing and being seen, is understood as the most insouciant form of social assembly.

As a social amusement, it is also obvious that the theater has contributed to the transformations associated with contemporary late capitalism. The social nimbus of the theater does, indeed, still have its force, but one no longer meets up with people in the theater, one simply goes there or drops in; the performance is reduced to a quantified option on the amusement market, which one purchases, when one wants. (There remains a vestige of earlier times only at great premieres; but even in these cases one marks the change all the more, since at least three-fifths of those present are there in professional capacity.) And since the social circle of those who are interested in the theater has widened, taking on a more or less shapeless structure, changing the theater performance from a predominately obligatory to a predominately advertised amusement, it has adopted the essential characteristics of a business. There is a notable conformance between the psychology of theater and that of business. The psychological technique of the poster emphasizes two qualities, which every adroit advertisement should have: it must not merely be noticed, but it must take advantage of a feeling of familiarity; an aggressive poster annoys the passerby for weeks, but the object of irritation is suddenly surrounded by a feeling of warm intimacy, if one accidently comes across it as reality in a shop.

We find both features reflected in our theater business today; the greatest possible sensationalism alongside the greatest possible intimacy, i.e., banality. Therewith we find an explanation for a contradiction that is not often seen to be one. This contradiction rushes with greater and greater force toward its main cause. It seems, namely, that amusement requires a certain sense of compulsion. I am no sociologist, but I have noticed that all ceremonies have their occasions and nowhere in the world do people gather together solely for amusement. Even the famous sexual excesses of ancient and primitive times wrap themselves around religious dictates; the courtly festivals gathered people together to serve the princedom; the days when Christians gorge themselves the most are the most serious celebrations. It very much appears as if amusement requires a certain compulsion, in order to suppress the opposing forces of boredom and tedium. One can thus understand that even in theater, the more it tends toward a pure amusement, the more lukewarm it becomes. And this condition between laughing and yawning, stimulation and apathy, indeed, precisely this latent condition of an enduring decline wherein our theater has made itself so comfortable, has inspired these reflections. We are approaching a condition of pure amusement that reduces the need for variety to a thoroughgoing boredom. Our epoch has created this condition. We appended a social-hygienic moment to it — as "diversion" — but apathy is

THE "DECLINE" OF THE THEATER (TS III)

the reigning feeling in the public sphere; the public still accepts the theater as amusement. But the psychological effects of such a condition are the same as with all conditions of relaxation. They rock back and forth on a small swing above an empty space for a long time, which is tolerably pleasant. But if they happen to be interrupted, they want to be shaken up.

This is the reason why the theater audience is sleepily satisfied with minor variations of what has already been there for a long time, but also expresses gratefulness for stronger attractions, without taking them seriously. I believe that this condition is thus correctly described, and now we can see that the apparent contradiction between the most banal and the most sensational, which has been proven to be no contradiction at all when it comes to business, is also the psychology of amusement.

But now we have arrived at the two paths upon which the current evolution of the theater moves. On the one hand, theater becomes increasingly levelled, dull, and flat. All of the French and pseudo-French romantic comedies, all of the so-called problem plays and masterly theatrical conceptions, the plays enjoying serious acclaim — in other words, none other than the amusement and cash-register plays — can be described as a maximum of insignificant gags to a minimum of significant ideas. Thus, fundamental infertility is just as important for success as the fertility of superficial variations; or, in other words, the ability to gain a new perspective on a thing is by no means more important than the ability to not gain more than one new one. The more tepid and stale the whole, the more unique the one idea upon which the clever presentation of the piece lives; such works are often charming, but with each one, our general distaste for the theater grows. On the other hand, the development of theater demands that everything become ever more brash and garish. One plays the wild man on the stage, whether as sexual lout or as apostle; one appears as a representative of an age or a tendency. In order to overcome the public's inertia, the directorial circus brings actors onto the stage like tame beasts, who are made to perform feats that our simple animal natures reject. In the end, we more or less eviscerate the intestines of the theater when we make an instrumental element such as space itself the bearer of an intellectual emphasis. Without a doubt, certain values are achieved thereby and, in any case, these performances are much more enjoyable than the culture of stardom, which also should be mentioned here. But it is unquestionable that they too are derived from the requirement to constantly increase the level of stimulus; if one judges them by their success, they are strong rousing attractions, pistol shots in the silence. But the public, who knows everything ahead of time, already knew that the shots were blanks,[18] even though they played along a bit.

18. See Musil's farce, *Vinzenz and the Mistress of Important Men*, (229), where shooting blanks is one scenario of many used to parody theatrical clichés.

THE "DECLINE" OF THE THEATER (TS III)

What is less well-known than this nexus — and I don't imagine it could ever be emphasized crudely enough — is that our critical evaluation also reflects nothing more than a dramaturgy of amusement, a business dramaturgy, a dramaturgy of exhaustion. Of course, we have some excellent critics with personal perspectives about all of these problems — they are not the ones I refer to here. But if one were to analyze the touchstone by which influential mediocre criticism judges, it appears to be at bottom nothing but instructions about how to keep people awake who are threatening to fall asleep. This is done, for example, with suspense, that childish, transparent technique of letting someone guess something that is no longer a riddle from the very first moment. The requirements of dramatic clarity, whereby, to the greatest possible extent, everything that happens must happen, end in the catchy simplicity of the illustrated children's primer. One praises this if one immediately falls, in the first scene, as if through a hole in a picture window; if very much happens; if the characters swiftly change; and elegant entanglements — ones one had already expected — provide surprising outcomes to small complications. If one goes to the theater tired, one wants something to happen on the stage to counteract this tiredness — a tiredness that is simultaneously taken into consideration. Almost everything that is called dramatic technique is of this sort. A good playwright works like a manufacturing engineer, who knows that in the first third and shortly before the end of the working day the number of accidents is the smallest; he instinctively takes into consideration that the attention wavers, which is why three peaks are more intellectually stimulating than a flat plain, because the man with three ideas — by contrasting himself with the accumulated elevations — knows best how to take advantage of his own empty expanse. (This relates to the journalistic style.) But the critic falls for it and heralds such factory knowhow as a dramatic law, which the theater is proud to have cribbed over the course of the years. It is uncommonly rare that one finds in our criticism a remark about the cultural-intellectual significance of a play, a discussion of its ideas, passions, or even atmosphere; in contrast, very often we do find emphasized the conception that dramatic literature was written for the theater and ends in theater or that it has no deeper source and no higher goal than to meld together in some appealing weave and woof. One finds this sort of wool-ware-critic[19] always busy remembering other characters and plays that have appealed to him, and since he has no will or ability to grasp intellectual form, he compares them by their most obvious elements, most external similarities, and the crudest possible typological summaries of

19. The weaving/wool metaphor and pun is smoother in the German, where Musil uses the word "wirken," which means both to have an effect and to weave, in the first sentence, and then goes on to talk about "Wirkwaren," i.e., knitted goods, in the second.

characters and scenes. The apparently positive "appeal" displaces everything else into a secondary sphere. That which is suspicious in life is thus transformed into the highest requirement of theater: to be concerned with appearance, rather than with the central, original cause.

Naturally everything that has gotten confused within these people's heads does have a kernel of truth; but they make themselves servants of this uncertain bit of truth instead of its master. From stockholder to costumer, everyone talks about the theater with a ceaseless enthusiasm, as if they were speaking about a mysterious world, exempt from the usual rules of life, at whose threshold all experiences of the usual world recoil. And the critic doesn't mind going along. "Technique" no longer plays the same kind of role in the novel as it does in theater criticism (although it is technically at least as difficult as is drama), but the novel does play a greater role today in the mind of humanity. Probably the reason for both of these things is that the novel is not as good a business as theater.

Cultural Education Crisis [20]

One can naturally counter, against this attempt to understand our theater experiences through the concept of a commercial amusement transaction, that there are also other explanations. We are, after all, used to explaining

---

20. In German, *Bildungskrise*. The German term, "Bildung," which I have translated in this passage sometimes as "cultural education"

the conditions of art as a battle and exchange of principles and the appearance of certain personalities. But that goes along quite well with the former abstract observation, since the process of the emergence and coming into prominence of influential persons of a particular kind is largely caused by social conditions.

And that a social moment plays an important role here, at least when it comes to what is stigmatized, is evidenced by the fact, already mentioned, that such things are a great deal less apparent in the novel than in drama, even though almost the same people come into question in both cases. Further, that the phenomena in drama and painting are similar, even though the circle of people is different, while the social requirements — business and so-called collective consumption — are practically the same. Even more compelling is the argument that the condition diagnosed for the theater is, perhaps, not only applicable today, but was not much different in Goethe's time. The intellectually third-rate in those days certainly had its provincial, folksy traits, but these took about as much hold as a certain metropolitan intensity has caught on in all the performances of our times.

↵ and other times just as "culture," is a central, but untranslatable, word in German literature and social thought, a part, of course, of the term "Bildungsroman," usually translated as "novel of education." It is important to understand that the sort of education implied is a wide-reaching cultural education of the whole person, in the tradition of Goethe or of Schiller's "æsthetic education."

THE "DECLINE" OF THE THEATER (TS III)

It is probably true, too, that there is not much difference. But this leads directly to the second part of this observation, which has treated the theater as much under the rubric of amusement as cultural education. To say it outright: even if the incongruity between the two components has always been just as large, there still remains a larger difference today, in that the developmental directions of each one have switched places since that time. "Cultural education" — or, more precisely, the desire for it, the disposition favoring cultural education — was in youthful ascent at that time and today it is in descent, dissolution, or at least has fallen into a state of precarious crisis. At one time, the bourgeois society laid claim to the theater — with us, through the great minds of the classical past, and even today, a distant holy obligation seems to still play a role, but this panacea of cultural education itself has shared theater's fate. A "culturally-educated person" was originally more or less someone whom a modern literary school today would call a logocrat; it is a matter of an assertion of power based on intellect, an idea, which developed later in bourgeois liberalism, so that today the term "culturally-educated" is frequently used synonymously with wealthy. Culture itself is only protected to a certain extent — in the manner of good housekeeping. In general, it is left to its own devices by the capitalist society and the free market. The symptoms exhibited by the theater today are only one part of the widespread crisis of cultural education, or, if one will, the twilight of culture in which we live. A comparison with the history of the English theater of the nineteenth century — where the influence of the metropolis and the sociology of their amusements was apparent a few decades before us[21] — exhibits some of our symptoms (the banal sensationalism) in an even cruder form; but the counter forces that overcame this condition were not as vitiated by cowardice and doubts as they are today.

It pays to summarize some findings from relevant research about the fate of our "cultural education" and to compare the example of the theater against the whole.[22]

The term "cultural education" in its current meaning arose around the middle of the 18th century. General education meant, in those days, universal education; to educate oneself, to form oneself; Kant used the word culture for it; with Herder, then with Goethe, the meaning of *paideia* and erudition were added to the term. But in the main, from that time until the end of the 19th century, "cultural education" was the same as spiritual independence or enlightenment. Formed in the age of

---

21. [Musil's note.] Very valuable: E.L. Stahl, *Das englische Theater im 19. Jahrh.* [The English Theater in the 19th cent.] (Munich-Berlin: R. Oldenbourg, 1914).

22. [Musil's note.] I take this from a work by L. v. Wiese in his *Sociology of the School System* (Munich-Leipzig: Duncker & Humblot, 1921), a work that I mentioned in this newspaper.

Enlightenment, this conception encompassed the opposition to clerical and political bondage and was originally rational — including a belief in the trinity of nature, reason, and freedom. Later, as the belief in the autonomy of reason suffered considerable losses, this concept was partially displaced by the belief in natural scientific realistic thought. An important factor — one decisive for our difficulties — was, furthermore, contributed at the very beginning under the influence of Herder: the ancient ideal of general human wisdom. The ancient ethos was recommended as an exemplar for direct and absolute imitation. "One becomes a culturally educated person in the fullest sense, above all, through intercourse with the Ancients, these ancient fathers of human spiritual and intellectual cultural education, these eternal models of the correct, good, and practiced taste and of the highest accomplishment in the use of language; we must form our ways of thinking and writing in imitation of them; in imitation of them, we must model our reason and our language. The meaning of humanity, i.e., genuine human reason, is revealed to that man who has done this; he becomes a culturally educated person and proves himself to be one in both small and grand ways" (Herder: *On the True Meaning of the Liberal Arts and Primary School Education*, 1788).

One need only read this quotation to see how far behind we are in the organization of ideological transformations, to what extent we have been stalled at a phase that should have been temporary, how much we stand with our backs against the future, and in what sort of an unsustainable position we put ten thousand young people every year in our advanced schools.

It occurs to me that there is, in every education — although this will be contentious today — a general human value; and no form of education is merely a relative ideal of its time, but rather, all forms of education follow one another as partial solutions of a task that remains fundamentally the same. Yet, on the other hand, every education is determined by the column or social class that supports it, is painted and stuccoed by the relativity of the expectations and perceptions this column raises. Indeed, its prevalence probably was never a matter of its internal value, but rather always it is a reflection of the fact that it is a prerogative of the upper classes and therefore an argument for social advancement. In this way, there is a continuity among the German people (*à la* Paulsen):[23] the clerical-Latin ideal of cultural education with the clerics as the leading class, the courtly-French idea of the aristocracy, and finally the bourgeois-Hellenistic-humanistic ideal in which end-phase we probably find ourselves now. For every one of these kinds of cultural education, and also all others that we

23. Friedrich Paulsen (1848–1908) was a German Neo-Kantian philosopher and educator, author of the book (mentioned in Musil's Notebook 10 from 1919–1921), *History of Scholarly Education* (*TB I*, 531).

know of, developed according to the same scheme: a generally invasive transmission into the social body that appears to constitute a strong attraction. At first it occurs somewhat peripherally and is hardly noticed as its own phenomenon, but merely as the result of a life directed toward other decidedly different goals (i.e., in the Germanic-Latin middle ages) or in the countless myriad small alterations to life that are gradually integrated into the scheme of life (transition to Scholasticism in the so-called Modern period). It then comes consciously to the surface in its second phase, which one can call the Heroic (Classical). At this point, exuberant expectations are attached to it, and it awakens fervent striving. This is the time period when it begins to be organized according to a plan. The third developmental phase, wherein the now officially-sanctioned new impulse arrives, can be recognized by its characteristic bureaucratization. In our case, this process of whittling down to the bone came to its perfection in the 19th-century school system, and it necessarily induces yet another phase, that peevish disappointment which we now suffer. New ways to achieve the goal are sought, and depending on the conditions, they lead either to revolution or reform.

When one attempts to describe our situation, one comes up against the following fundamental characteristic of the crisis of cultural education: cultural education today has lost its social halo — and not only because of the political emancipation of the working class.

It is well known that education never reached the whole people, not even the middle class, but really only a very exclusive class, and, as such, was paused much earlier than even at its half-way point. As a result, the entirety of the people has become extraordinarily heterogeneous and will become increasingly so. The public education system is hardly more than a stopgap. The public school system takes up new intellectual impulses only with the greatest possible hesitation and uncertainty; the newspaper has, quantitatively at least, had the greatest success, but makes no secret of the fact that it remains more or less in thrall to the ideal of sensation and that it accommodates itself to the lowest possible reading level that must be able to grasp its transmissions. We lack, therefore, the very foundations for the quick, apt comprehension of intellectual achievements; and a vast cycle of contradictory impulses must already be stirring furiously in the mass requirement for hero worship, cruelty, sentimentality, bigotry, greed for money, addiction to pleasure, and curiosity.

But all this is already true for the culturally educated classes too. The ability to incorporate new intellectual impulses and to follow them along deep and vast inroads as much as possible has not kept up in any way with the hurtling consequences of such impulses, nor with the daily increasing mass of human beings for whom they are intended and upon whom their fate rests. Yes, one can say that the institutions which incorporated themselves in accord with reigning conceptions of cultural education, institutions such as schools, political structures, and churches will themselves put up a resistance to these new impulses.

A great number of ideas accumulate here — ideas that have either not been thought about or have been thought about badly — and those ideas, which we must use to instill order or to simplify the situation (in general they consist of the remains of the fragments of an 18th-century ideology that has not been replaced by anything new), are insufficient. The accumulation of intellectual discourse all around the earth, reaching back into distant times, the historic and the ethnological revelations about new forms of life, continue to pile up ever-new intellectual material. And as a necessary result of this, a sort of self-decomposition of culture must occur. The culturally-educated class was overpowered by a feeling of weakness; it lost its confidence in its own education and therewith a large part of its prestige. Every one of us recognizes this confusion; uncertainty and cultural distress are the well-known accompanying stigmata. And every one of us salvages today what suits him — from what is left of the swooning, supine German spirit.

Aside from this, the educational material of the present tends to have advanced in the realms of positivistic knowledge, facts, science, specializations — the practical mastery of the world has made fantastical progress; the significance of the *real* in contrast to that which has been *thought* has become palpable to a degree unimaginable up until now, while the concept of cultural education that is supposed to organize this education has remained old and Herderesque. This well-known incongruity between the new influences and the form of the vessel that is supposed to contain them is a main cause of all the symptoms. The attempt to bring a realistic tendency into the school system was, to be sure, already present, but it both overshot and came too short of its goal, in that, on the one hand, it attempted to force the humanistic content into the realistic, and contrarily, because ultimately it merely piled content next to content, without this side-by-side accumulation giving birth to a new intellectual spirit.

Theater and Cultural-Education Crisis

If one transposes this general condition onto the case of the theater, the symptoms are the same, even when it comes to the details of the ameliorative attempts. I would like to just touch on three of them here:

Art and the school system both have been, for about 30 years, in opposition to so-called intellectuality. One has compared the arid rational education of the school tyrants to the ideal of education of the "heart"; has demanded "intuition" instead of the sharpening of judgment, "experience" instead of lecturing, photographs instead of gripping transcription and other things of this sort. The results of the same tendencies can be found in

THE "DECLINE" OF THE THEATER (TS III)

the realm of art. Impressionism already cultivated the partiality for writers who must speak to the heart or some similar organ that one conceives of as having no contact with the human cerebrum, and has thereby contributed considerably to cutting theater off from intellectual developments. It was forced to drastically deform itself into something simple, to function through action and emotional gesture in a kind of illiterate language. The one result was a noticeable lack of intelligence in dramatic writing; the other was the expectation shared, up to the present, that a great dramatic writer will come, who shall be able to speak to everyone in the most profound way. That this imagined writer with the common touch, of course, never does come, fits right in with the lament that our times are no longer capable of producing art, as well as a fully unnecessary dissatisfaction with our selves. Even the subsequent "generation" did not correct this error; the exaggerated reliance on stage design, dance, voice modulations, mimetic composition, was an attempt to find a new means of expression, instead of reorienting the old verbal one for a new intellectual use. Nothing more than an enrichment in a few cases was possible.

The second tendency that streamed through the educational movement was a social-ethical one; instead of personality, an expansion of the self through collectivity, a refinement of social sensibility and its strengthening through the education of the will, there is a radical break with the idea that education is the development of the individual human soul: everyone has often read of this in one form or another. To an extent, these demands meld with or combine with the former ones: insofar as they have had an influence on the theater, they, too, result in an art made up of a sort of holy, ceremonially-unified language of the people and of feelings. It is especially recognizable in the frequently concomitant rejection of "individual" art as something that has been outgrown. Well, one can certainly say that the old hero of our theater, with his specific tragic conflict of the free will, oppressed by the limits of bourgeois law, was truly a free market hero. But that already changed long ago — if not with the requisite awareness. I once expressed it with the formula: the tragic conflict between the individual and the law must now be replaced by an avowed conflict with the laws of earthly existence — a conflict that is often unresolvable, but always bearable. Therein lies the difference between the time of the Enlightenment, which believed in the autonomy of the moral laws and reason, and the time of empiricism, which recognizes an infinite task with only partial progresses. This empiricism is the great intellectual experience which we are up against, if our *globus intellectualis*, with its small educated class and its vast impenetrable masses, does not explode first. Socialism (wherefrom the socio-ethical reform plans of the theater mainly stem) will alter none of this, just as long as the tendency for world exploration and mastery are inherent to mankind, which is probable.

THE "DECLINE" OF THE THEATER (TS III)

I do not doubt — the whole first part of this explication already said as much — that the alteration of the form of society will also lead to the alteration of art; but when it comes to the basic problems of creation — and the conflict between individual and collectivity belongs in this discussion — these alterations may, with the exception of periods of transition, only shift the emphases and the form of the expression. Even Socialism carries the stigmata of the present in its cultural strivings, an inability to unite mechanics and the soul. In politics, it is certainly more likely to be too rational than not rational enough and, at least in Germany, without a strong heart, it abandons art to a kind of extension of the heart that shall come or already is there. Among those of its followers who are art reformers there are unfortunately many ostriches who stick their heads in the future, while they cannot understand anything that is strong, salubrious, evolving in even today's theater.

The immediate expression of a weariness with cultural education is ultimately reflected in the "anti-literary" position, which can so often be sensed in the discussion of theater questions. Liberation of the theater from the ballast of culture and intellect, reawakening of the pure boisterousness of the need for play, improvisation, actors' theater are all well-known slogans, whose influence extends from a theater calendar that is tailored only toward actorly achievements to the more serious attempts to revive the improvisational theater of the

Baroque era. After all that has been said, nothing more needs to be added. In my opinion, all of this can only result in a situation where the literature of men of letters is replaced by the writing of journalists, which is read daily in the newspapers by actors.

Even without this journalistic substitution, a great many of our writers already ensure this development. While one was busy defending and fighting against "tendencies," one had not bothered to account for the fact that the most influential and common direction of dramatic writing, encompassing all the various movements, is the one that lends itself to journalism. Stimulating, with smooth corners, some temperament, occasionally clever and with pointed emphasis and potent displays, being relevant and a few other things are the virtues that the talented dramatic journalist borrows from his colleague at the newspaper. And there is some real talent here. The downsides are: one searches for the new, but only finds the newest; all the different impulses that float in the intellectual atmosphere are blended together, but no single one is deepened and ripened. Naturally, the fact that this activity only serves a rather profane diversion becomes more and more clear, just as in the case of "entertainment," while its devotees fancy themselves to be maverick servants of intellectual culture.

I believe that if one familiarizes oneself with the sort of relationships that those people who participate in the daily experience of theater learn bit by bit, one will see that this is not without influence. But the attempt to extrapolate possible solutions for the crisis from there would be excessive. Thoughts like these do not pretend to be theories, which explain phenomena. Things hang together in this way, but they also hang together in another way. That is the difference between life and rigid order. But one can only follow the connection from one dimension at a time. I must also admit that the attempt to follow up even the smallest thing in contemporary literature already seems ridiculous to me, while we are swimming in a sea of foam. Nevertheless, I wouldn't want to go to the trouble of avoiding a few conclusions that present themselves. The most remarkable thing about the condition of our theater is, indeed, that we only recently enjoyed a high point and even today have some very significant individual achievements. The weariness, hopelessness, and indifference that has made itself at home in the atmosphere of the theater are much worse than is justified by the theater itself. They are a cultural-education weariness, a matter of uncertainty, lack of intellectual courage, not knowing whereto. The stimuli that the theater emits every evening evaporate into emptiness, because the cultural categories that could incorporate them are lacking. These categories would first have to be re-created. But therein one pushes up against the unravelling totality represented by every cultural crisis — and finds no end.

If I, personally, attempt the narrowest summation of the experiences I have gained over the years —and I believe that anyone who is at all capable of doing so comes to such conclusions in the same way — I can only say that nothing has exhausted me so much in my life as the breathtaking non-intellectual spirit that fills, not only the atmosphere of the theater, but our literature as a whole. One finds effortless success, if, say, one mixes two to ten portions of significance with 90 to 98 parts insignificance; even that gives the impression of being intellectual culture. The lowest degree of this admixture is enough if the thing is called German and healthy. The higher-level mixture will not be accepted from either side and is held to be worthless. The same can be said of soul, passion, strength and every human reaction whose existence will only be acknowledged if at least nine-tenths of it is run of the mill.

But if clever people (and today people are so very clever) relinquish an activity to this kind of idiocy, there is always a reason for it and this one is: *tua res agitur* — and the sort of relationship, through which something arouses the people's energy, is here lacking. If a normal, civilized person sits down in the theater today and sees a soul screaming and wailing: what can we expect from him? He suffers blows against some unspecified internal organs and he must find these actions either shockingly unpleasant or shockingly interesting; the difference is really almost only a matter of good will. And when it comes to experience, the two reactions merge into each other with ease. But if he finds them interesting and wants to say something about them, he will find himself faced with an immeasurably arbitrary choice of expressions. For the critic generally finds himself in a rather similar position. One recognizes critics by their expressions: temperament, chaos, knowledge birthed by blood, voice of our time, roar of an experience, dynamic between man and man .... I have grabbed a few quite at random. Do they make any impression? Do they describe an experience? Do they refer to a single human value? Something one could grasp? All of it is vague, imprecise, subjective, immeasurable, singular, accidental. I would like to highlight one of the causes: the training grounds for "intellectual culture" are in literature class, where, on the one hand, of course, critics and audiences receive their decisive preparation, but where on the other hand, the whole process self-perpetuates. What would one say, if university level physics students were to listen to or learn the biographies of Kepler and Newton, how their personalities, their times, and their works were related, but nothing at all about the interlocking systems that combine into a knowledge of physics? Yet this is precisely what happens in literature. The humanism that we practice is, at best, comparative, ethical, or fruitful for life only as an aside; generally, it seeks rather, as much as possible, to understand personalities, times, and cultures as a whole and to set up this whole as a model. The essential content value is neglected. We have the biographical, but we lack a consciously ideographic understanding, which is increasingly left, more or less, both in life as in school, to personal whim and taste. I know very well the significance of the "magic of personality" in art, and especially in the theater; but when another person ingests the personality of a work's creator, the same thing happens as with the ingestion of any nourishment: a depletion of elements and their assimilation. Every human work consists of elements, which also exist in countless other connections; but if one understands the phenomenon in only one particular way, the work disintegrates amid the motile categories of the soul — categories that have existed from the beginning and still exist today — and it transforms itself into an interpretation of life. That is what we understand to be objectivity here; and as long as we don't possess it, yes, nor even have a presentiment of its necessity — as long as we only wait for the overpowering personality (of the writer, the work, the actor), which we would like to slurp down as a whole like an oyster, we will not arrive at better conditions. If one were to ask oneself, for example, what differentiates times of religious revival from other times, one would find, not only the intensive preoccupation of man with God, but also an intensive preoccupation with life itself, a burning objectivity of presence.

This leads, by the way, right back to that common touch, which the theater has lost. If one ignores everything that separates the theater from the people, i.e., prices, performance times, and the like, ignoring even the exceedingly vast difference in niveau and expectations that cannot be overcome by universal public education alone, there still remains the unfulfilled requirement of a vast panoply of characteristics that might bring the theater to life. The first of these is the preoccupation of mankind with himself. Even on the low level of common conversation, someone from Rome is *in play* with another person with his whole person, the way a woman plays with her fan; he argues for himself and his thoughts, as he speaks. We, on the other hand, have the ideal of *action* on the stage and in life. This difference is, thus, a matter of ethnic culture and is not just a question of the stage. How then does one bring such a culture back to the prerequisites of drama, a culture whose ideal is the strong silent man of few words, the off-duty lieutenant; a culture, which received a criticism after its own heart, i.e., the sort in which spirit rumbles today like the noise in a classroom when the teacher unexpectedly is called away?

I don't know how. But herein we see again the relationship of such problems with the whole.

SELECTED REVIEWS

VIENNESE THEATER EVENTS
Vienna, March 28

[*Prager Press* (March 30, 1921)]

Premiere at the Burg Theater; *The Swan*, a play by Ferenc Molnár

A bourgeois gentleman, tutor of princes, is taken advantage of and induced to be the spur for an heir to the throne who is taking his time in finding a bride. But it is not insignificant that he is also an important historian, astronomer, and fencer. He "gives it" to the prince. He "breaks through" the ceremonial formality. He ... but the little princess too, who was supposed to be an accomplice in the depraved plan to stimulate the heir to the throne by flirting with the tutor, she too does not lack a noble heart. Sword, Regalia, Historia! — Should the game turn serious? She pities the tutor so much. She is ashamed of herself. What do princesses do in such situations? They kiss. They explain: a heart beats even in the breasts of princes and princesses. One suffers anxiety and anticipates the coming of the democratic republic in the last act.

But expecting such an outcome, one has underestimated Molnár. Up to that point, the decisive question of personal development had been considered from the servants' view of the bourgeois heart before 1918; the abolition of nobility was required (perhaps also the reinstatement of the monarchy in Hungary): thus, one can condone the sacrifice of the awakened heart to the national interest. Not: an inhumane state, but rather, one that is even considered necessary, one smiled upon by ascendant bourgeois observers of humanity. They do not end up together and Marlitt rolls over angrily in her grave; but precisely 180 degrees.[24]

Molnár is least successful in this last act, but it is, thus, the best one. In his otherwise extraordinarily precisely-painted watercolors, he leaves few cloudy or blank spaces, wherein one might reflect — usually, the author fills them in with something worse. Unfortunately, it happens like this: if an author masters the stage exquisitely, he will necessarily be mastered by it; and the stage is the stupidest place in literature, if not in all of Europe. Even the basic idea of *The Swan* — so fitting for the stage — could be elevated to something of spiritual worth. The prerequisites for this are not lacking in the play, and there are even places where it attains this height; but it would be difficult for it to remain so fitting for theater if it were to succeed even more. It is the same in life:

24. Reference to E. Marlitt (1825–1887), male pseudonym of Friederieke Henrietta Christiane Eugenie John, one of the most-read German writers of her time. Her formulaic works often featured orphan girls, struggling with the help of a bourgeois work ethic to attain independence.

a small head fits well on an elegant body, but a significant head never really sits upon a body that can give a tailor great pleasure.

The circle of authors for whom the Burg Theater is accustomed to work puts the theater in the comfortable position of being perfectly prepared to do justice to Molnár's works too with a suitable production.

Meanwhile, at the Neue Wiener Bühne, one experiences, under the violent commando direction of G.W. Pabst, the last night of Expressionism, which has been condemned to death. Killing is very beautiful; but to kill so many people in response to a bylaw or the appendix to regulation Number So and So, and to still be, when off duty and no longer under orders, a good-natured person: this is the original sin. That's the main idea, more or less.

This thought is capable of being developed and was in fact developed during the German collapse of 1918 — and in other places too. It remains valuable, despite the fact that it — half understood & half explained — has paralyzed a great people. But today it is hardly any more significant than a thought cloud. Anyone who wants to learn more about it can read the essay, "The Curse of the Objective Mind" by Walter Strich in last year's issue of *Der Neue Merkur*. The one-act play, which is the impetus for these thoughts, is called *The Hangman*. Its author is Maria Lazar. In it, the head falls before the execution.

But Maria Lazar published a book in 1920 with the Tal Press called *The Poisoning*. It is made up of youthful elbowing, a sometimes-reckless uninhibited vision, is rich in ideas and an agile facility for figurative language. But it lacked almost any trace of personality or intellectual consistency; a very nervous ego-impressionism as *Ersatz* is not, however, grounds to condemn. Thus, it is all the more annoying to see the talented author scribbling like this.

CORRESPONDENCES?
[*Prager Presse* (March 30, 1921)]

Empirically, the person who is condemned to experience the stream of so-called artistic events finds himself, soon enough, floating along melancholically and morosely. There have only been two of them recently that were able to hold one's attention for more than a moment. These were two cases of theatrical diarrhea. One was suffered by the masters of Viennese criticism and the other by the mayor of this city.

The cause was that we lack a law stipulating that one must write theater reviews — in certain serious instances — on the anniversary as well as on the premieres of a performance, and book reviews five years after the publication of a book. Further, that the critics must polemicize against each other for as long as it takes for a total knockout blow to emerge from out of the arbitrary whim and stench of subjective response.

This idea is naturally not for serious men, who have more important things to do besides bothering with æsthetic questions. But if someone were to write that he doesn't want to reflect any further about Saint Thomas Aquinas' confusing ideas, but that sometimes Aquinas does utilize some pretty expressions — these serious men would call this statement superficial. When everyone says the same thing about a writer, where it is a sign of the same sort of religious shallowness, they think nothing of it. With the exception of a few worthy examples, this was the case when it came to the criticism of the premier of Paul Claudel's *The Exchange* at the Viennese Burg Theater. In this case, great minds, who had only lately given their most profound donations to the Concordia Ball, did not even bother to hide their rejection in irony. One must regret that there was not one single voice raised against such a lack of understanding, despite the 30-year uphill battle that has been waged since Ibsen was received in the same way — a battle which we have to thank for what little artistic earnestness we have today.

I don't want to write about either the play or about the production, except to note that, with a very remarkable exertion of energy and talent, it almost succeeded in completely reversing the play's meaning. They attempted, namely, to perform *The Exchange* impressionistically, from the outside in, like the workings of a commonplace gear, which randomly manufactured a group of people. Instead of from inside to outside, instead of proceeding *à la* Claudel from the rocky foundation of general ideas, from which the "ideas" of individual people emerge as dryly as cacti, which nevertheless have incomprehensibly fleshy leaves. In *The Exchange*, this is his style more than in any other play. Every figure speaks its catechism and exchange: a square made up of two triangles is not formed between people, but rather between life principles or moral systems, not because of individual contingencies, but in a dialectic of values. It almost would remain merely a recipe and a game of patience, were not the most essential parts gathered together with *such* precision that these normal sentences are transformed in one blow into tangible individuals with their fates and their lyrical emanations. Whosoever does not think this possible, should remember that catechisms are not written for readers but for human beings, who are supposed to live by them; with the proper prerequisite, that whosoever does so, becomes a man after the catechism's heart.

The better the performance was, the less was the play able to reach its internal goal, and I am perhaps more of an opponent of Claudel than a devotee; but even so, it was like a blow to the heart. But many critics missed this. On the stage was an enormous debate about life and they thought that they were witnessing a reportage of a sexual matter, with an excess of lyricism. They did not recall that the stage is a moral institution. One must, however, in their defense, add that this has long been forgotten and, even among contemporary writers, few know this. Those who do, seem to substitute a moral public restroom for it; at least they are always in the greatest possible spiritual hurry.

More fun was the second event, the scandal of the pogrom surrounding *La Ronde*. I will only repeat the most essential facts.

The Federal Legal Council, Glanz, forbids the production of Arthur Schnitzler's *La Ronde*. The Arch-Deacon of St. Marx, Mayor Reumann, explains that this was his territory, and allows for it to continue to be performed. Mayor Reumann is protected from the suspicion that he supports literature, despite the literary prizes which the city of Vienna has given out during his time in office. So that one does not — God forbid — think that he has forgotten himself, he protests that he merely stands and falls by §7802 of the Ministerial decree of the year 623. Between the two parties — like a stubbornly indecisive dachshund who is lured from both sides: "Come to the gentleman!" — stands the chief of police, Schober, the strong man of Austria. The one side demands that he close the theater; the other, that it not be allowed to cave in. Suspense as in a street scuffle, where the honor of the audience demands that the opponents finally come to blows. The always-correct legal advisor admonishes the upholding of the higher administrative court, the Arch Deacon turns once again to the onlookers, demanding that they, for the last time, hold him back so that nothing disastrous happens. The lack of movement in the scene develops into a traffic obstacle. But luckily, at just the right moment — snorting modestly, with Nibelungen-brass-knuckle-rings in their pockets — comes along one of our leagues of young people of Christian-Aryan worldview, storms the theater one night and turns the somewhat passé *La Ronde* into a futuristic event wholly in the spirit of Marinetti, with rotten eggs, blank cartridges, opened hydrants and battered female audience members whose grooming is perfected by having their clothes torn off. Now the president can forbid any further performances in the interest of public safety and whatever happens in the higher administrative court is nothing but a theoretical sequel.

Since such things have been happening everywhere over the last three years, we should judge them, not from a Viennese perspective, but rather as a general test of the apparent preparedness of the German chief of police. In accord with the significance of this event, I do not want to conceal my opinion. The man from Berlin (*quel boche!*) placed the performances under the protection of the police, as if it were a matter of an interrupted business deal. I believe that he did, in fact, the only thing that was his duty. The nation should have only one relationship with art: to create structures that safeguard it. The stage is a moral institution; the nation's job is to protect the institution and leave the morality to the stage. If one takes art seriously, it will be serious and I am of the unmodern opinion that it can then be one of the most serious human endeavors. How easily could the mayor of Vienna — regardless of whether Schnitzler's dramatization is tasteless or not — have spoken about these things in a way that would have made one listen. But there has never been an official voice, which has admitted to the validity of these ancient truths. He could have indicated that in a short time, there would be something profoundly moral performed, that art has ebbs and flows, and that a healthy national sense must entail respect for institutions that are larger than their boundaries; just as one may not raise a row in the church if a preacher makes a mistake in the text. He could also have indicated that one does not do away with the murkiness of a well by spitting into it and that our nation — buried as it is beneath so much rubbish — requires, in order to find its way out, the flexible strength of cultural preeminence, not the naïve athleticism of iron-limbed youths with milk-moustaches.

But shall one demand that politicians discover a seriousness in art, which critics and artists, for the most part, have lost themselves?

MOSCOW ART THEATER
[*Prager Presse* (April 21, 1921)]

I.

Prague has the good fortune of seeing them perform again. Years ago, in Berlin, I was there when they presented *Uncle Vanya*, still in those days, under Stanislavski himself. I admit that I hesitated before the reunion; war lay between, and that which one calls art had changed its aspect in the meantime; the Russian revolution had kept Stanislavski and Nemirovitsch-Dantschenko, the spiritual forces behind this artists' troupe, behind in Moscow, while a portion of the performers and directors, who had fallen into Denikin's[25] hands, were banished or released to the freedom of the West — I don't know how to say it more correctly, but it is all the same. In any case it was not to be expected, even if one had the kernel of the troupe before one, that it would not have suffered from this distancing from the source of its powers. Unless it were a case of a miracle. But this is not a small troupe of actors, but rather a wandering human community, who carry their God and their soul permanently with them.

25. Reference to Anton Ivanovich Denikin (1872–1947), the Polish-born Russian general, leader of the anti-Bolshevik forces in the Russian Civil War (1918–1920).

Well, it is the kernel of the troupe. And it is a case of a miracle!

I saw *The Night Asylum*, *The Three Sisters*, *The Karamazovs*. These pieces constituted the strongest shocks and the deepest moments of happiness, which art, which life, is capable of providing. Despite the fact that I did not understand a word. It is the perfection of theater.

I will attempt to remember and refer to a few details that I noticed, without affirming that one should remember this or that in particular and not the inexhaustibility of so much else; the real work of art is infinite, says Gœthe.

Above all, there is the music of their voices. All of these actors can sing. One learns to with Stanislavski, before one depicts people. That is such a simple and splendid idea. We do it too — peripherally. But not even opera singers intone correctly and therein it is clear how much finer vocal cords and ears must be, if they are to depict the undulations of the speaking soul, which is often apparently speaking of something else entirely. That is why the choral yammering of the modish stage never coalesces into song — this impoverishment of the spiritual side of song is, to me, like having ink splattered into my ear. Here, one experiences the thousand convolutions and rhythmic fragments of expression that obtain between two human beings. Because they *can* sing, they do not; instead, they speak the most dream-like beautiful prose that I have ever heard. And if they really do sing sometimes, because the poet wants it, there is a moment of silence — I don't know whether it is really in the room or just in the enchanted soul of the listener — when one believes one is clearly feeling that something is happening to one now — a rhythm of the blood or still deeper inside — but the voices already have nothing more to ground them and they hover in a heaven of sorrow.

The eye is no less considered than the ear. One could keep one's ears covered and just look, without tiring. The gestures seem to grow out of the characteristics of the roles, to take on their own meaning — images that engulf and then dissolve into new configurations! — Without compromising the modesty of their role as servants to the action, the way the fluttering of a gown accompanies someone in the act of walking: this alone has never before existed. But that is not even the half of it. As an example, I will merely suggest one thing, the authority with which they direct the attention of the audience. They succeed in ensuring that one sees everything, when usually, otherwise, one is always hanging on some nail or other and has to chase after the backstory; if one had been paying too much attention to the hero, or had begun to ignore the hero because a clock was striking in the background. With the Moscow Theater, one misses nothing and their directors orchestrate the movements of our attention with such an uncanny artistry that these movements themselves are an enjoyment to behold. It is an artistry of nuance: of time and intense nuance, as never before experienced.

I believe they succeed in this because they leave so much out; although one hardly notices it. One believes that their performance grows naturally out of the scene itself, like a garden filled with a thousand freely sprouting ideas; but in truth, these people perform with a remarkable restraint and control and, in lieu of the many gestures that would be possible in reality — and which those actors bent on realistic portrayals would pile on, one on top of the other — instead of these many gestures, they choose only one, which embodies the entire significance of the moment, because it is a distillation of all the dimensions of this magical directing. In this way, they gain the necessary time to synthesize the single effects into a symphony that is ten-times denser than reality. They sound the pure note, uninterrupted by all peripheral actorly sounds, the note of poetry, and what they perform is no longer theater, but art.

II.

It would be, thus, a mistake to call their style Naturalistic or Impressionistic, even though the pieces by Gorky, Chekhov, and the depiction of Dostoevsky might mislead one in this direction — or to mistake their work as the late flowering of a faded artistic movement. What they enact — beside the fact that Impressionism is as much an asylum for homeless artists as is Expressionism today — does not seem to us like a twenty-year-old obsolete art form, but rather as the art of the future, insofar as the European theater could be conceded to have a future at all.

In order to check my theory, I sought them out and mischievously asked them what they themselves called their style. Just as I had imagined, they looked at me with big eyes and answered: We perform *The Life of Humans* by Leonid Andreyev with decorations by Aubrey Beardsley, we perform Maeterlinck, we perform *Hamlet* in the style of Gordon Craig, Stanislavski performs in the Moscow Chamber Theater amid stylized decorations: We play every piece according to its essence. — I am certain, just as they may softly elevate realistic plays (usually performed so badly) above the boards, that they restore to fantastical ones a dizzying sense of reality.

For they create the body of the play from out of its soul. If I have heard correctly, it happens that they work sometimes for three years on one piece. Vladimir Nemirovitsch-Dantschenko, the writer, watches over the spirit; Stanislavski conjures forth the bodily share. I would find it, in any case, quite natural, and it should be taken as a lesson for our dramatists, who ready their pieces in three months. One can easily come up with ideas and in the chaos of our times a versatile soul experiences all kinds of scenarios; usually, if one throws a costume (as new and as modish as possible) over this astral momentary body, the work of art is already finished. But it is not the kind of work, in the sense of that internal totality, which Goethe called infinite and inexhaustible. This totality occurs moreover only when — seemingly paradoxically — the soul of a writer has exhausted itself on a work; when it has transformed its shape so much within the work, that it can barely recognize itself anymore, so that it can barely encompass the work any longer, as if the soul were encountering the work, in its terrifying completion, as if it were a second nature. And in reality, there is nothing more natural than this seeming paradox. For whoever is a writer and not just a schmoozer, does not just arrange his ideas, but rather arranges his world picture, his world wish, his world will inside of every single idea. And insofar as struggle and work are larger in his whole existence than the contents of any one moment, these two things will be greater and more filled with rich associations than can be grasped by any one moment, and the work that has come into being will, in the moment of its completion, overshadow its creator, just as the many-branched crown of a tree overshadows the branch that bears it. — Of course, this doesn't belong in a newspaper. And yet it does. For, the fact that such rigor is hardly ever practiced these days is one of the reasons that our artistic fashions spread like galloping consumption and our educated public follows the competition of book-makers as if they were bookies.

The same is true for the actor. Nothing is simpler for a person with mimetic abilities than to empathize more or less with an indicated type, to rashly appropriate a "personal" interpretation of the stereotypical, and to let fall all manner of possible gestures into this empty infinite space. But the art of acting, if it is to be more than boring cinema, only occurs when personal whim is inhibited by a sense of responsibility toward the conception of a total meaning. The way in which the Moscow Artists do this is the strongest argument one can find against all the usual critical and theater blather about how something well written can be effective on the stage, or, how, on the other hand, something can be a nullity, but still a great piece of theater; inane talk, which comes, with its professional jargon about scenes, dramatic structure, and the like, half out of the literature seminar and half from the Operetta market. The Moscow Artists, on the other hand, take the intellectual vision of the writer, which has been seen, heard, thought, and felt simultaneously, that is all united, but they also take whatever is not fully clear, but which is alive, nevertheless, and they work through it, through all of its suggested dimensions, until, instead of something shrouded in shadow, they arrive at a completely embodied unison. This has, by the way, a social aspect to it. The repertoire of the Moscow performers is only 11 plays, enough, thus, for only one season. But if our standing repertoire theater no longer offers even the possibility of the highest achievements of art, it must be forced off the stage, and the thought of a future wherein fewer plays were performed is more comforting, after all, than the thought of the European stage slowly languishing of incurable dementia.

Today it seems as if the Russians had brought an exotic world with them, as if the sky of the steppes and the vast, deep homeland hovered over their performances. In truth, it is something that could become our own; it is the cosmos of a well-crafted literature, an arrangement of incommensurable associations, enclosed within the atmospheric arc of an enormous sky. There are actors under this sky, who are some of the greatest performers alive today, but even these strong individuals bow down before the spirit, no, they bow down toward it, the way someone does who lifts up something fragile. Their collaboration is neither balletic, nor a tyrannical discipline, but rather the life of a spiritual community. It is, in itself, a performance of human absorption, one of the most astonishing performances there is. Aside from in this troupe, it does not exist on the stage. Nor, either, aside from them, does it exist in contemporary life.

AN EVENING AT THE THEATER

[*Prager Presse* (May 4, 1921)]

There are two kinds of plays; those written by writers, and those in which a writer writes a play. The first kind are usually bad; the second kind always. In the comedy I am about to describe, a writer writes a play.

I no longer remember the scenes of the play that were quoted, but I do remember the style: "rolling gold, capricious luck; what is fame??!" Or: "I, leave my child?! Do you take me for the kind who lacks sacred maternal feelings, or…?!"

Now, of course, I don't precisely know how much the play's author was making fun of the author in the play; but I did notice how much he did not do so: he has someone say that he has a great talent, which was only made superficial through success. Like Hans Müller,[26] perhaps, before his catharsis. If I rightly understood, the serious nature of this comedy is hidden in this thought.

---

26. Hans Müller (1882–1950) was an Austrian playwright, screenwriter, and director. His plays were some of the most-performed works at the Viennese Burg Theater in the first two decades of the 20th century.

The writer who has been rendered un-serious meets a serious actress and is struck to his depths. He takes the leading role in his play away from his lover, a theater star — in the melancholy moment when she knows that she has outlived both the zenith of her fame and of her love — and gives the role to the up-and-coming rival. He even decides to get married, which obviously is as uncommon for writers as it is common that theater stars come running after them. But at this, the prima donna whose zenith as star and woman has passed, explodes.

There is a dark spot; on the lily-white frock of the serious young actress. Did she or didn't she ... ? There is in fact another white garment in this quickly darkening background. It belongs to an elegant frock coat and the frock coat belongs to a baron and the baron is co-owner of the theater. And when the serious young actress was still languishing hopelessly in the provinces, he went out, scouting for talent. What happened to her then, I dare not suggest. Did she let her innocence fall from her or did she wrap herself in it? If the former, then only out of pride, in order to make it seem less likely that it could have happened from sensuality. And so powerful women stumble. But the successful playwright finds this too much to bear. And while the prima donna explodes, this other business shatters his soul. He had thought that he would find a tender lily-white frock on his wedding night, but will instead have to deal with a suspicious dark spot on his bed; one looks forward to the honeymoon so much, but already in the first hotel there will be bugs! There is a terrible scene during the premiere; he hits the fiancé. In the intermission, before the denouement. But creative life is sometimes just like the gold-producing ass and the cudgel-out-of-the-sack from the fairy tales: life beats you up and the artist lets loose golden feelings; in her emotional sufferings, the serious actress performs smashingly. She makes his play a success, but afterwards she no longer wants to marry him. One can hope that she can still marry the noble theater sponsor, which, as far as my understanding of economic matters goes, would be more advantageous; in any case, writers like these I have never seen.

I would like to keep it a secret where this play is being performed, who has written it, and what it is called.[27] Why make trouble? One should simply take note of what can come of such a satyr play; how one can make a pleasant meal even from the thistles of life if only — one knows the right audience for it. The author is an irreproachable confrère of the feuilleton. A life with a little bit of wit on the side, and an eye for its weaknesses.

27. The mysterious play in question was *Behind the Curtain* by the Austrian playwright and journalist Marco Brociner (1852–1942). Fanta, *Gesamtausgabe*.

Without the will to fight them off. Without the arrogance to try to do better. A Parsifal, even when he looks at Pitaval.[28] A hollow pipe, through which the public spirit gushes year after year.

---

28. After the French advocate, François Gayot de Pitaval, who published several volumes of *causes célèbres et intéressantes* between 1734 and 1743.

THE DEATH OF DANTON BY GEORG BÜCHNER

On the Performance at the German Volks Theater, Vienna

[*Prager Presse* (May 22, 1921)]

How would I produce Büchner if I were the dramaturge of the Moscow Art Theater? Above all, beginning with his words. Büchner's words are like an outbreak of fever, conjuring up colorful, beautiful, irregular spots that merge into each other now and then to form strange figments. In the beginning was the Word: that goes for the whole epoch. And before the Word, was Shakespeare.

I must add that it almost cost Alfred Kerr — even though no one could come up to the level of this critic — his head and collar, when he said that Shakespeare's works are dead for us in large doses. I must repeat it: *in large doses* they are dead for us today. (Guardians of the dramatic, grim seminarians and thunder-hurling feuilletonistic non-seminarians usually use Shakespeare when they want to throw him at us moderns these days.) But that's beside the point.

What is important here, is that a baroque harangue of unprecedented contagious capacity springs from out of the burlesque figures that this Vulcan Shakespeare gave birth to (from the burlesque, more so even than from his great characters). Rank as warts. Like sponges.

A para-harangue that doesn't come out of the mouths of real people, but does not need anything to live on, is born of the air, is there, grows… and suddenly spreads among people. The word as formed air: and at the same time, an enormous creative force; this has always been for me the most astonishing aspect of the effect of this great writer. I have the feeling, when I tune my ear to Shakespeare like this — I think, one mustn't think now about *the thing*, but must enter in somewhere through *a word*; then one must let go of the word, the way one lets one's hand drag a pencil after it; yet in a peculiar way — and then Shakespeare's word-world appears, and along with the word, the world. Gerhart Hauptmann sometimes writes, when his own voice is not there, like a medium under verbal suggestion from Shakespeare; whole groups of writers, whom he has influenced like this, have done so; *Sturm und Drang*, for example. Georg Büchner, too, for example.

Palpably noticeable in his *Woyzeck* fragment.

But *The Death of Danton* is pervaded with something that is of different parentage; a sturdy skeletal structure. Büchner carried a wisdom with him into the grave — a still-young wisdom, but powerfully built. He died, hardly 26 years old, as a private lecturer, I don't know whether of natural science or even philosophy; in any case, he lived intimately with both, within the realm of both. He had no love for belletristics, only for facts:

only people like that are capable of transforming beautiful ideas into facts. When he died, the two tendencies of his nature had not yet coalesced, but they were already very close to each other. A cynical expression of strength, an almost boyishly prattling verbosity, that lets ideas arise out of the air, and a quest, amid dawning understanding, for the word from out of great depths. It is sad to reflect on how German literature might have developed through him.

The two factors that make up the essence of a writer are, namely, not often thoroughly combined. We have writers who can whip up foam very nicely with their tongues, but when it comes to a perspective on life, they have the suspicious depth of, in the best of cases, a conversation lexicon set to music; on the other hand, we also have very learned writers, and in those cases, they are mostly without foam, but, instead, whipped up by excesses brought on by too much reading. Conversely, Büchner possessed, practically imperceptibly, the ability to transform real unique and great profound thoughts suddenly, surprisingly, into life, so that not only his characters possess the thoughts, but so that they possess his characters, and so that these thoughts belong to the personal fate of these people, while each thought also marks a step forward in their minds.

In this scene, Danton is threatened and is weary of the defense:

CAMILLE: Quickly, Danton, we have no time to lose!

DANTON: (*Dressing*) But it's the time that is losing us. It is so boring to always put on one's shirt first and then pull one's pants on over it and to go to bed in the evenings and creep out again in the morning and to always place one foot ahead of the next; without any expectation that it will ever be any different. It is so sad, and that millions have done it already before and that millions will do it again like this, and, even worse, that we are made of two halves who also do the same thing, so that everything happens doubled — that is so sad.

This is weariness with the routine of politics, but also a person's weariness with the routine of being a person. One never finds such a passage in, say, a representative German writer like Gerhart Hauptmann. If human nature is revealed to Mr. Miller in a Hauptmann play, it is the miller-nature of humankind.

I must admit, that such passages thoroughly suffice for me to deem Büchner a great writer, and that there are enough of them for me to take *The Death of Danton* for a great, albeit immature, work. It continually astonishes me that critics find so much to object to in it. I also notice that, while some of the historiography in it remains on the level of preliminary reflection or even in the form of excerpts, some of the phrases uttered by these revolutionary men come rushing, one after the next, without either being reduced to empty phrases or being devoured by that tragic phrase-chaos we know so well from the realm we have learned to honor as political destiny. Both would have been possible by taking just one more step. There is also scarcely a doubt about what Büchner was trying to accomplish here: to level the step taken against the one he did not take. Sentences like:

> You want my head; go ahead. I am weary of all the slovenliness.

> What is it inside us that whores, lies, steals, and murders? We are puppets, pulled about by unknown hands; nothing, nothing on our own! Swords, which spirits fight with — we just don't see their hands, like in a fairy tale.

> ... if we only took off our masks once, we would see, as in a room with mirrors, nothing but the same, ancient, toothless, obdurate numbskull, nothing more, nothing less. The differences are not so great; we are all scoundrels and angels, idiots and geniuses, and, truly, all of these at once; the four things find space enough in the human body, they are not as vast as one imagines —.

Sentences like these contain the meaning of the play. Not to mention the soft voice of the little Lucille, just before Danton's execution:

There really is something serious in this. I will remember it one day. I am beginning to understand such things.

To die — to die — ! — Everything should be allowed to live, the little gnat, the bird. Why not him then? The stream of life should stop flowing if only one drop is spilled. The earth should suffer a wound from the blow.

Everything moves, the clocks turn, the bells ring, the people walk, the water runs, and that's how everything is until, until this! No, it cannot happen, no, I will sit on the ground and scream, so that everyone walking by will stop in shock, so that everything pauses, no longer moves. (*She sits down, covers her eyes, and lets out a scream. After a pause, she rises.*) It doesn't help; everything is the same as ever; the houses, the streets, the wind moves, the clouds float. — We will have to bear it.

Certainly, scenes and passages of this sort, even if there are many, stand isolated in the play; they do not build it up, but rather overflow it with their light, and sometimes there is not quite enough to reach from one of them to the next. But if one were to conclude from this that the play is not dramatic, that would be simply dogmatism. Büchner himself gave the right answer to this question in the play itself, an answer one should hang up in all the feuilleton reviews and theater halls:

I say to you, if you don't get everything delivered to you in wooden replicas, in pieces in theaters, concerts, and art exhibits, then you have neither eyes nor ears for it. If someone carves a marionette, so one can see the string that will be pulled hanging down, and whole limbs crack with every step in iambic pentameter — what a character, what consequences! If one takes a little feeling, a sentence, a concept, and dresses it in jacket and pants, makes hands and feet for it, paints expressions on it and lets the thing suffer and moan through three acts, until it is finally married or kills itself — an ideal! If someone fiddles an opera, which imitates the rising and falling of human emotion the way a clay pipe does a nightingale — *ach*, art!

Put the people from the theater on the street: *ach*, the miserable reality! — They forget their God for his bad imitator. The creation, glowing, roaring and glimmering, around and inside of them, being born again every moment, they hear and see nothing of. They go to the theater, read poems and novels, grimace at the faces therein and say to God's creation: how common!

There is only one condition for the dramatic: to be art. That is the difficult thing. If one attains that and if one reaches for it with the means of the theater, one will always have a right to it. Our contemporary position, that the writer should adapt himself to the stage, is perverse and deadly; the theater must find in writers the challenges that will keep it alive.

The Death of Danton is one such challenge — a chance to renounce the histrionic strain that obtains amid action and invented character. The piece was written on small scraps of paper, arranged so well along the same thread, that one part could easily be exchanged for another. The production can do no better than to emphasize the significance of these small, acoustically potent images, which the writer has usually clearly indicated; and for the rest, to let the consequences of these complementary and intertwined excerpts work themselves out amongst themselves. The effect will be, as Robespierre says, that:

> The night snores over the earth and waltzes around in a deserted dream. Thoughts, wishes, hardly intimated, confused and shapeless, the fear of creeping out into the light, now receive form and gown and steal into the silent house of the dream. They open the doors, they look out of the windows, they become half flesh, their limbs stretch in sleep, their lips murmur. — And is not our waking a bright dream? Are we not night wanderers? Is not our action like the action in a dream, only more clearly fulfilled? Who will reprimand us for it? In one hour, our mind enacts more thought-deeds than the sluggish organism of our body is able to complete in years.

Of course, this would demand a directorial talent unknown in any contemporary German theater. I have already suggested the reasons for this in my essay on the Moscow Art Theater. Nevertheless, we must thank the Deutsches Volks Theater, for providing an interesting production, which revealed everything on the stage that can be achieved by an ensemble that performs the same kind of stagecraft behind its curtain.

Characteristic for the imprecision of the instrument is that the relatively insignificant courtroom scene had the strongest effect.

ARMS AND THE MAN [29]

[*Prager Presse* (June 15, 1921)]

On June 12 in Vienna we read:

English-Bulgarian-Austrian literary-politico contretemps in Schönbrunn!.... We know Shaw's witty, biting, deep and sometimes superficial little play *Arms and the Man*, in the translation *Helden* [Heroes]. It is not necessary for me to narrate its events. It mocks the ideology of military fame and therewith a bit of the ideology of statehood. If it were performed in Paris today, French patriots would probably protest against its tendency to "destroy national idealism"; in Bavaria, Bavarian patriots would do the same. In Austria, it was not Austrian patriots who protested, but Bulgarian ones. That is a complication. An English writer has insulted a Bulgarian in an Austrian affair; one cannot fail to see the cultural

---

29. Musil's second theater review to deal with political questions (see *Correspondences?*, 81–86) was printed, not in the theater or feuilleton section of the paper, but with the political news. The review was accompanied by a footnote, reading: "Telegraphed from Vienna on June 14th: 'In the Schönbrunner Schloß Theater, yesterday and again on Saturday, Bulgarian students demonstrated against the production of Shaw's *Arms and the Man*.'" Fanta, *Gesamtausgabe*.

progress evident in the possibility of being able to insult a third party altogether. The internationality of aversion is at least a first step!

The Schönbrunner Schloß Theater, a branch of the Burg, is a small, charming, cramped little theater, that has a hard time finding plays that are neither too heavy nor too light for its scope. So, one can well understand that it snatched up Shaw's *Arms and the Man*, without bothering to acquire the approval of the Inter-Allied Arts Commission. Now, it cannot really be denied that the play does contain serious insults to the Bulgarians, insofar as a work of art can insult anything but art itself. An old Bulgarian Major declares, for example, that constant washing is unnatural, to which his daughter counters that she finds it necessary, "almost every day." There is more of this sort of thing. Indeed, one must concede, although the English drama only shows Balkan traits through a foreign lens in order to make its own Balkan traits palpable at home, it still profits from that somewhat reckless humor, with which every nation in its philistine psychology examines the mistakes of others. I can even understand it and excuse it, that Bulgarian youth living in Vienna felt insulted. I hear there was even a meeting between the forewarned Bulgarian Delegate and the director of the theater — a first! — but, since Thespis' cart, carrying the performance, was already rolling on to the stage, it could no longer be stopped. Instead, the meeting resulted in a prologue by the director, insuring the public of the purely literary aims of the Burg Theater. It was, to be sure, a surprise that the Schloß Theater had literary aspirations, but, in any case, these were not able to avert the scandal that broke out in the first and second acts. In the stalls and in the galleries a furious eruption of whistles, boos, and ejaculations of protest broke out, which inspired a counter attack by the other theater guests, who felt robbed of their sacred possession, their paid seats. Only after repeated flank attacks of the police, who finally managed to throw enough light on the conflicting opinions to make arrests, could one speak of a successful performance. Police President Schober celebrated therein his second victory in the history of theater.[30]

It is a natural human weakness of the young Bulgarians that they understood the polemical intention of the playwright crudely and personally; one should have assuaged them and provided them with an explanation, instead of yelling equally silly insults at them. Art, which attacks or distorts the reigning reality to show something higher in the background, is nowadays immediately lynched on account of the *lèse majesté* of inherently philistine ideals. What the young Bulgarians did with Shaw, German audiences did to Wedekind, Lautensack, Schnitzler, Sternheim. With just as little right.

30. See *Correspondences?*, 81–86, for Schober's participation in the scandal surrounding Schnitzler's *La Ronde*.

To reproach ourselves with this is the best thing that we can say in response to this *contretemps*, just as long as the manifest general will to peace manages to prevent a new war.

MOISSI EPILOGUE [31]
[*Prager Presse* (June 19, 1921)]

Report from Vienna:

I last saw him years ago; young, at the pinnacle of his fame; he played Gyges. His dissecting, his slowly dissecting manner was unforgettable. It suited Hebbel well; in a simultaneous production of Shaw, it did not make the same impression. But with Hebbel, it was as if a spiritual being had arisen from purely dead wood, as if he were breaking off pieces of bark, sentence by sentence, with every gesture; as if he were piling up the bark fragments, letting them collapse, leaving nothing but a husk, while becoming, nevertheless, more and more himself.

In Tolstoy's *The Light Shines in Darkness*, he plays Nicholas Ivánovich Saryntsov; he plays him as a neurasthenic of goodness. The man who cannot bear the injustice of the world, but who also cannot bear to do the right thing. Who takes his minions' hands and takes his wife — recklessly, from one pregnancy to the next. A matter

---

31. Alexander Moissi (1879–1935) was an Austrian-Albanian actor from Trieste. The most famous actor in German-language theater between 1910 and 1930, he worked with Max Reinhardt and frequently went on world tours.

of opinion. One could lay a greater emphasis upon the inner voice of the man, on the tested prophet, on prophecy altogether. On the Tolstoy of the Communist legend. But one feels that there is much in the play that justifies Moissi's interpretation.

The Light Shines in Darkness makes one think of Rousseau. A similar form of moral exhibitionism, public exposure of battles of conscience. Such a sincere squabble between two internal voices, that humanity seems to unite and the world seems to stop. Such natures are not doctors for, but rather squalling voices of, the birth pangs of humanity; their strength is not found in a final synthesis of their ideas, but in their impotence. Which also explains the utter rejection of Tolstoy by the western intellectual tradition.

It is to the performer's credit that he has managed to alter our assessment of Tolstoy. Perhaps it could have been done without so much emphasis on the neurasthenia. But that is for Moissi himself to decide.

He has one gesture, when he lifts his face to the heavens and spreads out his arms, another where he bluntly halts: these gestures are — yes, they are simply bluntly broken-off fragments of soul. Like a ball rolling in sand, like blows against a mattress. I did not like them. But they left behind an impression that would not diminish and seemed increasingly masterful. To exert such compulsion is the art of the actor.

*

Hamlet! He looks like a *Childe* from a Gothic wall hanging. His gestures have something only half-awoken, half — still-woven about them. Sometimes they flare up into life, flicker up, twist into fiery streamers; then they sink back down again into a dream.

He doesn't play a brooding Hamlet, not a Hamlet guided by the motifs of metaphysics, nor a divided shall-I-or-shall-I-not ego. Instead, he simply plays a young nobleman, who would be a hero if only the fate that has been lain upon his shoulders were not too heavy for his youth. He loves his mother but must contemn her; he abhors his step-father, but that isn't enough reason to immediately kill him, is it?! The ghost scene is rendered as naturalistically as if it were an inner voice. When he reunites with his school companions, he becomes a boy for a moment. This is all wonderfully unified and reflects the luster of a great, dark temperament, which one simply observes in this Hamlet. He never proves himself; he *is*; a young tiger doesn't have to show his papers to prove he has passed an exam in Machiavellianism either.

When he is carried out in the end, he lays there slenderly in the outstretched arms of the man Fortinbras, half anchovy, half Damascus sabre, exaggerating his youth even in his death. If I were a small girl, I would fall terribly in love with him.

*

The essence of a great actor is Being. Infecting through example. The way that the grace of one young dandy teaches a hundred dandies finer movements. A beautiful woman makes women more beautiful. Life is ultimately not made of syllogisms, but of wind, clouds, smiles and gestures. Irrational and exemplary.

Of course, this is precisely why acting is so often hollow. Imitation of imitations, unspiritual, clever, hostile to art. It must always be revivified by actors like Moissi, actors who also understand how to read the scripts.

MOISSI GUEST APPEARANCE

[*Prager Presse* (October 5, 1921)]

As Romeo: the Natural entered; he was not pleasing; but this Natural had transformed into something remarkable, in need of explanation — so much did he master the character. He played a Southern brother of Hamlet, an impulsive, more self-confident, more erotic brother, who nevertheless was cut from the same cloth; the similarities were not in his mind, but in his flesh, in his voice, in something instinctive, in the aura around his presence. The basic tone was dark; doom and the highest doom-bliss were sensed in the first moment when he glimpsed Juliet, and from then on, it merely fulfilled itself: the enemies of the fates will hand Romeo his sword; he is practically a bloody jinx, and the fact that he really dies with Juliet because of a misunderstanding is fully in keeping with his character. It would then be a drama of fate, if — if it were one. But Shakespeare did not have much patience for such over-saturated, modern (despite their stamp of *Hellas*) concepts. There are perhaps fates, there could also possibly be dramas of fate, but *Romeo and Juliet* is not — but, one can't say it is not one at all. Moissi's interpretation, checked against the text, is namely justified; step for step; and yet — how shall one say this respectfully? — Shakespeare is not the man to carry a total-conception throughout one whole work (his literary interpreters are, however, those kinds of men); he jilts, so to speak, any overly intellectual interpretation, and thus we are left with islands, wherein Moissi wonderfully conjures up some kind of inexhaustibility, elevations of endless sorrow, or wherein he fashions some kind of half-conscious self-lacerating manliness.

That he nevertheless — one may well say — is almost boring, is not yet quite explained. No matter how much I have reflected upon it, I can find nothing more than what young girls knew in the first moment: it is a physical matter.

Moissi is a *belle laide*; even the charming music of his voice is beautiful in a fractured way. But Romeo — Romeo is, in brief, with his tragedy, his tension, and his imbroglio, something out of Courths-Mahler;[32] but orchestrated with splendid lyrical padding by Shakespeare. (Whoever doesn't believe me, read it yourself. Shakespeare was in his twenties when he wrote it; he took the whole situation and the figures, excepting Benvolio, from an epos of Master Brooke; Brooke took it from the Italian fabulists; they in turn, from a Greek novel, thus really from Courths-Mahler, for she *is* a Greek novel.)

---

32. See footnote 4, p. 5.

Romeo is a grandson, with Family Magazine ancestors; and an ancestor with Family Magazine grandsons; he is — passage for passage! — English Baroque bombast; he is not the main character of the play at all, although the handed-down abridgements are falsely named after him and called *Romeo and Juliet*. They should really be called *Juliet*, for she is the richly, ingeniously-created character: but she is created out of the magic induced by the beautiful young fellow. A touch of the ruly unruly type; a splendid German youth, sitting with his mandolin; he is named Heinz and one loves him, even though one does not think him very clever, although he need not be dumb. But he must be *inconceivably* beautiful in his every expression. And Moissi is only *conceivably* beautiful. Nature has established a boundary here, over which the intellect cannot — or only very indirectly — escape. Moissi's defeat was honorable; it happens in life every day.

As Danton: when *The Death of Danton* was performed in the Spring on this same stage I already timidly expressed my opinion that this play, although incomplete, constituted a great literary vision and that it really, perhaps, would have to be played with the so-called feeling of the author in mind, and not just the feeling of the actor. But what is poetic in this piece is neither the character, nor the action, but rather the words. An almost feverish flowering word-fantasy under the influence of Shakespeare, along with sudden flashes of deep thoughts, sometimes translated into flesh and bone, and simultaneously a ghostly leave-taking from the earth, "weariness with the routine of politics, but also a person's weariness with the routine of being a person." One doesn't have to perform the works of poets, but if one does do so, one must perform them instead of producing "theatrical experiences" or preconceptions of the nature of the dramatic: in this case, one would have to present a loose chain of swiftly-painted episodes, which tremble beneath the breath of the words. (I believe that if the theater is not to succumb to cinema, it must find a way to tune itself to the poetic rather than to the theatrical; but it would rather die.)

The directors at the Volks Theater gave us, instead, great opera. Stiff curtains and illuminated stage magic. Among all this, Moissi performed Danton's great speech before the convent. It cost Büchner his head. For in this scene, the politician woke once more in his *Danton*, the journalist, the old lion; but he also collapses back, in this scene, from the height of the great, spiritual world-weariness to which he had already attained. This retreat, in just the moment when everyone including himself believes in the possibility of one last courageous act, could be performed; its opposite could be performed. But Moissi performed pure pathos. Therefore, he could not play world-weariness earlier on, but only civilian weariness; almost a silly Danton, an Epicurean, who observes sensual pleasures tenderly, as he nears his end, only to turn around to blow one last, blazing blast on the trumpet. It was a Danton by Richard Schaukal.[33]

It is probably due to the same question of taste that Moissi just scumbles Danton, instead of fully painting him in.

(This production makes one think of another actor, Hans Ziegler, who created a soft, womanly St. Just, by imitating a 40-something charming woman in trousers — the great, glittering, devastating hysteric arose unmistakably and impeccably from this hermaphroditism.)

In [Schnitzler's] *Green Cockatoo*, an actor acts very actorly. Not exactly true to the instructions of the author, cruder, but effectively drawn. Then crouching at the scene of the murder, bluntly, without posing; representing the persistently bewildering absence of reality behind the illusion — more or less comparing the much simpler heroic life of the trenches to that of the more heroic hero's life of the war newsroom. Quite stimulating in other ways, too; but I cannot refrain from thinking that more could have been made of this brilliant little play. With a virtuosic stroke, actor and passion cut a wedge out of the tree, and one saw its two new surfaces gleaming; but the trunk was missing; this Henri was qualities without a man; pictures. While Schnitzler had written a very perfect little thing, perfectly rounded on all its sides!

33. Richard Schaukal (1874–1942) was an Austrian poet and prose writer associated with Symbolism and Impressionism.

As Othello: one can come to understand Othellos if one remembers the war; these upstanding, honest "soldier natures," who are led to bloody decrees and mass murder by their distrust and a lack of civilian sense. Moissi has failed to give this typical harrowing symbolism to his Othello. One might expect a flop, a feather-weight-Othello to match his elderly-Romeo. But Moissi did well, and his interpretation was a delicious gift. He played what Flaubert calls Africa: cruel pitilessness, something close to a childhood fairytale, a skinny Othello with thick lips; he was a camel rider, a weedy hero from Bible stories, an ape, upon whose brow God's kiss of innocence still burned more palpably than it does upon the European man's; of the kind of power that, although it is unconquerable beneath a vast open sky, collapses amid sleazy whisperings — a power that Nietzsche calls a barren, glowing music; he was a being that does not exist, an artificial and magical being, a draft, a fabulous beast; found a stone, a piece of glass, held it in his fist and looked and looked at it evermore, as if it were all the wonders of the world: and it was Desdemona.

The play achieves — even this play pieced together out of a tangled mass of novellas — genius in its last act. The way that the chambermaid Emilia, initially merely disgruntled and glib, goes wild; the way that Othello breaks down and the way that the little dove Desdemona, by the thrashing of her innocent wings, incites the big hawk to attack.

Here Grillparzer's very sage words hold: "Shakespeare's truth is, namely, a truth of impression, not of analysis. The pregnancy of the accomplishment, the power of his embodiment, is so overwhelming that we do not think of the possibilities at all, because the reality stands before us. The gift of portraying at this level earns all the privileges of Nature herself, which we must honor, even when we do not understand her." These words catch, blaze up here.

Here was the place where disappointment was lurking; but Moissi avoided it cleverly; he did not venture to rise to a level of vitality, where his force would not have sufficed; instead, he decelerated, muffled his force and lifted himself suddenly from earthly to abstracted and aghast. No matter how much the Erinyes hounded this Othello: in the moment when the fabulous beasts with their flying flanks stood still and no longer knew what to do, they became a pack of yelping dogs. Measured against this, it seems to me irrelevant whether this interpretation suits the standard version or not. In remarkable distinction from this Othello, stood the Iago of Mr. Bonn, who was an excellent Tellermann in *Florian Geyer*, but, who, under the lax direction of a guest performance, became a devilish Iago, who threw his cap in the air, grumbled throatily, and let loose all of the tricks of an old, hackneyed comedian nature.

Tolstoy. *It's All His Fault*: this comedy in two scenes is painted with one finger of his left hand; arabesques on top of a Russian motif. Such knick-knacks have no place in literature; they float in the paradisiacal blue sky of accident. (If someone — like Tolstoy, who can do so much — had not made them.)

Herein, Moissi plays a dear, modest, young scallywag; with a sense for something higher, who strains for preposterous foreign terms and can do nothing to stop the other side of his self from stealing when he is drunk. He doesn't play him the way one frequently does, as an old-Moissi, but rather as if an irrational, wonderful figment of inspiration had snowed down like a star from heaven.

AUSTRIAN SUPPLEMENT

[*Prager Presse* (October 21, 1921)]

The adapted *Danton* of the Volks Theater, which I reviewed as *Moissi's Guest Appearance*, has been followed by a new version of *Woyzeck* in the Raimund House. It is bad enough in itself, when one dies, but it is even more dangerous when one leaves fragments behind.[34] That these scenes have been dashed off by a prodigious "fellow" will be grasped by anyone whose ears have not outgrown their heads; but where Büchner was ultimately going with them can simply not be known. It is my sense that he was heading toward a scurrilous, fantastical, tormenting and tormented world, in which case, the scene wherein Woyzeck is cutting up rushes with his friend would be a tuning fork against which to modulate the tone of the whole. The production that was offered was part E.T.A. Hoffmann, part tortured, egg-headed Woyzeck-creature; in itself, consistent, and adapted with surprising earnestness. It was — I don't know why — judged by a portion of the critics as Expressionistic. In that case, one could call every well-conceived stage production Expressionistic; I would prefer the opposite.

34. A note of warning to Musil scholars of the future!

This reminds me that there was also something new at the Burg Theater: the *Wilhelm Tell* of that still very emerging writer Friedrich Schiller. Apparently, also an Expressionist, at least if we were to judge by the made-to-order stage scenery. The text, of course, is more reminiscent of a Biedermeier milieu, but I hold the scenery to be the main thing; if one wants to reform the spirit of theater, one must do it like God: it is well known that he created the landscape first, and only afterwards the people, and he put the idea of consumption into Schiller's mind. That God did not stage modern history in the carbon era is only a result of the fact that he is, after all, not a true poet.

People have also been painting and in the last weeks there have been exhibitions. Hagenbund, Artists' House, and an exposition of Italian painters who call themselves *Chiaro di Luna*.[35] Conclusions from obligatory viewing:

---

35. The *Hagenbund* (1900–1938) was a group of Austrian artists who, like the Secession, separated themselves from the more traditional and conservative Viennese *Künstlerhaus* (Artists' House). Unlike the Secession, the Hagenbund was open to different styles and philosophies of art, paving the way for the participation of radical young artists like Oskar Kokoschka and Egon Schiele in 1911–12, and, in the 20s, Expressionists, Cubists, and artists of the *Neue Sachlichkeit* (new objectivity) movement. *Chiaro di Luna* was a group of Italian painters, showing in Vienna in 1921. Presumably named in protest to the Futurist motto, "Uccidiamo il chiaro di luna" ("Let's destroy the moonlight").

a concept. This concept is *a paintersmith*. The paintersmith. One knows what a wordsmith[36] is: someone who can have excellent qualities but is not really a writer; the only difference is that the paintersmith hangs his works on walls and creates a public nuisance. — At first, one is in a quandary for quite a while about what one should say. Among the Italians, for example, there are some excellent, cultivated works. Perhaps one should name names, as a good host? Zenatello, Sacheri, Pavan, Salviati, Grondona, Baruffi, Rossini, Zanetti, Vianello, Rescallo, Piantini, Gartorelli, and the others of the same niveau, who are members of a protest group against Futurism, as if some German authors from *Westermann's Monatsheften* and *Der Neue Rundschau* were to form a defense league against the excesses of the "newest lyric poets"? Then one has to spend a long time in the Artists' House, where a whole mess of ability and painterly culture is hidden, and then say important things in the Hagenbund exhibition about red, yellow, violet, blue, green and orange. Ideas, oh, even real ideas register, for it is a matter of competent painting on all sides. But what is painting? When seen only once like this? How can one synthesize it like this? Mastery of the material?

36. Musil's words here are *Schriftsteller* and *Malsteller*. *Schriftsteller* is a much more common word used for *writer* in German than *wordsmith*, but is a less lofty designation for writer than the word *Dichter*, which is sometimes simply translated as *poet*.

To be able to do something? A great deal can be said about how that is done; but I do not explain how a car is made, I treat its making as a given necessity. If our life were secured and only required splendor and representation, it would depend upon questions of craft and the like; but our life is decomposition, a swarming of ants, a self-relinquishment of one's unique self, record-breaking, but also — although still a heroic communal trumpet blast — never a triumphant entry parade. What shall good painting mean to us? We want to capture the optical aspect of our existence! We don't even see the world, but if we do happen to see it for once, we become as still as a picture. If someone manages to make us be still like that, it is well worth it to reflect about how he does it; compared to that, everything else is mere busyness. Even amid a thousand wordsmiths one finds not one writer, that is to say, not one artist.

CURRENCY SPECULATION OR: FROM MOLIÈRE TO STERNHEIM TO KAISER

[*Prager Presse* (November 18, 1921)]

To speculate is to reflect deeply. Currency speculation: deep reflection about money. It is lacking in the lost world of Molière, which was more intent upon sharp sketches of laughable caricatures and on the initially laughing and then gradually serious emerging awareness of the advent of a new civilization mirrored by an old one. I don't know how Molière should be performed. Not as a vision of our vision of the vision of that lost world, which would have preferred to have lived in the vision of an even earlier one — but somehow indirectly, with the shimmer of a mirror. In Sternheim's adaptation,[37] it has been set amid the atmosphere of "1913": fully direct and current. Lines are cut, sentences invented, and, creeping along in the old badger's burrow, quite evident, is Sternheim himself. Harpagon is one of us; this is a story of

37. Carl Sternheim (1878–1942) was a German playwright and short story writer, considered to be one of the major exponents of Expressionism. Apropos Musil's subject of money in this review, it is relevant to note that Sternheim married into a wealthy German manufacturing fortune, but that he is also known for giving his 1915 prize earnings (from winning the Fontane prize) to Franz Kafka.

our lives; the figure becomes symbolic of our time, filled with Sternheim's philosophy — but one retreats deferentially, one assuages the great author, acknowledging that a genuine Sternheim is still something very different than a demolished, de-Molièred Harpagon.

Yes, money rules the world: that is Sternheim's great discovery, only uttered before him in *Rigoletto*. Sternheim has made many other discoveries, some even witty ones, and aside from him (but after him), only Heinrich Mann has stirred up the sphere of middle-class culture like he does, even though, in Sternheim's case, everything happens between the walls of an iron cash register. This is his spiritual milieu. He need not speak of money and still he speaks of it. His language and his thought — from the start neither a very strong language nor a very strong thought — took on the abstract character of money: hasty, hard, shifty, stingy, and banished from life like Midas. This is a result of his first having learned to speak among money people. When he was still a young Don Juan poet, he was simply very talented; in those days, he was much thinner, but later he pulled himself together cleverly, coined himself, learned how to play the genius-role of money — that transforms all wishes and pleasures of the world with a simple device kept in his pocket. And thereby found his place in the universe. Perhaps the universe is somewhat larger than him; but he doesn't notice this anymore.

He is not diminished by it. He is one of those fundamentally well-meaning people who pretend to be caustic; he has adopted the skin of a hedgehog, a daemon, because perhaps he would otherwise have gradually become too smooth. But ever since he has become obsessed, he has developed genius; the most stubborn, soberly besotted, infuriating kind of genius that we know. One must be sure, however, not to regard his intellectual content, that which he has to say to humanity, separately from his general complex — and one is forced to do precisely that when it separates itself like an annex in this Molièresque comedy.

If Sternheim makes Molière smaller than they both are, then Pallenberg reduces their Harpagon completely to one single line on a blank piece of paper. He looks enormously intense, he has three, four, five masterful expressions for his mania, for angst, mistrust, elderly dotage, but in general, the same one rises and falls through all three acts. Perhaps his initial *forté* is too powerful to be able to vary; perhaps Pallenberg is more clown than actor; perhaps his caricature-style demands another setting in someone else's play, a silent dream gliding, with this elf at its center. Here the motto: "critique after seeing once more" has its limit. Of the few worthy people who write reviews, some estimate his performance very highly. I would be charmed to see what they see in Pallenberg, if only I had not seen it in Pallenberg himself.

I don't know: did I speak about Sternheim so well or so badly because I saw Georg Kaiser's *David and Goliath* right before in the same theater? Here too, money monomania, deep reflection about its governance of the world. It is an early Kaiser, later adapted to a new global awareness. A man has collected the contributions for a family's shared lottery ticket, but has not paid for it; the forfeited ticket wins the jackpot; he continues to swindle and finally everyone marries everyone else or becomes happy in some other way. When he is forced to admit that he has betrayed them, they have nothing more to win. In the meantime, one of them drinks six glasses of beer in a row, to characterize that he is a royal beer brewer, and to the great joy of all the mothers, a child wets a rug covering the parquet flooring. There is nothing more to add except that Karl Forest created a masterful swindler, while Kaiser's is only a raisonneur, and that one should read Kaiser's early works, if one wants to see him as one of the exceptions.

AFTERWORD TO THE MOSCOW ART THEATER

[*Prager Presse* (November 25, 1921)]

One might have hoped that a long-term performance residency of the Moscow Artists, such as was necessitated by their circumstances, would have had a decisive influence on the German theater; but after everything I have read about them, it does not appear to be the case. That which is exotic, the astonishing is — as is quite natural — incorporated into our own theatrical experience; insofar as our theater today is uncertain and corroded with displeasure, it could happen that, suddenly, its utter obsolescence and its stiff bones and joints would come to light. That would be a decisive day for the culture of a people, for without a doubt, it is not only life that proffers a model for the theater, but the theater that offers models, models which are copied by seemingly widely disparate areas of life, such as politics or business. The proposition that certain occurrences of the World War would not have been thinkable without the operetta, had nothing paradoxical about it whatsoever, and I would wager I could prove that a great deal that has happened since then, despite all alleged *Realpolitik*, would have looked quite a bit different, had not the outmoded catastrophe technique of the European theater, its kitsch requirements about exits and entrances, its false heroic dynamic and its ridiculous conception of what action and heroism consist of, eaten away our minds.

We can see now how the Moscow Artists were most likely received: a new conception of what the theater can be comes up against old categories in a cultural moment when thoughtlessness and an enterprising spirit of comfortable self-satisfaction freeze the foundations. One praises them relentlessly, using the old, unaltered thoughts; feels that these laudatory thoughts aren't really sufficient, and calls them exotic; as if one were praising with this word too. But in reality, one is hardly conscious of maintaining a mental reservation. Forthwith, the experience is degraded to a merely æsthetic one, and transformed from an existential experience into a subject of conversation. In this case, exotic means "Russian" or also "their realistic art of depiction." Right from the beginning, which was not difficult for a writer, I warned against these misunderstandings, as misconceptions that blocked off the road to understanding. What the Moscow Artists perform is not realism. It is the theater as a work of art, and, as such, it is not Russian, but European.

It should be European. In fact, the European theater has gone in a different direction. It has become a theater of actors, if it is not more correct to say that it has remained a theater of actors. For, of the two factors that interact on the stage, the writing and the acting, the latter has always been the stronger, and has eaten up the former. Already in Shakespeare's time, the actor's moment decisively overpowered, quantitatively, in terms of ceded space, the literary, and German dramatic literature hardly existed on the stage when it came to its highest achievements, since it offered too few "roles." Now, if one were to ask oneself just once what the difference is between one of Goethe's or Hebbel's characters and a "role," one would find that a role merely provides the actor with a pair of vulgar spiritual categories; rather, provides practically nothing more than the tonality and the *forte* or *piano*, and leaves everything else to extemporaneous improvisation. The work of literature, by contrast, demands of him a difficult intellectual achievement, and a much more exact assimilation of his eyes, arms, and legs to a completed conception that is foreign to him. It is thus quite natural that the actors generally prefer the bad or old, so-called-authorless plays, and that they avoid literature like the Devil avoids holy water. These great helpers and allies of literature have a fierce mistrust and a comparable presumption toward their associates. That the theater directors have sacrificed the writers up to the actors, does not surprise these commonly rather narrow-minded men who are under the influence of a horizon filled with immediate sensations. The results have been a very respectable elevation of the individual actorly achievement, which the German theater enjoys, and an increasingly baser condition of dramatic literature. If, however, two beings are bound to each other for better and for worse, and one of them grows fat at the expense of the other, there eventually arrives a point when the suffering of this other leads to the collapse of the first. And if the signs are not deceiving us, we have already come very close to this condition. There can be absolutely no question that literature must be the source of the theater's true life force; since, however, the traditional nature of the stage and a so-called dramaturgy have created obstacles for literature's participation, it has turned away from theater for two generations, and the real artistic development continued in the novel. Whatever is left of theater faces a public that — and herein lies the real essence of our contemporary crisis — ultimately, and quite rightly, prefers to go to the movies.

In recent times, we have not only experienced the phenomenon of the actors' theater, but also that of the directors' theater; an interpretation — more that of the directors than of the writers — commands the stage; the advantage in this is that an interesting work is possible even without exceptional actors; the downside is a certain Frederick the Great-style parade ground desert. It is better for writers who themselves need assistance than for those who could help the theater. The Moscow Art Theater, in contrast to these two Western European forms of the actors' and the directors' theater, represents the *writers'* theater. While in the West, when one returns to the peep show after a long pause, one cannot repress the feeling that it is nothing but theater, with the Moscow Artists, the scarcity renders the productions auspicious. It is theater. But theater not as an ersatz life for those who want to be told about life or need to be entertained, nor is it a society amusement; it is, rather, meaning-making, interpretation of life, a ministering to humanity.

I have already suggested what techniques are used to bring this experience into being. One can never reproduce the essence of a work of literature other than in its full totality, otherwise it would not be something living, but rather a product of that cooled-off rationality that we study in mathematics or psychology; no one is in a position to explain it unless he commences to follow a path from thoughts to feelings that always suddenly stops somewhere or other, so that one must always begin again anew somewhere else. Unless one is foolish, one can only want to approximate the essence of works of literature, albeit in increasingly narrowing circles. And the exact same thing can be said for the truly apt method of the Moscow representation. The characters in a work of literature are always connected to each other; none of them could really, if they were to step outside their frames, stand up on their own (our star theater knows nothing of this); every one is a reflection of all the others. If the actor really wants to bring them to life — not to that life that sits in the orchestra section, but to their own life — his mimetic impulse must be determined by all of these relationships; his conceptions must modulate until they fit, not only in one, but in all directions; and he will only allow them to emerge from out of this profound relationship to the whole. A work of literature contains such a wealth of thoughts and feelings that are connected to each other, without always being distinct, that it is always more than its interpretation. And precisely its quality of not being able to be translated back, this incontrovertibility of the process is what gives a work of art its own life — its organic nature, its sense of having been created, the essence that cannot be expressed, and the inexhaustibility of its effects. The sum of these spiritual relationships is wholly indeterminable, and one cannot say how much of them the Moscow Artists incorporate into their performance: from a certain level of richness on, the work of art begins to open up and breathe. It is then as ambiguously unambiguous as life itself and — art, which for those who understand it, also has another side, wherein everything is bundled together with everything else — is also something for which we do not yet have a name.

That is the mystery of their performance, that knows no diminished roles for its participants. It fails palpably in unpoetic plays, like [Surguchev's] *Autumn Violins*, and it is, as a result of their life of travel and the separation from Stanislavski also not always up to the same level. But one notices it all the more in the exception:

sometimes it descends a bit into miniature painting or cheap propaganda, and then in the next moment rises again to its full magic. And this magic consists in that which is seen by us to be the ruin of theater: that the stage lets itself be led by literature.

JESSNER AND *BRAND*

Vienna, December 26th
[*Prager Presse* (December 28, 1921)]

It is almost laudable again to perform Ibsen, and that among his plays precisely *Brand* was chosen by the Volks Theater in Vienna, which has committed many sins against intellectual culture in the last year, pays up their sin-account. The play has become remarkably fresh. Once it seemed older than the society dramas. In the time of the urge for realism, it was, with its glacier-spook, a bit off program, and with its pastor-conflict, its narrowness and its rather meager symbolism, also not to the taste of those who were still too young at that time to have a say, but who already felt that Ibsen and Hauptmann would not become the leaders of the new period that all young people see in their future. I think that even today, the proxies for ideals with which Ibsen works must be unbearable to very young people; this church, which must be brighter and more free; those artist-butterflies who long for the south; Gerd, that glacier bumblebee: it really has something of the oppositional fantasy of the apothecary apprentice from the Norwegian town, something of the heavy tread of someone who came from narrowness, which Ibsen never lost his whole life long. One thinks of Nietzsche, the breadth and sprightly richness of his horizon, which had such an effect upon the German youth in those days at the same time, or even of Kierkegaard, and one will understand it. It is not attractive the way Ibsen, while making one assertion here in one moment, also whispers just the opposite. A fake and a true friend (the famous Ibsen double bottom!) advise: Brand, go away, you have conceived of your duty too narrowly. You are simply ruining everything! — But to what avail? Brand has taken on the task of striking sparks upon the human stones of a northern glacier. It is conceivable that this is of the highest importance, but this question is hardly even mentioned; even if it were the highest, a different play would arise from it, one of renunciation of the breadth of spirit for the sake of proximity to Biblical people, one that Ibsen did not want to write at all. But if Brand's task were not the highest, well then Brand has acted as Napoleon would not have; he does not take over the leadership of the slaughter, but rather puts his own life personally on the line in a patrol skirmish. He dies because of a mistake and not because of the nemesis of the spiritual warrior; again, that sort of death would be a different play than the one Ibsen wrote. In Ibsen's play, Brand acts like a man who stands with his back to the sun, and makes gestures as if the sun stood in front of him. He acts like a man who sacrifices himself for something lofty, but is also supposed to represent a man who fights for that lofty thing: these two men would act in opposite ways. The particular case betrays its nature and appears as the general one, but it does not fit with the consequences: therein lies the non-committal nature of all of Ibsen's symbolism, the weakness of his theater, which works with likenesses that do not match in decisive points, but for all that move easily amid the scenery. Although I speak from principle about this, I do not want to say the slightest thing against the greatness of this man, who at the moment may even be under-appreciated. But particularly because the present seems to have turned against him, the direction from which any critique might be leveled should be established: today one decries his realism in general, that side of his world-picture that is far-seeing; but one childishly and vulgarly imitates his symbolism, his relationship to the spiritual, that technical method dependent upon a meagre expressive ability. I question this as a contemporary path to a spiritual art.

The famous Ibsen depth has become transparent today for eyes with even a medium-strength vision; but something emerges from this that was once less visible: the drama of a will. Greatness is not just a matter of character, but also of intellect; strength of will is almost entirely a matter of disposition; therefore, it can also be represented by this pastor, whether he acts upon small-thingamabobs or upon greatness: this symbol has no wrinkle in it. It has an enormous youthful freshness. This Brand chars everything that he approaches. Child and wife die on him, he himself leads a life of increasing torment, at the end of which his goal is even further off than at the beginning, but the spirit rages through him, the spirit that lifts mankind up, in that it builds a staircase out of the cadavers of its sacrificed favorites. With an enormous bitterness and enormous experience, Ibsen has written this drama of manliness, and it burns like a block of iron in contemporary times.

The direction should be credited with having uncovered this side of the work. The happy choice of the actors brought out the hardness and the obliteration. Mr. Klitsch struck the first note fiercely and radiantly, and achieved the miracle of exhausting neither himself nor the audience by the end, in that he followed the meaning of the author's words very exactly and did not make any superfluous naturalistic gestures, but rather reproduced everything as if it were made of one material — a material that was harder, in a way barely comprehensible, than normal human flesh. Mrs. Janower was not only a victim, but also the companion of a man who was himself a victim. The imagery of the scenery around them both was, at best, almost at the level of a *Kunstwart*[38]

38. *Der Kunstwart* (1887–1937) was a German magazine of literature, visual arts, craft, theater, and music, aimed at the cultural education of young people. As an organ of the *Lebensreformbewegung* (life-reform movement), it engaged in a critique of materialism, industrialization, and urbanization — celebrating a return to nature.

magazine, wherein many weaker images competed in vain to suit a somewhat dirty stage magic, made up of cardboard cliffs, wind machines, and choppy figures; one had the impression that there had originally been a will to tighten up the lineaments, but that somewhere along the way, it was realized that one really should not allow all of the props of a well-funded theater to go unutilized. Why Jessner did not snatch up *Brand* is incomprehensible to me.

At the matinee, he had staged *Richard III* in the Raimund Theater, with Kortner in the main role. In I do not know how few days, he turned the undisciplined actors of this house into an ensemble that was hardly recognizable, an ensemble that enacted every small gesture, in any case, with an unprecedented contagious commitment; even only as a directorial achievement, it was the sign of a master. But it was more.

The external elements of this Jessner *Richard III* are: large colored surfaces, curtains, walls. Creating a peaceful rest for the eyes in a comfortable mode of concentration, simple and fluid scenic changes, cutting away all of the distracting naturalistic excess.

Substitution of battle tumult and the like, which never really works on the stage, with acoustical attractions: music, instrumental as well as half-consonant humming.

Small scenes played in front of the curtain. Along with this, the more surprising, ambush-style charm of the uncommon; variety; also shortening of the deadly pauses. Repeated, adopted by low-voltage writers, this will probably become unbearable in five years, but here and now it is a boon. It must be noted that the presentation of the scenes in this way is naturally not new; the Burg Theater is imitating here; but what is new is using the style for the whole production, where, unlike in other cases, it is not out of place.

Cutting away all of the distracting naturalistic excess in the gestures as well. Great, slow, flowing gestures; the meaning makes waves, not ripples. Not living images, but imagistic living, in a somewhat slowed-down, sustainable life rhythm. Indeed, it sometimes was a little reminiscent of an art-historical repertoire. Grünewaldian finger claspings were there, were indelibly beautiful, yet disturbingly posthumous.

Finally, the famous staircase: what is it?[39] A relief for the eye, surprise, the expansion of height and depth on the stage, of the space contained on the stage, discovered to be a powerful device. But the main thing is the blotting out of reality. Those who have died in the battle do not lay upon the field that is not a field; instead, they lay upon a staircase, that neither is a field nor wants

---

39. The famous "Jessner staircase," designed by Emil Pirchan in 1920 for Leopold Jessner's production of Shakespeare's *Richard III*, was used in many subsequent plays and became an iconic example of Expressionist stage design.

to be one, that is not even a symbol of the "mountain of corpses," but rather a powerful offering unfurling itself. At its top, Richard appears with his diadem-spider crown; it is an image that has no more direct connection to the real outcome of the lost battle, but which hangs together with the whole, like music and words. One could, if it were otherwise beneficial, use a trapeze and acrobatic rings instead of the staircase; the main thing is the breaking down of the common, associative, sacrosanct relationships, and the yoking together of the real, capricious, artistic ones through impressions of various derivation.

Altogether, the most powerful part of this direction has the effect of pure music. An art of fantasy. Exuberantly emphasized parts of reality are placed next to each other through the power of the dictate or rhythm of an internal voice. Something emerges from this like the dance of medicine men, intoxication, cult, an irreality that transcends reality. Kortner plays in this way, as well; he and the direction were one.

These achievements are not isolated; they may be the most impressive result of a decade's worth of developments in literature and the visual arts; Jessner is also unthinkable without Stanislavski. Despite all the admiration, I cannot yet relinquish my mistrust that these developments could have an inhibiting effect on living (not just contemporary) literature. This kind of staging requires a certain type of already-known work, work like Shakespeare's, where the audience understands the faintest suggestion, or work that is inherently typical, like the simulation of dramatic Expressionism, which could hardly be made more content-poor by the greatest simplification.

Nevertheless, next to the Moscow Artists, it is probably the strongest European theatrical achievement of the day. And those critics are right, who don't want to let the "Berliners" interfere with Viennese theater. The Berliners could spoil us.

VIENNESE THEATER I
[*Prager Presse* (February 5, 1922)]

Miss Julie, The Father: Strindberg was 40 years old when he wrote both of these plays.

In *Miss Julie* many strands combine. Firstly, the impatience of a twenty-six-year-old "little Miss," who wants to lose the diminutive. Secondly, a little spleen; the kind that grows out of social pamperedness, and is sometimes nothing more than the tiredness of a dauphin condition of a royal soul without any task. Mrs. Albach-Retty of the Burg Theater found the perfect tone for both of these. The third strand is also mixed up with Strindberg's harem hysteria. Fourthly, it is a social commentary on the imbroglio of the valet whom Miss Julie seduces, as compared to the entanglement that has been created by Miss Julie's neurotic errors. And fifthly, the whole one-act nocturne is infused with the baritonal melancholy waft of the song: *post-animal triste*.

These five elements allow the direction — supported by good acting — to have a fairly strong immediate effect; other impressions were not lasting. The play strides on in proper theater boots, with powerful theater steps until the ending in suicide, and does not allow that one considers other ways to help the poor countess; for example through the advice to postpone death at least as long as necessary to discover whether consequences other than moral ones were to be awaited, during which time the question of the moral ones sometimes changes too. The moral collapse, to which we — like the citizens of that not yet fully lapsed good old time — are also irretrievably subject, depends upon a dramatic morality from the time of the Romans — a morality which Lessing would have still thoroughly enjoyed. Strindberg seems to have understood this, since he underpins his ending with hysteria and suggestion. Almost innocently enraptured, he paints throughout a ghastly sketch as the pinnacle; at its apex, he declares: the last link of a rotten chain must be exterminated, and, as a biological man of progress, he blows the little life's light out.

As usual, the public managed to lift itself up out of the tragic depths of death to rush off to an after-theater dinner. In the suspenseful excitement, one almost forgot to mention the guest performance of Jean the Valet, by Mr. Heinrich George, made up of a haunting mixture of naturalistic elements and stylistic exaggerations.

*

The cavalry captain in *Father* is played by Paul Wegener, who has left Berlin to perform on the Viennese stage. He plays his role nervously, quietly, tormented, and quietly, nervously tormentingly, with an artistry that has the great form that Nature does, when all its props have been cleared away or pared down.

Different elements contradict each other in this drama. The defeat of a man through the innocent perfidy of womanly nature, defeated despite his spiritual, higher but lesser stalwartness by a short-armed instinct; and the defeat of a weak man by a woman, a man with a mother complex and neurasthenia. The second divests the first of its validity.

Today, looking back, one is really just as confused about Nietzsche as about Zola. Nietzsche writes of the play: "It has surprised me beyond measure to come to know a work, in which my conception of love — at its basis a war, in its foundations, the deadly hate of the sexes — is brought to expression in such a grandiose fashion." Zola complains, in his bittersweet foreword to the French edition, that the persons in the play are "almost ideal beings." They are common beings. Drawn from a narrow, but vital milieu of emotional experience. Not common due to the intelligence of their creator, but due to their passion, their mania, their uniqueness. This is all hacked out with a remarkable theatricality and a remarkable crudeness; clever and barbaric, harrowingly wailing, but not harrowingly analyzed, ingenious or querulous; irreparable and off-putting. But perhaps one should never admit such things.

Between the two Strindberg plays, *The Rashhoffs*, by Sudermann, was a friendly relief. One act, wherein a

Berlin coffeehouse girl is overcome by the virtuousness of a pure woman, is the purest kitsch; the others are not half bad. This must be said, since so many "little Suders" are given leave to versify with priestly countenances. An old regular conducts his son's Circe to their estate, to examine the bacillus germ close up. The result is named Wally, who probably comes from the vicinity of the Café des Westens, and the old man falls in love with her himself. God yes, this sort of imbroglio could have come from Marlitt, if one had only made sure to use powerful smelling salts to keep her from falling into a swoon while writing it. And the ending, with the preservation of the pure hearth — but also Wally's interests — would have been quite in her powers: but the roles of this old landowner and the coffeehouse girl are good sketches.

Magda Garden played hers with "racy," but diamond-sharp strokes; Wegener was a damned agreeable country squire, expansive in words, expansive in girth, who can be damned disagreeable and who can stomach a glass of wine now and then without getting too soused. One couldn't help but sympathize with him. Of course, one only needs to see one hair of this sort of fellow to know him fully; one has seen him somewhere or other a hundred times, and in this way, he makes one feel quite at home; but Wegener makes a perfect little genre picture out of it. It is true, the playwright forces the actor to remain superficial, but a well-painted surface has its own worth, even if it is not particularly lasting.

GOAT SONG BY FRANZ WERFEL

Premiere at the Viennese Raimund Theater
[*Prager Presse* (March 15, 1922)]

One element of writing is the vision, the sight, the waking dream, the passivity, being overwhelmed with lights, shadows, the shapes that life takes; the writer lays beneath the tree of life and suddenly he sees the existence of something that is not himself. A farmhouse parlor beyond the southern Danube, almost a manor; about a hundred years in the past; semi-Byzantine, semi-rigid peasant splendor in garments, words, and gestures; the lord of an old peasant dynasty; in his youth, master of all the women; today still powerful. The writer lays beneath the tree of life and watches the workings of a mystery; shadows fall on the faces, tigers' stripes; the mystery breaks out; it sizzles like steam out of the cracks in a kettle; the people turn into bells, which begin all on their own to ring, more and more wildly. The writer sees something that is not himself before him, the throng of people without land or homes, those who have been disgorged from the system, standing at the edge of beggary and theft, who want land, fallow land, that the farmers must leave unworked; "a piece of land, oh, yes, that is like sleep for the tired," as Werfel's apt phrase runs.

The writer sees the mystery itself; perhaps on one panic-stricken afternoon, when the world goes almost dark in its hard-tender purity, when the hard-tender taut order of light hardly seems capable of holding together; "Oh, deadly silent noise," says Nietzsche. Werfel says, "The Ancients believed that at the sunny hour of noon, something can spring from rapt nature, formless but visible, terrible and filled with splendor, killing every wanderer whom it assaults, as if it were the momentary vision of everything, pressed together into one whole." This last vision has a thousand sides; one doesn't know what it is. But also, as in the workings of any mystery, this general dynamic of hidden uncanniness has often been created; by Maeterlinck in *L'Intruse*, for example, though in another key. But the situation also, the horde of beggars, the seer, the one who has returned from America, the fictive southern Slavic history, the master farmer, his spiritual liberation through material annihilation, this too already existed; in the lovely little novel, *Awakening*, by Fontane. I included passivity among the visionary elements of literature on purpose — receptivity. But one must understand it correctly: aside from the role that coincidence can play, Hauptmann often also takes a much deeper honorary quaff (*Schluck and Jau*, for example)[40]

---

40. Reference to Hauptmann's play *Schluck und Jau*. Schluck and Jau are characters in this play, apparently inspired by Shakespeare, but the word *Schluck* also is a noun meaning "quaff" or

in memoriam of Shakespeare, and Shakespeare, for his part, was practically a habitual tippler of Italian novellas; one can only apply this very indirectly as a measure of originality, and as a diagnostic criterion only in tandem with other elements.

Because being able to immerse oneself in the not-self is the one half of writing; the other half is the opposite: to be able to immerse oneself in one's self — to be able to will, to impart meaning. The writer sees the existence of his Not-Self before him,[41] in fragments, sounds, or echoes: what does he do with them? He begins to interpret them, to connect, to amplify. I will try to briefly convey how this is handled in *Goat Song*. For my objection begins with the way in which the elements are connected. Alright, the mystery lives in Gospodar Milic's house; only four people know it, know that Gospodar's first child emerged from his mother's womb as a gruesome monstrosity and has been kept hidden for 23 years like an animal in a stall: Gospodar, his wife, the old nurse and midwife. Even Mirko, the well-developed second son, does not know, and it is Stanja, his bride, who awakens the question in him — an old longing,

↩ "swig," and is used in the earlier part of the sentence when Musil mentions Hauptmann's honorary drink (*Ehrenschluck*).

41. This extremely irregular construction (in the German: *Der Dichter sieht das Nicht er Seiende vor sich*) is reminiscent of Yeats' concept of the "Anti-Self" as an important element in creation.

an uncertain certainty. The mystery is already so ripe and has martyred their consciences so much that they are practically on the verge of revealing it themselves in the moment when an accident lets it spring to the surface; provided it does not have symbolical significance that the doctor — the Voltaire enthusiast — who has just paid a visit, was the one who forgot to bolt the stall. In any case, the shapeless being escapes, falls among the dissatisfied throng, and is proclaimed as a patron God by the rebellious students. A rebellion is staged; both parties are crushed in a bloody struggle; even the animal is destroyed; but the "she" of the play, Stanja, has been impregnated by him first; his seed lives on. Thus the play ends in destruction, from which, at the end, two beautiful love songs ring out: the song of the two who have consecrated themselves to each other in the beyond — the student and Stanja — and the song of the two old people, freed of their greed and possessions, who finally find happiness.

The unfolding of the events in the play is hardly any more meaningfully related than it is here narrated, and when I reread this, I must say, it would make a very good opera libretto, with an ingeniously obvious beginning, but a somewhat arbitrary plot garland for its continuation, unless a deeper meaning were developed in it step by step. The meaning that is not present in the figures, then, must be found in the para-figures. Briefly, the play must be a symbol. For a symbol is something through which the unspoken meaning is co-created in an elemental way; in contrast, allegory would only be an allusion to well-known figures, like Mars and Venus on the sandstone fountains of old castle gardens. So, let us agree: if it is a symbol, then there is a cast of grandiose simplicity right in the midst of its operatic nature, which, ultimately, makes it just an allegory, and, as such, it remains a libretto.

The "mystery" — this is what the beautiful symbolic fundamental idea is called — that which has been hidden, the monster, is the animal, the early stage in man; but what is the animal? Is this something meaningful enough to fill the vessel of a metaphoric plot? I will not let myself be convinced that my well-rounded, clever friend X hides an animal inside him. I admit to animalistic traits in all of us, but an animal is primarily — if it remains at this level of explanation — only a summary allegory. Naturally, psychoanalysis exists; and looked at from a humanistic perspective, there are wars, revolutions, crimes and other eruptions; there are atavisms. "Listen, Andres, something's afoot?! Cavernous! Everything cavernous! An abysm! It's shaking.... Do you hear, something is wandering among us, something down below wanders among us!" — says the good Woyzeck [of Büchner]. The good Woyzeck is shaken by his prescient unknowing, but the writer has not done enough yet. If a writer says: the animal, one must accordingly know something more profound about this or have seen its effects in a mirror, or else it is not a question of a symbolic form of writing that has directly approached our emotional disposition, but rather something completely opposite: an approach to the most rational sphere of all through the mechanism of a general presentation taken from the sphere of literature. One says, the animal, but if one understands comprehensively, one can just as well say, the ungraspable, the irrational, the anti-Christ, the eternal opposite of fixed possession, the subconscious, the repressed, the greed, the chaos and also everything else altogether, because here everything has become one thing. What does it reflect then, when Juvan, the intellectual agitator, and Mirko, the groom, play "cavalleria rusticano" in the moment when the great bell of fate is struck? What does it symbolize when Juvan relinquishes his success at the high point on account of the "hated beloved" woman? ("Because I have hated, the woman has to destroy me —"!) What does the animal in me say to the "black mass" orchestrated in Act 4? The point is: wherever there is room for such things, there is no room for anything else.

All of this is not contradicted, but rather proven, by the fact that this play gripped some people. I have, for example, heard the following interpretation: the animal is the force that claws at our times, the addiction to collapse; the people without land represent the Communist Party; Juvan, the student, who proclaims that the animal is a God, is the intellectual, who suffers today, but, on the other hand, hates the bourgeois society, without knowing them; the people who have no possessions are not able to build a new order, they can only destroy the old one; in contrast, the old masters are chastened by the revolt, and, furthermore, the animal, the daemon of the revolution, also came from their land; yes, a new generation will also bloom out of the union of the bourgeoisie with Communism.... That this drama is a powerful symbol of our time! That is all a little bit correct and one must accept it with Werfel's phrase in mind: not the murderer is guilty, but he who has been murdered. Were someone to conclude therefore, that Werfel is the greatest dramatic talent since Wildgans, one would have to say that it is naturally not as bad as all that. There is much that is significant in *Goat Song*; indeed, some things, like the figure of the Jew, are delineated with an unexpected dramatic precision, and it goes without saying, that with a poet like Werfel, there is beautiful melody in the prose too. Everything else, the rest, I would like to call a kind of Farmer's Almanac of the theater, an unscrupulous repetition of the same contours that have been drawn by generations of artists, which have been corrupted, and then, in this form, have been taken up again consciously by a new artist; this is a form of eclecticism that renders self-conscious and artificial that which Schönherr and other theater writers make unconsciously and therefore awkwardly; and it's possible, too, that it no longer even matters what it was that inspired the essence of this style, but I don't believe that more can come of it than: musical passages by Werfel and texts by tricksters.

For years, Werfel has waged an energetic battle for deeper significance; in my opinion, he wages it too cleverly, too little against himself; which may not hinder the fact that this time, perhaps, he will be pronounced successful.

LE PAQUEBOT TENACITY
(Premiere at the Viennese Burg Theater)
[*Prager Presse* (March 18, 1922)]

The translator is Theodor Däubler. The author, Charles Vildrac. The Burg Theater may congratulate itself upon an artistic feat.

Vildrac belongs to that other France, which was an illusion of German literati during the war, but which afterwards turned out to be just a handful of good people who have practically no influence. Romain Rolland wrote an introduction to this premiere, filled with resignation. It is said that he has been ostracized, and it almost looks as if the writers had now fled, weary of "humanity," to live among the animals in the wilderness. Well then; welcome!

Aside from a few trifles, I only know this one play of Vildrac's — which constitutes a great achievement; if it can be taken to represent the intellectual physiognomy of the best of France, one would also have to add: Chekhov; that is: a sage, calm, renunciative art, not a titanic one. Clear vision, comprehension, melancholy, curtain.

Two young men from the class in all of Europe that apparently has kept its humanity most intact, from the proletariat, want to leave France. Canada! They know very little about it, but have let themselves be lured by the promises of some human export business, have the self-confidence of youth, and are sick to death of their fatherland. One is the sanguine, energetic, striving type; the other is quiet, slow, strong. (The usual will and heart's will.)

Due to some damage to their boat, they have to wait in a harbor town and both fall in love with the waitress of their inn, the quiet one in a good and proper and deep fashion, with serious conversations; the other one: just because he thinks she's there for the taking. And she is. His frivolity arouses hers; they drink a bottle of champagne together, just as he had planned it, one night after closing time, and the seduction happens of itself. In life, those merry natures who don't take things too seriously and therefore make these things easy for other people are much more dangerous seducers than even those "demonic" Don Juans and even worse than the true lovers. I believe that this has been expressed in this way for the first time here. "There is so much to think about," says Thérèse, tersely pitying the earnest one in the moment when she lets herself be taken by the other.

By the other, who provides pleasure instead of depth; there is something sort of symbolic around here. The frivolous one is, after all, not a bad guy; he falls in love with the charming girl who is also in love and betrays his friend with her, both of them feeling very sorry for him. The characteristic touch is that he doesn't go to Canada after all. And the calm, slow, stronger one goes alone — in the future? I think that is what is intended. Otherwise, nothing much happens in the play. But there is a deeper meaning: the good, nice, happily-energetic people never change the world; they are and remain at home in it, the way it was and is, before and after the war — for there is a good deal of talk about the war in the play. Comprehension, melancholy; at the curtain, a weak gesture toward Canada.

It is only when one reconstructs the sequence of the scenes, that one realizes how excellently, how carefully, how densely this play has been constructed. The heroes are types, all around them harbor workers and innkeepers; unconsciously, one is somewhat bored by the content of the main dialogues (which represent no foreign humanity, but just a weaker version of our own — white collar proletarians!), but one's attention does not flag for a moment. The impression is supported by a production that, with the exception of one of the actors, is extraordinarily unified and good, yes, partially masterful, and that showed possibilities for the Burg Theater that were surprising.

VIENNESE THEATER II
[*Prager Presse* (April 21, 1922)]

The Raimund Theater brought us Nestroy's *Love Affairs and Wedding Bells* in an old ornamentation that was quite nice. It is astonishing: one wanders for weeks through the Viennese theater world, like a lost wanderer and sees, since it is totally dark everywhere else, that one is in the Raimund Theater again and again. In Nestroy's directness, allowing thoughts to speak out of the mouth of a man whom he names Fat, there is a fresco-like panache, and in the shamelessly-improvised character of the acts, a certain spiritual greatness: yet, in between elevated points, the play is brought down by vast lows that are unbearably silly. Aplomb, the tip of the nose of someone stuck, like Vienna's Metternich period, on the path of its evolution; but the other parts? If one reads many plays of Nestroy in a row, one has the discouraging feeling one gets from contact with shallow people.

Tilla Durieux from Berlin plays the Basque, Yanette, in Brieux's *Red Dress*, wielding an Erdberg-neighborhood Viennese dialect, with the force of a thrown brick. Elementary in her face makeup, in her heavy, powerful movements and in shattering explosions, grand and audacious in their conception (she kneels down, astonished, next to the man she has murdered, in a way one has never seen before). Nevertheless, one is almost ashamed — as if one were committing an act of ungratefulness — to note that this primitivism is somewhat like the way that refined people imagine primitives, a Gauguinesque art salon Tirolianism. This is caused by the fact that the artist throws herself instinctively into essential elements and high points within a fully alien world, while the bourgeois-clever play is not up to such vehemence.

Ludwig Hardt, most renowned of the reciters, also from Berlin, came for a series of declamations. Small, bold, ancient Roman profile, a voice more hard and cracked than beautiful (which, nevertheless, imitates Moissi's golden tone wonderfully when he does a caricature); it is interesting to see how this man instills a readiness for listening in his audience. His literary taste was not the finest on these evenings, Heine and the *Goyim-Heine*, Liliencron, dominated; nevertheless, one eagerly followed his boyishly unrestrained joy (delicious in the comic parts), while he delivered important messages, that absolutely needed to be uttered *now* and listened to with the greatest attention. Surrender; but that is one of those great ethical factors of which the essence of art is made.

Surrender is also the watchword for the best and naturally least-known theater of Vienna, the Jüdische Volksbühne. I saw Ossip Dymov's Yiddish drama, *Der zinger fun zayn troyer,* directed by Dr. Siegfried Schmitz, in a production that, in its perfection, was reminiscent of the Moscow Art Theater. I will never forget the round-rectilinear, eccentric face of Isaak Deutsch, who played Joschke, the fool, around which a real Reality — transformed by sorcery into a magical one — swings on silent hinges. Formula for this Moscow-artistry: it is a naturalism, but everything profane is removed from it. No; profaneness is removed from the souls of these comedians, while they perform.

If I were the archbishop of Vienna, I would subsidize the Jewish People's Stage.

VIENNESE THEATER III

[*Prager Presse* (April 29, 1922)]

The general's daughter, Hedda Gabler, whom Mrs. Durieux plays at the start of her guest appearance, contradicts to an extent the abilities of this actress, but ultimately, one need not look frigid and proud and cowardly to aim a pistol at men and to hit *oneself*; such swans, Nordic and otherwise, do exist, and it is also not very certain what Ibsen meant by it all. The Hedda that Mrs. Durieux plays is a woman who terrifies her little school friend and who tears at her hair, who throws her beloved's work into the fire out of cruelty and this cruelty is filled with a strength made up of a mixture of hysteria, lustfulness, cowardice, but also something of her earlier girlish wildness, the impotence of an imprisoned woman, and blindness — such a strength is perhaps well worth seeing. I believe that these interpretive possibilities may also be present in the play, in which case, Ibsen is damned lively — if only the public were sober enough to pay attention to this and not, instead, in a state of disenchantment, misled by a belief in a mystagogy, which the author never possessed. Unfortunately, Mrs. Durieux does not consistently sustain her interpretation, but was quite detached in some parts; there, she did not perform individual passion, but merely that nervous impatience of a race horse, which is the occupational tic of all female stage stars.

A very interesting comparison appeared in the production of H. Leivik's milieu play, *Schmattes*, by the Freie Jüdische Volksbühne and Georg Kaiser's *Krehler the Clerk* in the little *Akademie Theater*. *Schmattes* means, namely, rubbish, and suggests the human rubbish of life, who in this case sort rags under a Jewish-American boss, strike, succumb, and then hopelessly continue sorting; amid this dirty melancholy of the dark underbelly-side of life, is a quiet-earnest Jewish man from an elegant family, physically frail from a tendency to intellect and the old texts or perhaps only incapable of taking on a battle against a life like this one, and who therefore is bitterly prepared to consider himself a *schmatte*; I can't follow the Yiddish, but that is how it seemed, and it ran its course in a rich naturalistic sorrow and shoulder-shrugging bluntness. The mode of depiction was excellent, a miniature painting of what it is to be worn down. In characteristic contrast to this play, stood Kaiser's, sprung from the contemporary milieu. Krehler the Clerk is a *schmatte* too; for God knows how many years of work, he has only seen the world on Sunday, and cannot free himself from the experience of a terrestrial revolution, when, for once, he has a weekday free, because his daughter got married the night before. He is forced to see that the world, which for him has consisted of an office cubical, teems behind his back in an overflow of irregularity and confusion. He goes mad and commits a murder. It cannot be ignored, that 20 years ago one would have played this on a cello, the way that Leivik has. But Kaiser blows ironically on a child's trumpet. The effect is stronger and more essential, because no time is spent on peripheral details. But after a first act, which begins brilliantly, it breaks down precisely where the tragedy should begin. Krehler is a symbol. He stands for many; his whole life, he has asked himself: what do I live on, and now suddenly asks: what do I live for? One can just as easily raise oneself up in response to this question as come to collapse; he is a *schmatte* and thus collapses, but then he collapses not from this question, but rather because he is a rubbish specialist. It fills him with hate toward the weekday rationality, represented by his wife; he runs amok, like others have: this is how it should be, one feels the writer say behind him, but — it *is* not this way. An idea has uncoiled itself, but no existence has developed. From this perspective, the drama, despite its liveliness, is stuck in the didactic genre. This is in its style. A realist would draw a creeping madness or a broken, but not mad clerk, consecrated by a tear. An essentialist — ? I don't know, but it seems to me that the singular case of a murderous end is not suitable to present the essence of an average existence, even if the motifs were not meant to be personal, but were supposed to remain abstract. This breaking point, where, in a drama, a new, particular achievement of the writer would have to takeover — the closest thing would be a turn from tragi-comic to comi-tragic — is not rerouted by the production either; chiefly by the fault of the main actor, Forest, who seemed to not feel the awkward nature of his task and who did not alter his half-hungover, half-visionary character, which was only interesting for the first five minutes.

Aside from this hardly avoidable quirk, the direction, led by F. Th. Csokor, in a debut in this new arena, was sharp, witty, and completely refreshing.

THE LIGHT
Premier in the Viennese Stadt Theater
[*Prager Presse* (June 21, 1922)]

One motive for the production was doubtless to put a blind person in the middle of the stage, to take advantage in this way of an interesting theatrical performance; ultimately this is something different for once; the beloved Mr. Otto, whom one had borrowed from the Volks Theater, walked about on the boards for four acts with a cane, bent over and fumbling, with a hearkening expression on his face. He managed to create a powerful effect in the first ten minutes in this way; for the rest of the evening, it's a matter of opinion. He was supported by Miss Nore Gregor in the liveliest fashion; this young actress is the source of a simple, noble, transparent stream in this play's events, which are otherwise not always very clear. But perhaps the play was chosen because one wanted to avoid shallow theatrics, and was looking for works that explored interiority. In which case one would have performed it more accurately in Germany. Since truth is always a compromise, the truth is that Duhamel's play was performed in Vienna because it has already been performed hundreds of times in Paris.

And now some earlier German writers can expect to be lifted up by a wave coming from France, that will at least allow them to be recognized as imitators of their French descendants.

But the question of who came first is naturally not that important. Over the last 30 years, Germany was advanced when it came to interiority in literature. But this German literary movement was preceded by Maeterlinck and Bergson, without whom it is unthinkable. On the other hand, there are Germans who were the ancestors of Maeterlinck and Bergson. Contrasting and continuing, this game can be played ad infinitum. What is significant is not that there are plays like *The Light* — for they exist here and there — but that there is an audience for their success in Paris today, while here such a success would be doubtful. The path of human evolution is not determined by the creative spirits, but by the others, the ones who resist them.

Duhamel's *The Light* has internal action, not external. Nothing happens, except that a girl, who loves a blind man, herself goes blind, partially because of her own actions, and that two souls unite, although before her blindness one of them had only anxiously been drawn to flutter about the other. When I say that the way this has been executed has something of Maeterlinck's interiority about it, I mean that the state of blindness has been explored here with feeling, so that we experience more than just the depiction of two very particular souls and their God-given blindness. The internal occurrence is really not much more than an underpainting, but an underpainting made with very tender, loving, and broad strokes.

The stage design could have attempted to remove any separation between the figures and this background; the work would then have had to have been performed in a lightly elevated, somewhat declamatory style.[42] Instead, the play was set in a thoroughly bourgeois geography, with the consequence that the spiritually invisible aspect fell away. Leaving only a few concrete effects: the aforementioned novelty of the blind actor, two blind people lost in a storm, the symbolic effect of their being lost at the edge of an abyss, and the like. If one had read the play (it is in a good translation published by E.P. Tal in Vienna), one would more accurately appreciate the anatomy of those scenes that came through even in this production. Something remained of the play's beautiful, one might say girlish, soft body, the way it does in a radiographic image — something like a lesser version of this heightened internal human experience, attached firmly to a skeleton made of action, like the ribs of a corset of happenings, fastened around it from the outside in.

---

42. Compare to Musil's own set directions for *The Utopians* (229), another work that features internal rather than external action, which stress the irreal and open nature of the play's occurrences.

REINHARDT ARRIVES IN VIENNA

[*Deutsche Zeitung Bohemia* (September 16, 1922)]

Ballroom of the former Hofburg: gold on white, ceremonial rectilinearity, swoop of two stairways at the end; tapestries on the walls, and divine clusters of glass grapes as chandeliers. One doesn't think one is seeing a stage at all, but merely a part of the room without chairs. What is necessary for the scene is brought in at the ring of a bell by servants, and if great transformations are needed, a curtain, which doesn't reach up to even half of the room's height, is closed. Max Reinhardt makes his entrance in Vienna here and in this way, after one had heard for a year that he desired to do so, having to overcome multiple different obstacles, seeming to be securely re-established, but then called away again.

[Goethe's] *Clavigo* was performed.

The events of this little drama — that consists of five vignettes that call themselves acts — run back and forth between extremes, but always prettily straight ahead. One moment Clavigo is good, the next, faithless. One moment he is pulled toward Marien, the next to all the others, whom he has not yet enjoyed. One moment he is a man, the next a genius, who laughs at man. One senses something experienced faintly below the surface. More strongly, the preoccupation with principles. There is something that does not alter, amid all of Clavigo's alterations: once it is established that he oscillates, he oscillates regularly and without complications. One does not even miss "psychology"; but one does miss a more complex ethics. It is an early play; written when Goethe was 25 years old; at the same time as *Werther*. The synthesis of reflection and feeling, bestowed upon the subsequent epoch of sentimentality, with a soulful zeal comparable to that of the Reformation period, had not found its final form in this play. But it introduces the synthesis, and that is just as important, and is even its own form of perfection.

For our time, the language of that period has something papery and unnatural: one fell upon another's bosom and expressed one's feelings in long speeches. The young Goethe must have thought it a natural expression of the situation to allow Carlos and Beaumarchais and Clavigo to say what he, the writer, found to be proper, fitting, and exhaustive. But we, today, who have had a glimpse behind the curtain of Expressionism, can hardly imagine that the people of that time were really as long-winded in talking as they were in their writing. And, in truth, they will have experienced things really intellectually, and their discourses, even if they were not always spoken aloud, certainly always floated behind their words. The director is herewith posed with a problem. He can either allow the illusion of this time its free play, a sense of pastness with a light accent on former times, or he can allow the illusion of that time its play, as if these long speeches and dogmatic feelings were the most natural thing in the world. The former would remind us with a slight shudder how ages sink into their graves, and would alone be commensurate with our true relationship to that art; but, remarkably, it would appear to most people as an artificial, historical interpretation, even though no theater connoisseur will doubt that the most extreme deviation from our nature, as long as it is completed retroactively, will appear natural on the stage or will not even be offensive in the slightest way. Thus, everyone will grasp that Reinhardt, who has cast the play with his best Berlin stars (Moissi, Lossen, Dieterle, etc.), directs it, without batting an eyelash, as if no time has passed at all, and also that it was a success. He really superimposed the unnaturalness of the writing style upon the second unnaturalness of the theater staging, featuring images that turned carefully around each other, passions held together by a tiny nail; Dieterle every inch the consummate French monk; Moissi, a little golden-pheasant-man, gifted with the loveliest song, modulated tones and hues, every old tapestry, velvet and brocade, taken out between the lines and spread out artfully. Exceedingly subtle, complexly developed comedy.

I believe, therefore, that the Viennese will find their

theater longings — the ones they refer to with that hardly comprehended concept, National Theater — fulfilled with Reinhardt, and that he will find in Vienna the foundation, from which his art will perfect itself, an art, which, if I am not mistaken, is a superior form of society art. There are clever and elevated people in Vienna, who see the peak of theater in this. I belong (with respect) to the other party.

ROBERT MUSIL

THE REINHARDT GUEST APPEARANCE IN VIENNA

[*Deutsche Zeitung Bohemia* (November 14, 1922)]

I wrote about it when it first began; now I have to fill in the subsequent developments. The first impression — with *Clavigo* — was: unfolding images that circled around each other, passions held together by a little nail, a theatrical staging superimposed upon the emotional nature of the writing style. With great respect, which it deserved.

In the Hofmannsthal adaptation of Caldéron's *Lady Goblin*, one might have still been undecided. Charmingly dressed puppets. A puppet plot. Play within a play; play with the lifeless distance of a play, that once, when it was still fresh, probably still was paradoxically effective through its great nearness to life. A contemporary archivist's stance toward the art of the theater; an odd burial of living word-wisdom. Furthermore, something of the charm of contoured church facades. Of the rendezvous charm of evening Baroque ruins. Charmingly spiced past; perfected from the standpoint of culinary arts, but perhaps somewhat low on caloric content.

The turning point came for me with the third of the five acts of *Stella*. How splendid, how cleverly naïve is this play! Somewhat thick with emotive speeches, and at the beginning one resists, when Reinhardt expressly transposes all of Goethe's exclamation points into gestures: but when Cecilia (played by Mrs. Lossen unsurpassably), sees her faithless friend Fernando again, one human moment filled with the endlessness of suffering and the reverberating silence surrounding the fate of two souls, the whole production, in every one of its vertices, becomes as transparent and as perfectly-formed as a crystal.

Once again: how cleverly naïve is this play, even today. Its essence is not in the fact that Fernando oscillates between Cecilia and Stella, but that he really does not oscillate, but rather entirely honestly, intensely, is with one woman and, almost in the same moment, just as much with the other. That is an irritation, not only to the good Christian, but also to the libertines in the coffee houses — one that is far beyond the simple division of a heart into two. But the real lesson is in the way that this heart remains true to both the hearts and to itself and the way that it melts into two other real and filled hearts. The first version was performed, in which both the women remain with the man; Goethe preaches in it with fiery tongue: be good, and it will work; and see, it did. ("He felt humanity! — He believed in humanity....") Behind a perfected stylized theatrical production, a moral sensation was concealed, in the most unobtrusive way possible.

Certainly a good enough reason — even if I don't know if it was the decisive one — for the currently reigning Christian-Socialist Party, which is inordinately interested in moral choices, to direct their organ, *Die Reichspost*, to report, during their most recent discussion of the Burg Theater crisis, that it would be unthinkable to appoint Reinhardt as the director of this artistic national institution. I don't know if he even aims for this position, but he staged [Rey's] French comedy, *Beautiful Women*, with his actors, even though it is a piece of rubbish, with that inimitable elegance known to all admirers as the peculiar privilege of the Burg Theater — a privilege of which it does not always take such full advantage itself.

THE VILNA TROUPE IN VIENNA
[*Deutsche Zeitung Bohemia* (December 18, 1922)]

The turmoil in the East has displaced a large number of wandering theatrical societies into the Western world, among these the various Yiddish troupes, whose language is a mixture of Hebrew, with German and Slavic elements, thus — if I am rightly informed — really a motley language, which however, schooled in old tradition and in recent Yiddish literature, is quite estimable in its musicality and expressive powers. The theatrical culture of all of these troupes is influenced by the Moscow Art Theater, which, without a doubt, embodies the highest directorial artistry of Europe, and which far exceeds the average metropolitan European theater. I am only able to judge the literature that it imports by two examples, but their quality cannot be denied. Isaak Deutsch's troupe, which played last year in Vienna under the direction of this extraordinary actor and director, presented — along with a fantastic drama by Ossip Dymov, who himself is the leader of a Yiddish theater in America but also a writer with a European reputation — only "milieu plays" from the Jewish-American émigré circles. These pieces seemed like a rare transplant of the naturalistic "problem literature" that we had in Germany 25 years ago. In contrast, the Vilna troupe, which came next, takes its characteristic performances from the world of Hassidic legends, a fantastic world — insofar as a critic who is unfamiliar with the language and the milieu may judge — a mixture of conceptions culled from all sorts of mysticisms, onerous dreams, and a somewhat spooky belief in ghosts.

But this mixed world of religion and superstition is a good foundation for theatrical performances that abduct the mind in a dreamy way. It sings and intones, softly and incessantly, the old rites amid the plays' scenery, lifts itself to full-throated song, and sinks away again in the half-melody of a speaker, so that one never knows when the reality ceases or the dream or perhaps it is only a strange prayer that begins, or already again it is common reality returning once more. There is, in this art, a constant oscillation between two directions, the profane and the religious, just as there is in the people — whom it depicts as people who are just as much at home in their agreeable shopkeeper existences as they are in a thoroughgoing spiritual one — a spiritual existence, which they appear to fear as much as they love. In Noe Nachbusch, the troupe possesses an orator like none I have ever heard. Perhaps I should call him a singer, for the basis of his sonic construction is doubtless a temple liturgy; but just as rhythmic prose is not merely a verse minus something or other, but rather an artistic form all its own, his speech-song is a wonderfully swaying plant, grown in isolation from out of his being — a plant, which has never existed in the wide world except in him. Shuffling across the stage in a splendidly frozen mask, this actor incites a breathtaking silence around himself, slowly lets his words arise, swallow themselves, and sink together again in a little heap of stillness. He does no more than this, and one is gripped by a desperate longing to see this word-architect of sound-fairytale castles try his skills on other tasks, which he seems, however, to eschew.

The second theatrical rarity in this troupe is Miriam Orleska, who is the most beautiful actress to take the stage since Duse. Perhaps she is not beautiful in the bourgeois sense, but the beam of her eye, the pleading of her hands, the movement of her youthful body, silently command the whole surrounding room, like a God in the moment when he enters a world: when one follows the play of her amorous depictions, one feels that the old, abused phrase, *divinely beautiful*, does not express a *degree* of beauty, but rather its internal source. It is difficult, here as well, to avoid the effect of exoticism upon one's judgment, and one wishes one could see this actress, who would be a great prize for the European stage, just once in a Western role, perhaps playing Desdemona. The rest are good actors. But very good.

RUSSIAN CABARET

[*Prager Presse* (March 24, 1923)]

Imagine some familiar thing with one or the other characteristic missing. Then develop the remaining characteristics to their highest possible perfection. Then you will get an impression that is, at once, strangely under- and also extra-real. Remove, for example, the life-size quality of a horse, its ability to move, and the indefinable essence of its realness, and it remains a small brown papier mâché pony, with a swan's neck, tiny black hooves, gracious little leather straps; it stands behind the magic window of a pastry shop and it penetrates, along unreal passageways, into the soul of a child, shining with a glittering splendor that is never again attainable.[43] Perhaps the strange magic of primitive sculptures and drawings, the enjoyment of sketches or extreme stylizations, the overwrought ornamentation of our fashions, yes, the whole essence of human art and artificiality, is based on nothing more than such internal amalgams of the under- and the over-real.

43. This miniature toy pony is a recurring motif for Musil, which plays a significant symbolic role in *The Man Without Qualities*, along with the cut-out cardboard figures Ulrich remembers from a childhood circus poster.

Now do the same with a cabaret song; let go entirely of the little bit of sense that it may have. And, instead of that, sing nothing for many minutes except, "*Ach*, that is the little hunter," or "Occarina-Macaroni," and you will arrive at the same borderland. On the far side of this border lies idiocy; on the nearer side, however, the little hunter spins — blond, merry, round, and as green as an illuminated billiard table — around three singing farm girls, who prod him around in circles with a melody that shimmies from their hands and their hips; and right there on that border, exactly in the middle, you are sitting, and are so happily sad as if you were sitting in water and wanted to make puppets out of it. Out of an extraordinary fantasy of design and a disciplined power of coordination of the many details, this Dadaism truly reflects a magical stupor, in which sense and non-sense blend in a wonderful way. A non-sense of a higher sort ensues; perhaps it is the ultimate sense of our *Dasein* [existence], which really, for damned sure, mirrors a Da-*Dasein*.

To be truly accurate, the "Blue Bird," the best of the Russian cabaret theaters that have opened in Berlin, is the only one which holds itself suspended on this fine line; the two others, the "Carousel" and the "Russian Cabaret," slip down, sometimes on one side and sometimes on the other. In the "Blue Bird," the spirit of Stanislavski and the Moscow Theater Collective — where nothing was considered minor — still lives on most palpably. This spirit transforms itself from theater into a playful theatrical, but not like something that just happened to fall under the table of art; instead it becomes a non-Euclidian world of illusion, wherein one gropes about for one's bearings like a newborn. The two other theaters haven't achieved this yet, although the program is mostly the same and their production is indeed astonishing; they are just a nuance more tame in their interpretation of their task; not sloppier, but less spiritual. And the fairytale splendor of their costumes and musical tableaux almost seem like a sort of artistic military campaign; instead of Stanislavski, the weaker moments have an expressionistic Makart[44] as their demiurge; but it is mostly a matter of the surprise of the first impression and the critical mood of the second, and I really do not mean to quibble.

A preface to one of the programs explains that these cabarets evolved out of private entertainments of actors, singers, and dancers; one need only think of our own Operetta-mélanges, which evolved out of similar occasions and which have achieved a certain modest critical success. Just the same, I do not believe something else that the program professes: that these little theaters have sprung up because the days of great dramatic art are over.

44. Hans Makart (1840–1884) was an Austrian painter and ornamental interior decorator; the sensual and luxurious grandiosity of his paintings and home décor is representative of the Ringstrasse-era in Viennese art and design.

Instead, I believe that such theaters can only evolve to such a high level in cultures that have also brought forth the best serious contemporary theater, and that the Russian cabaret separates itself from the performances of Fritz Grünbaum in Austrian and German cabarets because — and in the same way that — Dostoevsky is to be differentiated from [the homeland writer] Waldemar Bonsels.

YVETTE GUILBERT

(Guest Performance in the Chamber Salon)

[*Der Abend* (December 22, 1923)]

They call her a "diseuse," from the French *dire*, to say, which can also mean to recite, and which we German speakers have translated into the clumsy "Vortragskünstlerin." But what it really is, is neither to say nor to recite, but rather to say what you mean, to "tell *them*" — the ones who are clattering their plates down there, and who have forgotten to eat for the length of one moment, with their mouths agape. For Guilbert was already a European celebrity when she performed at the Parisian tingle tangles. This separates her from her trained sisters and daughters, these performers of *Lieder*, these grand-piano horses and ponies of Germanic upbringing. She was a battle cry, and she came from below.

What made her famous in those days, when she first became the "Divine Yvette," were street songs; original, you understand, for the street has no poem before the downtrodden human with his more fruitful intellect, the artist and bohemian, manages to loosen its incendiary tongue. It was about the same time when Aristide Bruant performed those broadside ballads in brothel-bistros for his cash-rich audiences, those songs that also became very famous in book form. "I don't know if I'm from Grenelle (from Montmartre or from La Chapelle), from here, elsewhere, or below. I only know that idle people without a rudder found me one morning in the dirty gutter." Such songs had an effect as if one were to suddenly throw an *Ottakringer Heferlberg* at the sideboard of a fancy restaurant; even if they were no more than a titillation, the pleasurable shock of a saucily-coiffed world of sin and misery, they still contributed a great deal to an airing-out of views, which has made the life of morals slightly more enjoyable since the nineties.

In those days, Yvette Guilbert stepped before the public with red hair, red flowers, red lips, and black eyebrows; her simple dress, with deep décolletage, on her angular-flexible body, was white; she wore long, black gloves, a black belt, and black shoes. Her face and her songs were ugly-beautiful. What enraptured the people was the laughing effrontery with which she recited the sauciest verses, and the fury that occasionally flared up behind the most pleasant ones. It was the contrast between what was considered not-beautiful and not-moral, and a persona wherein such things became beautiful in a new way. This same contrast was to be found in her large mouth, which could fold itself into the sweetest expressions, and in her nose, which was in reality what the Viennese call a "croissant," but which in moments of anger appeared to be like the bolder inversion of the boldest eagle's beak. I saw her for the first time years later, when she already performed only in black. The program, too, was no longer that of the young Gilbert; already in those days she mostly just performed old *chansons*. But the power of her presence was palpable even then at the very first verse. A ringing energy, like when bronze drums are touched, sometimes reverberated suddenly from a sweet playfulness. It was the power which the offensive once had to give offense, the power to stimulate.

Today, after some wanderings, she lives in Brussels, where she recently founded a school where young girls are trained for opera, drama, cabaret, and film. She presented some of these students here too, and she performs with them now, no longer on an empty stage, as before; for she has added the charm of colorful scenery, simple backdrops, and bright costumes. The demi-theater that presents these young girls is a bit like the Russian Cabaret; they too sing little dressed-up songs with droll gestures; perhaps with a bit less sophistication and a bit more natural charm. It seems at first as if Guilbert's direction is like a loose bouquet of wildflowers; but the amount of work it really requires can be appreciated in a little vignette based on an old Catholic church, in which the early Gothic wooden images of holy virgins awaken; while the conception and the staging are not particularly original, the production of this scene reveals an admirable discipline and precision in every detail.

Stronger than the director Guilbert, is Guilbert the singer, and truly, she has become a new singer altogether, although she still performs "songs from all centuries." She has grown broad, the lithe one, and when she comes on stage, she does not hide her age at all. Her singing is mellow and measured. The performance is understated and of an incomparable artistry and maturity. She does not make her face young with makeup, but when it begins to move, a miracle occurs. As the feeling that she is expressing travels across her face in a richness of infinite forms, one believes suddenly that one is looking at the face of a young girl. The City of Brussels has dedicated a piece of land to this great artist for her school, and Cardinal Mercier has presented himself as a patron of this new enterprise. Guilbert's whole life has been proof that it is not what a person says and does that makes her worthy, but *how* she does it. It seems that a nation which cares to educate spirited *diseuses* also necessarily wins spirited Cardinals.

ERNST TOLLER'S *LAME MAN*

Matinee at the Viennese Raimund Theater

[*Deutsche Allgemeine Zeitung* (February 23, 1924)]

When Wilde first saw, once again, the light and shadow of the open air brightly contrasted with each other, when the meaningless, delightful whir of sounds reached his ears, the faint scurrying of a world, that was, despite everything, brilliant and precious, with Reading Jail still very close at his back, he turned around to look once more at the torment. But the walls that had castigated him lay in the same light as everything else and were a part of the whirring beauty. Wilde never managed to turn this moment into a paradox, and I think that he ultimately collapsed precisely because his gracefully-dancing mode of thought could not overcome this simple contradiction. Something similar — but without the added *de profundis*, instead rather, packed with a youthful, resistant spirit — is at the root of Toller's drama, *The German Lame Man*.[45]

---

45. Ernst Toller also spent time in jail, for his participation in Munich's 1919 Soviet Republic. He wrote this play during his imprisonment. According to Fanta, this is "one of the most thorough and thoughtful" of Musil's theater reviews. Fanta, *Gesamtausgabe*.

This lame man was a healthy, well-behaved factory worker before the war, a worker, who, like thousands of others, led his life with the faithful trust that, "as is scientifically proven," the materialistic historical development will one day give birth on its own — "from the womb of the historical development of circumstances" — to a happier existence for us all. He then went to war, like everyone else, proud of his brave manhood, which placed him on the same level as everyone else, and returned — to his wife, castrated by a bullet. The tragedy slips into this clearly-prepared noose. The noose, above all, of the war cripple. Why it is called the *German Lame Man*, I could not discover; I take the German-part to be a post-hoc glued-on allegory or a repressed second motif, that never was developed, but that still remains meaninglessly in the title. The lame man could also have lost his legs or his eyes; every mutilation (consolidated as a deformity of the sexual organ!) is repulsive to the peacefully gossiping person. As long as it is not over-compensated for by the mood of war victimization and heroism, and the feelings remain in their usual place, the emotional atmosphere of horror or also of ridicule rises up once more around the altered person, as around everything unfamiliar. The inherent tragedy of betrayal or the farce of oblivion is not German, but rather cultural-human! Toller carries it off as if it were a legend. In the woman, disgust and sexual desire fight against love. A friend of the man reaps the benefit. While the lame man is forced to bite off the heads of rats and mice at a side show to afford bread (to at least be a manly nurturer), his wife enjoys herself with his friend. She regrets it later and jumps out of the window, since he cannot get over the thought that she also laughed at him for lowering himself to the level of an animal for her sake. And the lame man just lets them both be reduced to a fatal despair, because he no longer has the strength to understand their coexistence. The fatherland had celebrated him as a hero, a fine specimen of a man, before he could even show that he really was one, but as soon as something happened to him that is as much of a hero's fate as any other, he became ridiculous, and then the fatherland would permit his wife to divorce him? He still believes in the future nation, where everyone will have his rights, even those carrying heavy burdens and the sick, but when he despairingly tries to find support for the belief from his friends, when it is a matter of his own case, there is no longer any room for it? It is as incomprehensible as that his wife loved him and then laughed at him. As incomprehensible as the fact that she didn't really laugh at him — but even if she had done so, she would also have to have been a good person; for he only needs to look into her eyes to see: "Where is the beginning and where the end? Who can say this of a spider's web?" — So, the world gets mixed up in his brain. This is no longer the tragedy of the war cripple, also no longer of the unmanned, but rather the suffering of Everyman, when he notices his loneliness among his fellows in that moment when it is a matter of the deepest things; demonstrated by an effective case. Another writer before Toller expressed the lame man's experience like this: everyone "must push along his own plank alone amidst infinity," and this previously expressed concept of fate, that one collapses if one loses the strength for dreaming and imagination, is also expressed like this: "to lose the strength for transformation";[46] since the few truly tragic conflicts (and not ones that are actually improvable) always can be traced back to the same basic contradiction of our conscious existence, even if they seem to be only slightly similar.

It is utter madness to interpret a play with this kind of mood, as one does in Vienna, as political. In contrast to how it is performed in Dresden, in Vienna it has been performed under the auspices of the Workers' Defense League (as a matinee in the Raimund Theater). It is — if one must use such formulæ — at its core an anti-collectivist, individualist play, more an anarchist than a socialist one and at the deepest level, not any of these things, but a work of literature. If one insists on calculating how its lights and shadows are allotted to different party platforms, one sees the left coming out in a worse light than the right, the critique of love hits harder than

---

46. Both lines are paraphrases of lines from Musil's own play, *The Utopians*.

that of the animosity that is satisfied that "all types and peoples of the German street" are therein reflected. But I believe that one can see from this play that (no matter what one says against them) literature and politics, even in the person of the same author, are two very different spheres; up until the penultimate moment of creation, they may seem to be dependent upon each other, but then one outlook separates itself from the other and often, surprisingly, comes to quite different conclusions. There is something in artistic conception that is objective, truthful, a force that comes from opposition that persists no matter what path one has arrived at it from: the application of this principle for an impartial observation of artworks is obvious.

From a purely artistic standpoint, the most remarkable thing about the drama is the surprising thematic depth in combination with a milieu that is apparently not conducive to it. There is really more thought stuffed into the lame man himself than a person of his qualifications can really bear, and often the thoughts seem to come out of him like paper words; neither are the other people in the play always safe from speaking a little too prettily in the Defregger-style,[47] like salon proletariats, and on the whole there is more overblown soul than dramatic

---

47. Reference to Franz Defregger (1835–1921), Austrian painter of rustic and historical Tirolian genre scenes; he represents, for Musil, the parochial Austrian folksy tradition.

bones; but for the first time since Hauptmann, people who make up a large portion of our populace are moving naturally on the stage, and the coarse figure of Grosshahn (played uncommonly vividly by Werner-Kahle in Vienna) is conceived with a strength of observation and vision that, aside from Toller and old Hauptmann, no one else possesses these days. Further, some scenes are spurred on with a whip, swing, smack and bang; I personally don't esteem this sort of thing so greatly, because it has contributed so much to the intellectual inferiority of our stage, but it contributes to a particular kind of dramatic talent; and it is worth admiring how much content can be found in Toller, on the surface. That the figure of the side show owner is reminiscent of Wedekind (as the scenic rhythm of fragments is of Büchner) is unimportant; such figures are common property; it all depends on how they are used.

DOCTOR KNOCK BY JULES ROMAINS

[*Deutsche Allgemeine Zeitung* (March 18, 1924)]

This play, performed at the Wiener Volks Theater in, as far as I know, its German premiere, was the most interesting disappointment of the last few weeks. As far as I know, Romains was only known to us up until now due to a lovely essay about his ideas written by Ferdinand Lion in the *Neuer Rundschau*. He is one of the younger French writers, like Duhamel and Vildrac, who flourished during (and in part by being against) the war. They appear to produce a weaker sort of literature than their somewhat arrogant predecessors Claudel or Suarès, but a more human one, which holds its nose closer to the earth and which, therefore, shivers more at the messy complexities of existence. Romains' *Doctor Knock, or the Triumph of Medicine*, was a Parisian theater success; despite this, it really contains particles of a new kind of humor. They were not emphasized in the Viennese production, and were, thus, fully unnoticed by the reviewers, who merely saw parts of a comedy that contrasted with each other dryly and awkwardly, while — because they admire the usual kind of French comedy — they felt justified in expecting something else. I would like, therefore, to analyze the concept of this play a little.

Dr. Knock is a man who understands very little about medicine, but, on the other hand, has accurately learned, through the most diverse experiences of a very irregular biography, just what one can sell or buy in life, and what artistry such business demands. But he had no luck in it until he gave in to the voice of a youthful wish. He has himself named a doctor of medicine, purchases a meager practice from an old country doctor who wants to retire, and plans to manage it according to his modern sensibilities, to ennoble it and raise its income potential: and his success grows at a fantastic rate. The principle, which he has to thank for this, mixes philosophy with medicine and can be summarized as: without sickness there is also no health. He develops the idea in the first act, and, by the third, the success of the principle is total: a previously healthy community of fifteen-thousand souls now suffers from fear of every kind of sickness, but prospers economically through doing business in every kind of medical paraphernalia. Besides, the satisfaction of possessing a doctor who heals all illnesses — illnesses created by suggestion — outweighs the illnesses themselves, and one can well conclude that the sum of Dr. Knock's benefices in this community ultimately outweigh their bad effects. There is, in the end, nothing to hold against him but that he freely applied the principles that honorably rule nine-tenths of our lives instead of the left-over tenth, where they rightly or wrongly — and precisely this is the heart of the joke —

are judged to be humbug. One sees that the spirit of this play, despite circumstantial similarities, is different from that of Molière's *Malade imaginaire*. Molière depicts in an individual — whose name, Argan, everyone revealingly always forgets — the immortal type of the hypochondriac. The young Frenchman of today does not only extend the individual into a mass phenomenon (Shaw did just this, with much more wit and maturity than Romains); moreover, instead of merely making fun of the delusions that make up a man, he experimentally takes them seriously, and constructs his comedic world around them. It is very likely that Romains took his inspiration from what we today call the Second School of Nancy, which attained remarkable successes in healing through the simple recipe: "imagine that you are healthy," and that he wanted to spoof them; but insofar as delusion is not only the basis of physical health, but also doubtless the basis of the creation of needs, persuasion, impressing, and advertising in healthy society and, thus, if one will, of our own world, then his irony extends into a broader realm. One can define the difference between these two kinds of humor in this way: that in place of a generic depiction, in place of a single type, in place of the phenomenon of a humor of caricature, today, if only as a passing fad, we have the appearance of a social-utopian kind of humor, half ironic, which — in response to doubts about the goodness of existence — alters it fantastically. The old kind of humor always made fun of some individual thing, but, in general, always remained a serious and honorable business. Even when it came to a satire of a whole society, like *Vanity Fair*, for example, it went without saying that the depicted perversities corresponded to a normalcy that existed somewhere, which was only briefly suspended. In contrast, today's new humor doesn't take anything at all seriously. If the former directs itself against something in particular, the latter directs itself against everything; the former against a specific object, the latter against the collective reality — the contemporary reality, in which we live. For the former, the swindler Dr. Knock would have been the main point, or the gullibility of his patients; the latter bases its shattering effect on the confusion of the times, which makes everyone dizzy and gullible. This new comedy uses the contemporary situation and the current intellectual atmosphere of this murky orb to explain the lifestyle of someone like Dr. Knock. This kind of humor is neither an invention of Romains, nor of the French; a similar way of handling material seems to be afoot in Russian literature; and in Germany, too, it has already broken through the logic of the stage. This seems very natural to me in a time when the most gargantuan exertions of energy are accompanied by an unprecedented ideological confusion; the single, steady point from which a satire can attack an object is lacking, the atmospheric medium in which all events can be humorously connected is missing.

I have to admit that I have misused the example of *Doctor Knock* a bit in order to elucidate something of more general importance. Romains suggests that he intends this sort of satire, but he fails to really bring it off. After determined attempts in the beginning and in the overall plan, the specific elements of the second and third acts return to the more solid ground of traditional comedy, without being really at home there — unless of course something essential has been lost in the translation of the dialogue.

VIENNESE THEATER IV
[*Deutsche Allgemeine Zeitung* (May 9, 1924)]

The Wiener Kammerspiele is a small theater, led by the playwright, Siegfried Geyer, the author of the witty *Mary*. Among very well-acted entertainments, it sometimes also brings a sacrificial offering to high art, upon which art may live a bit longer. This time it was — after much moralistic-political back and forth — Wedekind's *Solar Spectrum*. It is rarely if ever performed, because it only consists of a fragment of one first act, which tells the story of how a full-blooded virgin, who can no longer bear her single state, flees into an idealized bordello, which, in Wedekind's ethical world, plays the role of a spiritual cloister. Wedekind's ethos is somewhat like a freethinkers' or crematorium society; but directed with charm, performed by the actresses with roguish enjoyment, his imagined Love Shop presents a practically South-Sea mood of moral innocence. One must admit that the police are not entirely wrong in fearing that some citizens who have come across this Hörselberg,[48]

---

48. The Hörselberg is rumored to be the Venusberg — Mount of Venus — discovered by Tannhäuser. According to the legend, he was disappointed by the Pope, who had told him that it was

will leave it, if not quite in the fashion of Tannhäuser himself, at least like Suchandsuchhäuser; but it will have done them no harm, so long as they are able to glimpse — behind the filthy stupor of the everyday — a shimmer of the possibility of beauty and goodness.

There are various opinions about whether or not one should perform Paul Claudel in Germany. Mine is that it should be done, because the success of each of his plays is evidence of the possibility of inspiring theater to the depiction of deep passions and correspondences — a practice that has become as anti-French as it is anti-German, with the result that one has unlearned the belief in it everywhere. Propelled by Ida Roland, the Burg Theater performs the *Break of Noon* (not in the large hall, but in the small Akademie Theater). This production — that featured a particularly great achievement by Mrs. Roland in the first act — is otherwise inadequate, because the actors did not live up — not even in their physical attributes — to the uncommon and very particular spiritual-sensual requirements that this play calls for. Nevertheless, nearly half of the content — and this is very important — wrung a success out of the stagings over the course of many performances. It is strong evidence against that theater superstition, which

↵ as likely that his sins would be forgiven as that a dead branch in his hand would sprout new leaves. Tannhäuser then decides that he may as well wile away the rest of his sinful days in the Venusberg, when the branch sprouts.

believes that a drama dare not be anything more than an effecting placard advertising a few commonplaces. The spiritual costume of Catholicism comes to Claudel's aid in his other plays, in that it explicates meanings that he only needs to suggest (a remarkable internal parallel to the superficial history play); but in *Break of Noon*, it is almost only the pure presence of the dialogue that renders the effect. Admittedly, dialogue that is a substitute for life.

On the 50th birthday of the mischievous Karl Kraus,[49] Berthold Viertel also arranged a performance in Vienna (*Neue Wiener Bühne*) of his poems, *Dream Game* and *Dream Theater*, welcoming the public with a diplomatically fiery speech (which achieved even greater success later) to a celebration of this satirist, whom he really would have preferred to silence, while Kraus lay, already richly anointed and interred, in the royal grave of a pyramid of devotees' skulls. It is impossible to sketch his figure as an aside in a theater review; I must restrict myself to the conclusion that even this bellicose spirit has his Achilles' heel, or, if I may express myself fully mythologically, that the lyre that he holds to his chest is strung with Achilles' strings. His language, more laden

49. Musil is known to have been consistently critical of his brilliant contemporary Karl Kraus, possibly out of envy of Kraus' relative popular success. This review is one of the only places in Musil's writings where we find any praise for Kraus' considerable contributions to Austrian cultural discourse.

with associations than meaning, is perfectly suited to the realm of satirical prose for which it has been developed, but loses its personal expressive power in literary prose and verse. His rigid morality, when used as support for attacks upon dubious newspaper features, is of the highest worth, but becomes, without this opposing force, somewhat bourgeois. His will, bravery, and fanaticism, his extremely fierce storm, levelled against the unclean, his inimitable police-grip style, his ability to take the times as wares that have only been half manufactured and then satirically complete them — all the characteristics that make up his image in his publications, have a much less powerful effect in his literary work.

Six Characters in Search of an Author by Luigi Pirandello is a framing innovation of such charm that the title, accompanied by little explanation, had already spread through the press of half of Europe. On top of the ever-popular promise of making the theater the subject of theater, in this case, the spirited cross-over between the world of ideas and the world of objects is constructed with all the informality and formality associated with a good theatrical conception. What was left of this, however, in the production of the Raimund Theater, gave the impression that the lightning blast of genius had come to alight upon a spiritual atmosphere of rather average poetasting. In any case, the production altered the text very much, believing that it was gussying it up with locally-colored theater jokes.

ARTHUR SCHNITZLER'S *COMEDY OF SEDUCTION*

[*Der Morgen* (October 13, 1924)]

Comedy comes, according to the standard version, from *Komos*, the song of a swarming, buzzing mass. A comedy of seduction therefore means something like: the enthused, the revelrous, the agitation, the swarming and buzzing mosquito-dance around one's life's center, in other words, somewhere between the foot soles and the skull.[50] Schnitzler has always observed this swarming with pleasure; a little melancholic, a little bit in love himself, gently sinking, yet sharply observant. A doubter in love with life. His world picture, as is the case with all gentle, doubting people (what can you do!), has something to it that is never fully closed off; but since he was a sharp observer and since this picture of the world, perhaps, really, after all, doesn't allow itself to be as securely closed as we would like, it was pulled from infinity through the remaining openings. In this sense, Schnitzler is a realist; it made little sense — as an earlier generation, hungry for intellectual models attempted —

50. These sentences are worth dwelling upon as partial explanations of the title of Musil's play, *Die Schwärmer* (translated in this volume as *The Utopians*), which carries as one of its meanings, an association with swarming bees.

to place him, with an unappreciative gesture, with the Impressionists or Naturalists; his strength never lay, in fact, in intellectual composition or in the capture of new ideas, but rather in musical intervals and resonating overtones (not to mention his extraordinary dramatic skill). He will not rise up on judgment day as the great denouncer, defender, or law maker, but rather as one of the most famous lawyers of heaven and hell, who enforces a declaration of nullity on the grounds of mistakes in the process. He is perfect proof that style is not a matter of school, but rather is related to the internal makeup of the spiritual character of a man.

Having established this, it goes without saying that a drama of ideas that does not gather diffuse light, but rather moves characters through certain intellectual rays, which, as well, must emanate from out of the characters themselves, requires a powerful effort, reorganization, and transformation. Ideological passions and talent for construction are needed; for here it is not only a matter of creating people, but rather also of creating the picture in which they stand, the frames, the wall, the house, yes, a new space; and this all must not only be built upon the passion of a thinker, but it must also be both transparent and opaque, so that one perceives the framing only by the movement of the people who live within it and, gradually, as it teaches the audience to comprehend it. The last writer who achieved this was Hebbel, regardless of how one may feel about the content of his ideas.

With Ibsen, the people may have lasting substance, but the ideas that move them do not have the personal strength that makes them as independent of truth, falsity, and the relative alteration of the times as the worldview of a madman or a genius might. Skepticism would not hinder such an achievement (we live today in a time that severely undervalues skepticism), but the obsessive idea does not let Schnitzler be. When he undertook, with the *Comedy of Seduction*, to construct something like a philosophy of love, or rather something that could not be realized without such a philosophy, he began with the elements of the atmosphere, with the characteristics of mood, lanterns on a midsummer's night, a garden party in one of Vienna's princely baroque parks.

Now, that is always very pretty and rewarding. Pairs come and go, knots are tied and untied, nature is dreaming, and human fates wander amid artificial light as if over the bright tableau of a dream-consciousness. The only thing that is really lacking is music by Offenbach, which is also very lovely. For the casual musicality of the beginning is well-justified in advance by the expansion of the second act into three scenes, each independently standing beside the other, as the air-ducts attached to the life- and love-threads of the first act. Subsequently, these threads, extremely loosely wound, detach themselves, one by one, from the play. Or perhaps these are only arbitrary pairs. For love here moves in a circle. It never hits the right person, and the seeking has no end.

It is a very long play, but what is remarkable is that most of the action nevertheless happens in the *entr'actes*. People meet and part from each other in the scenes, but in the *entr'actes* they fall in love with each other, sleep with each other, fight with each other, and exchange each other. Aurelie, the Countess of Merkenstein, has three suitors waiting upon her before the first act, and has already chosen one for her lover; she announces it in the act, begins to have deep reservations, and meets up by chance with a fourth, for a boat ride. In between the first and second act, she becomes his lover; between the second and third, the lover of another man; and suffers, in the same *entr'acte*, the decisive breakthrough. This leaves only her death, along with the return of the shy lover of the first act, for the last. One notes a similar pattern with Judith Asrael, who sleeps with man number 4 and also invites suitor number 3 to share her life's journey between the second and third act. Seraphine Fenz, too, makes an acquaintance in the first act, kisses chastely in the second, and is, nevertheless, impregnated in the following *entr'acte*. Never do we experience the actual, only the *entr'*actual.

The acts themselves mainly consist of previews and retrospection. A philosophy is thereby suggested, more or less: that the moment is nothing but the nostalgic point between longing and remembrance. That passionate action is nothing but a mask, behind which a person remains isolated. To be sure; but this observation, which is often so charming as an occasional gloss in Schnitzler, is not enough in this case. All of these women have a philosophy of profound carelessness — a thoughtlessly straight-ahead back and forth; all of them are little Katharinas, who will not exactly allow their grenadiers to be decapitated, but always have already begun standing up with their left foot, while they let themselves be laid down with their right, and the men assist them in it. Perhaps this is harsh in retrospect; but nevertheless, the embarrassing cry of contemporary sexual need inadvertently rings out loud and clear. It would only have been different, had the previews and retrospections, wherein the main activities take place, been different; but this is where Schnitzler pushed up against a boundary line that he does not overstep. All of these women have eaten of the tree of knowledge, but they speak an erotic officialese. Instead of saying: it was all the same to me whom I danced with, they say: "Whom does your hand await?" Their tongues have wooden feet, like an iambic phrase, and they speak like party platforms for denominational soul-searching. Even the main speaker, Falkenir, who hearkens to eternally rushing internal streams. This is uncommonly noticeable with a writer like Schnitzler, who is a master of the epigrammatically pointed phrase, and it can only be explained by the fact that these sage imitations and commentaries of realistic life have tumbled out here into an alien milieu of figures created on the basis of absolute ideological formalism.

When one considers how, for example, even with Büchner in his unfinished sketches, the passion of the idea shoots through the shape of the whole and the words sprout out like the leaves on a tree, so that almost every one expresses the uniqueness of the whole, one immediately recognizes that in the *Comedy of Seduction*, the spiritual roots of language are not deep enough and not densely enough entangled. The characters do not arise from out of the thought concepts, but remain half swaddled within them; but since no one can deny Schnitzler the talent for depicting people, the fault must lie with the concepts themselves.

The production was therefore challenged with the awkward duty of cutting the play's head off a bit, at the vertebræ — of the action. With a swiftly rushing tempo like this, the production should be so quick that the audience learns to blink with its ears and to hear, not so much the random utterances of the characters, but rather their prevailing keynotes, which were explicitly composed by the writer.

The Burg Theater substituted for this possibility a production featuring ceremonious speeches and emotions, against a beautiful backdrop, from which only Mr. Aslan emerged as excellent. Mr. Günther, who played Max, a seducer from the sphere of *Anatol*, the right man at the right moment with a soft touch, the tender midwife of the feminine soul, who wins every woman only to lose her again, was fully charming solely in the first act.

When, however, the *Comedy of Words* is performed in modern theaters, the significance of Schnitzler comes alive. These three one-acts, *The Hour of Recognition*, the *Bacchus Party*, and *The Great Scene*, fill an evening with a light heaviness, charmingly well-sketched, technically apt, clever, witty, with fine little wrinkles and also strong lines. Arnold Korff demonstrates his great and powerful acting ability, free of all the bad traits of the traveling actor; and in Alice Rhode we seem to have gained another unknown talent for Vienna.

SAINT JOAN
[*Der Morgen* (October 24, 1924)]

Shaw founded the necessary institution, "First Aid for Critics"; its name stands over the preface to *Major Barbara*, but all of his prefaces are thoroughly in service to this cause, including the preface to *Saint Joan*, whose seventy pages are more instructive than anything that any critic, including myself, may uncover in the play. But why is the critic a person in particular need of aid? This question leads us right to the life of the saint.

The critic is, namely, neither an especially evil nor an especially stupid person, despite the fact that naïve or offended people assert as much about him. Such people are caught out in an error. Many critics even surprise the connoisseur once in a while through a generosity that, upon acquaintance with intellectual mediocrity, declares it to be the work of a profound talent, if not of a genius, just as long as it takes the smallest trouble to utter words within an effective theatrical form that are more or less already popular. Without factoring in this generosity, it will be incomprehensible to later generations and will throw a bad light upon us, when it comes out how much has been deemed great among us, without discriminating about whether these pronouncements have been issued by conservative or radical wings or by the enterprising wag of theatrical justice's tail. Furthermore, as mentioned already, most critics are not thoroughly stupid. I just wish that those people who think ill of criticism could observe the assembly of people at a large dress rehearsal or a premiere; they would be corrected by the large number of significant and expressive faces present, who might be lent as ornament to every comptoir, every general assembly, and every ministry. I am convinced that a large number of critics have missed their true calling. These critics also miss something when they critique, but they always do it well, cleverly, and with a wealth of knowledge. And there is only one single case wherein they become radically stupid and evil: as soon as they come across something essentially new.

Over the last 20 years of literary developments, which have created a type of writer who, as martyr to an idea, makes the public shudder with his missing clauses, the critics have even grown accustomed, whether encouragingly or mockingly, to the literary career revolutionary. This fact, however, will never stop them from bitterly persecuting any truly individual phenomenon, no matter whether it deviates from the norm or from the kind of abnormality that has already been accepted. The — I don't want to continue to use that somewhat questionable word "new" — the *independent* challenges the critic's sense of superiority and simultaneously incites his dislike, in a completely unconscious and incomprehensible way. These feelings are expressed by an attempt to prove that the new element already existed, and by an attempt to quickly assemble it out of what is already known to him; he will, thus, un-self-consciously declare that everything that contrasts greatly with Wedekind, Kaiser, Sternheim and other writers with whom he is well acquainted, is imitating them.[51] Insofar as he does not succeed in demonstrating his desired superiority this way, he disposes of the new phenomenon, forgetting to remember that he did the exact same thing 25 or fewer years ago with Wedekind, etc.

But is this at bottom any different than what humans in general do? Wouldn't every ass, no, even every person who rightly considers himself to be experienced, but who has never seen a zebra, declare that a zebra is nothing but a black and white striped imitation of an ass? The critic is thus, in fact, not an exceptional person, and his particular fallibility is really only the result of the fact that his duty sometimes puts him into contact with uncommon phenomena. It doesn't make a difference whether we are talking about writers, saints, or other innovators: the collision of bureaucratism with irregular phenomena always ends the same way. The bureaucrat researches earlier documents, and one can attain anything from him if one alludes to these com-

---

51. This is a direct response to Musil's own critics, who, much to his annoyance, compared him to these writers. See *The Utopians Scandal*, below (216–223).

mon examples, but he declares everything unbearable that approaches him on no basis but its own inspiration.

And this — says Shaw — is the relationship of saints (who are always somewhat irregular) and those institutions, churches, which are formed out of the bureaucracy of belief. His Maid of Orleans has three main activities: she is the first female Nationalist; one of the first, or at least one of the fiercest campaigners for women's rights; and the first protestant. He settles for making her nationalism evident; the role it plays in the drama is more or less the role played by Mr. Siegfried Löwy's gossip column. Her girlish ambition is inducement for the most wonderful conceits of Shaw's humor; but her protestantism, as general, diplomat, and saint, the — in two words that mean the same thing for Shaw — unusual and autochthonous nature of her gift, along with her confidence in a clash with the powers that be, is the deeper concept of the play. One could summarize it in the formula: the Inquisition responds to Joan just as every bureaucracy responds to its protestants; including the bureaucracy of criticism itself, which probably shows us the road that led Shaw to his knowledge of such matters, although we may ignore for a moment that in this case we are dealing with much more serious shortcomings. For if one takes the concept of bureaucracy to its conclusion, it will be identical with all general forces of inertia, and it is evident that it is an inescapable phenomenon, because it pulls together everything that is antithetical to genius, but orderly in mankind, so that the expressions of genius, the personal, the heretical, can only find their form in opposition to this inertia. Saint Joan is placed in this situation, as comic as it is tragic, and this is why Shaw does not draw her, to use his own words, operatic-heroically as his predecessors did. Because she really only becomes interesting through the forces that oppose her, forces that are, in the world plan, almost as important as she is.

But this was not emphasized in the Volks Theater; the cuts went against the grain of Shaw's intent; the actors who represented the powerful church and the feudal system of the 15th century were excellent, to be sure, but they did not bear its proper old severity; this must be said, since it touched on the essence of the play. The rest of the performance had an admirable verve, enhancing the collaborative performance, and brought a palpable elevated will to the stage, which inspired all of the other actors too. This theatrical direction by Karlheinz Martin is extraordinarily worth seeing and the scene at the court counts as one of the most beautiful and most original directorial achievements ever.

Mrs. Steinsieck as Joan gave the impression of not being quite finished with this extremely complex character; at first, she surprised us precisely though a simplicity, in which, nevertheless, all the colors were given play; but later, her qualities grew more meager. The sense of superiority felt by the inferior person, with which Shaw so deliciously imbued the figure of the Dauphin, was performed ravishingly by Mr. Edthofer, with wonderful drollery.

THE UTOPIANS SCANDAL
[*Das Tage-Buch* (April 20, 1929)]

I send my greetings to those who have whistled and hissed! Perhaps all of them did not know precisely why they did it, but they were nevertheless on the right side.

Let me just briefly summarize the pre-history: a theater had prepared a so-called premiere, without informing, beforehand, the shocked author, whose permission it never would have received. There are some people who would call this artistic bravado. Bravado, certainly — to the point of impudence; but artistic? In that case, someone who staged a break-in — where he knew there was a precious art work — is an artist!

The collaborators had engaged a theatrical publishing house without asking or informing me. Whether it thereby committed a crime against *civil* law is a question that has been taken up by the Society for the Protection of German Writers, out of a proper awareness that something like this concerns all of us who write. Thus, I will not speak about that at the moment. Yet I may say one thing: this theatrical-wholesaler has acted, according to the most blameless business practices, against *spiritual* law; following the principle of selling off goods that have long been on the market at lower rates. Congratulations to the first playhouse in town to have launched a business model purely on the basis of commerce!

I distanced myself from this production as soon as I heard of its existence; but, because I heard about it so late, I could not, due to various legal reasons and complications, stop it from proceeding. Now the critics have spoken, and I may observe the mess. I know that one should not directly respond to a critique; this is actually a rather good convention of our sphere, a way of maintaining a sort of professional order, with the admirable aim of keeping everyone from speaking over everyone else; thus, he, at least, who is the most involved should be silent; and truly, I have always respected this rule. But in this instance, I find myself in a special situation, in that it is not *my* play that is being discussed — may I not, then, participate in the discussion? I take this permission for granted and allow myself to say a few things that are, I feel, important and worth noting.

It is remarkable to me, for example, that of all the reviews that lay spread out before me, more than half of them do not say a single word about the fact that I protested against this production and that I declared it illegitimate. (One that does mention it, adds: this is well known!) Obscurely, I remember a legal principle: that a criminal is innocent until proven guilty; and I was not the criminal. I was also not the material, which the researchers had before them when they were coming to their conclusions. And it is, after all, a principle of research, that one may not call a creature a singing ass when one has not heard his voice! There were indeed people who did not let this hold them back at all. They wrote about the torment that I had inflicted upon the audience, about the crapulous crap that I dared to present, about the meaningless dialogue that I "served up" to Berlin, about the clique that was attempting in vain to save me — this is a florilegium. Even if most of these friends of my writing have never read a single one of my books, least of all *The Utopians*, they would have to have known of my protest from the newspapers.

Let us leave them to their continuing advancement! More important to me is that Mr. Lherman[52] has once more mentioned that I am in debt to Wedekind, to Schnitzler, and to Shaw. I presume, of course, that Mr. Lherman's interpretation is in debt to these models, but I must add that some other critics are similarly in that debt — since this is not the first time that I have been accused of this. I pity the aforementioned great men terribly, who have not been able to protect themselves, over decades of theatrical success, from the "burden" of having such a poor student as myself.

52. Jo Lherman, the director of the production under discussion, was a director, theater manager, and impresario, known for his theater obsession and for his con-artistry. Later, under the name, Gaston Oulman, he was the radio commentator at Radio Munich for the Nuremberg Trials.

As far as I am concerned, I can only say that my relationship to these three writers lacks any preconditions out of which one could invent a dependence. Schnitzler's intellectual world touches mine only in the slightest way. I abhor Wedekind, but I admire Shaw — but only since the rather late date upon which I have made his acquaintance — for the nature of his wit, with the utterly helpless awareness, that I would never be capable of writing one single passage that is witty in the way his are. It seems to me that the root of the alleged similarity is inside the heads of the critics themselves. It is well known that a child calls all men Papa. And I fear that I must conclude, that when it comes to the development of theatrical comprehension, there is a not inconsiderable number of critics who are approximately at a similar stage.

I touch upon the painful part of the whole episode when I consider the individuals who wish me well, whom I treasure, but who have, under the impression of this production, distanced themselves from me. Among these people, the question seems to be: is *The Utopians* a stage play or not, and what does the piece mean in general? It hurts me that I cannot make better use of this extraordinary opportunity to talk about this question with an example that I understand as well as my own, but I don't have the time for it. So, I will just begin randomly with the difference between a creative and an illustrative theater — concluding with a discussion of the kind of theater that strives for creation. For by illustrative, one can understand — as part of the spirit of this question—all theater that relies upon a static web of perspectives and rules for life, of which it presents merely a single expression, an example, or, in the most audacious case, an exception. The politicized theater, no matter which politics, is of this kind. Anything there that is already extraneous to art cannot be added to it. But the common bourgeois theater is also of this kind. Really, a good play is a perused anecdote, in which characters appear whom one easily recognizes, also passions, which one easily recognizes, and then there need only be a few structural characteristics, like suspense, tempo, contrivances, and the like, also a bit of lyricism. Between Sardou and the theatrical genius of tomorrow there is no difference in this regard; if one of them presents an anecdote that is an intrigue, the other one presents an aperçu that has been culled from the philosophy that is in the air, instead of which a hundred others could just as easily be used and illustrated. (To be continued: the popularity of this sort of play for directors and actors, who illustrate it further.) Within this illustrative art there is, of course, a great latitude for personal talent, beauty, disposition, etc., but the intellect just spins around and around in the same way within the same circle. It is not changed, merely given a new hairstyle. The problems of life are sketched, mucked about, but never drawn out.

And it goes without saying that there is only a relative difference with the performances — and yet a difference of degree on one side and another of a critical point! — when the illustrative is compared to the challenge of a creative theater, one that reflects the fact that we are actually made of spirit. Do not fear, we can still eat lobsters, conduct politics, and do everything else that is human (we should do this!); and as far as I am concerned, one can conceive of the spirit as materialistically as one wants. But we do not want to deny that the most meaningful moments are those wherein we are enlivened by some mysterious thought that carries us beyond ourselves and into the vastness of the universal. I admit that I don't know how to express this; since all of these words, *thoughts, spirit, idea,* have been abused and have earned, thereby, a bad name. Nevertheless, we know how to differentiate quite clearly between whether we are doing something in our lives in response to an internal spur or not. We know quite well that we can be vehement, and nevertheless remain hollow inside. We know quite well that we can have the most noble feelings and can express the grandest convictions, but that in the next moment nothing remains of them but the dregs. There is such a vast difference between our growth and our ossification, a difference that opposes all of the worthy distinctions we flaunt — a difference that resists all of these exclamations mightily. And, briefly said, one must create a growing, evolving theater.

This is why art is here; one could just as easily say the same thing about a novel or a poem. And since I am discussing my personal case here, I may say, that I have done nothing else my whole life but attempt to find the correct proportions of these things in our art. It is all the same to me what I narrate or whom I describe; I only want to imbue it with the maximum of spiritual life that I can attain. I have often been called a psychologist; dear God, today psychology is the same thing that geography was in Marco Polo's time, nothing more. I have been called an unraveller, but I struggle to achieve synthesis. I have been called subtle, but I aim for the whole, as long as it is visible to my foolish eyes.

Arrangers of attractive shop-window displays of contemporary times have, meanwhile, promenaded through literature, and have had themselves photographed, leaning against a pasteboard boulder, the winners of the world record for sneering.

Is *The Utopians* a stage play then? I still maintain today that a correct performance of *The Utopians* would be. It is uncommonly difficult to shorten — or, as one more properly says — to adapt, but it would not be impossible to, as one says, proportionally minimize, without the imposition of distortions, even though, naturally, some substantial loss could not be avoided. I am convinced, that when it is brought properly to the stage, the life from which the words and thoughts were born will re-animate them, and that then they will not be so difficult to comprehend (as I understand, was the case with the provisional deplorable impression made on some critics by this production). I have said a great deal about criticism here: I do not want to neglect to also thank some critics for their help! In difficult hours such as these, one really has need of a pause, wherein someone else takes up one's travail. And I do not think myself presumptuous if I say that *The Utopians* can wait to have its day; the genre won't become overcrowded. I am also not afraid that it will become obsolete, although many people have already assured me that they themselves are already beyond it. For it is my belief that one can never get beyond something that has spirit, but can only abide beside it. But I would very much like to see the experiment repeated properly during my lifetime, since, to come back down to earth just to see it, after the general reception that I have received here, would be a rather harsh fall.

PLAYS

THE UTOPIANS

A Play in Three Acts

DRAMATIS PERSONÆ

THOMAS

MARIA, *his wife*

REGINA, *her sister*

ANSELM

JOSEF, *Regina's husband; university professor and high-standing official of pedagogical administration*

STADER, *owner of the detective firm Newton, Galileo, & Stader*

MISS MERTENS, *doctoral student*

A SERVANT GIRL

The play is set in a country house that Thomas and Maria have inherited, near to a city.

All characters in the play are between 28 and 35 years old; only Miss Mertens is perhaps a bit older, and Josef is over 50.

With the exception of these two, all the people in the play are beautiful, however one may imagine that.

The most beautiful of them all is Maria: tall, dark, heavy; the movements of her body are like a melody, played very slowly. In contrast, Thomas is almost small, thin, and wiry, like a beast of prey; likewise, his face almost escapes notice under a masterful, strong brow. Anselm's brow is hard and low, wide like a fanatically-tightened belt; the sensual part of his face is fascinating. He is taller than Thomas. Regina is dark, indefinite; boy, woman, a fluttering dream whatnot, mischievous magic bird.

Miss Mertens has a kind face that is reminiscent of a school satchel, and a backside grown wide from long listening in the halls of wisdom.

Josef is lean, haggard, and has a large, angular Adam's apple, which moves up and down over a collar that is too low, and also a wan, brown, fin-like mustache.

Stader was once a pretty boy and is now a capable person.

ACT ONE

The scene is a dressing room, connected to the bedroom by a large closed sliding door. Entrance door on the opposite side. Large window. Ground floor. View of a park.

The scenery must be designed with as much fantasy as reality. The walls are of cloth, doors and windows cut out, their frames painted; they are not fixed, but fluttering flexibly, within bounds. The floor is painted fantastically. The furniture suggests abstraction, like wire models of crystals. It must be real and usable, but as if it resulted from that process of crystallization whereby, for a moment, sometimes the flow of impressions freezes, separating out a single impression, unmediated, alone. Above, the whole room flows into the summer sky, where clouds swim. It is early afternoon.

Regina sits on a chair, hastily pulled up against the bedroom door, a letter in her hand, drumming on it softly with her knuckles. Miss Mertens, baffled, stands more toward the middle of the room, facing her.

REGINA: You mean, you are really not superstitious? You don't believe in occult personal powers?

MISS MERTENS: What can you mean by that, really?

REGINA: Nothing at all. As a child, and still as a young girl, I had an ugly voice — as soon as I spoke out loud — but I knew that one day I would surprise all the world with a marvelous song.

MISS MERTENS: And did you receive the requisite organ?

REGINA: No.

MISS MERTENS: Well then.

REGINA: I don't know how I should answer you. Didn't you ever have an inexplicable feeling about yourself? So mysterious that you had to take off your shoes and sail through the room like a cloud? In the old days, I often came in here when Mama was still asleep next door. (*She points to Thomas and Maria's bedroom.*)

MISS MERTENS: Yes, but for heaven's sake, why?

REGINA: (*Answers with a shrug of the shoulders and bangs loudly on the door.*) Thomas! Thomas! Why don't you come already?! Joseph's letter is here!

THOMAS: (*From inside*) Coming, little crow; a moment. (*One hears the door open; he sticks his head in and notices Miss Mertens.*) All right, then another moment; I thought you were alone. (*He closes the door again.*)

MISS MERTENS: (*Goes warmly toward Regina.*) Tell me, just what do you hope to prove with all of this?

REGINA: Prove? But love, how could I prove something? It's all the same to me.

MISS MERTENS: (*With tender persistence.*) I mean, when you say that you sometimes see your first husband, who died here years ago.

REGINA: Then tell me, why shouldn't I see Johannes?

MISS MERTENS: (*With persistent compassion*) But isn't he dead?

REGINA: Yes. As certain as we stand here. Officially confirmed.

MISS MERTENS: Well, then, it's impossible!

REGINA: I don't want to explain it to you! I just have powers that you don't have. Why not? I also have faults you don't have.

MISS MERTENS: I get the feeling that you don't really believe what you are saying.

REGINA: I don't know what I believe! But I do know that all my life I have done everything in opposition to what I believe!

MISS MERTENS: You don't really mean that. Here everyone talks about powers that only people who are here have! That's the spirit of this house: a revolt against something that is good enough for all the rest of the world.

(*Thomas has entered. Not yet fully dressed; what he is wearing is fitting for a beautiful summer's day. He busies himself with all sorts of morning duties, since, for the moment, no one pays him any attention.*)

REGINA: Oh, I'll tell you something: All of us come into the world with capacities for the most unimaginable experiences. Laws do not bind us. But then life always makes us choose between two possibilities, and always we feel: one possibility is not there; always one, the undiscovered third possibility. And we do everything that we want, yet we've never done what we wanted. In the end, we have lost our talents.

MISS MERTENS: May I see the letter again? It must be this letter.

REGINA: (*Gives it to her; in the meantime, to Thomas*) Josef is going — to come here.

MISS MERTENS: What are you saying?! Really?

REGINA: With Joseph, everything is real.

THOMAS: (*Very — but apparently not unpleasantly — astounded*) When?

REGINA: Today.

THOMAS: (*Looks at the clock*) Then he might be here before midday? (*Takes a deep breath.*) This — is all happening rather quickly.

MISS MERTENS: I am convinced that His Excellency Josef wants nothing more than openness and a little compromise. You will communicate your grounds for divorce peaceably (*with a palpable barb at Thomas*), without insulting him. And when the last remaining bit of dishonesty toward this man — whom you never really thought of as your husband — has been cleared away —

this spook that haunts your nerves will disappear all by itself. You were a saint! You have no need whatsoever for the fiction that you deceived your husband with a dead man! (*She turns with fervor back to the letter. Thomas and Regina step slightly to the side.*)

THOMAS: You two were talking about Johannes again?

REGINA: She thinks I'm lying.

THOMAS: She doesn't understand; she takes it for real.

REGINA: It is real!

THOMAS: (*Lays his arm around her shoulder and taps her on her brow*) Little crow, little crow! Little, nose-picking dream princess, insulted like a child who has lied or stolen sugar and gotten punished by Mama.

REGINA: It's practically real. It's probably much more real than —

THOMAS: (*Doesn't let her finish*) You are wrong: that's the whole thing! You are wrong; and it's just the same, whether one has done wrong or suffers from it. (*He has sat himself down in front of her and has unconsciously wrapped his arm around her knee in a brotherly fashion.*) Nowadays, I too am always wrong. But the more one feels this way, the more one exaggerates. One pulls one's own skin ever tighter around one's head, like a dark cowl with a pair of eye holes and openings to breathe. *We should be the siblings now, Regina.*

REGINA: (*Half turning away*) Truly, you have always been heartless like a brother, no matter what happened to me.

THOMAS: Distant feelings, Regina; like yours.

REGINA: (*Setting herself free*) I like that; (*bad-tempered*) but what does it mean?

THOMAS: (*Pursuing her persistently*) Not immediately graspable, like Anselm's feelings! Branching out over the whole sky like sheet lightning! Better to be apparently lacking in feeling. (*He notices that Miss Mertens, having finished reading, wants to join the conversation. To her*) Well, what does Josef write? Is His Excellency, the Master of Knowledge and its servant, very angry at us?

REGINA: He threatens to destroy your career and future if you don't throw us out of the house.

MISS MERTENS: Master Josef has no right to do that! No one can raise objections to the fact that Dr. Anselm brought you to your sister's and his friend's house, where you all spent your childhood together. He only has a right to the truth. Well then, you will receive him with the truth; you really don't have to tell him that, privately, you plan (*again, with a palpable barb aimed at Thomas*) to marry Dr. Anselm after the divorce.

REGINA: Josef can't just be re-tuned like a piano.

MISS MERTENS: Your long dutiful self-sacrifice, justice, love, all human feelings are on your side. He is a human being. Trust in that which all humans have in common, and you will not have done so in vain! But I fear that this must all sound rather pedestrian to Herr Doctor Thomas.

THOMAS: (*Sanctimoniously*) On the contrary, I agree with you. If we had behaved like that immediately, we would have been able to avoid all of this.

MISS MERTENS: (*Warmly opening herself up*) But why didn't you always think this way??! Why did you write that letter, in which you merely made fun of all of it, and angered Master Josef — obviously the cause of his answer?!

THOMAS: Because I was an idealist.

MISS MERTENS: Excuse me, Herr Doctor, I dare not doubt that you are an idealist — a scholar with your achievements must be one. But every human being is good and can be won over to noble feelings, His Excellency Josef too, and I would have imagined, that an idealist would have to do that, would have to try to do it; by a — I imagined an idealist — in a word — with ideals!

THOMAS: (*Laughing out loud*) But dear Miss Mertens, ideals are the worst enemies of Idealism! Ideals are dead Idealism. The dregs of rotting — —

MISS MERTENS: Oh, oh! Now I don't need to hear anymore; I see that you are making fun again, and this time of me! (*Previously she had tapped on the door while* *waiting for an answer. Now she exits with an aggrieved, but restrained expression.*)

THOMAS: (*He is suddenly transformed.*) You are the only person here I can talk to without being misunderstood: tell me, what is wrong between you and Anselm?

REGINA: (*Refractory*) Why wrong?

THOMAS: You both know that something is wrong between you. Don't you trust me anymore?

REGINA: No.

THOMAS: Right you are! ... We once believed we were new human beings! And what has become of it? (*He grasps her shoulder and shakes her.*) Regina! How ridiculous; what has become of it?!

REGINA: I made no plans for a new world order. That was you others.

THOMAS: Yes, fine. Anselm and Johannes and I. (*Still moved by the memory*) There was nothing that we would have accepted without reservation; no feeling, no law, no greatness. Everything was connected to everything else, and interchangeable; we leapt over abysses between contraries and tore apart things that had grown too close together. All that was human lay within us in its total, vast, fresh, eternally creative possibility!

REGINA: I have always known that whatever one thinks would turn out to be wrong.

THOMAS: Yes, alright. Those thoughts that make you sleepless from happiness, that drive you, so that you run in front of the wind for days like a boat, must always be wrong.

REGINA: In the meantime, I prayed to God for something especially beautiful for myself alone, that you all couldn't even think up!

THOMAS: And what has come of it?

REGINA: What do you mean! *You* have achieved everything that you wanted!

THOMAS: Do you have any idea how easy it was? First slowly, but then: the accelerated fall upwards! On the sloping plain, it is just as easy to go up as down. — In a half year I will be a full professor, if I don't let this thing with Josef ruin me beforehand. In my whole life I have never come across anything as shameful as success. But quickly now: what is the meaning of this Johannes story?!

REGINA: You can all talk and help yourselves with words. I don't care to. With me, things are only true as long as I do not speak of them.

THOMAS: We don't even know if it's already a honeymoon or just an engagement trip, and you both invite a dead man along!

REGINA: I don't want to talk about Johannes!!

THOMAS: But in the old days you never even — liked him that much!? And today!? Today he has advanced to the level of an ideal! — Anselm connects the story with a particular intention. What is it?!

REGINA: Anselm connects everything that he does with a particular intention.

THOMAS: Yes, that's how he is now?! It wasn't like that in the old days, was it? But now, whenever Maria is listening, he becomes simply unbearable. Everything that he does is somehow a kind of soul betrayal!?

REGINA: (*Softly*) Yes, that's it.

THOMAS: (*Looks at her uncomprehending. Then restraining himself by force*) Fine. But what does it mean?

REGINA: And you will see that he retreats when Josef gets here. He will insist that we are only here with you because this is where Johannes died.

THOMAS: Well, we'll see whether he carries it to such an extreme.

REGINA: He never wanted it to go this far.

THOMAS: But what *did* he want, then?

REGINA: (*With an undertone of contempt that Thomas does not notice*) *I* seduced him!

THOMAS: You *him*!? But God knows that you have never run after anyone in your life! You took Josef, after all, as one takes the veil!

REGINA: He was moved beyond all measure, when we found each other again.

THOMAS: (*Faster than he wants*) But was he in a bad way?

REGINA: He will always be in a bad way. If he can't get close to a person, he is like a child who has lost his mother.

THOMAS: Yes, yes, yes …. Brotherly love for all the world. All the world's lovechild. That's what he pretends with Maria too.

REGINA: (*There is something passionately foreboding in it, despite herself.*) He is infected by other people as if by an illness! He completely loses his mastery over himself through the other person; he must immediately set up a resistance!

THOMAS: What kind of a resistance?

REGINA: You wouldn't understand; I can't tell you. A resistance. An ugly feeling. A preparation for something evil.

THOMAS: You, at least, affirm that something unreasonable *just is*; you were always like that; the more you felt that others couldn't believe you, the more true something became for you. But he doesn't say: it *is*; only (*imitating a sensitive mode of expression*): it could very well be so… for someone with an abundance of feeling. He lets uncommon experiences *shine through*. He surrounds himself and his life with secrecy. Regina: Does he have something to hide?

REGINA: (*Comes close to him; emphatically*) He will fall to pieces and do something desperate if you obstruct him! If you even force him into doing the smallest thing that does not fit with the pose that he is striking for Maria!

THOMAS: But you don't believe that it's genuine, do you?!

REGINA: Of course, it is false.

THOMAS: Well then?.... Tell me then!

REGINA: But it's genuine, too. (*In an outbreak of despair*) Have you never heard someone sing a false note with genuine feeling?! Why shouldn't someone feel genuinely with false feelings?! Don't imagine that he has just talked himself into it to spite you! Just believe that one can kill oneself for a feeling that one doesn't take seriously!! One doesn't have to take something seriously to live it; we all live like that.

THOMAS: (*Stubbornly*) We'll see what this is about when Josef comes. (*Then changed*) But Regina, despite everything: I will always believe that we are all as close to each other as two sides of a card.

REGINA: (*Passionately, in a mixture of fear, mockery, and foreboding*) Don't sacrifice yourself! Send us away! You are much too strong to understand weakness. You are too — transparent, to see through dishonesty.

THOMAS: And he? But he is, too! Regina, you know he can't lie! He can only —

(*Maria and Miss Mertens enter and wait, Maria with the letter in her hand.*)

THOMAS: Be true...in a more complicated way. From a certain point on, for him, as with every spiritual being, a lie is no longer the opposite of truthfulness — the opposite of truth is barrenness!

REGINA: (*Hardened*) Yes, perhaps you're right; one should let it be the way he wants it.

MARIA: (*Softly and slowly*) I believe we should think about making some preparations for Josef.

THOMAS: (*Jolted out of his thoughts, then with some mockery in his voice*) Yes, of course, we must take some precautions for Joseph.

MARIA: He may be here any moment. Haven't you read his letter?

THOMAS: No; I forgot. (*He turns toward Regina.*)

MARIA: I have it here. He writes that he's coming to speak with you. He calls your harboring of Anselm and Regina here "abetting of abduction and adultery"—

MISS MERTENS: (*To Maria*) No, absolutely not adultery, I am a witness.

MARIA: — And if you do not put an end to the murky situation in your house, you will have to suffer the consequences.

MISS MERTENS: I am witness, that something — so primitive — for a woman, whose conscience even demands that she remain faithful to a dead man, and for a man who befriends a suffering woman with such unspeakable tenderness — is not even a possibility.

MARIA: Yes, yes, but Thomas has, after all, practically pressed this weapon into his hand. (*To Thomas*) He believes that you, as a man of level-headed consideration, in a man-to-man talk, as he says, will understand — —

THOMAS: What if we all simply went away; let's go on an outing.

MARIA: But by evening we would have to come back again; and he would wait.

REGINA: Can he really harm you?

THOMAS: He certainly can.

REGINA: (*With the satisfaction that one feels from the fulfillment of even something unpleasant*) Then he will do so; you should not underestimate him. So long as everything holds together on the outside, he can bear all moods, all revulsion, all scenes like a lamb. He always had the idea that happiness was a strain. And when it results in strain — good; so be it, that means nothing to him; on the contrary, it's a form of earnestness.

But against the smallest public scandal he would defend himself desperately!

MARIA: He already calls her Potiphar's wife.[53]

MISS MERTENS: A martyr to a more delicate arrangement!

REGINA: But he maintains of Anselm —

MARIA: But there he contradicts himself, no? Doesn't he simultaneously suspect adultery?

REGINA: Of Anselm he maintains, that he is a celibate out of necessity, who is really — (*she tears the letter away from Maria*).

THOMAS: Oh ho!?

MARIA: Regina, you are unkind!

REGINA: But those are *his* words, not mine! That he is a celibate by necessity, who is really a voluptuary.

---

53. A favorite reference of Musil's, to the Biblical story in Genesis of the attempted seduction by Potiphar's wife of Joseph, her husband's favored servant. When Joseph refuses to betray his master and sleep with her, she revenges herself on him by falsely accusing him of attempting to seduce her, so that Joseph is thrown in prison. Since, as we find out later, Anselm had become a trusted friend of the household of Regina's husband Joseph's house, and that Regina herself seduced Anselm, this comparison is not entirely off. And yet, it is odd that Joseph, who believes his wife a victim of Anselm's treachery, would also compare her to the seducer and betrayer of the Biblical story.

THOMAS: Now this is getting interesting. (*He takes the letter from Regina.*) Why didn't you say that right away?

MARIA: Voluptuary is not in the letter; he only says that you have both seduced and confused each other.

REGINA: And a swindler!

THOMAS: A swindler? (*Searches for the place.*)

REGINA: On the third page.

THOMAS: A swindler incapable of love. A vampire. Adventurer. What gives him these ideas?

REGINA: (*Shrugs her shoulders like a kobold*).... Nothing.

MARIA: Perhaps we shouldn't take it so seriously. Certainly, he is debased by jealousy. He's just slandering because he feels how far superior Anselm is to him.

THOMAS: Aha! But that is practically visionary...! Anselm is almost 35, and what has he achieved?

MARIA: I thought he was an associate professor, like you.

THOMAS: For one year, and eight years ago! Then he quit teaching and disappeared. And remarkably, what Josef writes has a certain apparent probability. (*He looks spitefully for the passages in the letter again.*) He ingratiated himself with Josef under the mask of someone with common views; as a caring friend; sympathetic feelings for all the world; as humble idealist.... But we know how he was in the old days: What has Anselm become in reality?

MARIA: You are being tactless!

THOMAS: But Miss Mertens admires Anselm so much that she won't even listen.

MARIA: He is an important man!

THOMAS: (*Suggestively*) Oh, certainly. Probably. He has ideas! Naturally. But — does he have ideas? Really? Not just in the way every other person nowadays does? That can't be ascertained quite as simply as all that. (*Parodying thinking*) Does he have grand feelings? But a passion, as great as it is, can only be as great as the person who is possessed by it.

MISS MERTENS: He would almost have killed himself, when the success of our departure seemed threatened!

THOMAS: Is that so? Would? And almost? It just depends on the ability of the feeling to metamorphosize; a torn off thread might have been the umbilical cord of many great works and only a stupid person really just goes and hangs himself.

REGINA: But a swindler?

THOMAS: That's precisely what is visionary about it; a swindler, too, merely *almost* hangs himself; great men and swindlers have the first step in common.

MISS MERTENS: Oh, I am very much afraid that these reflections are merely an expression of your prejudice against Dr. Anselm.

THOMAS: You are mistaken, Miss Mertens; as bad as I am, I have never been worthy of having a friend in this life — and that friend was Anselm.

MARIA: (*Conclusively*) Anselm is certainly an important man; one mustn't immediately jump to such unnecessary comparisons. You are the one who has conjured all of this up with your letter.

MISS MERTENS: His Excellency Josef is simply responding to your own words!

MARIA: And you fed him the idea that they were fleeing from him.

THOMAS: Indecisive people fleeing from the decided one!

MARIA: Fine, Thomas, I don't want to argue; but in three hours at the latest Josef will be here and will demand a decision. What is going to happen?

THOMAS: Nothing.

MARIA: Nothing?

MISS MERTENS: (*At the same time*) Nothing!

THOMAS: It will all be cleared up soon. Anselm and Regina will stay, of course.

MARIA: Will you speak with Josef then? Because Anselm refuses to do it.

THOMAS: (*Shocked*) Anselm refuses…? (*Almost yelling*) He refuses! (*He looks at Regina, who readies herself to leave with Miss Mertens.*)

REGINA: (*Mockingly*) He has his resistance!

MARIA: (*About to retreat to the bedroom again*) Because you wrote this letter.

THOMAS: Well, then I will welcome Josef with a party!

MARIA, MISS MERTENS, REGINA: (*Standing still again*) With a party? ... ?!

THOMAS: (*Viciously*) Yes, to the devil, with a party, to get him in the mood right from the start. If I can find some old empty cocoons — ones from which the butterfly of human ecstasy has fluttered — I'll string them up all around him! Negro dancing and drumming, divine intoxicating piss-pots, feather robes, in which the little man dances for the little woman!

MARIA: (*In the doorway*) But the man is furious. He's certainly prepared to ruin you if you continue to behave so unwisely!

(*She leaves. Thomas looks toward Regina, takes a few steps toward her; since she continues to walk toward the exit with Miss Mertens, he turns around and follows Maria reluctantly.*)

MISS MERTENS: (*Remaining in the door*) You are in the right; you shall not allow yourself to be placed in the wrong by anything. Stop this party!

REGINA: Thomas can't be stopped when he gets something in his head.

MISS MERTENS: Then let us flee!

REGINA: Thomas has risked his entire existence for Anselm.

MISS MERTENS: And isn't this marvelous person worth even more?! But Dr. Thomas will spoil your case. I implore you, remove yourself from his influence; let us travel further with Anselm!

REGINA: Anselm doesn't want to go away.

MISS MERTENS: I understand. A man of honor does not want to run away. So, he will speak with Master Josef himself; he has, it's true, the gift of speech to such an enchanting degree.

REGINA: What for? It's out of the question that I marry Anselm.

MISS MERTENS: But how cowardly! Don't you see that Dr. Anselm has only refused to speak with Master Josef because he was insulted by your brother-in-law Thomas? Dr. Thomas turns everything to ice with his theoretical ruminations.

REGINA: (*Mysteriously*) But darling, don't you notice anything? Not anything at all?

MISS MERTENS: What is there to notice?

REGINA: Shh! Softly! (*She leans carefully out the window, to see whether Anselm is listening.*) Oh, one can never be safe from him.... Don't you notice, that Anselm loves Maria?

MISS MERTENS: But that's a crime, what you are saying! Your own sister! The wife of his only friend! No, no. (*Grabs her arm*) Regina! Oh, these silly, silly delusions, and as smart as you usually are!

REGINA: But why not? What would be so awful?

MISS MERTENS: What would be so awful?! Don't speak so revoltingly!

REGINA: You overestimate it wildly. A new person stands before him: he is curious; perhaps ... moved. But what am I saying? Not a new person. It was only chance that it was not him, but Thomas, who married Maria.

MISS MERTENS: (*Letting her outrage subside*) I thought that it was by chance that you had married Johannes then and not him.

REGINA: Or not Thomas; that made practically no difference with us. Now he sees another man walking in his own suit, the one he gave away; that has a mystery. It's really not the kind of silly story that usually begins with a woman; with him, it begins somewhere, and just happens to tumble out with a woman! —Yes! Really! — Love is never love! It is a physical encounter of fantasies! It is (*as her eyes wander, looking for an analogy*) chairs ... curtains ... trees ... becoming fantastic. With a human being as the middle point.

MISS MERTENS: Oh, come now, come now! There is an atmosphere around Dr. Thomas that is not good for you.

Let us walk outside a bit before breakfast. (*She pulls the reluctant and resistant Regina with her. Standing still again near to the exit door — the conversation had led her back into the room.*) And Maria?

REGINA: My sister is a fat, stupid cat, who arches her back whenever someone scratches her.

(*Exit. In the doorway they let a Servant Girl go by, who puts down a breakfast tray, knocks on the bedroom door, and leaves the room again, while Thomas and Maria enter.*)

THOMAS: (*Breathing deeply at the window*) I woke up, wanted to speak with you, turned on the light; there you lay with your mouth opened, sunken away....

MARIA: You're revolting; why didn't you wake me?

(*Both begin to attend to their grooming.*)

THOMAS: Yes, why? Because I almost got down on my knees like a hermit! Your large body lay there, so homely and silent. It moved me so much.

MARIA: I am not even allowed to sleep in peace.

THOMAS: When one is never alone —

MARIA: And married for years; yes, yes, yes! I really can't take this anymore!

THOMAS: When one has been married for so long, and always walks on four feet and always breathes with a doubled breath and every drift of thought moves twice and the time in between the main things is depleted twice over with minor matters: then naturally one longs sometimes like an arrow for some high-altitude thin-air space. And rises up in the night, terrified by one's own breathing, which was going along, just moments before, perfectly regularly without one's consciousness of it. But doesn't spring out of bed. Doesn't even really kneel down. Instead, one strikes a match. And there lies someone like that, bundled in flesh. That is the beginning of love.

MARIA: *(Covering her ears)* I can't hear anymore.

THOMAS: Don't you ever hate me?

MARIA: *(Letting her hands fall immediately)* I? Hate?

THOMAS: Yes, straight-out hate. I would have believed it this morning. You were walking barefoot, with your full weight, and I stood there, small and aching in the opening of the room and my beard stubble jutted out, sharp and brittle, into the passage. Didn't you hate me then like a knife that is always in your way?

MARIA: *(Painfully calm and convinced)* That is the end of love.

THOMAS: *(Jubilantly)* No! Its true beginning![54] Just understand: Love is the only thing that doesn't exist

---

54. This exchange is taken almost verbatim from the play *Love* by Musil's nemesis, the successful sentimental playwright Anton Wildgans, whom Musil also parodies a bit later in this scene. See Rogowski (*op. cit.*), wherein we also read of Musil's acknowledgment in a diary entry that Wildgans had touched the "periphery of an issue of existential importance" in his play *Love* (159).

at all between man and woman. As its own condition. The real experience is simple: an awakening. (*Lively*) I have seen you grow up beside me; brotherly, but naturally without the same interest I had in myself. Then I — excuse the expression (*he gestures mockingly to her height*) saw you grow more and more. Beyond me. And finally, you passed the moment by; suddenly you appear as gigantically tall and immeasurable as the world. That was the lightning strike, the intoxication. Everything that surrounded me, clouds, people, plans, was surrounded once more by you, just in the way one hears the heartbeat of a child under that of its mother. The miracle of opening and union came to completion. (*Undercutting*) Or however the terminology goes.

MARIA: And today it's as if we had been dreaming in the gutter.

THOMAS: If you want, yes. We awaken again and lay in the gutter. Globs of fat, skeletons; sewn into a leather sack of insensible skin. The ecstasy up in smoke. But it will become what we make of it. True human bitterness can be found in it; everything else is a belittling exaggeration.

MARIA: I only wanted your success. When you came into the bedroom at 2 AM, tired from too much work, sulky as a child, I was understanding. I didn't know what you had done, but it was my happiness, my value as a human being; I could be sure that I was this unknown thing. But now it's different. You have distanced yourself from me.

THOMAS: Because I can't watch the way you creep into the honey trap!

MARIA: What are you saying?!

THOMAS: He smothers you with flattery. Because he is vain and can't deny himself the pleasure of being gratefully admired by you.

MARIA: I do often find his exaggerations rather strange.

THOMAS: But you allow yourself to be influenced by this revoltingly sweet stuff.

MARIA: I am not the sort of goose that always only clacks "love," "love"![55] But don't believe that even *I* sometimes don't have the feeling that one should do something else with oneself aside from this settled life?!

THOMAS: Since Anselm's been here. He keeps you from understanding me.

MARIA: (*Pulling herself together; going to him*) But you, you yourself raved about him, before he came; and even when he got here! You said that he had what we lacked!

THOMAS: And what is that?

MARIA: Don't ask; I lacked nothing. But now, just because something has entered your head, you want

---

55. Another reference to Wildgans, whose name means *wild goose* in German. See Rogowski, *ibid.*, 159.

to make him out to be bad again; purely as a trial of strength; that's how you are.

THOMAS: Tell me, why don't you, how I am.

MARIA: Without a living concern for anyone, that's how you are. None of this comes from your heart at all — that's what's so chilling about it!

THOMAS: From my head instead?

MARIA: (*Riled up*) But I really can't bear this constant "activity," this fiddling with all of existence anymore! Is nothing at all worthy of just being recognized and left in peace?!

THOMAS: Now you're just repeating yourself —. But I can't answer you now. His holiness is here!

(*Anselm, visible to his breast, has popped up in the window.*)

ANSELM: How did Madam sleep last night?

MARIA: (*Coldly*) How ceremoniously you ask!

ANSELM: You must sleep like the earth.

MARIA: Do you mean: as deeply, or always with one eye opened?

ANSELM: I imagine that a crown of green mountains grows around you while you lay quietly.

(*There is a small, awkward pause.*)

MARIA: Thomas disturbed me; he was terribly restless last night. (*She becomes embarrassed.*) No — I mean —

— well, why shouldn't one simply be able to say something like that?

ANSELM: (*Ironically*) But naturally, why not...? What is true, shall one say!

THOMAS: And what do you think about Josef?

MARIA: Regina probably hasn't shown him the letter yet.

ANSELM: No. I haven't spoken with Regina yet.

THOMAS: She can't be far. It upset her very much.

MARIA: (*Since Anselm seems to be withdrawing with hesitation*) No, here. I have the letter here. First you have to read it, of course. (*She gives Anselm the letter. Thomas remains near the open door for a while in the bedroom. Anselm stops reading immediately and stares at Maria.*)

MARIA: Read it, why don't you? (*Anselm climbs through the window into the room.*)

ANSELM: Have you ever dreamt that a person whom you knew tenderly to the very core met you in the dream as a strange other, made up, even in the smallest gestures, of a torturous mixture of desire and possession?

MARIA: What happened next was like a pile of restless leaves, where something was hidden that could spring up any moment?

ANSELM: Well, okay, Maria; I was your friend long ago, when you were the girl Maria; and now you live under Thomas' name and I can't just spring up.

MARIA: But you are looking at yourself in the mirror the whole time!

ANSELM: (*Caught*) Do you really believe that I see myself? God, yes, like a spot on the mirror. Eyes are hands that one washes one's whole life long; even so, they never lose the dirty habit of touching everything. One cannot help that. Sometimes I wish I could sterilize them, so that, purified from all of the other touches, they could only behold your image.

MARIA: God, God, God, Anselm!

ANSELM: Yes, you find that ridiculous; because you hold it for an exaggeration, which deviates from good, spiritual taste. Just another arrogant seer. How pale would this wraithlike taste become if my eyes really would sizzle up, like damp burning steel? And drop out dripping wet?!

MARIA: Ugh!! Don't keep wallowing in such disgusting images!

ANSELM: (*Fiercely*) Without remorse, I would twist a knife even into your heart! If I could only bring you back just once more from the threshold. Where the women have to remove their corsets. The acquired "bearing." The understanding of a beast of burden, which accepts everything: children and sick people, men, and the thoughtless death in the kitchen.

MARIA: Will you start to read, already?! We really have much more urgent things to discuss.

ANSELM: (*Chastened by her decisiveness*) Oh, it is so heavenly, the way you can never surprise me. I know beforehand everything you will do. I feel it inside me beforehand, like a painfully taut bud.

MARIA: Naturally, the common ideas of a homebody are easy to guess!

ANSELM: I don't want any uncommon experiences! The everyday experiences of human beings are the deepest, once one liberates them from commonness. (*Softly*) That is just what he doesn't know. And you don't know yourself anymore. His influence has made you smaller.

MARIA: I have already answered this: I love Thomas.

ANSELM: I'm not asking whether you love him; there is no answer whatsoever to that! …. (*Pulling himself together*) Decide whether what you feel is like what I am about to tell you. Once I was enraptured by … a pasture. On a wide pasture and beside me there was nothing there but this tree. And I could hardly keep myself on my feet, because the same thing that had convulsed and entangled these lonely branches, this same terrible stream of life, I felt it inside me, still warm and soft, and it coiled itself around me. Then I threw myself down on my knees! (*He waits a moment for the effect.*) That is the whole experience. Just like it is with you.

MARIA: Anselm ... these exaggerations are useless. You felt it; but: threw yourself down? Not a bit of it.

ANSELM: No? ...! Thomas really has destroyed all the depth in you.

MARIA: You are behaving brutally toward me and Regina.

ANSELM: Someone, like you, who will never let herself be thrown down again, should not cast blame! Everything that I could have achieved in life, I was forced to surrender. Because one stumbles when one believes. And because one only lives as long as one believes!!

MARIA: (*Fearful and anxious*) Read; Thomas will want to talk with you.

ANSELM: I would rather give you another example: when I was a monk —

MARIA: What? You were a monk?

ANSELM: Quiet!! Thomas must not know this under any circumstances!

MARIA: But Anselm, now you are telling me an untruth.

ANSELM: I will never tell you an untruth. It was in Anatolia, on Akusios Mountain. I saw the sea from my cell — through a little glassless window cut in the wall.

MARIA: (*Fending him off*) Read! Read!

(*Anselm doesn't want to, but they hear Thomas coming and Anselm looks at the letter.*)

MARIA: What can you have been doing all the time we have been sitting here?

(*She goes back to her activity again. Thomas enters.*)

THOMAS: You're not finished yet?

MARIA: Just read it one more time. (*Anselm tries to catch her eye, in order to deepen the little helpful understanding hidden in this subterfuge, but she avoids it. Anselm shrugs his shoulders sulkily and flies through the letter.*) Thomas wants to welcome Josef with a party, to provoke him even more. But I don't want us to behave like that. Josef is our close relative; this has to be resolved!

THOMAS: (*In his apparently playful tone*) I want to hear Anselm!

(*He sits down and looks at Anselm. There is a suspenseful pause. Anselm, increasingly uncomfortable, finally looks up slowly into the depths of Thomas' eyes, coming to a firm resolve.*)

ANSELM: Your letter has destroyed everything.

THOMAS: My letter, you say. — But you were in agreement with it, weren't you?

MARIA: That's why Thomas has to try to make it all better again!

ANSELM: No, Thomas may not speak with Josef; I will not allow it.

THOMAS: (*Eagerly*) So, you — — will speak with him yourself?

ANSELM: (*Throwing the letter down*) I can't.

THOMAS: Is that so? You can't? (*Looks at Maria questioningly.*)

MARIA: But do you really want to just accept what Josef accuses you of?!

ANSELM: I don't know what I should answer him. Isn't the gist of it that I am a swindler?

THOMAS: Yes.

ANSELM: And — — aren't I one, really? Isn't every human being, who reaches for another— — do you understand, even more violently than with arms! — — who wants to convince that other (*boldly*) despite the fact that no one can be certain of his case at the core … a swindler?

MARIA: (*Resistant, while Thomas instinctively watches her reaction*) That's hyper-sensitive!

ANSELM: (*Becoming agitated*) I myself don't know whether I had the wish to save Regina or to do something to Josef. Sometimes one is as grandiose and reckless as in a dream. Today I regret it.

MARIA: (*Enthralled*) What do you regret, Anselm? Speak now, while there is still time!

ANSELM: I don't know what I should answer Josef; every heartfelt principle is enormously contagious. Leave me.

MARIA: Then speak.

ANSELM: One did something. It can't be altered. One has crushed another person like a beetle. Under one's boot heel. But then suddenly the other rises up. Imagine a glass divided in two: he rises as high in us as he does in himself, this other person! He pours into us and knocks us down! All it takes is not wanting to be petty (*as if threatened*), then he reveals himself, this other person!

THOMAS: (*Who had been watching the effect on Maria with suspense*) Then there is only one thing to do: without any fuss, do what all the world would do. Put some small worldly pressure on Josef. We hire a detective and a good lawyer; there is surely one painfully sensitive point to be found even with Josef.

MARIA: (*Horrified*) You would sink to such means?!

THOMAS: Josef once confided something to me. Long ago. We would only have to send a detective after more specific details, and even if Josef's soul were innocent (*suggestively*), the facts can always be connected! The facts like to paint the soul in a bad light, don't they, Anselm?

MARIA: But that would be so base! Josef has only been good to you his whole life!

THOMAS: And I to him, whenever I was able! Even now I am honestly grateful and could, with just as much pleasure, do something good for him, if only the situation were different.

MARIA: You are unrecognizable. If you were not always a decent man, I don't know who is one.

THOMAS: Who? Anselm. Because he will reject the detective.

MARIA: Thomas, this is only an outbreak of overexcitement! You can't be serious! You're acting just like a scoundrel!

THOMAS: Anselm, what do you think? May I do it? Am I then a scoundrel? Or am I so much of a scoundrel that I may not do it?

ANSELM: You already know that I agree with Maria! You are letting yourself get carried away to do something that you can't condone.

THOMAS: A detective would be nothing but a sign of how little we are bothered by these idiotic imbroglios on which he lives. He who is untouched by them can make use of them!

MARIA: Thomas leaps immediately to extremes!

ANSELM: (*With mocking modesty*) Oh, maybe he's right. He who harbors a new humanity in himself, naturally has little tenderness.

THOMAS: You couldn't do it then?

MARIA: Thomas, if you can do this, then you really don't have even the slightest human feeling left!

THOMAS: (*Smiling, but forcing his voice to jest with difficulty*) Anselm, if one of us has to be the scoundrel in this business — and it can't be you .... (*He goes, in order not to lose his composure, immediately into the next room; the doors stay open.*)

ANSELM: (*Mockingly*) Reformers probably have to be heartless; anyone who wants to turn the world a hundred and eighty degrees must not be involved with it in anything more than an intellectual capacity.

MARIA: But didn't you come here specifically to be together with him again?!

ANSELM: And then a time comes when I deny myself. When I have to pull myself away — — like a scarecrow who has left its captured leg in the hand of someone stronger.

MARIA: I don't understand you.

ANSELM: (*Smiling*) I am afraid.

MARIA: Those are just words.

ANSELM: (*Serious*) I am really afraid.

MARIA: Words!

ANSELM: Afraid of every person whom I cannot infect to believe in me, whom I feel I can't give something or take something from.

MARIA: But what is it you want?

ANSELM: I don't even know anymore! Thomas won't let me find myself!

MARIA: I want you to talk this over with Thomas. You're a man, after all!

ANSELM: I don't know what you imagine a man to be. It is not a talisman of strength, ensuring that one is never weak. I can't!

MARIA: At bottom you're really afraid of Josef? Are you really fearful?

ANSELM: Yes. If I can't make others feel and therefore can't feel myself, I am horrendously afraid; otherworldly afraid.

MARIA: (*Mockingly*) And when you *do* feel?

ANSELM: Put your cigarette out in my hand.

MARIA: That would hurt you more than a sensitive man like you could bear.

ANSELM: If one does it slowly, it hurts. (*He grabs her wrist.*)

MARIA: But what are you thinking?! (*They fight.*) Let go! You will let go in the end anyway ... don't make a face like that! I'm not afraid ... No, you're not that strong. No, no, enough joking!

ANSELM: (*During the struggle*) You are mistaken if you believe I am docile. Or cowardly because of a weak heart.

(*Breaking Maria's resistance, he presses the glowing tip of her cigarette and her hand against his palm. His expression, to Maria's dismay, is fanatic and almost sensually ecstatic.*)

ANSELM: (*Afterwards, attempting to joke*) You see, when it must be, I spring into the fire.

MARIA: How can one be like that!

ANSELM: (*Brushing a few little ashes from his hands and clothing*) Yes, how can one be like that?! I am not a sweet-tempered person.

THOMAS: (*Now fully clothed, returns from the bedroom and notices that something has happened.*) What happened? Something happened between you two?

(*Silence*)

THOMAS: I am not allowed to know?

MARIA: (*Sullenly toward both of them*) I don't understand how you two cannot find a way out of this situation.

THOMAS: But everyone is still against the detective idea? (*Maria shrugs her shoulders.*) Oh, I thought so.

(*He stands for a moment helplessly before them both, wants to leave, but turns back again. Looking at Anselm*) And I only need to look at you and I know: that's not you! Anselm, we were back together again, like years ago, and sat up half the night, without sensing the time. And you agreed with me. You even agreed about the detective!! (*A small, embarrassing, involuntary pause ensues.*)

MARIA: (*As if she were surprised that she had not said it at once*) But one can change one's mind, can't one?

ANSELM: He attacked me and persuaded me! (*With unconcealed distaste*) But I can't bear a world filled with judgments and disdain for ever!

THOMAS: Shall I say what it is you're trying to hide behind all of this? Like someone who covers up a missing finger? That your life was a failure? And how could it have been any different?

ANSELM: (*Fiercely and mockingly to Maria*) He has always lived in his thoughts. Absolute ruler in a paper realm! That creates massive surpluses of confidence and despotism. Encounters with people are compromising and constraining.

THOMAS: Anselm!? Is Josef inventing what's in the letter? Or did I really provide him with it? (*They look at each other.*)

ANSELM: Naturally, he is inventing.

THOMAS: (*Fiercely and impatiently*) I really don't know what sort of revelations he is threatening to expose! I am certain that you are capable of anything!

MARIA: (*Defensively*) Thomas!

THOMAS: (*Cutting off the retort. As if he wanted to encourage Anselm to reveal himself*) There are people who only want to know what could be, while the others, like detectives, establish what is. Those people search out something that changes, while the latter remain on solid ground. It's a presentiment of the ability to be different. A directionless feeling of neither taste nor distaste, between the exaltations and commonplaces of the world. A homesickness, but without a home. That makes everything possible!

MARIA: There you go with your theories again!

ANSELM: Yes, they are theories. You have found the right word. But how horrible it is when theories get mixed up in life and death. (*He nervously picks up the letter again.*)

THOMAS: (*Bitter, accusatory, increasingly more impassioned*) Fine, they are theories. When we were young, we had theories too. When we were young, we knew that everything that the old people would live or die for "in earnest" had already been done long ago in spirit and that it was disgustingly boring. That there was no virtue and no vice that could be compared to a human adventure with an elliptical integral number or a flying machine. When we were young, we knew that whatever really happens is entirely unimportant compared to what *could* happen. That all of the progress of mankind consists in that which does *not* happen. In what is thought; its uncertainties, its fire. When we were young, we felt: passionate people have no feelings whatsoever. No, passionate people are formless, naked storms of power!!

ANSELM: (*Just as agitated*) Yes; and today I know simply that that was false and adolescent. There are trees, but the wind does not shake them. What is lacking in these ideas is that small bit of modesty that realizes that ultimately all thoughts are false and that they must, therefore, be believed in; by warm-hearted humans!

THOMAS: Your modesty! Anselm! Your modesty! Anselm, Anselm!

ANSELM: But have you ever even learned what that is?

THOMAS: Modesty, that is wanting to be the last one; in other words, the first one from behind! (*He breaks out in agitated laughter.*) Doesn't Josef, even, write about your modesty and love of mankind? Is Josef making this up?

ANSELM: He is wrong. Wrong! But in his wrongness, he is a human being!

THOMAS: And you really love Regina? Or you are allowing her to infuriate Josef only to torment her?!

MARIA: Yes, Anselm, Thomas is not entirely wrong there.

THOMAS: (*Still trying to move him*) Anselm! There is something in you that keeps any man from giving anything to you. Something no one can give to. It plays recklessly on the flute of human love as one plays with the breath of a dying man. This recklessness is in everyone. But there is also something inside you that cries out for others. If only it were toward your fellow misanthropes![56] A fear of endorsing iniquity, but all the same somehow supporting all of it. What have we achieved, after all? In our studies, considering how best to crack a nut like an ape with a stone in his hand?! Without even coming close to a single question that touches our redemption as human beings. Or emasculated, like you, having turned your brain into a comfortable womb that presses up against everything that is solid. Anselm, we bore it easily, so long as we were young and did not think about death. And later one gets by with fleeting distractions like work and success. But a little later still you come alive for the first time to the fact that it is no longer three or four or twelve o'clock, but that there is a silent rising and setting of stars all around you! And for the first time you notice that something inside you follows along, like an ebb and flood, without having been aware of it.

---

56. Here Musil has provided the translator with an untranslatable pun: *Mit-Nichtmenschen*, combining the words *mitnichten* (certainly not) and *Mitmenschen* (fellow men).

And the ascetic slings a cord around his heart and the other end around the largest star that he can see, and fetters himself. And the detective type has his nose in his tracks and doesn't need to lift it up. And I? And you? Can you be sincere, even when Maria is listening? Anselm, one person alone is a fool; two are a new humanity!

(*Exhausted pause.*)

MARIA: (*Who now, finished with her grooming, is cheered up*) But you are both fools! I see now for the first time how far gone you are. Have you said a word about Josef? (*Both turn to her astonished, as if to a voice from another world. Maria, laughing*) Anselm is absolutely sheepish. If you just have a long talk with Thomas, he will surely relinquish his symbolic detective!

THOMAS: (*Still fully confused*) Of course, I relinquish him.

MARIA: (*Continuing*) And Anselm has burned himself; Anselm is in pain; let me just quickly apply something cool to the burn. (*She begins to improvise a bandage.*) Go out first; he will come after; he will join you in your room in a moment.

ANSELM: (*With strained compliance*) But that is precisely what is dangerous about him; that he persuades everyone.

THOMAS: Shall it be then, Anselm? (*He looks at him questioningly, and Anselm forces himself to affirm the ques-*

tioning look. Nevertheless, uncertainly and with bitterness) Will it really be so? I will wait. You will not dare to disappoint Maria.

(*Exits.*)

ANSELM: (*Hardly has Thomas left the room when he pulls his hand with the unfinished bandage away from Maria*) I will not join him.

MARIA: What are you saying?

ANSELM: That, naturally, I will not join him.

MARIA: I will never speak with you again.

ANSELM: (*Untroubled*) Ever since we were boys, he always knew everything better. But I didn't want to answer to him! I don't have to answer to him! (*Exultantly*) I don't have to, Maria!! I don't have to. I can close my eyes, my ears, all my openings, until it grows completely dark around what I know: and outside, the great safecracker thumps and bumps about with his two pry bars, Reason and Revelation! (*Since Maria makes a dismissive face and does not answer*) I will sooner leave than give him access!

MARIA: Do so! It will be the best thing.

ANSELM: Will you come with me?

MARIA: What did you say?

ANSELM: Come away!

MARIA: (*First speechless, then*) But you must be crazy; what can you be thinking?

ANSELM: (*Lets a little time pass, then changes*) Of course, you will take this suggestion in the wrong light; I expected that.

MARIA: I do not take it at all. I have remained here because I want to put things in order. If you still have something else to say, do so; you surely do not intend to insult me.

ANSELM: I don't know if this insults you: I love Thomas much more than you love him. For I am much more like him. The crisis that he is now going through — is merely another version of my own. And if I am antagonistic, it may be out of fear for myself. But you suffer in vain with him, without admitting it to yourself.

MARIA: *He* suffers! This strong person, who has always been able to do what he wanted, is no longer sure of himself.

ANSELM: (*Enviously*) Thomas can do everything; but he cannot suffer!

MARIA: It's ghastly to watch and not be able to help him.

ANSELM: You could help him.

MARIA: I? Oh, Anselm, in this respect you are not seeing so clearly! I understand nothing of these inhuman ideas.

ANSELM: There is a way.

MARIA: Well, then say it right out, why don't you?

ANSELM: I already have said it to you.

MARIA: (*After a while*) But those are fantasies; that is fantastical.

(*A pause.*)

ANSELM: Do you think that I dispute Thomas' superiority, that I don't consider my intellect unsatisfactory compared to his?

MARIA: I heard that you had to leave the university because you acted up?[57]

ANSELM: I made myself impossible. Maybe I should have lived during the century of the Inquisition. If someone has another opinion than me, it's like a stone, grimacing at me; the bestiality! Whoever has eyes to see it is exposed to the shameless resolve of a drowning man, fighting for a place in the boat.

MARIA: But one must be able to have differing opinions, no!?

ANSELM: Maybe I'm just too stupid for it. Oh, Maria, we are both too stupid for him. I need to feel that I am

---

57. The original, "weil Sie Auftritte gehabt haben," can mean either: "because you went on the stage" or: "because you had fights." An actual theatrical career is not justified here, but the relationship between Anselm's life and an act is.

the ultimate for someone, the decisive one. Or else I feel rejected. Thomas can do without people, but even you say it yourself: what a monstrosity this is!

MARIA: You are possibly not completely wrong about that; there is something inhuman about Thomas. I, also, have often told him so.

ANSELM: (*Quickly taking this up*) He looks down on everything. The only thing he trusts is the power of a brandished stone; for this, namely, is the power of Reason, this Reason, which today rules the world. Those powers that dwell in people's faces, in the swallows in autumn, those unproven powers, powers of warmth, of blushing, even the powers of horses in a stall, that friendly or fiendish togetherness, these — perhaps he knows them. (*Mockingly*) Oh, certainly he will *know* them. But truths that can only be understood in seconds of shattering and that flare up like a spark between two people, these he does not sanction.

MARIA: I can well understand what you mean. But something is hiding in what you say, something that instantly flies away if one tries to name it. Something unreal. Something that is not worthy of belief.

ANSELM: And when *you* are so blissfully filled with such powers! Every gesture of your body is moved by them and radiates them. I am not exaggerating. Maria, I am sometimes so flooded by them that I suffer from the fear that my limbs and facial expressions will involuntarily imitate yours, like plants on the bottom of a flowing body of water.

MARIA: But these are excessive exaggerations!

ANSELM: The most natural in the world! Human nature itself! Do not diminish yourself! You know that one cannot understand anything at all with Reason, not even a stone lying there. One understands only through love. In a nameless condition of approaching and somehow relating. Which is why this question of Man-Woman is nothing but an overestimated particular case. But Thomas has taught you to forget this. Admit it, do, that he represses you to the point of helplessness. What can his concepts and analyses mean to you!

MARIA: Oh, they are always stimulating and valuable!

ANSELM: Oh! Really? But you have a deeper connection with man and objects than he does. I, for one, still remember what you were!

MARIA: Those were childish foolishnesses.

ANSELM: Thomas did not allow these powers to persist in you, just as he does not suffer any power to exist aside from his own. Now he suffers from their lack. That is his catastrophe; I have gotten him to the point that he suspects it himself.

MARIA: But what is it you are really after?!

ANSELM: What does it matter if you suddenly go away with me and Regina?

MARIA: But for what reason?

ANSELM: Mystery. Only an unexpected blow like this could shake him up and bring him to conversion. Otherwise he will destroy himself.

MARIA: But what would Regina say about it? She must want order and marriage as soon as possible?

ANSELM: Maria, she doesn't dare object! I must confide another secret to you: I have never promised Regina anything more than friendship.

MARIA: But then what has the point of all this been?! We've talked of nothing else but marriage from the beginning!

ANSELM: I only wanted to help her! Do you know why Josef calls me a scoundrel? Because he doesn't understand that I could have wanted to help Regina get away from him without loving her in this narrow and pedestrian way.

MARIA: But then why does he refer to Potiphar?

ANSELM: Just because he came up with it from somewhere. But I just wanted to teach her to live again, to awaken feelings in her, to force her to feel significance; to free her from the ghostly airy emptiness that had risen up all around her.

MARIA: But this story about Johannes is in itself a real fantasy?!

ANSELM: That's another reason why Thomas calls me a scoundrel. So, I must admit it to you as well. I suffered it in order to protect myself! Regina had a tendency to misunderstand me; she was in such a bad state. But I dreaded the thought that, once again, a human relationship would be reduced to a mere spasm; so, I had to use Johannes as a distraction. Everything that he was, I was not!

MARIA: Frightful, what you have involved yourself in!

ANSELM: Perhaps out of my own weakness. I supported these stories; she communicated with this dead man like a living guardian angel. Who guarded her against nothing; against nothing! She is really a person without any true connections to other people. Her feelings sit in her head, like Thomas'. Such people exaggerate everything. Then the paltry shiftlessness of this lie moved me somehow. But when I was just about to wean her off this morphine, ever so gently, Thomas came and interfered. Marriage. Letter to Josef; detective: you alone can measure what he has set in motion.

MARIA: I do not agree with everything you have said, Anselm, but I do begin to glean some connecting thread between some things that I didn't understand until now.

ANSELM: Thomas is the very merciless man of rationality whom he battles in Josef; the very one he battles in Josef!

MARIA: Indeed, you are not totally wrong; you're a little right.... It would be necessary to do something drastic to drive him to a conversion.... And you were really in a monastery?

ANSELM: Why do you ask? I was there.

MARIA: Anselm, because you must always tell me only the truth! I would be devastated if complete truthfulness did not exist between us all now!

ANSELM: Maria, even if I wanted to, I could not lie to you; you know how I worship you!

MARIA: But you really must speak with him.

ANSELM: I can't do that! I could bow down to someone thirsting for reconciliation, but I cannot speak with Thomas. You can tell him everything later. *Could* you tell him what we have discussed?! Or would the words lose their powers between your mouth and his ear?! — You must run away from here, secretly and suddenly. He will search for you. The place which his mandate has allocated for you will be abandoned. You will be on your own. That is the only thing that can bring him to conversion!

MARIA: Do you know that you are running the risk of becoming a bad person? You intend something good, but you have absolutely no scruples in your choice of means.

ANSELM: But what does that mean — choice of means, when I already feel that you, out of your innermost strengths, will find the right ones; it would be to shoot at the sun with pistols. Oh, Maria, I am less than a bad person; a scholar, who has lost his scholarliness, and a person who fails, again and again, in his choice of means. Only you can help us.

MARIA: Anselm, we must speak of this some more. About Regina too. But you will promise me then to speak with Thomas? (*Since Anselm is silent*) Oh yes, you promise me. Come then, we will now walk in the park a little. (*Since Anselm turns toward the other door*) No, not that way, through here (*she points to the bedroom*); it's closer. But you must close your eyes; it's such a mess. I think that once we have discussed this fully, Thomas could really help.

ANSELM: (*With muted fury and malice*) Oh, I would rather you would climb through the window! Don't you want to go out that way?! You would have to crouch and contort yourself to fit yourself through and to pull your skirts together, until you transformed into something incomprehensible; as in an accident! But you are too beautiful to risk something like that.

MARIA: What has gotten into you now?

ANSELM: That you have *slept* in there, for years and years!!

MARIA: Nonsense! Eyes closed! Give me your hand!

(*Exit. The stage remains empty for a moment.*)

REGINA: (*Entering*) If you really think it's a good idea, then in here; here no one will disturb us now.

MISS MERTENS: Oh, I know that it seems scarcely bearable to trust a strange man. Who could understand you as well as I?! I know what it is to lock oneself up in one's innermost self. You! Tenderest of saints!

REGINA: Thomas said something about a detective, no…? But I don't like that at all!

MISS MERTENS: No, of course that is wrong of Doctor Thomas; one of his cold conceits! You see that!

REGINA: Ascertain! Observe! What can be achieved this way!? It's so stupid.

MISS MERTENS: But perhaps this man can help you; he has expressly asked for you. (*She gestures out through the open door.*) And even if he looks a bit common, his face is not unsympathetic. I will leave you two alone.

(*She lets Stader walk by her and retreats. Stader comes closer, sniffing at the room with all his sense organs. He was once a pretty young man and is now a capable person. His clothing imitates the correctness of a well-to-do scholar, but with the addition of a small black artist's tie. As he enters, he puts a surly mature expression on his face and nudges his large blue eyeglasses, as if he had just put them on.*)

REGINA: You have been sent by … a bureau? Won't you sit down?

(*They sit down. Stader hesitates and clears his throat. Since he has not succeeded in impressing Regina in the desired way, he takes off his glasses and makes a natural face.*)

STADER: These dated, old-fashioned tricks still really do work sometimes! A pair of glasses, a little authority in one's expression suffice in most cases! So, you didn't recognize me.

REGINA: I still don't know…? (*She looks at him, a wide grin spreading slowly across his whole face.*) What do you mean?

STADER: You don't remember?

REGINA: N… o. Oh, yes…. You were a servant at our house?

STADER: Hmm… er… yes; indeed, quite so; I *was* a servant…. Stader, Ferdinand Stader… *Ferdinand*!? But even in those days I was already something finer in my free time, a singer and a writer.

REGINA: I know. You performed as a singer at night in resorts, even though you were not strictly allowed to. I liked that.

STADER: And how many times did you breathe a kiss into my hair and say, you —

REGINA: Don't behave tastelessly now!

STADER: Tastelessly? You bit me with your teeth and all of your ten fingers were in my hair and you said: you in — you in — ; dear God, I knew it just a short time ago and now I have forgotten it again! It was something with genius.

REGINA: You — ingénue. My God! (*She throws her hands in front of her face.*) I could kick myself today!!

STADER: Calm yourself. It's true, that you did me a great wrong when you ... well, I was going to say, when you simply threw me out. I had not known that fine ladies could be that way. But I don't hold it against you. Because, in so doing, you gave me a shove in the direction of the truth. And I have the truth to thank for my advancement! You were, it turned out, not mistaken about me, and your declaration that I was a genius, it accompanied me and gave me such strength; it wouldn't do you any good if you tried to take it back today. I was never merely a servant, and I gave it up altogether right after that. I was many things. Taxidermist, piano player, a second at duels, a photographer, even a dog catcher; I was a comprehensive man, even before I discovered my career. And I must say, it requires not only the discipline of research, but also some artistic blood: today I am the proprietor of the largest contemporary research institute.

REGINA: Research?

STADER: A detection institute.

REGINA: You want money?! How much? I don't have any.

STADER: (*Nobly*) Please consider me to be standing before you as a knight! I merely wanted to beg a small favor of you. (*Correcting, with disdainful tenderness, her error.*) Not that kind; you haven't changed at all, have you? My institute is the largest and most modern research institute of the day: Newton, Galileo, & Stader. In earlier times one would have called something of its ilk "Argus." But because I know how much I owe to modern science, I have incorporated its two founders into the name of my firm.

REGINA: (*Who is confused*) Yes, then, so … you must be the detective whom my cousin Thomas spoke of?

STADER: Your — ? Who is Thomas?!

REGINA: My cousin Doctor Thomas — well, it is *his* house you are in! He spoke of wanting to hire a detective.

STADER: (*Very agitated*) In the case of His Excellency, your husband, and a certain Doctor Anselm Mornas?

REGINA: In all probability, certainly!

STADER: (*Extremely emotionally*) He has a detective! And not me! I am mortified!

REGINA: But I'm not at all certain that he has really done it.

STADER: It's not yet certain!? You must arrange a meeting between us immediately. I am His Excellency's detective; but I will sell all my secrets to him. I will give them all to him, if he will only grant me a hearing! You must recommend me whole-heartedly to him immediately!

REGINA: But that's not possible.

STADER: Not possible? You mean, because of — ? What's past is past. A man has higher concerns! Listen to me: my institute works with the most modern scientific methods. With graphology, pathography, family history, probability, statistics, psychoanalysis, experimental psychology, and so on. We investigate the scientific element of the act; because everything that happens in the world happens according to laws. Eternal laws! The reputation of my institute rests upon these laws. Countless young scholars and students work in my service. I do not demand the paltry details of a case; I only need be provided with the basic laws that make up a man's being and I know what — under given circumstances — he will have been compelled to do! Do you understand? Modern science and detection narrow the realm of the accidental, the disorderly, the allegedly personal more and more. There are no accidents! There are only facts! Yes, indeed! There are only — scientific correspondences. Yes, this is what has become of your "little Neapolitan," your "street singer"!

His Excellency, your husband, attracted by the extraordinary reputation enjoyed by our institute, has offered us the honor of his case. It meant a great deal to me to provide satisfaction to such a high-ranking scholarly personage: here is the written material. (*He points at a thick portfolio, which he has not let out of his hand.*)

REGINA: Material? You don't mean? About whom?

STADER: Naturally, in addition to the aforementioned modern techniques, we also use undercover investigators, bribes, women, alcohol, servants, estates; in short, the so-called classical methods of detection science. Do you want to see? (*He opens the portfolio.*) This postcard here is from Doctor Anselm Mornas to his tailor and concerns the ordering of a winter suit. If you will, observe that the card must have been written in August. That is proven by the date of the postmark and by the conjecture that it is a matter of a pure and simple so-called purpose-result situation, whereby there would be no use in misleading the tailor.

REGINA: (*Baffled*). I don't understand. What can be concluded from this!?

STADER: Oh...! Ordering a winter suit in August, that could mean: foresight; thrift, for in summer, winter fabric is less expensive; lack of style, for one would not yet know the newest winter fabrics; fourthly, some mysterious reason. He is not at all pedantically foresightful; he is not thrifty; not lacking in style: what remains now? The mystery. There you have the whole human being! And the analysis of the contents fits the handwriting completely. Just look at this upward-striving check mark: a love of adventure. This low 'u': secret passion. Oh, it is a pleasure to spread before oneself, so effortlessly, the hidden essence of a man! Here! Do you see this shaded stroke: suicidal ideation! And now these practically disappearing middle letters: a roving instinct; it is the handwriting of a man who disappears from time to time and spreads the rumor that he is going to his death. I don't even need to notice that he writes the word "betroth" so that one could read it as "betray," because I already know, without this, that his urge to live is keen: this steeply climbing serif! In sum, he has the feeling that he cannot live without the person whom he will meet in the winter in this suit.

REGINA: So, he already knows her?

STADER: It was you!

REGINA: How in the world can you know that?

STADER: Of course, as an agent of His Excellency, I will be cognizant of when Doctor Anselm came to your house for the first time. (*He looks at his watch*) But I am running out of time; just look at this one document.

REGINA: But that's my handwriting!

STADER: Yes, it is. I took it way back when as a memento; it was your budget book.

REGINA: What can you see in it?!

STADER: I have given it no little attention. In this case, I must say, all the scientific indications did not provide me with anything more than what I already knew. (*While he leafs through it*) Heartless. Sleeps long. Unwise. In short (*in slow, lengthy, saved-up triumph*): scientifically considered, a thoroughly substandard personage. And…! (*He has finally found the place he had searched for and holds it before her very carefully, so that she cannot tear the book out of his hands.*) And here "Ferdinand" is written and next to it, "*colon* little Neapolitan." And then: "Johannes, when will you return?"!

REGINA: Give it back to me.

STADER: But what do you think? (*Friendly*) Yes, tell me, I heard something before; there was not too much opportunity, but the lady, who was in your company, exclaimed, "Saint." Do you still really do that? You explained it all to me, remember? At the time. Your love for me was meant for the holy Johannes and I was involved only the way someone is married by proxy. It impressed me mightily at the time. I was innocent — excuse me that I laugh: you told *me* that, the future Newton & Stader — and I believed you. But it really was a beautiful invention and later it made me into a psychologist. Only: something so unusual is not accessible to everyone. And if one repeats it too often and fully worthless individuals get involved in the act: you will have great troubles! Do you know, by the way, that your current groom is already married and will not get divorced so that he doesn't have to marry you?

REGINA: (*Having pulled herself together in the meanwhile*) Yes.

STADER: This information was gleaned from an analysis of this letter to his lawful wife — that is, it says as much.

REGINA: I would like to see that; show it to me.

STADER: (*Putting it back into his portfolio and closing it with care*) You would tear it up.

REGINA: So, you have been engaged to spy on me?

STADER: His Excellency the professor and I both serve the truth, each in his own way; I, ever since I arrived at manhood!

REGINA: (*Stands up*) You are a swindler! You know nothing at all! I never knew you! I am prepared to swear an oath to it at any moment.

STADER: Ah, but I have not shown you everything — by no means. I still have entirely different material: Are you missing anything?

REGINA: What should I be missing?

STADER: A notebook, for example? A very small yellow book: wherein you have written your life story and also Doctor Anselm's?

REGINA: But I still have that — — !

STADER: No, in fact, you no longer *do* have it.

REGINA: I put it in my suitcase. I am quite sure of that.

STADER: Could be. But not only in simple natures — no, not at all; I can say no more, except: even in scholarly circles one can find subjects! — But let us leave it be. You see, we are familiar with these outbreaks of impetuosity; you have not insulted me.

REGINA: (*Who has made her decision*) Yes, we shall leave it be!

STADER: Truth is always subject to attacks, but it rises above them.

REGINA: If that is truth, then truth is a terrifically filthy trap for catching humans …. I look at you; you stand there like a ghost. You stand there as if: —I could calculate and then give you the exact number; you could then put it in your files. How can I make you understand that all of that was never true?!

STADER: (*Who finds this twist awkward*) You don't need to.

REGINA: But it was true! Don't you remember?! Have you forgotten how I gave myself to you like a dog in heat?

STADER: What's past is past.

REGINA: You cannot get off that easily! Before, I saw you as you were; afterwards I saw you the same way: but in between I simply could not bear it — you were so disturbing to me!

STADER: Yes, yes, yes; one always hears something like this after affairs such as these.

REGINA: But I just couldn't get enough of compromising myself — of throwing myself away on you! Sometimes, when I am alone in my room, I cannot bear to see my bureau — the way it just stands there; sometimes I notice that it has changed and that it makes faces. Then I have to rush to open it and look inside: otherwise I might call it Johannes too.

STADER: (*Warning her, but just as determined to come to his point*) I can only advise you to confide in your cousin, Professor Thomas. That is a man whom one may trust. Such a reputation in his field, people have told me; but, moreover, such a vision for mankind! Scholars don't always have that; particularly in my field, one sometimes has to fight against the contempt mankind feels for our work. It's quite unjust, of course; for, from a modern perspective, a detective is something as lofty as a researcher; yes, even loftier, when one considers that our subject of research is mankind itself. In any case, one could always use some support. (*He has stood up*) I want to win him over to a great idea. That you did not throw yourself away on the most unworthy has been proven. You only have to make Doctor Thomas take notice of me, as a person with whom it would be worthwhile to be in constant contact. If you wanted that, everything would remain strictly among us three!

REGINA: I will not do this; I cannot make such a thing happen anymore.

STADER: Regina! Get a hold of yourself! You treated me badly back then, but I founded my institute on your hush money. I wish you well. But ever since I have heard of Professor Thomas, I cannot rest! I am prepared to do anything! I have incalculable artist's blood in me! Without it I would never have come so far in my profession. Be decent!

REGINA: I don't want to.

STADER: But I could do you too much harm!

REGINA: Go ahead. I know myself as I really and truly am; you have me in your hand. I want you to deliver this portfolio to His Excellency.

STADER: Yes, but have you no shame at all? All the details would come out at the trial! You must have some shame; you would allow yourself to be so totally exposed! Have you no fear!?

REGINA: Listen, "Ferdinand": One can be as holy inside as the steads of the Sun God, while outside one looks like what you have in your files. That is a mystery that your institute will never decipher. One does something and it means something completely different on the inside as on the outside. But in time, one has only done what happened on the outside. One no longer has the power to transform it!

STADER: Well, I could testify under oath that you certainly seemed to be very conscious of what you were doing, every time.

REGINA: — ?! Yes. You are right. That's the horrible thing about it. — But you must leave; we can't stay here any longer.

STADER: Yes, I'm already quite late, I must get to the train. (*With one last try*) Professor Thomas is threatened! A sinister threat hovers over his head. You don't know what's in the letter you have seen; Anselm isn't here on your account; he is here to seduce his friend's wife!

REGINA: Is that so? You have to go this way. Then comes a door, it leads to a bathroom, then to a hall and a few steps — I'll show you the way myself. (*She leads.*)

STADER: (*In the door of the bedroom*) I am going to go to His Excellency now. I'm going to give it to His Excellency. But before I give it to His Excellency, I can still be met at the train. And perhaps even afterwards…. Stories like this, I don't understand; a man has logic! I thought you would do anything to keep the portfolio.

(*Exits.*)

(*The stage stays empty for a moment, before Anselm enters from the other door. He looks around carefully, walks quickly to the bedroom door and collapses, leaning on the door frame, and sinks into reflection. His expression is one of the* visio beata. *Suddenly he flinches, as if he were embarrassed in an illicit act, and attempts to make himself look harmless. Regina has returned through the bedroom, walks in, and stands across from him.*)

ANSELM: You were in the room?

REGINA: No, I came from outside, but you didn't notice me at first.

ANSELM: Yes, yes, I was looking for you; I left you standing there, but then I couldn't find you anywhere.

REGINA: But that's not true.

ANSELM: (*Looks at her with surprise, but then says calmly*) Maria? But what are you thinking! She amuses me.

REGINA: Is she waiting for you?

ANSELM: I was supposed to fetch something for her, a shawl; but she can wait a good while for it. She sees me as a romantic hero and expects medieval attentions from me; she has a hard time understanding things, like all stately women.

REGINA: (*Convinced*) Have you watched her eat? She chews slowly like a cow. She would love to always have flowery conversations too, vast green word-landscapes to graze on; you are so good at that, by the way.

ANSELM: (*Attempting to outdo her. And since he now, after the previous passionate scene with Maria, finds himself in an opposing phase of spiritual disgust, he speaks at first as if filled with even more conviction.*) Yes, she requires lyricism, ideally dappled with butter. It drives me mad. After time spent with her, Thomas is like a delightfully dry desert wind. Do you know, I would not be at all surprised if she were to suddenly leave him, when the spirit moves her; these 180-pound souls fall down like sacks.

REGINA: Would you really like to see her like that? She makes me want to scatter pepper on her body to make her jump, so that I could then say to *her*: my dear Maria, a hygienic aroma of virtue surrounds you like the pure carbolic air of hospitals. Such leaps are nothing for her!

ANSELM: Don't hop like that, old virtue! I would love to see her face then!

REGINA: You still remember, don't you, how thin her legs were, and how the goody-goody's knickers were always falling down. Now one can't see, but since we have been back, I am plagued by the question of whether her legs are still so thin.

ANSELM: (*Can't join in anymore*) All of us together from morning till night: let's not speak about her anymore; it makes me shiver to think of her.

REGINA: See! You're lying! Oh, how you lie!

ANSELM: But would I be able to talk about her like this?!

REGINA: Oh, you! You only speak well of a person as long as you are indifferent to him. As soon as you feel something for him, you smear him with filth, to hide it! (*She suddenly stops.*) Come away!

ANSELM: (*Unwilling*) Why?!

REGINA: Come away, Anselm! We'll travel! We'll flee! When Josef comes, we will already be gone. You have gotten caught here; you can't get free of Maria.

ANSELM: Don't be so horribly womanish right off. (*He considers.*) On the contrary, you must beg Maria to come with us.

REGINA: And?

ANSELM: If we live outside of this house together, your husband can cause us the greatest troubles; if you travel with your sister, he can't do anything to us at all.

REGINA: And — ?! Beat that idea out of your head. I will not play the decoy for you two much longer.

ANSELM: You imagine you have dragged a secret out of me. Okay then: your sister is superb! Superb and bland, like water. Smells as good as a laundry room; for all I care, if you like, just as filled with vapors.

REGINA: And I?

ANSELM: Josef, too, is a superb person. We allowed ourselves to look down upon him. Certainly, they are maddeningly sluggish in temperament and spirit, these people. But I will tell you something: even the unconventional experience is nothing but an upside-down conventionality. And life is richer, even among a team of oxen, than inside a head like Thomas'; and a carriage driver who sleeps with his horses knows more about the world than he and you do!

REGINA: Should I go back to Josef then?

ANSELM: God, I mean, how about getting out in the fresh air for once first? Here you will never get free of these crippling experiences with Johannes. Here it's like a room the morning after a bacchanal.

REGINA: So, I should dunk my head in "splendid" fresh water! But I don't want that. I would rather kill myself. Do you hear me? But not on account of you.

ANSELM: Doesn't everyone say that, when they believe they have been abandoned?

REGINA: I have borne other humiliations. Have you been scheming about this for a long time?

ANSELM: What do you mean?

REGINA: Did you perhaps take our little yellow book out of the suitcase again and leave it out for Josef?

ANSELM: So, you know it? From where? I could deny it, since you leave everything lying around. But: Yes! I did — because I already knew what awaited me with you. You came too close to me. You don't want to get out of my way anymore! I am not strong enough to save you, either; definitely not you. Your blasted weaknesses have stirred up all of the crypts inside of me!!

REGINA: And you will surrender to Josef? These superb people seem to have a great influence on you all of a sudden. It was always unbearable to you before when anyone knew the slightest thing about you, as if you were in their power if they did. You would have preferred to tell a nasty lie about yourself than admit to something good that was really true.

ANSELM: By the time Josef knows any of this, I'll be God knows where. I will change my name and begin again. I want to begin again, do you understand? I must begin once more! You will not hold me back!

REGINA: So, you wanted to begin a new life again. And that was the day when you hit yourself in your face with your fist and almost cried. (*She mimics him mystically*) "It's a miracle that I have found you! It has floored me, like a miracle. — I would rather die than have to survive this."

ANSELM: Yes, that was the day! I felt that I had to save myself. We were so unfathomably one. My life was so repeated in you. Another I, you stood in my path and there was a fluttering stillness all around us and a sudden gliding out into this ocean that was in us and around us, so that I felt: if there is a shipwreck, only one of us will reach the shore again…. How insipid that already sounds today. How inglorious these futile attempts.

REGINA: Oh, every word has been etched in my memory and I was able to repeat it to the detective, so that today Thomas and Josef will know precisely as well.

ANSELM: What do you mean? Are you feverish?

REGINA: There was a man here; right before you came. A detective, a former servant. He was once my lover; he left me, since a man, as you know, has higher interests! He knows everything about me; much more than is necessary to arm Josef; he has collected it in a thick portfolio, and I told him all the rest. But he also knows more about you than you were going to disclose to Josef in your relinquishment of me. He has letters to your wife, in which you confess. He knows your whole life. And what he did not know yet, I told him.

ANSELM: You were out of your mind. You must do something right away to silence the man. Where did he go?!

REGINA: No! Josef shall find out about it all!

ANSELM: What do you mean, no?! Do you want us to be exposed before Thomas and Maria like a pair of toads?

REGINA: Yes!

ANSELM: All for an idiotic tale of jealousy! A love story, oof, the devil! Do you have any idea whatsoever what you are doing? All these absurdities, that were only possible in the darkness between two people, are now to be — all tawdry as they are — exposed in bright daylight?!

REGINA: Anselm, you are in denial. You did not give *me* up to Josef, you gave us both up. Because you had the courage then. It was an escape from the crypt of reason! Oh, immediately when you appeared! Your first word, when I asked you how your life had turned out, was: it has been one long humiliation. And out of the seething cloud of memories, out of this stag herd, whose stinking swarm had concealed the heavens from me, came the lightning flash: suffer humiliations — that is what we do!

ANSELM: Don't say: We! You should not press yourself upon me as if I were you! I hate your humiliations! — Yes, yes, I know, you told me your Johannes story and I encouraged it.

REGINA: And you believed in it as little as I did.

ANSELM: But it gripped me unspeakably! This ghost, who was always watching when you gave yourself to another, was our ghost. Our fear of being alone.

REGINA: And our fear of *not* being alone. Of being watched. Of being smothered! Weren't you trembling in anticipation your whole life for the moment when, like a barracuda, you happened upon it and tore out a piece of fear's flesh before it could grab you? One who shies away, you; one who shoos away. Everyone approaches his brother gruesomely, like a fish to a corpse. And we all carry a sea around with us!

ANSELM: You infected me with these delusions! I only seemed like that. As if all sympathy, all nature, were only dread and decay!

REGINA: You are still really just burdened by your fear of Thomas and Maria. And the shame about everything that you've done. You beast! Anselm! We are not anything real! Whether we lie or not, are good or throw ourselves away: something is intended for us that we can never rightly interpret. You knew this and you have given away all our reality. In the one moment when you had courage!

ANSELM: I can't hear any more of this. One cannot continually uphold something that resists reason to such an extent. It all seems so unbearably dishonest and unnatural today. Where is the man?!

REGINA: (*Looking at the clock*) I don't know where he is.

ANSELM: Ah, you are nothing but a festering wound that doesn't want to heal!

REGINA: Once you had courage. Shall we retreat again? Let us, rather, take every humiliation upon ourselves. When one no longer has the strength to be something different than what one does, one is no longer a human being!

ANSELM: I want to know — where is the man?!!

REGINA: The shawl, Anselm! You were looking for the shawl. You must bring Maria her shawl!

ANSELM: I want to know — where the man is!!!

REGINA: (*Looking once more at the clock*) So, now it's too late. Josef's train is arriving, and the man is standing at the station and is giving him the portfolio. (*She becomes weak and begins to cry.*)

CURTAIN

ACT TWO

The scene is Thomas' study. The walls are covered with a strange pattern made of book spines. In the background, at an angle, a large opened window. A park. Deepening darkness. At first only one small lamp is lit. The set is in the same style as the first act, except that the furniture is scant and heavy, spiritually overweight. Above, and even in some places between the books, a starry night.

ANSELM: (*Coming from the opened window*) How the trees rustle. One doesn't know: is it the ocean?

MARIA: We are waiting in vain. Thomas must have been held up.

ANSELM: Why did he really go into the city?

MARIA: He didn't say. He went away shortly after the conversation with Josef.

ANSELM: The reception was pathetic — that party! Josef should have wandered from the park's entrance to his room along a Disillusionment Allée! Allée of the contingent century! Why didn't Thomas set up gramophones in the bushes, to whisper lovers' vows in extinct languages?! Dummies of beautiful women who collapse into bone-dust the moment one looks at them?! Let out his frogs and mice?! Hung an x-ray image of the beautiful Regina in his consultation room?! Trailed intestines from the branches!!

MARIA: Disgusting! You are always mucking about in these phantasmagorias!

ANSELM: Because I am filled with rage! If I *wanted* to think like Thomas — not to believe in the immortal portion: I could do it much better. I could come up with an infinite amount of filth! (*He goes to the window again.*)

MARIA: It looked preposterous enough without any of that. But it amounted to nothing, Thomas felt that himself; he wasn't really engaged in the thing. It's your fault, Anselm! You had promised to go and speak with him beforehand.

ANSELM: (*Turning around while walking*) And Josef didn't even notice it at all, it didn't register, you say?

MARIA: Right off, he just said: I have things to tell you that will alter your perspective. I had the impression that he saw and heard nothing before that.

ANSELM: "Important" things, did he say?

MARIA: Sure, yes; probably, no?

ANSELM: He could have also said, terrible. Or revolting…?

MARIA: Don't torment yourself again! What can it mean that even you persuade me that there are unworthy things in this portfolio? I almost have the feeling — that you want to prepare me.

ANSELM: And then Thomas silenced you? You should not have allowed him to!

MARIA: Don't get so worked up; Josef wanted to speak with *him*.

ANSELM: The portfolio came from a detective? Thomas must have told you what was in it, before he went to the city to check on its accuracy!

MARIA: But who says that he's doing that?! I find this assumption irrational and invalid!

ANSELM: (*With condescension*) He is envious!

MARIA: He fears more than there is cause to.

ANSELM: He is envious of my ideas. And would like to destroy me using moral reasons, like a bourgeois!

MARIA: Only because you're so secretive.

ANSELM: Give me the portfolio!

MARIA: But I have no right to do that.

ANSELM: Is it here in this desk?

MARIA: Yes, but Thomas has the key to the drawer.

ANSELM: Open the drawer!

MARIA: Like a sneak, without having discussed it with him? I will do no such thing.

(*She stands up indignantly and walks over to the opened window.*)

ANSELM: (*At the desk*) I will do no such thing, I will do nothing! We are in the dark, in a nameless catastrophe: let me lead you!

MARIA: I don't want to be complicit!

ANSELM: One must have the courage for short cuts. You will make yourself guilty by not doing this.

MARIA: It would be stealing!

ANSELM: You believe that everything one does must always be speakable and nameable; that's Thomas' dread legacy! But one must act in such a way that one cannot say it, not think it, not even understand it, but just does it! Nobody at all understands how to act today.

MARIA: (*Turning away, then quickly turning back again*) Where is Regina?

ANSELM: (*Stubbornly*) I don't know…. No, I do know; she has locked herself in her room.

MARIA: Still? Weeping and screaming? Lets no one in?

ANSELM: Apparently.

MARIA: Listen! … ? I believe I heard screaming before. (*Distraught, coming away from the window*) I can't bear this; the trees are still rustling so senselessly.

ANSELM: Like water!

MARIA: No, the wind runs through the trees; as if it had feet; runs; runs. It's so pointless.

ANSELM: And what happens? So many things happen in the world. As if there were nothing but ticking clocks hanging in a room, each one telling a different time.

MARIA: Runs, runs, without taking a breath, listen to it! It's frightful.

ANSELM: Yes, it is frightful! Why did this leaf fall in front of the window just now? Don't imagine that there's someone who knows. Everywhere: two, three steps further an answer; then fog. Every second, demands glide by you, facts with red, green, yellow eyes and foghorn cries. Decisions threaten and glide away in the fog. (*He has taken his head in both hands.*) My life, God, if I wanted to think about my life, it's filled with eyes like these!

MARIA: What kind of a fit is Regina having?

ANSELM: Faintheartedness. Nerves ... a wild swoon!

MARIA: But she's practically hysterical, no?

ANSELM: Or it's a lack of restraint. I don't want to think about it!

MARIA: And you're certain that these documents are the cause?

ANSELM: They must be stolen for her sake; they expose her utterly.

MARIA: And what do they say?

ANSELM: But I have not read them.

MARIA: And about you? There's nothing at all in them — about you?

ANSELM: It could only be inconsequential things. Or lies that I don't know about.

MARIA: And they're supposed to be in this drawer?

ANSELM: I've already told you everything.

(*Maria tries to open the drawer with a bunch of keys. It has grown dark and Anselm turns all the lights on so that she can see.*)

MARIA: (*Stops*) Let me speak with him.

ANSELM: (*Fiercely*) No! .... You must do something surreptitious. Come away. You must grasp a resolution. It's not a thought, Maria. A grasping: as if, in the most insubstantial darkness, your splendid hand were to close and suddenly you felt a part of an unexpected wonderful body in it!

MARIA: That's all so unnatural. (*She interrupts herself again.*) Even if you were to say, we will live together like man and wife: I could speak with Thomas. But this way it's nothing and just the same, something frightful .... Can't we just be friends?

ANSELM: I don't want anything for myself! As a boy, understand me, as an innocent child, the moment I saw you, I experienced such a feeling of happiness, spreading out over my entire body — that I had no idea how to save myself. How much stronger is such a feeling — in a man, where it localizes like a blister and erupts!

MARIA: (*Moved*) I cannot be rid of the feeling that all of this is happening just because you want to take revenge upon him for something or other ...!

ANSELM: Believe me: I didn't come into his house for that. If there has ever been a human being, no matter how far away I was, who, like a beacon, let me dream of home, it was he. If ever a human being's face bore the power of all human faces.... But hate? Yes, perhaps despite all, hate! Perhaps therefore hate? Sometimes I believe that one may only do evil to someone whom one loves: otherwise the evil is as dirty as a love that one carries into a bordello!

MARIA: You shouldn't speak of love if you have to feel anger, dirt, and evil along with it!

ANSELM: (*Despairingly*) But what then?? What shall I call it?! To need human beings! Anyone who is a human being cannot just hang suspended in his own web of thoughts the way Thomas does! He must be won over, loved, cheered on! To swing together! Is this not a tormenting need?! Not to be alone, Maria!! Being alone means: not knowing where to go. In the unbearable confusion of truths, wishes, feelings! Have some mercy for every disappointment, evil thing, lie, that has served to soothe an indescribable fear that you, yourself, do not understand.

MARIA: Quiet! Listen, rather; didn't she just scream again?

ANSELM: She screams without ceasing, but one only hears it sometimes.

MARIA: But we must help her; why don't you help her?

ANSELM: Why don't *you* help her?....

MARIA: What are you trying to induce me to do? You've changed entirely! The way you are dragging me into this; I told him that you were his friend.

ANSELM: Sometimes I seem like someone who has arisen, a haunted man without a foothold, falling. But just consider how much suffering there is every moment in the world; what an ocean of suffering and uncertainty, in which we all fight against drowning: should it depend upon whether one ends this one affair crudely or gracefully? It only depends upon how one situates it within the whole.

MARIA: And you believe that Regina's condition won't worsen if we three all travel together?

ANSELM: No; the portfolio must be removed from the world. Then these excesses diminish. The release will gradually be complete; like something unfurling to a standing position. I promise you.

MARIA: Listen! Again!

ANSELM: (*Grabbing her hand wildly*) You can feel too how much she suffers! How she struggles; like a little cat that is being drowned!! (*They go to the window together.*)

MARIA: Regina will do something to herself.

ANSELM: (*Pressing her hand*) Do you think so?! Ah, I am abandoning her! And I feel the right she imagines she has to me, as if her heart were thrashing about in mine for a way out. (*They listen.*)

MARIA: What is she screaming?

ANSELM: Johannes.

MARIA: This delusion.

ANSELM: It's no delusion. She's calling *me*. She called every man Johannes. It was her justification. Oh, her frenzied subterfuge from the truth! (*There seems to be nothing more to hear. Maria has gotten free and has gone back to the desk.*) She drove him to suicide; you know that, of course; because he doubted himself: she only wanted to love him like a sister.

MARIA: (*Trying the lock again*) Regina, love like a sister?! Do you really believe that?

ANSELM: Yes; she was like that then. And he was excessively sensitive; he was much more tender than Regina.

MARIA: I don't think that Regina was ever tender at all; how else could she have borne this life that you've told me about? (*Stubbornly*) None of the keys fit.

ANSELM: Try this one. (*He hands her one of his own.*)

MARIA: No, no. I don't want to anymore.

ANSELM: (*After he has tried the key in vain himself*) I'll try it with a knife. (*He opens his pocket knife.*)

MARIA: Let's just let it be, instead.

ANSELM: (*Pushing her aside*) No; I want to! (*He tries to spring the lock.*)

MARIA: (*Trying to stop him*) Leave it. I don't want to anymore! (*She flinches as if at a wild cry.*) Again! .... (*They listen ....*) No, that was a door. Thomas? Terrible. Go! Listen: steps. (*Anselm quickly puts the knife away.*)

MISS MERTENS: (*Rushing into the room*) Oh God! I'm coming from Mrs. Regina; she won't let me in! Just listen!

MARIA: Oh, it's appalling ...! Yes, we've heard it too, but what should we do? Call the doctor?

MISS MERTENS: No, she doesn't want a doctor.

ANSELM: Of course not; we have to let it run its course.

MISS MERTENS: (*Having gone to the window*) Really, everyone can hear it. (*She turns to Anselm, sharply.*) Doctor Anselm? I'm asking you: are you the only one who does not hear the way Regina cries?

ANSELM: (*Lacerated by pain and self-irony, altogether reckless*) She is singing! It wasn't a lie; she is singing filth! Not humiliation before swine, nymphomania. Not weakness, artificial excuses, superstition; sickness, an ailment. Such things can only be sung. In common language it *would have been* that.

MISS MERTENS: (*Almost speechless with outrage and surprise*) Doctor Anselm ...??

ANSELM: The men never meant the slightest thing to her, oh certainly, I know! She let Johannes die, she married Josef, the way one hires a caretaker. But sometime or other she began to believe that she must make it up to Johannes in some way, by throwing away on other men that which she denied him. After death, some people are declared holy, after all, and the wish is often enough the father of a thought.

MARIA: But be silent, do!

MISS MERTENS: You are abusing the delusions of an exceedingly tender womanly conscience!

ANSELM: So, you love her that much? Then you'll want to understand it: even as a child, while we others talked, she would crawl under some bush and put earth in her mouth or little stones, put worms in her mouth, pick her nose, taste the excretions of her eyes and ears. And she thought: someday something wholly miraculous will come of it! What's wrong? Are you feeling nauseous? Don't you love your saint? Your Saint Potiphar?! Men — they are not anything else, they are nothing but — the mystery that one takes into one's body.

MISS MERTENS: You slander her!

ANSELM: (*In nervous despair*) But don't torment me! Do you believe I don't want to help her?! If I only knew myself — how to help her!

MISS MERTENS: I will lay myself before the door if she doesn't let me in! — and to think that I believed I had never seen a more sensitive paragon of erotic delicacy. (*Exits.*)

MARIA: How could you speak so roughly!

ANSELM: (*Walking back & forth excitedly*) She's heard enough. She won't even come along now; no matter how much she loved Regina. Is there anything as unappetizing as virtue?!

MARIA: But you never should have sacrificed Regina like that!

ANSELM: Why does she have to make such scenes! With the whole journey here!

MARIA: Is it better then, if one does something in secret?

ANSELM: Yes! For the hundredth time, yes! I will always prefer to do wrong in secret, instead of parading an exceptional good thing in public as a cover; it's more worthy. Thomas does everything publicly. Men of reason are always overt. But I'm able to lie only for this one reason: because I am terrified of the smugness of a strange man who believes that he keenly understands me. A man like that clings more dreadfully than an estrous woman; it is as if one had stepped, by accident, into someone's brain!

MARIA: (*Shivering from the memory*) It's the most repulsive thing in the world, a woman who forgets herself like that.

ANSELM: (*Changing suddenly*) Oh, not so simple. It's not at all that simple, either. When Johannes was dead, Regina ate almost nothing for weeks; a few crackers daily was all. She grew thin, she wanted to force an otherworldly communion with him. It was very beautiful, very strong. A glowing condition of goodness. She didn't love him, she just *loved*. She shone! But then came reality, which — even though Thomas triumphs over it! — always upholds its rights; all the thousand hours, which had to be spent somehow. And every one leaves only one very tiny mark, like a smallpox scar, a mark of: look, it has passed. And all of a sudden, one's whole face has the blinking expression of a complete person. You have no idea how many people are devastated by the fact that they manage to live! But we're losing time. Didn't you want to try to open that drawer?

MARIA: Finish speaking and then I will answer you.

ANSELM: (*Looks at her mistrustfully, testing her for a moment*) Yes! I *can* understand it! ... I knew that you were waiting for that. I can understand how every faithlessness that she committed in this life seemed to her to be a faithfulness in the other. Every external humiliation like an internal elevation. She painted herself with filth the way another woman uses makeup. Isn't that beautiful too?

MARIA: No!! (*She looks at him with questioning disbelief and then throws away the bunch of keys.*) I won't do this anymore!

ANSELM: (*Decidedly*) All right, then let me do it. (*He opens his knife again.*)

MARIA: No, I won't have it! There is something mysterious about you that you will not admit to me: that binds you to Regina! (*She ensconces herself in the chair at the desk.*)

ANSELM: (*Walks back and forth in front of her and sometimes stops excitedly.*) What do you think? Should it be? Haven't you heard, she's begun again?.... She is sitting all alone in the star-sea, in the starry mountains and cannot speak. She can only make ugly faces, little evil Regina.... Even a grimace is a world of its own, from the inside. Without any neighbors and alone with her music of the spheres spread out across infinity.... She couldn't speak with the beetle and put it in her mouth; she wasn't able to talk with herself and so she ate herself. She also couldn't speak with other people and yet she felt — this terrible longing to unite with all of them!

MARIA: No, no, no, no! That's the lie!

ANSELM: But when one is subject to foreign laws, lies are the evaporated sense of home in dreamt of, nearby countries — don't you understand?! They are closer to the soul. Perhaps more honest. Lies are not true, but aside from that they are everything!

MARIA: But this excuse with Johannes is so repulsively fraudulent!

ANSELM: She doesn't believe in it either. No, Maria, she doesn't believe it. She doesn't even believe that there's a reason to scream. She just does it. And as she does, she feels that she is a mystery that cannot make itself understood. It's the last, random, false expression of what is left to her. A gigantic human need lies in it; perhaps the same need we all have!

MARIA: (*Springing up*) I can't listen to this anymore. (*It's unclear whether she means Anselm's talking or Regina's cries, which seem to be heard again.*) This sensuality is appalling! (*She wants to go to the window, but Anselm stands in her way and she grabs onto him with both her hands and holds him tight.*) Why don't you go away with her?!

ANSELM: No. I can't. She can come along, for a little while longer. Give me the keys.

MARIA: I just touched you for the first time and I'm supposed to run away with you; it's really too ridiculous!

ANSELM: Trust me with the keys.

MARIA: No ... I can't trust you! (*He tries to pick up the keys. Maria stops him and picks them up herself; they stand there for a moment fighting and pressed against each other.*)

ANSELM: (*Takes her hand and presses her nails against his neck, lips, and eyes*) Touch me! Hurt me! Here!

Here! Take a knife and cut designs in me like a tree! If you don't believe me, torture me until I am unconscious and you can do with me what you will.

MARIA: (*Tearing herself away*) You're a bad little boy and I am supposed to seduce you; you demand it.

ANSELM: (*Throwing himself in her chair*) I demand nothing for myself … except the permission to leave your shoes outside your door, to brush your skirts. To breathe the air that was in your breast. To be the bed that may bear your impression. To be allowed to abandon myself to you! Aside from this, all other reality becomes uncertain.

MARIA: (*Parrying and placating*) As long as we have known each other we have never seen more of each other than our faces and hands.

ANSELM: But when I leaned upon you just now, it felt as if my life, far removed from all the world's events — without arms, without hands — could hold and touch yours. (*He tries to grab her hand again.*)

MARIA: (*Uncertainly*) But we're no longer young.

ANSELM: That only means: Thomas has made you cowardly. It's considered unnatural when, for once, the path of two people's communion is not approached along the same paths as eating and digesting are. I want to possess your life. To partake in the grace of your being!

MARIA: But why does it have to be a woman?

ANSELM: Because you are a woman. Because it is unspeakably confusing that you — on top of everything else — are also a woman. That your skirts wander across the floor like bells around what is invisible! (*He buries his head in his arms.*)

MARIA: No, no, those are excuses, Anselm ....

ANSELM: I don't know what else to say. Betray me to Thomas!

MARIA: (*Touches his hand to make him look up. He does not. She sits on the arm of the chair.*) Anselm, everything you're saying is all so disturbingly unnatural. Silly childish things. Long buried things.

ANSELM: (*Lifting his head*) But everything "worthy," "important" that you're doing now is so incredibly insignificant to you.

MARIA: No, no! ... Yes. — But I don't want to!

ANSELM: (*Straightening up*) There is something in you that gets nothing at all from all this. And you have not had the courage to live for it! In the old days, you would have despised the kind of life you now lead!

MARIA: In those days, if we slept two hours too many it was like something we could never make up for, that, even days later, was remembered with a sudden pain as a great loss; you're right about that. We felt, we *are*. We ate very little, did not grant the body too much space.

Sometimes I held my breath as long as I could. But in reality, it all came to absolutely nothing. (*She says this while scribbling on a piece of paper.*)

ANSELM: Did it really come to nothing? At 8:20 every morning it was your practice to come into this park. I can still see the hands on the clock in my room. I took one of my books where you had written your beautiful name, and traced its lines: following your hand through space exactly as your hand must have gone. Then I ran after you.

MARIA: (*Sloughing it off by standing up*) Those are childish foolishnesses; they have nothing more to do with us.

ANSELM: (*Springing up*) Those were acts! Inexpressible forms of friendship. Acts are, after all, the freest things that exist. The only things that one can do whatever one wants with, like dolls. World of wishes, having grown so unfathomably spacious! (*Once more as if terrified by memories*) Nothing that happens to us can be understood and it is only when we do something ourselves that we are saved, in the midst of the unfathomable itself.

MARIA: Do you still recognize this? (*She shows him her drawing.*)

ANSELM: (*Interrupted, almost irritated*) A sugar loaf?[58] An angel?

---

58. Up until the late 19th century, sugar was transported in sugar loaves, which looked something like those white cones to which one affixes wings, heads, and halos at Christmas time.

MARIA: Close the window. I keep having the feeling that someone is going to come in through the window.

ANSELM: (*Sensing an advantage*) First tell me what it is.

MARIA: It's also from back then. I had drawn your face from memory, it didn't look any more beautiful than this, so I wanted to make up for it by drawing myself in a nightgown also. (*Anselm quickly shuts the window in order to take advantage of the situation. In the moment when the window is closed, they hear a door nearby.*)

MARIA: (*As if caught*) It's Thomas! Go! (*Foolishly, she turns out the light.*) Go away, I can't stand it! No, stay, turn on the light; I've already torn it up. He knows this drawing, I told him about it once. Please, turn the light back on!!

ANSELM: (*Confused*) I can't find the light....

(*Thomas walks into the dark room. There is only a little light in the area around the window. He moves around there, going back and forth. In the darkest corner of the room, he suspects the presence of Anselm and Maria.*)

THOMAS: Is someone here?

ANSELM: I am, Thomas. Good evening.

THOMAS: Are you alone there?

ANSELM: No, we were waiting for you. Maria is here. (*Trying to sound casual*) We were chatting and can't find the light now. (*He feels along the wall.*)

THOMAS: But why bother? It's really very nice in the dark. (*Pause.*) Why don't you two keep talking? Am I interrupting again?.... But for heaven's sake, continue to converse; what were you talking about? Is it something I may not know about?

MARIA: It wasn't anything good. Regina is unwell.

THOMAS: And Anselm was waiting for me here to explain to me why he did not come see me.

MARIA: I'll turn on the lights.

THOMAS: Please, leave it dark. It's truly a more remarkable thing than you would believe, two men in the dark. Can your eye tell us apart? No. You just don't hear it yet: each of us also says exactly the same thing as the other. But I assure you; that's how it is. Thinks the same thing. Feels the same thing. Wants the same thing. One sooner, the other later; the one thinks it, the other does it; the one escapes, the other is caught. But whether one is the detective or the criminal, the one who burns or the one who extinguishes, honest or lying: if each one takes a role, it's always the same game of cards, only shuffled and dealt out differently.

MARIA: (*As if she wanted to ask, horrified, Thomas, are you drunk?*) Thomas, are you...?

THOMAS: What? Thomas, are you *what*? One has friends so that one doesn't become vain. Don't let yourself be deceived. It's only an error when one murders someone on account of differences. The similarities are what horrify us! The envy, because one wants to differentiate oneself, even though one stays glued together in *one* block! Admit it, Anselm! (*Silence.*)

Oh, only darkness and silence. (*He waits.*)

But in the drawer lies my pistol. Ever since we were boys, you wanted to be stronger than me. If I were to shoot now? I can aim well at that somewhat darker blackness over there…. (*He waits. Silence.*)

Naturally, you're patient. You grind your teeth. You won't open up. Maria is to believe you have feelings that will survive even death … but have you heard me? I have turned the key … now I've opened the drawer … two minutes more and I am free of you; I can smear your brains on the wall! (*He waits.*)

If you have not answered by the time I count to one hundred, you never existed. One … two…. You were only a delusion. Oh, I would be so happy. Three…. He has no work; he has achieved nothing! He creeps around and rubs himself on people. Do you understand, Maria, he has no self-esteem; he must be loved, like an actor. But he can be loved, no? No? He can, can't he?!

MARIA: You are dreaming, Thomas …?

THOMAS: Ah, you two don't believe I would do it. But he has stolen my position in life away from me —

MARIA: But that was what you wanted!

THOMAS: You're right, you're right. (*He stands up and moves closer to the place where he assumes Anselm is.*) I wanted that! For that's how it is in the world of dogs. The scent in your nose decides. A soul scent! There is the animal Thomas, there lours the animal Anselm. Nothing differentiates one from the other but a paper-thin feeling of an enclosed body and the hammering of blood underneath. Do neither of you have the heart to grasp this? Will it hunt us down to our deaths or ... into each other's arms?!

MARIA: (*Has jumped up frightened and stood in his way*) Thomas, you *have* been drinking!?

THOMAS: (*Lighting a match*) Look at me, Maria! (*He searches for Anselm with the small flame; Maria quickly turns the light on. The drawer is opened, but Thomas stands there without a weapon.*)

(*Still looking for Anselm in vain*) Just look at me, Maria.... (*Anselm is gone.*)

Gone? Disappeared without a sound? ... Arrived without a sound? What was there between you two?

MARIA: (*Intensely*) There was nothing!

THOMAS: Nothing? But that's everything! I know that you would never say an untrue word to me. Nothing has stirred; but the whole earth, with everything that is on it, moves.

MARIA: (*Firmly*) Is it true that you went into the city to investigate this — report?

THOMAS: Josef heard me come in. We must be brief. Anselm didn't come. I ripped open my heart for him and he didn't take the trouble to come!

MARIA: So, it's true …. (*Decisively*) Give me the report; I want to burn it!

THOMAS: (*Looks at her at first, with speechless agitation*) That's a noble idea! Truly, it has Anselm's dash! Naturally, I won't give you the evidence.

MARIA: You are conducting secret proceedings against Anselm. You accept Josef's presence in the house, a fully impossible situation. You drive into the city, while he guards the house. All without asking me. Anselm is my friend as well as yours: I don't agree to his being treated like this in our home!

THOMAS: Fine, I will give you the portfolio. But you must listen to me without prejudgment. If you still want it, then …: I will give it to you. Why didn't he come to see me? Because he had something to hide: he's a swindler!

MARIA: But you always say that. And then you say again that he's a fellow misanthrope!

THOMAS: Nevertheless, he's performing a farce for you. Why? Why did Johannes kill himself?

MARIA: But none of us knows that.

THOMAS: Oh? … Because he trusted Anselm.

MARIA: Rather, because Regina tortured him first! Go on!

THOMAS: There could be evidence there in the drawer. That's not what I have to tell. But listen to me, will you?! I want you to see it for yourself, finally! Johannes lacked — like all of us — that stupid drop of belief without which one cannot live, cannot admire a friend, cannot find one, that bright drop of stupidity without which no one can become a capable human being or achieve anything. Every human being, every work, every life has a crack that's only glued together! Only swindled closed!

MARIA: Wait! You mean that without a drop of stupidity, one cannot love?! Everything has a crack, if one is clever and doesn't believe? Continue.

THOMAS: No, not like that! Sometimes I believe that because of this we could become new human beings; sometimes I believe I am falling apart! I blame myself, Maria! Everything I've done was raw power! Hurtling away wildly from one place or another. But don't believe that Anselm is any better! Johannes may have been better. At least what you call better. He was weak. Tender. He believed that some other person had to help him get beyond it. And Regina was hardly the right one; still too curious and not jaded enough; a door, that didn't let itself be closed. So, he went to Anselm. Anselm seemed to adopt him. But deepened his lack of courage even more and encouraged Regina simultaneously in her impatience toward him. Anselm won both of them over — for *himself*! Until Johannes could no longer bear it!

MARIA: But why would he have done all of this?!

THOMAS: Why? Because he suffers just like Johannes did! Because he needs assurance and people! If one achieves nothing, one must be loved in order to feel justified. He steals love, he breaks in, he robs it, when it must needs be! But — when he has it, he doesn't know what to do with it. Already, when he was at the university —

MARIA: Oh, that was different.

THOMAS: Yes, he's already worked you over well. But don't you notice, that he — like all people who are always in love — is only interested in himself? That it drives him to be enraptured with every new person; like an illness; he must flatter them and persuade them.

MARIA: He may commit reckless acts. But he does care. And it comes from inside, like a spring.

THOMAS: Don't let him fool you. It's just like the methods and swindles of mediums who have long ago fallen out of their trances. He doesn't love; he hates every person, like the accused hates the judge whom he must lie to.

MARIA: But what are you really talking about here? Don't you feel that these are fabrications?

THOMAS: Don't you feel that every one of your objections is a torment to me?! He lures people using deceitful promises, because he must manage to survive on his own plank in the middle of infinity! You don't understand that. But don't you see that you and I, the way you are staring at me as if I were mad, are the miserable proof of this?!

MARIA: But is some of what you have claimed up to now proven in there?

THOMAS: It says ... (*he hesitates and masters himself*) nothing in there.... No ... I meant, yes, I believe, only: I presume. (*Sounding like someone who knows he has lost his case*) It cannot be proven; one must believe it.

MARIA: But that's ridiculous; Thomas, poor Thomas.

THOMAS: Ridiculous, if I say it; and if he had said it, a spring.

MARIA: You yourself described him to me every day when he was not here and was on his way. He had, you said, something that you lack. This ability to be bound to all human beings through interest, without strife or work. But now you have allowed yourself to be emotionally involved; no, you yourself are the one whom Josef agitates! And Anselm, too! As if you had to make him bad again. Obstinately, with your greater strength. Give me the portfolio. I will burn it — for your sake!

THOMAS: (*Flinching*) No, not yet, no! Now we don't have any more time; I hear Josef already. Go, go to *him*!

I beg you, go to him once more! (*He pushes her toward the door.*)

MARIA: I don't want to go to him! I want to talk with you!

THOMAS: I can't listen to you! Go to him! Perhaps — look at him and think of what I said.

MARIA: No — (*but then, since Josef enters through the other door, she can't contradict him; exits.*)

JOSEF: (*Dressed in dark clothes. Expression as if at a burial.*) You are delaying your decision too long; I am in an untenable position here. Regina refuses to speak with me, just as she has not answered my letters. She has obviously not yet abused my forbearance enough!

THOMAS: Return home; give it all some time to work itself out on its own!

JOSEF: Are you convinced now of the accuracy of my analysis of the situation?

THOMAS: Yes. (*He retrieves Stader's portfolio from the desk and lays it before him.*)

JOSEF: Regina hardly knows what it means to wound a man right at the core of his existence. But this sick liar, this confidence trickster must be made harmless! …. At first, I thought: a little refreshing vacation, a nervous mood, this sudden leaving without saying a word. I was prepared then to accept this impropriety. Regina was commonly cold, a saint, so to speak. You understand, that also has its good sides: she was never susceptible to warmth from the masculine direction. But then — when I looked for a word of explanation, of goodness; instead of this brief message that she had gone to her sister's — I found this little book, filled with the most revolting verbal excesses, which I was hardly able to comprehend...!

THOMAS: They wrote that they wanted to come here because Johannes had lived here with them?

JOSEF: Regina wrote it, but I am convinced: under his dictation. How stupid, otherwise, to present me with weapons: she claims she has always betrayed me! So that she could stay near to Johannes! Can you understand that?

THOMAS: Yes.

JOSEF: You can understand that? Oh well, you are all this way; an idea need only be exaggerated: you immediately have a weakness for it!

THOMAS: I can think of something similar. It's like homesickness.

JOSEF: Oh, she will of course have "thought" up something too, while doing it: for it's certainly not at all true! The cold, chaste Regina: that's where the crime is, the incomprehensible part begins there. To maintain a lively remembrance of a dead man for years, despite the fact that... well, we were really happily married! But one could come to grips with even this, even if it is exaggerated; it's even noble; although naturally really very exaggerated, to be sure. Just think, nevertheless: faithfulness? That's abnormal! It's also a lie! And then, lasciviousness! As a sacrifice to the dead!? A nearly ceaseless chain of adulteries, over years and years?! Ignoring even the animalistic part of it, just the filth of the secrets and lies: can you even imagine such a thing of such a shy and fastidious — I can speak to you, can't I, as to a brother? — of such an unsensual person as Regina?

THOMAS: One would have expected her to be too proud for it.

JOSEF: And was she ever proud! It was sometimes practically embarrassing how loftily she judged strangers. But then this fellow began his work. I'm convinced that he wanted to protect himself with some kind of counter-insurance for all eventualities.

THOMAS: (*Like someone who, despite long efforts, has not been able to understand*) But why would he have persuaded her to do that?

JOSEF: To hurt me!

THOMAS: Were these notes addressed to you?

JOSEF: No. Regina is simply so terribly unpractical that she just left all the papers lying around in the drawer... But they couldn't have been written for anyone else but me. He probably arranged it all with some intention or other, the scoundrel! Because my detective's conclusions — you know, the fellow is rather pompous, his scientific method is certainly absurd, but he is skilled — and all his materials support it: Anselm cajoles people with flattery. I, for example, didn't like him at first either, but he manages to seize you, so softly and humbly, at your weakest point, wheedles your thoughts out of you until you believe that you've never been so well understood by anyone else. All so that: when he has you, having carefully spied on you, he can hit you with a precisely-aimed, cruel wound. He has repeatedly even used false names and documents to do this! Pretended he was a nobleman, that he was rich or poor, learned or simple-minded, apostle of natural healing or a morphine addict, whatever was needed, in order to drive some innocent — but still somehow suspecting — soul to madness. As you know, some of these stories would cost him his head.

THOMAS: (*Stands up*) But how do you explain all this to yourself?

JOSEF: Sick. He is a dangerous, sick man. But that doesn't obviate his responsibility.

THOMAS: I keep wondering about that; but it's too little and too much.

JOSEF: I'm telling you: a common, but dangerous, sick man. He convinced Regina of the whole thing with his arts. He hates me from before; I don't know why; I certainly treated you all with kindness then; even this hatefulness is sick! And the idea is constructed with the refinement of an abnormal person; one can only have put it all into a logical order — with great difficulty! And so it goes: as long as she believes in Johannes, she may do whatever she wants. For he is nothing but her own fate; the one that died young, you know. Not a memory, not a dream, which one could, if necessary, understand, but rather (*Taking these words like shapes in his hand like an incomprehensible piece of machinery*) what she wanted to be, her belief in herself, her illusion of herself, freed from reality! She — herself — as — good! Which must then mean that she wanted to do good. But failed. The worse she becomes, the closer she comes to Johannes! For the more one loses oneself, the closer one is to oneself! And suffering humiliations is the fate of the spiritual person in the world! Humiliations, that — you understand — am I not then, why I am not, then, just as good at spirit as Anselm, who has not achieved anything, I do not know. I'm telling you: Regina would never have come up with aphorisms like this on her own, not in her whole life. But once she has let it go so far, she's forced to accuse herself of all manner of ignominious acts! He was hoping to secure his own return with this. But I'm not that stupid. When he had her write that she desired him and had wanted to seduce him, but that he had only wanted to direct her soul, that he would have rather struck himself down or threatened suicide than have allowed a transgression against "that upon which I and others place the greatest importance": that was when I became very suspicious, and my suspicion has increased. (*Confidingly*) It was merely a reflection of his own abnormal condition.

THOMAS: But please, at bottom Anselm is not all that different than we are; there are only shifts of emphasis.

JOSEF: I would have to pity you. He seems in fact to fear ... well, to fear ... that he may have gone too far. It's difficult to clearly imagine this. Least of all, since he has a wife. But most of the time he seems to suffer from an entirely uncommon case of shock. In the form of a woman, suddenly a human being has come too close to him! He seems to have undergone a hysterical crisis; this has produced these perverted hateful actions. It would be better if he would stop doing them, "in accordance with my requirements," if he must continue to play the "martyr"!

THOMAS: So, you are certain that all of this really is a matter of friendship alone? In that case, he certainly would transgress this border only against his will.

JOSEF: Stader — the detective, you know — came up with the illuminating theory that: if it had gone further, they would have stayed in the house. For in those cases, the lovers are afraid of a scandal.... And I say to you: if he were at least a man, I would know what to do! But he is a deviant, a fool, a womanish sissy! (*He tries to* *calm himself down by walking around aggressively.*) And you, Thomas — so gullible. You love your wife gullibly, and she, infected by such foolishness, offers up your honor to her partner in foolishness...!

THOMAS: I prepared you in my letter for people who are difficult to characterize.

JOSEF: And you set me up as the reactionary in your very unnecessary theory of morals — when it isn't even your field; well, at least you understand the process. But I believe that you are ashamed of your mistake; the facts have provided me with more satisfaction than you could have. You have, have you not, become convinced — since our first discussion — that the data are correct?

THOMAS: Yes. What I could check on was correct.

JOSEF: And, in that case, you are now obliged to show him the door.

THOMAS: Yes. I am obliged to. (*After a short struggle*) But I cannot. Especially, right now, he shouldn't go. He must stay now. Don't pressure me. (*He puts the portfolio back in the desk.*)

JOSEF: (*Looks at him with astonishment, walks back and forth again.*) You do not misunderstand me? I will to no extent relinquish the authority given me by the law. I only hesitated out of consideration for you; and out of a distaste for a scandal in the family.... I demand that you renounce him in front of the women and close your house to him.

THOMAS: I appreciate your kindness... but I cannot do it.

JOSEF: All right then .... That doesn't discharge me from my duty to restore order. Give me back the documents.

THOMAS: (*Finally, fully resolute, removing the key from the lock*) No. I'm sorry. I cannot.

JOSEF: (*Shocked*) So you really are fond of him...! That's how it always begins. (*After some effort*) He's here to betray you and Maria just the same way that he betrayed me and Regina.

THOMAS: I know it. But... you believe ... it's that simple? So completely in the same way?

JOSEF: You don't know everything.

THOMAS: But it's not true! He cannot have come here to do me harm!

JOSEF: But you fool! You deluded fool! You think that the simple truth is not good enough for you; the one times one of facts only convinces you when it is also a "higher truth"!

THOMAS: Maybe that's just what I was trying to say. If you were to convince me that Anselm wants to betray me, and if you were to convince me that — Maria wants it: That can't be true! And it can't be false! It can only mean something that cannot be said like that at all.

JOSEF: So, you are enchanted and under his spell too! Alright. Then I will stay here.

THOMAS: How do you mean that?

JOSEF: I will remain in your house. You will not show me the door when you leave it open for this rogue.

THOMAS: (*Confused*) Naturally not, no … but it can't be done.

JOSEF: And I say to you that I will not leave here before I have forced this "headhunter" — yes, you see, that is the right expression, I invented it for him — before I have forced him to lick my shoes in front of all of you! You will see, he will do it; he is cleverer than you all are! He will not persist, as soon as he sees what it all means!

THOMAS: (*Bitterly and with rising emotion*) You would regret it. As long as nothing has really happened, a … a turning away is not to be rejected out of hand. You would want to speak with Regina. She would avoid you. You would provide her with evidence and she would simply not hear it. Do you understand: a deafness of the soul. You would clearly show her that he is a rogue, and she would not see it. You would lose your mind, truly; you would no longer know whether you had been speaking nonsensically or if your words had flown away?!

JOSEF: I will find a way to make her listen to me. I will not have to blame myself for having made myself an abettor of guilt out of a lack of resolution. (*Exits.*)

THOMAS: (*Casting an eye in deep despair a few times around the room*) You would think, being together for so many years would be something spiritual. Then someone comes; nothing has changed, but everything that you do is meaningless and everything that he does means something. Your words, which used to penetrate deeply, fall from your mouth unnoticed. Where is soul, order, spiritual law? To belong together, to be held, to hold? Truth. Real feeling? The abyss of mute loneliness swallows them all up!

MARIA: (*Stepping in carefully*) I didn't really know… are you alone again? I was waiting.

THOMAS: And … you heard?

MARIA: I didn't listen. I don't want to know what you two talked about. Give me the portfolio.

THOMAS: (*Shrinking back as if from an inescapable danger*) Then …? Really?

MARIA: I spoke with him about it once more. He's beginning to confide in me. Let him be my friend. *Especially* if he is bad.

THOMAS: Okay then, you really do mean it …. And what I told you?

MARIA: If you believed it yourself, you would approach it differently — not just from the inside. (*Pained*) Why have you involved yourself in this? Because you believe that he is influencing me. Yes, he does; isn't that allowed?

THOMAS: He may? Can! He can, Maria! Look at me; what has changed? You lose your darning egg, that dear round thing that you sometimes stretch your stockings on; then you find it again in the street days later; you hardly recognize it; what made it yours has decayed; now it's only a ridiculous small wooden skeleton. Then you return to me like this. A child of *his* spirit: with repulsive shreds from its alien womb still clinging to you!

MARIA: You are a hard, violent person.

THOMAS: Say envious. Say filled with hate. I would like to corrode this strange being — who battles me without us even being able to touch each other — with the most powerful acids! I find him in your thoughts; that leaves me even more helpless than if I found him in your bed.

MARIA: You are a hard, jealous person; you demand, without wanting to give anything in return. May I only listen to you? Must you be right about every question?

THOMAS: So little, that I sometimes don't even understand anymore why you have always been with me instead of with him? There is something in me, something stubbornly resistant, that protects you like a mother protects the pleasure of her child. When you come from him, this part of me feels — stupidly, happily suffering — something refreshing, new.

MARIA: Don't you see then that it's not at all on my account that you are stirring up troubles and dangers for our existence? You're doing it because you sense that he doesn't — desire — me! But *values* me more than you do!

THOMAS: Ever since it began, you've been telling me that it's not love, but a spiritual experience —

MARIA: It is only that.

THOMAS: (*Tormented*) I've been trying to show you for almost just as long that he is a counterfeiter when it comes to internal experience. But you don't believe in me, only in him. That sounds so simple and is — the horror.

MARIA: I still believe in you! But what have you made of it?! Something never finished. Something that can never be clear. Threatened by every new idea. Like ersatz, a vague feeling of belonging together, like travelers in a compartment. Without compulsion or passion! I don't want to think! One can also live in some other way! Thomas, what grips you and tears you and shakes you is yourself! The shame over the hours when you don't think; when you come to me, because you don't want to think, more exposed than naked in these shameful "weak" hours, when your viscera are exposed. What have you made of us! "Little one" and "there, there," "mousie and cat," "itsy bitsy little man and little missy"!

THOMAS: Silence! Silence! It's horrific! I can't hear it! …. Don't you feel the enormous helpless dependence in this? Everything that a human being can give to you lies in the consciousness that you do not deserve his fondness, that this person finds you good, even though there's nothing in all eternity to prove your goodness. That this person takes you as a whole, you, someone who can't speak for yourself, think for yourself, or prove yourself. That he's there; is blown toward you; toward warmth, to bolster you up! Didn't you feel it like this once?! Did you always feel it differently?

MARIA: And you're even proud of it! You have let me lose the courage to be myself!

THOMAS: And Anselm is giving you a counterfeited self!! You will be terrifically disappointed!

MARIA: He may be counterfeiting. But I have a right to it, to be told such things, told by someone: that is how it is! So that — even if it were only a delusion! — something stronger than myself might grow. That someone says words to me that are only true because I hear them. That I am moved by music instead of being told: don't forget that it's only a bit of dried gut being scratched! Not because I am stupid, Thomas, but because I am a human being! Just as I have a right to water flowing and stones being hard and something heavy sewn into my skirt's hem so it will hang straight!

THOMAS: We are talking past each other. We are saying the same thing, but with me it means Thomas and with you Anselm.

MARIA: Is that all you have to say? Something never, never, never stands there, large, exciting, necessary, grasping for your hand! You won't even take me away from him.

THOMAS: One can't take someone away from the place where he stands. But you will — (*he searches for words and doesn't find better ones*) be terrifically disappointed.

MARIA: Tell me, if you really know something! Don't leave me so all alone!

THOMAS: It can't be proven.

MARIA: (*Irritated*) I think that the only proof for or against a person is whether one rises or sinks in his presence.

ANSELM: (*Storming in, extremely agitated, impatiently abandoning all prudence*) I must speak with Maria one more time. I have to speak to Maria at once.

THOMAS: I will leave you two alone.

MARIA: Thomas, not like this! The fact that he is a man is so irrelevant here.

THOMAS: And if that were his specialty? Anselm, did you hear?! Have you understood that Josef is waiting in the house?! (*Since Anselm does not answer him, he is overcome with fury, grabs the pillows from the divan and throws them on the floor.*) Lay yourselves down on the floor … there! … there! …. Get it over with, before we speak any further! Blood is rushing through your heads! That one point that has not yet united is floating in the deep-sea of your bodies like a coral reef! Images are streaming through you like the wandering meadows of schools of fish with flower-petal-skin! "You" and "I" press themselves, mysteriously magnified, against the rounded glass of their eyes! And the heart, too, is swept along!

MARIA: (*Beginning to collapse in tears*) Aren't you ashamed of yourself?

THOMAS: And while Josef waits, too!! — In this situation, there is no longer any room for shame. (*To Anselm*) Say just one honest word; one word that crawls around innocently inside of you like a small animal. So that I know that Maria will be able to caress it, that Maria won't grow numb from disappointment! One word so that I can believe: they were only humiliations, because it was our fate to suffer them, the peculiar privilege of the intellectual among the inhabitants of the world! And I will bear all of it! Will protect you from Josef instead of calling for him, and comfort Maria in her fear and in her contempt for me and tell her that one is never so present as when one loses oneself.

MARIA: You tell me not to believe him and then offer me up to him totally: you have no more dignity!

THOMAS: (*In the greatest horror, tugging at Anselm's sleeves, as he remains rigid*) It's repulsive, the way you stand there in front of me. Repulsive the way we all stand here. It's so extraordinarily physical. The way you master Maria spiritually is so extraordinarily physical for all of us. There's something repulsively sexual between us — person to person! What do I care about you! What does Maria want with me! You're standing there like pillars of flesh! (*Leaves, to fetch Josef.*)

ANSELM: (*Finally giving free vent to an insane agitation*) Don't cry!! I couldn't move in front of him! So that he wouldn't suspect anything! But I will kill myself before I let you cry!!

MARIA: Anselm! By all the saints! Would you ever lie to me …? I would be devastated if you were lying …!

ANSELM: (*Mistrustfully, growing cold*) Has someone said something to you?

MARIA: How shall I trust …?

ANSELM: We don't have another minute to lose. Can I win your belief again through a sacrifice? Your belief in yourself! (*Threateningly*) I will do anything; just don't hesitate!

MARIA: But I can't get free of the idea that you just want to seduce me to make me different than I am. I feel that. Certainly, you must have always been this way.

ANSELM: Yes. I have always seduced people to be better than they are. But I have suffered torments.

MARIA: And with Regina, too.

ANSELM: Yes, but I hate her for it!

MARIA: You will hate me, too! Your life was always filled with friends and lovers.

ANSELM: Have they told you that? Then you know: out of impatience. Out of weakness, that doesn't want to wait any longer. But that carries its disappointment in it from the start. Carries the hate inside itself already; hate that only tries to be love out of fear! Already, when I was a child, everyone kissed me, these mothers, nannies, maids, sisters, girlfriends. The pachyderms! The arrow of longing for human beings gets stuck in their skin and a scar forms around their cheerful and healthy digestion! I can't be without people! And that's what my kind gets! You know it yourself.

MARIA: Thomas says, you *want* to be loved; only because you do not achieve anything. Oh, he's frightful. One can't trust oneself anymore.

ANSELM: And you will understand me, after all: my whole life has been destroyed by it. How often has hopelessness touched me already. The will against myself. Competitors, mad men, outsiders among them. Perhaps I *have* done something. But if you disappoint me too, the only great person that I have found, there is only one thing to do: a rope: a gentle, soft rope. And a silky smooth, green bar of soap to grease it with. To be able to do that once, after all, is the last great comfort for me. I don't fear the decomposition; it's mild and soft; mother of all, quiet and colorful and enormous; blue and yellow veins will cover my body —

MARIA: How shall I trust you when you persist in mucking about in such disgusting images!

ANSELM: (*Interrupted; looking angrily at her*) Even when I look at you, I tremble sometimes. I am afraid, because you are only a woman.

MARIA: Just be my *friend*.

ANSELM: (*Mockingly*) Your soul is mine; your love is Thomas'? (*Passionately*) Always this depraved separation! — Understand me, I speak wholly without desires: You still believe it's a matter of what is called possession. But if it were that, I would have just poisoned Thomas. You believe, because you are beautiful? Yes, (*with an undertone of cruelty*) because you are beautiful! But there are children who are avoided on the playground because they are so good; that was the kind you were. Some sort of spell emanating from your goodness warded off all impotent evil; you secreted that away. You are miraculously beautiful and have given away your stateliness with a touching gentility. Yes, you *are* — divinely beautiful! And I already understand that you are not allowed to be evil, you *must* want to be good to Thomas. But — your beauty already contains an invisible danger; your mild amenability is something of which you are secretly ashamed. You are wonderful, but — *also* alone. Thomas can never guess this. I understand you perhaps only as something related to myself. But I experience you as an enormous comfort. As an angel with a ram's hoof. In the midst of my breakdown, you descended to me like an angel; but an angel who belongs to me a little under her gown. (*Maria is silent. Anselm, a touch nastier, but still genuinely moved*) Your awesome womanliness softens something that otherwise would be too humiliating for me …. Don't keep silent! You don't know if you don't love him? Neither do I!! That need not be an obstacle! There is a unifying rapture that rips through everything in the world. I feel it confusedly, even in your resistance, as I hear your silence. Give yourself up to it! Hoist yourself loose! Your soul has come for you, the eternity!

(*They are interrupted. During the last words, like an underpainting, the noise of stormily approaching people and excited discussion is heard. Now the door flies open. Insensate, Miss Mertens rushes in with a disturbed Regina behind her. Almost at the same time, Thomas. Then Josef, angry, awkward; he closes the door carefully and accurately, making his entry infinitely embarrassing.*)

MISS MERTENS: (*To Maria*) For God's sake, help her; she doesn't know what she's saying anymore.

JOSEF: (*To Regina, from the door*) But I beg of you, you are exaggerating again; a sanatorium is not a madhouse at all.

REGINA: He wants to take Anselm there, too, if he does not leave! Or to jail!

JOSEF: (*Still near the door*) I wanted to have it out with Regina. She had been abandoned in her room by everyone and was crying so much it was not to be borne. I said to her, that in the interest of all of us, the best thing would be a stay in a sanatorium. Only a short stay. This is, after all, a sickness! (*He turns to her and sees Anselm near her. He walks, in his usual way, a few stiff steps forward and then one back; his breast rises and expands, his chin is raised, his lips search for words. Anselm stands slight and innocent before him.*)

MISS MERTENS: (*Meanwhile whispering to Regina*) You have been abused; Doctor Anselm is a small soul like all men! Or else — — now he had better prove himself!

THOMAS: (*Explaining, seemingly with peaceful pleasure*) Josef demands that you leave our house within 24 hours. He has, naturally, no right to issue commands in my house, and I leave it entirely up to you whether you want to obey him or not.

JOSEF: (*To Maria, embarrassed by her presence*) You forgive me; naturally I did not want to do it this way... not in your presence, but Regina could not be stopped. I only wanted to talk with her and — this one.

MARIA: (*Surprised, with the beginnings of outrage*) But what is the meaning of all this? Why should Anselm leave?

THOMAS: It is up to him to explain that to you; but I believe: ... you will see, that he will leave.

JOSEF: It's embarrassing, Maria; like I said, I did not want ... not in front of you.... But Thomas knew about it!

MARIA: (*Decisively*) I remain .... I find it necessary, if a paid arrogant detective runs my house, at least to be present!

JOSEF: Didn't Thomas think it necessary to prepare you?

MARIA: But for what then?!

THOMAS: I told Maria everything. I just didn't tell her that it had been proven by a detective. And she didn't believe it!! (*He opens the desk, inviting Josef to the portfolio, with a gesture at once apologetic and resigned.*)

REGINA: (*To Anselm*) Come away! Don't look inside, go out the door! They've set a trap for you! I betrayed you, I could have stopped it! Don't get entangled in their reasoning!

MARIA: But Anselm, just tell them that none of that can be true!

THOMAS: Tell us that it cannot be true! Tell us! But first look at this. (*He points to Stader's portfolio, which he has taken out of the desk.*)

REGINA: Don't look at it; that's the man's portfolio! Go! You still can do it. Kiss their hands humbly and go;

creep out the door to the street. Let them run you over with a wagon. Let them call you dog! Be a dog! But do not entangle yourself in their reasoning. They want to capture the invisible creature inside you!

(*Anselm, attracted by the unavoidable state of things, denying Regina, walks as if on a narrow road, his face completely withdrawn, concentrated internally, toward Thomas, who hands him a paper from the portfolio. Anselm looks at it, then at another two pages.*)

THOMAS: It belongs to Josef....

REGINA: I wanted to see once and for all, if you were courageous. Oh, if I *were* courageous — I am so afraid of being dead.

JOSEF: You unhappy soul! This is the work of this person, of the malign spirit, which he injected into you!

ANSELM: (*Returning the pages to Thomas again and turning toward Maria*) I already knew it. (*He goes in the same way that he came, back to his place.*) I leave the pleasure to Thomas. I have only one bit of evidence to add: that I never said an untruth to you! Can I speak with you alone?

MARIA: (*Monotone*) You must speak in front of everyone, everyone....

(*Pause. Anselm — smiling, embarrassed, or contemptuous, in any case in a forced stance — stands there in the middle.*)

MARIA: (*Horrified*) But how? Did you really — ?

ANSELM: But you already knew it all.

MARIA: I??! You said that these notes contained only harmless things. That we should destroy them only for Regina's sake!

ANSELM: Haven't I told you that I am a bad man?

MARIA: You played with such thoughts. Played and sparkled with lies and badness!

ANSELM: What more can I say to you?

MARIA: Whether or not it is true?!!

(*Anselm shrugs his shoulders, with a smile, and looks as if he were about to leave. Josef moves from afar to block his way; Thomas, who also had started to do so, lets it be. Anselm immediately abandons his plan; Josef goes to the door, locks it, and gives the key to Maria.*)

JOSEF: Please take the key. He will not leave this room until you let him go! (*To Anselm*) You will acknowledge your deceptions and promise Regina that you will never come near her again, or I will have you arrested in this house!

(*Anselm turns to Thomas, as master of the house, with a questioning look; but Thomas just responds to Josef with an ironic gesture. Anselm sits down and gazes calmly straight ahead. Short pause.*)

ANSELM: (*Looking at Miss Mertens, who sits in the furthest corner, her hands covering her face, then at the others*) We are together again almost like in the sweetest days of childhood; I only fear that we could offend Miss Mertens.

MISS MERTENS: Oh, I am going; this is the most torturous disappointment of my life. (*She stands up uncertainly, and since no one seems prepared to unlock the door for her, she remains standing thus.*)

REGINA: (*Who had been sitting close to her, goes and presses her softly back onto the chair.*) Stay with me; there is still much more to hear. (*Short pause.*)

MARIA: Then it was only because of this business with these notes that you and — (*She betrays the word "Regina" but does not speak it out loud*) wanted to go away, because you must have feared …? Oh, God, how can someone lie like this?!

(*Regina laughs.*)

MARIA: (*Irritated*) She shouldn't laugh! It's horrible, the way she laughs!

REGINA: I'm not laughing at all. When I was a child, I was sure that one day I would have a wonderful voice. Pay attention. Be quiet. Do you hear it? (*Laughing*) I don't hear it either. Anselm sings with my voice. But one can sing beautifully on the inside and be mute on the outside!

JOSEF: That is the malign influence of this man — like Herostratus, who burned down the temple of Artemis to get attention!

REGINA: — Johannes was well sung with this voice! It was simply the feeling: something will still happen to make life's troubles worthwhile. (*Bitterly to Anselm*) And then comes the day, when one admits: nothing more will happen.

JOSEF: She has fallen victim to a human-catcher; Regina, if you want to come to your senses, even if it costs me some effort: I offer you my protection one more time! Do you know how much he has betrayed you? His life has been a chain of betrayal and filth —

REGINA: I know that.

JOSEF: A chain in which you are but one link. He left a wife secretly waiting at home: I'll bet he never told you that!

MARIA: (*Screams half-aloud.*)

REGINA: I know that.

JOSEF: (*In a suddenly illuminating realization*) But then —? But then —? Then it is…!? No, it must not be… But then perhaps everything that he made you write here … was not at all so … everything that seemed so incredible … everything criminal … was not just his idea?

REGINA: What does Anselm matter to you?! He's done with me; he wants Maria!

JOSEF: (*Cries in despair*) But it's true!! I can't do anything more to him.... He should go or I will kill him!.... Give him the key, Maria, quickly! He should leave this room! (*He buries himself in his chair. Maria wants to hand the key to Anselm, but he doesn't take it.*)

REGINA: He can get a divorce, you know. But none of you know what a love affair for Anselm looks like! He needs this leash that holds him; just as he wanted me to go with him and Maria, so that he did not lose himself in her. (*She accompanies this by gesturing mockingly at Maria's majesty.*)

JOSEF: (*Annihilated*) Then I can't do anything to him. Then he only succeeded in exposing my shame.

REGINA: But he can't see any person without wanting to be like him! He cannot bear it if someone doesn't say to him: You are good! He finds you all horrible! But he's vain and weak! (*To Maria*) Do you know what he really thinks of you?

JOSEF: (*Despite his state of shock*) But please! We must not let her go on!

REGINA: You are unbearably natural. You would be supremely qualified to potty train children. You grab a man the way a kitchen wench takes a carp by its scales. To hear *you* sing the great aria, one would have to take a good deal of trouble. To bring you to trot. Some dynamite from behind —

JOSEF: (*Still feeling responsible, has sprung up and tries to close her mouth*) But that is absolutely — a

REGINA: A vigorous — a

JOSEF: Repulsive, like a fallen woman!

REGINA: (*Having torn herself loose*) One would have to give you a vigorous kick in the stomach! You chase after him, he said!

MARIA: I — — chase after you?

THOMAS: (*Holding himself back*) Did you really say that...?!

REGINA: He said it only yesterday. (*She turns for support to Miss Mertens, who shrugs her shoulder coldly, insulted.*)

THOMAS: But be silent you, you devil!

JOSEF: (*Automatically, as if he were duty-bound to defend Regina*) He is the one who said it! .... Now it's better that one says everything: ... I thought I should remove a few of the sheets before giving you the portfolio. I have suggested to you with what intentions he entered your house.

THOMAS: (*Groans, laughing. To Maria*) Your feeling and thought cannot discover the swindler in his feeling and thought, what a shameful, crude method: to show that the external man is the swindler! But a detective is so wonderful: what appears to you as melancholia, he explains as constipation and — — he cures it! Whom will you believe now? I don't know. Both of them. That's the eternal mystery!

ANSELM: (*To Maria*) Why are you not away from here...! It would not have come to any of this. I would have been a good person. (*Maria retreats. Regina throws herself at Anselm's feet, who pulls away from her.*)

REGINA: I will remain like this on the ground as long as you stand upright there. Is there nothing more in you that doesn't care whether you behave correctly or incorrectly? They proscribe to you what you should do, what you should feel, what you should think; no one says to you how you should *be*. You are unguided and unprotected, with something dark, untouched inside you. What do you want now? It's over! I lie on the earth and revenge myself and triumph! Because you no longer have confidence in yourself ... and neither do I ....

MARIA: So, stand up, Regina. Aren't you ashamed? (*She prods her softly and with disgust with the tip of her foot.*)

REGINA: Just prod me! Something is coming out of your dress and prodding me.

JOSEF: (*Repulsed*) I cannot watch this; I'm going.

MARIA: I'm going with you.

JOSEF: One should form an association of healthy people to defend against such sick ones.

THOMAS: Rather, rather, one would have to form an association of all the expelled ones so that they were not defeated like this. Speak, Anselm! Find *one* honest word!

ANSELM: (*To Maria*) I remained in the house up to now because I believed in you; I will kill myself if you leave the room.

JOSEF: (*To Thomas*) I will keep my house clean; do in your own what you will. I have fulfilled my duty. (*He and Maria prepare to leave.*)

ANSELM: (*Pointing to the knife that has lain open on the desk since the attempt to spring the lock*) Maria: do you recognize this knife? I will take it, if you can no longer believe!

MARIA: (*In the doorway*) I will never believe anything you say; the trust is lost, Anselm. (*She turns away and follows Josef without looking back.*)

ANSELM: (*Calling after her, weakly*) Maria?... Maria! (*Then he goes for the knife and — no one knows what has happened, since it happens so fast — he collapses. Thomas, who has been watching him the whole time carefully, stares astonished at him, but rigidly. Takes a few steps toward him and looks at him again with the same astonishment. Stands in front of him harshly and tensely. Regina has scooted across the floor and grabbed Anselm's arm and squeezes it with all her strength; pressing first just with her hand, then applying her fingernails.*)

REGINA: He can talk himself so deeply into something that he lets himself be martyred for it.

THOMAS: I don't see any blood; I wager he's pretending now, too.

REGINA: He takes something on and carries it out, even if he no longer wants to, just because he doesn't know any way out.

(*She has bitten fiercely and long into Anselm's hand, until it involuntarily reveals a sign of pain. Thomas throws himself right down next to him, kneels beside him, shakes him, twists his arms, pulls his hair.*)

THOMAS: Faker! Swindler! So, under your skin you're more beautiful than everyone else, huh?! If you don't open your eyes, I will trounce you! I will rip your face off!

REGINA: Don't hurt him! He's defenseless!

THOMAS: He's only shamming.

REGINA: Let him! He is good — *behind* himself! (*She pulls Thomas away and returns to biting Anselm's hand.*)

THOMAS: (*Fighting his way back to Anselm*) He still hopes to be proven right, after all. You corrupted man! Sordid defective wretch! Who tries to simulate health! (*Anselm has opened his eyes in response to the abuses.*)

(*Triumphantly*) Have you had to admit the truth even once!! (*But in the next moment, disgusted by himself, he stands up.*) Qualms! Is the lamp screwed on too high? The petroleum lamp, I thought, might explode. Ah ... (*laughing*) I know, we already have electricity ... for a moment I thought that mama was still alive and we were small ....

REGINA: Why do you rage against him so?! He hates you no more than he must hate everyone else, but he loves you much more.

THOMAS: Me he loves?! Coming here to steal Maria away!

REGINA: He loves you like a brother who is stronger than him.

ANSELM: (*Having straightened himself up with difficulty*) I hate you. Wherever I wanted to go, you were always there first.

THOMAS: (*Throwing the sentence at him*) No one believes you .... But what have you two done to us!! Everyone despises you both, persecutes you, ostracizes you!

REGINA: They crawled over me and away. I sacrificed myself, let myself be mastered, felt, as if I gradually really became what I appeared to them to be, and — I felt myself hovering at an even higher level; with parts that were still invisible, awaiting their counterparts. (*She stands up.*) Now I stand in clarity and everything is terminated. Today I have become a reasonable human being.

ANSELM: (*To Thomas*) You have persecuted me, whether you were there or not. Like a person who lures someone else to do him harm; you are to blame.

THOMAS: Of course, that's easy to say, but —

MARIA: (*Who sees that something has happened*) What is it?…. What happened?

THOMAS: He attempted a fake suicide. But true and false feeling are really almost the same in the end.

REGINA: There are people who are true behind lies and crooked behind truth.

THOMAS: One finds a companion and he is a swindler! One reveals a swindler and he is a companion!

MARIA: I don't understand a single word.

MISS MERTENS: (*Whom no one had paid attention to until then*) I beg to be able to leave. I can no longer follow this. Obviously, I cannot understand such "volcanic people" in whom "a fragment from the creation" has not yet solidified.

THOMAS: Such people are just scammers nowadays. These times only bear short feelings, long reflections.

MARIA: I don't understand one word. Have you made up? I will not forgive him!

ANSELM: I have spoken ill of you in order to protect my soul from an alien influence!

THOMAS: Be silent, Anselm, you must go to bed. You must sleep. Tomorrow, early, you have to leave. I almost wish I could go in your place, lulled by aimlessness. You are right. One is never so present as when one loses one's self.

CURTAIN

ACT THREE

A hall-like middle room on the first floor. Doors. A wooden interior staircase runs through it. Strange arabesques in the carpet. In the back, a very large window with a view of a landscape. Daybreak. Heavy, comfortable wooden and leather furniture.

The character of the scenery is the same as in Act Two; but the area feels more enclosed, like the inside of a closet. Regina and Thomas in fantastical house clothing. Thomas gets up from a leather couch in the back, stretches himself and comes forward, where Regina crouches.

THOMAS: I am ashamed of myself.

REGINA: Not to look at any man at all or at every man is the same thing. A woman can throw herself at their hearts, just because she is insane from feeling strange; from not being able to understand how she might hold their hand longer than necessary in her own.

THOMAS: Before I came here for the rest of the night, I read these notes of yours or Anselm's about you once more: I am ashamed.

REGINA: (*Agreeing*) Cooled-down fantasies. Repulsively naked, like birds who have fallen out of a nest. (*Even though she is staring straight into the light*) I can't look at the light, this nauseatingly beautiful morning; it heaves already, like a putrid world-stomach, up into vapid clarity.

THOMAS: And while I read, this Stader was in our house. And in another room Josef was sleeping. And in a third room, Anselm. I was afraid to ask myself whether one of them was sleeping with you once more.

REGINA: Why don't you say: Depraved woman?! Why don't you try to lift me up like a fallen girl?! At least look at it as natural, even if one no longer has the strength to see something behind it! — In the town there were no vacancies; Josef had brought home this adjutant. Could we just allow him to sleep in the park?

THOMAS: *Naturally* not! It's this accursed human "naturally"! We crouch down under it as the entrance to every baseness.

REGINA: (*Continuing*) And by now, Anselm is *un*natural!

THOMAS: (*Stressing the narrowness of the ambiguity*) And Anselm is unnatural.

(*Pause.*)

THOMAS: (*Tormented*) If you knew how men contemn a woman like that!

REGINA: Of course, I know. And they are right. I noticed it every time, but it was always a revenge for me; deeper inside. Because it's not, after all, about today: that one has done it. Rather that one was overcome by it; that one becomes what one does! Revolution, enormous will, nameless power rush into the world and become — — well, in your case, they become a professor.

THOMAS: (*Half agreeing*) Yes, perhaps everyone remains a prisoner of unintended success. Perhaps I have to get used to that.

REGINA: Blissful maidenly feeling, to hover along like a magic bird in the swinging ring of the world! It's only later that you realize that you have been sitting in a travelling cage that suddenly stopped moving.

THOMAS: Yesterday, when I spoke with your husband, I still believed in your aversion to men; now I have to get used to it, my wild sister, that you were just expressing this aversion in a perfidious, hateful way.

REGINA: There is something in me that was never touched by it.

THOMAS: I always found it so nice that the two of us never wanted too much from each other. There was a freedom of movement between us. Never any of that forced idealistic togetherness that extinguishes hearing, seeing, and thinking. Instead — even when we didn't see each other or write to each other for years — the calm sleep of an indissolvable relationship from our childhood on. Like everything far off, at its furthest boundary it was like music. It even fit well that you married Josef. The most human mystery of music is not that it is music, but that it manages, with the help of a dried-out sheep gut, to bring us close to God.

REGINA: Maybe I'm just evil; it could be; I don't like anyone. I do everything in secret. But I was always comforted by the thought that if it finally all went to hell, you could fix it; you would arrange it so that everything I had done would turn out to be good. But now you have been cast down!

THOMAS: Don't worry, I — will rise up again!

REGINA: Come, let us remove our shoes and stockings; come into the park! On the wet grass. (*Thomas refuses, but relaxes.*) Do you still remember that old Satan, Sabine?

THOMAS: Our nanny, who kept us virtuous? Finally, I realize who your Miss Mertens always reminded me of!

REGINA: Come over the wet meadow; the immaculate morning dew will wash our feet viciously clean like her sponge once did. The sun will steam on our shoulders. Look how it rises! Daft as an explosion! (*Jeering wildly and grotesquely at the sun*) A-a-a-h! That is beauty!!! Our naked soles will feel the earth — the animal, from which we have sprung — and it won't be able to throw us off. Then they will find us dead under a bush. And will break their heads over why our feet are bare.

THOMAS: Are you still playing with it?! You remind me of Anselm!

REGINA: I never thought of it; not even after Johannes' death. But I believe that from the beginning one is either intended for it or not. It grows underground and one day one recognizes one's calling.

THOMAS: But — you don't really mean it seriously?

REGINA: You have courage for two, don't you? Or should one just lay there at the end like an empty sack? Won't we all? What are you still waiting for?! This is the only thing we haven't tried yet; maybe it's a swindle too, maybe it is — — but to know that it is close by makes one blissfully free and fearless.

THOMAS: (*Grabbing her by the shoulder and shaking her*) Nonsense! It's beautiful! To be abandoned is beautiful! To lose everything is beautiful! To be free of Anselm's wisdom is beautiful! One eyes one's life, like a pupil that contracts smaller and smaller. Sees nothing, takes a false step from the highest point. And swings like a leaf through a deep, vast space.

MARIA: (*Entering with a candle in her hand*) It's light in here! (*Blowing out her candle*) Are you two awake? You couldn't sleep either? After Regina left me, I slept, at most two hours. I didn't know what Anselm would do, what you would do, Thomas. You didn't come into the bedroom.

THOMAS: Anselm will sleep it off; he has to leave today. (*He observes Maria from time to time, with astonished looks, trying to encompass and elevate her.*)

MARIA: (*Sits next to Regina and wraps her in her shawl.*) He certainly does much that is bad, without rightly wanting to, like a boy, out of clumsiness. And then runs away from it.

THOMAS: Please, Maria, we're over 30! Even at 80, one is still a little child inside. Admittedly. Even when one is looking death in the eye. But it remains unutterably revolting to wear this soft internal fur turned outward like he did yesterday.... It's bitter cold. Is your bed still warm? I want to lay in it.

MARIA: I'll make tea; none of the servants are up yet. (*To Regina*) Maybe he was not entirely wrong. If I had only trusted him! If I had done what he wanted and had gone away with you two!

THOMAS: (*To both of them*) Oh? So, you two spoke about it, did you? At the deathbed of the healthy one!

MARIA: You are always so disdainful. I'm no longer entirely sure; perhaps I owe him a bit of an apology. Didn't we make the same mistake with Regina?

REGINA: Oh, nonsense!

MARIA: (*Tenderly*) No, if I could only make up for it somehow. Now I understand for the first time why she married Josef; and I always judged it so harshly. But when Johannes' death came so suddenly, she just thought: wait. Make yourself small. What are 30, what are 50 years — if one has something to wait for!

THOMAS: You forget: that was a real death, not a feigned one!

MARIA: *You* forget, that years and plans are as smooth as a dance floor, when the first resolve of a young woman to be strong and worthy of a companion flies over them. Only later does one notice the repulsive parts.

REGINA: Nonsense, nonsense, nonsense! (*She tries to cover Maria's mouth.*)

MARIA: (*Stands up and starts to set up a samovar, but then lets it be.*) No, he should hear this. We didn't advise you or help you then.

THOMAS: And? What followed? She must have explained it all to you, too?

MARIA: Why won't you understand it? If she had already climbed into the grave alive, was she also supposed to just stay lying there?

THOMAS: Fine, *once*. But the next one? The one after that? The tenth, and then and then?!

MARIA: It didn't have to turn out that way, but I know this at least, if all one gets at home is mockery: to face up to that, a person would need the deepest love. Johannes himself would not have judged as harshly as you do; he knew that Regina was still much too young, and not long before his death he begged me: tell her, whatever happens, I will forgive her anything.

REGINA: (*Standing up*) I can't listen to this. I'd have to howl from ambition and chagrin like when I became first in the class at year's end by mistake.

MARIA: He believed in her: that is a power that makes one good!

THOMAS: And Anselm? Now I know what you two are driving at! Have you forgotten that you chased after him?!

MARIA: (*Almost ridiculous in her piety*) It was one of his lapses. One must not let oneself be scared off by it. One must not adapt oneself to his delusions. One must want to listen for the good in a person; then he will find the words for it!

THOMAS: (*Mockingly*) One must only take care not to think petty thoughts, and then he will reveal himself to you, this other human being.

MARIA: You only ever hurt him where he was weakest.

THOMAS: So, what am I to do?

MARIA: We must not just let him degenerate. We must not let something that could be good be ruined.

THOMAS: Maybe I should ask him to stay with us a while longer?

MARIA: Yes. You didn't warn me about him; you only mocked.

THOMAS: (*Calmly and decisively*) No. I will not rescue someone who has attacked us like this.

REGINA: (*To Maria*) Don't talk about it beforehand! Don't you remember: aimless swindlers like Thomas and I have the first step in common with important people; but the last step, Thomas makes alone!

(*Exits.*)

(*Maria suddenly moves very close to Thomas and looks at him helplessly. Thomas steps back sadly.*)

THOMAS: Do you see now? That you have been fooled by him?

MARIA: I have seen it. But Thomas! Thomas!! If one foresees everything, wants it, sees it safely arrived — that doesn't amount to happiness.

THOMAS: (*Hiding a tremor*) Explain yourself.

MARIA: I can't keep up with you two. I'm only a simple person. But you can only be happy through something unexpected; through something unpredictable; something that just occurs to you and is there and maybe isn't even right. — I can't express myself well. One has so much more power than words inside! Perhaps I should be ashamed: but Anselm gave me something!

THOMAS: Something you lacked with me?

MARIA: Yes…. What would you do if I were to go away?

THOMAS: I don't know. Go ahead.

(*Pause. Maria fights back tears.*)

MARIA: Yes. That's how you are. Renouncing everything if a new plan seems better to you! I know that you're fond of me. You know that I will never forgive Anselm. Never! But even this wretched person doles out more peace and warmth than you. You want too much.

You want everything in a different way. It may all be quite correct. But I am afraid of you!

THOMAS: You are beautiful. Have I never told you that? You are as beautiful as the arc of the sky — (*correcting his poetic tone*) or something like that — something that stays the same for centuries. It seduced Anselm as well. — Certainly, it's all my fault. I can't be different than I am. You see, Anselm and I think differently than you do.

MARIA: Anselm *and* you — ?

THOMAS: Yes. He was just too weak for it; he couldn't bear it. He intrudes suddenly on the people who feel at home in this world, and starts to act in their play, in fantastical roles that he invents for himself — — But I still believe that Anselm and I can never forget the truth.

MARIA: And I? So now *I* am the liar?

THOMAS: Not in that sense; in that sense, *he* is the liar, yes. I mean more that — more the truth that we are standing in the middle of an equation that is made up of nothing but indeterminate values and that only is solved by way of a ruse that presupposes some elements as constant. One virtue as the highest. Or God. Or one loves mankind. Or hates it. One is religious or modern. Passionate or disillusioned. Warlike or pacifistic. And so on and so on, along this whole intellectual country fairground, which, today, keeps its stalls open for every spiritual need. All you have to do is enter and immediately you find your feelings and convictions for life and for every possible situation. It's only difficult to find your feelings if you don't accept any other certainty but that this evolved ape, our soul, crouching on a heap of clay, is hurtling through God's unknown infinity.

MARIA: Perhaps you are right to complicate everything like that. I can't refute it. But I also can't bear it. To always face up to such problems. You even brought Anselm to collapse!

(*Regina comes in, agitated.*)

REGINA: He's gone!

THOMAS: Risen from the grave. Only fitting for a miracle man.

REGINA: (*To Maria*) There's a note for you in his room. He will wait for you until tomorrow at noon in the city.

THOMAS: What does that mean?

MARIA: That he wants to speak once more. That he wants to be heard once more.

(*Thomas shrugs his shoulders. Maria goes out.*)

REGINA: (*Intensely*) Do you know precisely — how Anselm is?

THOMAS: Yes.

REGINA: Then you are behaving cruelly toward Maria.

(*Pause.*)

THOMAS: Because I am letting her do as she pleases?—The ponderous, helpless Maria, you understand? All she needs is to set herself going! Do you understand? Like a weighty spinning top, she follows her own path. I'd like to whip…!

REGINA: I would have liked so much to start something bad with you, just to get my revenge on Maria; I couldn't do it. Anselm broke that in me. The way one awakens a somnambulist. (*Thomas looks at her astonished and expectant.*) I believe that I once wanted to become a very good person. Praised by everyone; nuzzled like a dog, to whom one says: good puppy! Never was I able to be good.

THOMAS: Yes, it's also much harder. Only stupid people find it easy.

REGINA: Not Maria; I can't bear it. Frenetically good. Performing a somersault between the highest trapezes of goodness; while the masses hold their breath, in that soundless moment when the spark hovers between the match and the tinderbox. When we were in school, I wanted to secretly adopt a little boy and raise him up to be a prince. I even wanted to marry our governess, because an evil loneliness made me sad. I thought that I would someday be able to make people happy like a fairy. When I was seven years old, I had discovered a magical formula to do it, and I sang it for hours at a time loudly into the ear of the gardener's little daughter and pinched her and beat her up, because she cried instead of becoming more beautiful. But later all of that just shattered because of people. One sees them truly and exactly as they are. One cannot love them.

THOMAS: No. But one must love them; sometimes; if one does not want to evaporate into a ghostly being!! That's it.

REGINA: Just like sleeping and eating: but I can't do it anymore!! (*Pause. She searches for a new beginning.*) Thomas! Don't laugh at me: I would like to make a sacrifice. To no one, no one but you. I don't want to be good for an alien rule; but for you, since you are like me, only stronger: I will return to Josef.

THOMAS: Such a pointless idea, Regina; I won't allow you to even consider something like that.

REGINA: But I want to .... Don't laugh at me ... I want, for once in my life, to serve an idea!

THOMAS: But I have no concerns about Josef. He won't do anything to Anselm now, or to me ... me? .... Well, it no longer matters to me if he harms me.

REGINA: I don't matter to myself anymore either. Don't reject the idea; it's hard enough for me as it is .... No, now that I have had time to consider, I can hardly go on.

THOMAS: Don't be so fainthearted! I beg of you, do not be fainthearted. (*He throws himself angrily and impotently onto the couch where Regina had been sitting.*)

REGINA: You are certainly good... but who knows what you have just done to me...?

THOMAS: What does that mean?

REGINA: Listen: someone is coming. I can only tell you when we are alone.

(*Exits.*)

(*Thomas sits, his head supported in his hands. Josef and Stader enter from out of the darkness, blinded; Stader is carrying a candle.*)

JOSEF: It's shameful. We are sneaking around in a strange house at night.

STADER: To uncover the truth justifies any vulgar concomitant circumstances.

JOSEF: But be silent, why don't you? You are always philosophizing!... At least not so loud.... (*He cleans his glasses and looks around without seeing; Stader has opened a door and has half disappeared inside it, which explains how he, too, has not noticed Thomas.*) Do you know exactly where the portfolio is?

STADER: This must be the way through; the study is all the way at the end. I know and observe everything.

JOSEF: (*Whispering in rage*) Don't scream like that! You will wake someone! The situation is shamefully improper. Naturally, you don't understand that.... (*Sighs. Says to himself*) But I can't rest for a moment as long as I know that these papers are in someone else's hands. (*He has put on his glasses; Stader has turned around, to take the confused Josef with him. Now both of them notice Thomas, who stands up. Stader quickly and absurdly blows out his candle.*)

THOMAS: I will give you the key. The portfolio is in the middle drawer of the desk. (*He hands the desk key to Joseph, who mechanically gives it to Stader; Stader disappears with it, happy to remove himself from the situation, nevertheless casting a tenderly inquiring glance at Thomas. Josef, uncertain, shamefaced, follows him, but turns around in the doorway to explain.*)

JOSEF: (*Apologetically*) It must be destroyed .... I would really have stolen it. If it were not murder, I would even — murder — this fellow (*pointing at Stader*) who knows everything!

(*Thomas pulls Josef, who tries to smooth over this intimacy with a stiff willingness, back into the room.*)

JOSEF: I have begun to ruminate once again about the facts. I have recently come to the conclusion: it can only have been a matter of a perverse confusion. It was not a love story!

THOMAS: No, it was no love story. (*He lets him loose, with a strange laugh*). Search, search! Arrest him! Set your police dogs on him!

JOSEF: You ... (*Gesturing at him*) are overtired.

THOMAS: (*Throwing himself on a chair*) Very tired.

JOSEF: (*Standing in front of him*) Too much feeling, my dear Thomas; only principles can help here!

THOMAS: Too much feeling: yes, yes, yes, yes. Maria says I have never had *any* feelings.

JOSEF: Well, yes, women; but even she would think differently today. In any case, yesterday I already said my last word against this infectious sick man whom you endure in your house!... In any case, I will really have him arrested, as soon as day really dawns and offices open and one can telephone.... (*Softening his tone*) It all comes from exaggerated feelings. One ought not to have that much feeling; or at least only for the great and the lofty things, where it can't be harmful like this.... It was a great disappointment to you?.... Well, yes, I mean, you are still a man of the most lucid rational ability; you only let yourself be overthrown a bit, because the exalted emotional testimonies of this fool infect everyone at first.

THOMAS: (*Tired, indulgent, but still feigning friendliness*) Can't you stay and sit with me awhile?

JOSEF: (*Preparing to follow Stader*) No, not that; not, at least, until you have come to your senses again.

THOMAS: Just a bit more patience. Your victory is assured.

JOSEF: (*Softening again*) I couldn't bear it either; I had to study the documents of this confusion once more.

I require a firm, dependable foundation in order to be able to exist.

(*Exits.*)

(*Thomas sits down at a heavy table in the middle of the room and supports his head in his hands again. Maria enters, sits across from him, looks at him; he looks up, she cradles her head in her folded arms and cries. Thomas stands up, sits down silently next to her, and caresses her.*)

MARIA: (*Looking up*) I feel like an adventuress.

THOMAS: You must do it. If someone does something for a cause with his whole soul, it becomes worthy of it after the fact.

MARIA: I want it but I am afraid of it.

THOMAS: One is always weary and worn out when something is on the point of being realized.

MARIA: It feels as if everything that I wanted to do were already long behind me. Why am I doing it then?! Why?! But a clockwork keeps ticking in me.

THOMAS: You must do it. Ultimately, you can only know what it was by whatever comes after it.

REGINA: You said the same thing about Anselm; you are throwing me out.

THOMAS: It has to be like a dive: there is the will, but that's not yet really anything; then suddenly, already, the new element and you are moving your arms and legs.

One is really always absent when it comes to life decisions.

MARIA: But do you even know what I want??

THOMAS: (*Looking into her eyes*) I no longer want to put pressure on you.

MARIA: I want to talk to Anselm one more time. Perhaps … I will bring him back here …?

THOMAS: I see your danger; but if it's what you want, I must accept it.

MARIA: (*Testing him further*) And if I didn't come back? What would you do?

THOMAS: I don't know.

MARIA: You still don't know?

THOMAS: One shouldn't always say: this must or that must not happen. Wait. I don't know what will occur to me. I really don't know!

MARIA: (*Springing up*) I can't stand it!

THOMAS: (*Gently*) When I look at you like this, it's as if I were already telling someone else about you. She was so beautiful and so good and something wondrous happened. But after that, I don't know what comes next.

MARIA: (*Hesitantly*) You are so stubborn.

THOMAS: There could be a hurdy gurdy playing in the street. It could be Sunday. Full of the gloom of a grey, used-up week. I could long for you now almost to the point of tears. But the idea of imprisoning myself with you in a relationship as frozen as love or any other total communion seems childish to me .... And yet I could ... perhaps, for you ... be grateful to someone who can.

MARIA: Do you know what you are like? Despite everything that you do to counteract it? The great desire to be good that one sometimes felt with a beating heart as a child at bedtime.

THOMAS: (*Resistant*) Don't forget: tender blisters now will possibly be dried skin in a few days.

MARIA: No. You can't just wipe away all your past life like that! I would at least like to preserve a clear idea of it!

THOMAS: Go; it's time, if you still want to catch the train.

MARIA: I can't leave you like this. Am I supposed to just get up from this table and leave you alone? I would still like to pour you some tea ... pay the laundry bill ... I don't know what else; nothing, nothing is there. (*She uncovers the tea pot that she had prepared earlier, lights the flame, and spoons tea into the water.*) Do you forgive me?

THOMAS: Let us part sincerely: I haven't really thought about it at all. I feel as if everything had sunken down and was still moving beneath the ground, and that someday and someplace it will erupt onto the surface again. There is a tidal marsh in me, no present .... Go, Maria; you must.

(*Maria stands, silently battling herself.*)

THOMAS: I am sad, too.

MARIA: You're not sad. You are sending me away. It is so difficult for me to go away from you; I don't know why. We women love more deeply!

THOMAS: Because you love men. The world breaks in upon you in the form of men.

MARIA: You're already looking forward to something else.

THOMAS: Reflection perhaps.

MARIA: Tears fill me like a column, from my feet to my eyes.

(*Thomas wants to approach her. She lets the tea stand and runs out the door. Thomas remains standing a moment longer, stricken, then goes to the samovar and finishes the preparations. A door has cracked open. Stader pushes himself in. Thomas, drinking tea, doesn't notice him at first.*)

STADER: (*Clearing his throat repeatedly*) I don't wish to intrude …. May I … ?

THOMAS: (*Interrupted in his absorption*) What is it?

STADER: In my current mission I should not really allow myself … but, if one considers it precisely ….

THOMAS: How — ?

STADER: I am more sympathetic with you! Despite all respect for His Excellency. I have admired you for years.

May I permit myself to advise you: do not involve yourself in this futile case. May I speak man to man? You are bringing pointless disappointments upon yourself.

THOMAS: Oh, I see ... I really have no idea what I have to do with it; but if you, as you say, admire me, I ask that you keep silent. As a grave; do you understand?

STADER: But I would like to suggest something to you; you can rely upon me, Herr Professor.

THOMAS: You were here by coincidence?...!!

STADER: Yes.

THOMAS: You did not intend at all...?

STADER: Certainly not.

THOMAS: Please, take a seat.

STADER: Thank you. His Excellency has deepened his reading in the meantime. (*He sits down carefully; is silent, searching for words, then blurts out*) You see, I have been following you for years, Herr Professor.

THOMAS: Why? What am I supposed to have done?

STADER: (*Charmed*) Oh, even you don't have a completely clear conscience. I saw it in your eyelid. In a microscopic twitch. Everyone nowadays suffers from subconscious delusions of guilt. — But not like this, not like this: I follow your *creation*, your wonderful work!

THOMAS: Do you understand any of it?

STADER: Yes, well, not really. That is to say, insofar as my career does not ... my career puts me in affiliation with all the realms of knowledge ... but, well ... it was years ago that Regina told me about you.

THOMAS: Don't call her Regina. Call her: Her Excellency, or say, your honorable cousin. Never mind. Do you want a cigar?

STADER: (*Refusing*) I am still engaged in a so-called professional business matter with your cousin; thank you, no.

THOMAS: A cigarette?

STADER: (*Unable to continue to play the insulted one with Thomas*) Thank you, perhaps. (*He takes one.*) But it would be immeasurably awkward if His Excellency found me like this. (*After every inhalation he hides the cigarette in the hollow of his hand.*)

THOMAS: So, what have you heard?

STADER: Oh, a great deal; and I was not idle. I have written down a few statements word for word! (*Pulling out a notebook*) I understand them quite a bit differently now than I did in those days. I even must admit that I did not understand them at all back then. But I had a presentiment even then of the enormous possibility of this sort of person, whom I now see clearly before me. (*He leafs through and quotes:*) "We are standing on the threshold of a new time, which will be guided or destroyed, but in any case, will be ruled, by science. The old tragedies are dying out and we don't know if there will be new ones, since today, in experiments with animals, one can inject the souls of miniature female creatures into miniature male ones, and vice versa. Someone who cannot solve an integral equation or who is not a master of experimental technique should not be allowed to speak about spiritual questions in these times." Do you still remember to whom you said this?

THOMAS: Yes, naturally.

STADER: It's from a letter to His Excellency. It made a strong impression on me. Do you understand? Just imagine the significance for morality and criminalistics, not to mention from the perspective of the investigative art of disguise. (*He stands up.*) Herr Professor! Should one allow such ideas to exist without exploiting their practical possibilities?

THOMAS: Her Excellency told me about it.

STADER: *Her* Excellency? Her Excellency told — ? You about — ?

THOMAS: Don't you want to save them from an embarrassing situation, out of gratefulness?

STADER: Hmmm. I already know what's coming. You mean that I should steal the portfolio? I am quite loath to cultivate this branch of my business.

THOMAS: Oh? Well, then; it was just something that occurred to me. But isn't it really quite improper, the way that you behave toward my cousin?

STADER: (*Disagreeing*) A man has higher interests. (*Once again overwhelmed by his emotion*) Yes; I, too, was a utopian! But I have come to see that that is not enough. Let me make you an offer; if you agree, I will do everything for you! (*He sits down again.*) I offer you the opportunity to honor the firm, Stader, Newton, & Co, by becoming a scholarly associate.

THOMAS: (*Amused*) This is quite a surprise. I really don't even know what such a thing would mean.

STADER: When it comes to a man such as yourself, I will not speak about the financial gain first; if the mind does not squander itself on books, but instead is applied to business matters, it cannot fail to succeed. Did you know that I used to be a servant?

THOMAS: Yes.

STADER: At that time, I was only a servant. At night —

THOMAS: (*Fending him off*) Please!

STADER: No, no, in the night I slipped away; always; I was a singer, that is to say, a poet. A folk singer, you understand, in the woodshed, so to speak, and I only had time at night. But I gave that all up later; then I was a dog catcher, a second for duels, an informant for the police, a salesman — oh, and many other things. One has something inside one that cannot find satisfaction in any career. A restlessness of mind, I mean. One final conviction is missing. Something remains and leads one on further and further. One would like to just keep going, straight along the street, straight ahead. There's something inside one! — But Herr Professor, am I talking too much — — ?

THOMAS: (*Has lit a cigar and listens attentively. His shattered mood has transformed into a bitter, giddy one.*) No, no, continue; it interests me more than you can know.

STADER: Then it came to me that only science could provide us with quiet and order. And I founded my institute.

THOMAS: I have heard about it.

STADER: Do you know about its scientific facilities?

THOMAS: People have informed me. Very ambitious.

STADER: Add your leadership to all of this and we'd have — a smashing success! I don't have to tell you that we sometimes still have to struggle against occasional inaccuracies in the methodology. Science has never been applied properly enough to practical matters; one experiences disappointments. But even more disappointing is human understanding! Particularly in scholarly circles, my institute does not yet enjoy the sympathy that it deserves. Your help would be particularly indispensable in this area: the development of Detectologistics as the Life Science of the Superior Scientific Human Being.

It's only a detection institute, but its goal is really the completion of a scientific world picture. We discover connections, we confirm facts, we insist upon the observation of laws; but that is only the basic part; I would not burden you with any of that. My *grand* hope is: the statistical and methodological observation of human conditions, which emerges from our work.

Let someone pick a card from five concealed ones. Seventy-percent of people will take it from the same place. Test readings of thermometers or millimeters, if fractions must be guessed at: all people will guess either too high or too low, depending on the space between the two neighboring marks. I have been told that there are eye-, ear-, and muscle-people, who can be differentiated from each other by flaws that lay-people do not notice. I have been told that the poets, from the beginning of time, have always used the same small number of motifs and that they could never invent a new one. I have been told that the format, which the artist allegedly gives to his pictures out of caprice, expands or shrinks depending upon certain wholly regulated laws, if one only observes the changes over the centuries. That lovers always say the same thing, is well known. In summer there is an increase in fertilizations; in autumn, suicides. I have been told: all this is even the same as the whitecaps of the waves: it's only the layman who believes that this white rising and falling is an enormous forward-striving movement; a few splashes lead us astray, but the whole mass of the wave pitches a scientific curve on the spot, without budging an inch. Shall one allow oneself to be made a fool of — by oneself? One does something and mysteriously it becomes a law! It's simply unbearable if one knows that someday everyone will know all of this precisely, but one doesn't know it oneself yet!

THOMAS: My dear friend, you have certainly been born too early. But you overestimate me. I am a child of this time. I have to be satisfied with sitting on the ground between the two chairs of knowing and not-knowing.

STADER: No, you are not already refusing me!? Give yourself some more time to consider!

THOMAS: Someone might come in at any moment. Listen, we can keep in touch from time to time. I might have an offer for you; not so interesting, just a very common one. You have seen my wife. Doctor Anselm left during the night. My wife is following him on the next train —

STADER: (*Looking at his watch*) According to the schedule, it must have just left.

THOMAS: (*Repressing a minor emotion*) Yes. Then they will meet in the city and have a discussion.

STADER: And you want material, just like His Excellency?

THOMAS: No. I only want you to report to me precisely how my friend looked during the discussion, what expression he had and also my wife's — if she was very agitated, if she gave the impression that she suffered, or a liberated, fresh impression; in short, very precisely, as if I could see it myself. And then keep me posted on everything new that Doctor Anselm does.

STADER: If I can stay in contact with you, this is a very small thing in exchange; I have also been able to serve His Excellency to his complete satisfaction. (*Josef enters, looking for Stader, with the notes already wrapped up as a package under his arm.*)

JOSEF: (*Annoyed*) There you are!

THOMAS: (*Quickly*) We will speak again later.

STADER: Excellency, let me be at your service — dutifully! (*He offers to take the package from him, eager to serve.*)

JOSEF: (*Holding it tighter*) Leave it, leave it; I'll deal with it myself. (*To Thomas in a peaceable, gentle tone*) Can you perhaps give me a piece of twine?

STADER: Here already, Excellency! (*He pulls a ball of twine out of his pocket and begins respectfully to tie up the package while it is still in Josef's arms, so that he unwillingly lays it down on the table.*)

JOSEF: But we also need some sealing wax. Would you be so good?

STADER: Prepared for everything! (*He pulls some wax out of his pocket*). Your Excellency should really not underestimate my foresight in this demeaning way. (*He tries to help Josef.*)

JOSEF: No, no, leave it, Stader!

(*Stader retreats discreetly a few steps. Josef begins, with clumsy, hasty, and trembling movements to seal up the portfolio. Thomas, in order to show his readiness also, lights the candle that has been provided by Stader.*)

JOSEF: (*In an undertone*) It was no love story!

THOMAS: No, it was no love story. But what was it then? (*He begins to help Josef.*) Sealing the coffin! Earth strewn on top. May flowers grow.

JOSEF: You seem to take it all much too lightly.

THOMAS: If I were you, I would clear the way for Regina to have a new life.

JOSEF: I beg of you, Thomas, no names! We are not alone.

STADER: (*From a distance*) Does Your Excellency perhaps have a seal on him, a signet ring? (*Josef turns to Thomas. They let the package go, so it opens up again. Stader takes over with a few skillful moves.*)

THOMAS: Just use a coin. (*To Josef*) Alright. Without names: but all the same, I would lay the way straight open; it is, after all, simple, moral ABC.

JOSEF: (*Firmly disagreeing*) I beg of you!

STADER: (*Mollifyingly*) Does Your Excellency recommend heads or tails?

JOSEF: For heaven's sake! Just do what you want without asking!

THOMAS: Losing doesn't mean anything anymore; winning also is nothing.

STADER: (*Triumphantly*) This is another of those cases. (*Suggestively*) One believes it is "accident," heads or tails; in reality, it's a simple matter of the laws of probability — and an occult power rules us.

JOSEF: I have already mentioned that you seem somewhat overwrought. One is not only responsible for oneself, but for the stability of everyone involved.

THOMAS: (*Doggedly. Pointing at the package*) I would burn it completely.

JOSEF: I won't hear any more!! (*Using Stader as a distraction*) Are you finished? Go then, go with it already!… (*Calming himself*) Wait in my room for me! Please.

STADER: (*With dignity*) Herr Professor, I will be permitted to speak with you once more later? His Excellency seems to be suffering from a momentary rise in blood pressure.

(*Leaves. Thomas slowly blows the candle out, with pleasure.*)

JOSEF: Thomas! If you really still wish to discuss it: I cannot do so, as long as this person is still in your house; I must call your attention to that fact.

THOMAS: He is gone.

JOSEF: Which he? I meant Anselm, of course.

THOMAS: Anselm has left.

JOSEF: (*Relieved*) Then you finally understood that he deceived you? I would like to speak with Regina.

THOMAS: That can't be right now. She is feeling unwell.

JOSEF: (*Making sure that Stader is not listening. Voiceless with mistrust*) She went with him??

THOMAS: (*Calmly*) Maria went with him.

JOSEF: You're joking? I don't understand how anyone could do so now, but you must be joking?

THOMAS: I have exaggerated perhaps. He left by himself. But Maria is also presumably gone by now; she is following him.

JOSEF: Following him? (*He becomes mistrustful again.*) You two have still not distanced yourselves from him totally?

THOMAS: (*Firmly*) No, it's not like that. It was Maria's own choice to leave. She condemns what he has done; but the way in which he did it captivated her.

JOSEF: But what is that supposed to mean?!

THOMAS: Firstly: that someone broke my bones — or at least my ossifications. All in all, the persistent primordial slime is still alive. Secondly: that the person closest to me has gotten free of me — and I will now free myself; perhaps this person only preempted me out of fear of me.

JOSEF: But Maria! A wife like Maria? This soul-thief! Oh, but now I am beginning to suspect another connection: from the very beginning he only intended to humiliate her in front of Maria, this wretch? Don't you think I needed to protect Regina? Ever since the time I stood there myself, I don't know how, suddenly in that sleeping unguarded room with a candle.... I am really still so confused.... How much more can even a resilient person like Regina.... Yes, now I take it as quite possible that she only acted out of confusion, when she — let herself be accused of such misconduct.

THOMAS: Sit down with me instead. I am so happy to talk with you; I was really looking forward to telling you, to you being the first person to know. (*He sits down and pulls Josef onto a chair.*)

JOSEF: You are strangely calm. Don't you understand: the hand that used to pass your plate to you at supper has possibly already committed an indecency? The mouth, that you believed just because you saw it opened, has lied? You moved around as if you were in a home, but strange eyes were looking in through all the walls? The worst shame that can be inflicted on a man has befallen you! ... (*He tries to repair what he's said.*) I, of course, do not *want* to assume that it definitely really happened.

THOMAS: (*Answering quite sedately*) Do you know what I see in it? That the love for one chosen person is really nothing more than a revolt against everyone else.

JOSEF: I believe that you … yes, in your case I really believe: you have no feelings.

THOMAS: I have feelings; they are just very loosely arranged.

JOSEF: No, no, I want to speak with Regina. She belongs in an orderly, stable atmosphere. (*He stands up.*)

THOMAS: (*Holding him back*) What are you going to say to her, then? What will you do?

JOSEF: (*Affronted*) Indeed, what will *you* do? (*Suddenly*) Thomas! Let's forget all of this! I will not bear you a grudge. We must bestir ourselves. We both have the same enemy.

THOMAS: (*Doggedly tranquil*) The cases are entirely different. Nothing happened between Maria and Anselm; at most, something is beginning. Between Anselm and Regina something *did* happen and has ended between them — or has died!! That which you call her misconduct.

JOSEF: Oh, so you say?

THOMAS: Regina and I have spoken about it thoroughly enough. Where are you going?

(*Josef has stood up.*)

JOSEF: I first need to have it out with Regina. In my misery I will, at least, have a clear, pure resolution. She shall admit this whole terrible confusion to my face, if she is able, without collapsing into shame during her speech.

THOMAS: She will not even start talking at all. For she knows that she cannot explain it away to you as mere daft adventures. Any old blockhead, a word-maker, emotional agitator, or even a sensualist, an athlete — even if he doesn't have the strength of a little horse — suddenly grows into something stupendous: Love! Just the way fear is: the hostile, unknown entity grows. The unknown grows in both cases! Can you imagine that? — Quite: I almost can't either. The unknown entity that seems to surround us apparently only grows for certain people from time to time. There seem to be people in whom something that sits firmly in everyone else is somewhat loose. It tears itself loose …. What's the satisfaction in ascertaining, after the fact, that the cause is named Franz or something else or those stupid words and assurances that lovers infect each other with! Naturally, she knew, too, that it was unworthy.

JOSEF: Once one begins to even entertain such ways of thinking: she should have confided in me from the beginning!

THOMAS: You would merely have pointed out the moral defect and would have been correct. She could just as easily have gone to a doctor and he would have told her: erotomania, a neurasthenic hysterical basis, frigid iteration with pathological lack of impulse control, or something like that; and he would have been correct, too! Then she would have inhaled the so-called adventure like a chain-smoker, with excess as the only limit. Eventually, she probably wasn't able to see any man at all without —

JOSEF: Without what? Don't you feel how unbearably depraved this is?!

THOMAS: Without grabbing hold of him, the way you can't see any handbook of your field, without leafing through it, even though you are certain, without doing so, what it contains. Don't ignore the fact that we often behave just as profligately — only with good things.

JOSEF: Oh, always these inappropriate clever jests, with which you love to make yourself important! One should have taught her to demand little and to have respect for the stable foundations of existence.

THOMAS: Josef, that's just it: she doesn't have it, this respect. For you there are laws, rules, feelings that one must respect, people with whom one must take especial care. She tried to ladle it all up — but she was using a sieve; and then she was astonished that it never worked for her. Amid an enormous well-meaning order, against which she doesn't have the slightest substantial objection to raise, something in her remains disordered. The essence of some other order, one that she does not dream of. A fragment from Creation's fire-essence, still molten.

JOSEF: So, you would like to set her up as some sort of model of an exceptional human being? (*Stands up. Ironic, with feigned ceremonialness*) I thank you; you have taught me to see. Do you realize that you have also defended the man who has run off with your wife?

THOMAS: Yes. I know that. And I still mean it. You demand ideals; but also, that one doesn't make any extreme use of them. You allow the widow to marry again, but declare love to be endless, so that the remarriage is successful only *after* death. You believe in "the struggle of life,"[59] but you ameliorate it with the commandment: Love Thy Neighbor. You believe in brotherly love, but ameliorate it with the "struggle of life." You apply the law *unconditionally*, but pardon afterwards. You are for property and beneficence. You explain that man must die for the loftiest things, because you make sure beforehand that no one would live for them for even an hour —

JOSEF: (*Interrupting him*) In other words, you're trying to say that I demand too much; ultimately, that I was too rigorous. Or the opposite: that I am nothing but a common compromiser?

---

59. This phrase in English in the original.

THOMAS: I merely mean to say, what no one denies, that you are a capable human being, who needs to establish a solid foundation! I don't mean to say anything else. You walk above a stretched-out safety net; but there are people who are drawn to look down by the holes in between.

JOSEF: I thank you; now I realize who you are. You are someone who has become sick by association with sick people.

THOMAS: I believe that one must fight against people like you for the right to be sick once in a while and to see the world sideways.

JOSEF: (*Approaching him*) Do you believe that someone with such perspectives has merited the right to have students and to be allowed to profess at a university?

THOMAS: I couldn't care less about that either. Do you understand: I — couldn't — care — less. What I want is to preserve the feeling of walking through an unknown city, where enormous possibilities stretch out before me.

JOSEF: So, in this regard you are in agreement with our exiled associate professor?

THOMAS: (*Yelling at him*) I find him ridiculous!! ... I only defend him against *you*.

JOSEF: Thomas, you are still very confused! You have labored 10 years on your scholarly work; and I must say, very capably. You are speaking irresponsibly; yet I feel responsible for you.

THOMAS: Look around you! Our colleagues fly off, drill through mountains, dive under water, don't flinch from any of the many innovations in their fields. Everything that they have done for centuries is a bold analogy for a stupendously adventurous new humanity. That never arrives. Because, immersed in all your activities, you have long ago forgotten the soul. And if you want to have soul, you lose your reason the way a student takes off his school colors before he goes whoring.

JOSEF: This is insufficiently earnest! Do what you want! Yes, your poor father, on his deathbed, entrusted me with the care of your siblings and cousins, but God is my witness, I can no longer be involved in this. I don't want to have anything more to do with you people. Nothing! (*Angrily exits. Thomas laughs behind him. Regina softly opens the door.*)

REGINA: I was eavesdropping.

THOMAS: (*Playfully*) You shall no longer do such things, Regina.

REGINA: (*Brushing off her skirt*) What does it matter if I end up doing that also? Oh, I wanted to try once more; but (*saying it the way one speaks of an evil omen*) I was ashamed.

THOMAS: Little Regina, little dreamerine, you may not do that; it is not done. You are now a noble, grown-up, earnestly striving human being. Did you know? Maria has left. Don't cry! Naturally: Anselm!

REGINA: (*Fighting back her tears*) Not because of Anselm, not because of Anselm! Maria can have him! He was never even congenial to me; he was always somewhat strange; his scurrying legs, his sniffling nose. I never had the basic physical sympathy with him that I have had — as long as I can remember — with you…. But I felt that my life would improve; he was so interested in me; he discovers something in everyone; nothing was allowed to just happen casually anymore….

THOMAS: Oh? And the foolishness with Johannes?

REGINA: Thomas, Johannes lived for me, only for me! He recognized no other goal or life purpose besides me! I was never so crazy as to forget what had been; to forget reality. But that this being no longer existed in the world; I revolted against that. It was a flight into irreality, well and good — (*She reflects and repeats it without the disapproval in tone.*) a flight into irreality; Anselm used to say that too…. Into the not-yet-reality, on the mountain top. There is something in us that's not at home among these people: do we know what it is? But he just didn't have the courage for it! … I suddenly became utterly stupefied and chaste when I realized that it was about something else. It was no longer a simple dreamy matter of luring a person behind the four paper walls of fantasy. His ideas resisted this. For the first time, it was not this meaningless direct woman's way, from the eyes to the place beneath the heart; I understood: strong human beings are pure. And even if you laugh at me: I always wanted to be strong like a giant, the kind that people still tell tales about generations later! And anyone can do it; anyone can be packed up inside himself, as in a small suitcase. But he did not have the courage! He saved himself! Thomas! What he is doing with Maria: that is a cowardly flight — *into reality*!

THOMAS: It won't be that simple with Maria either, you'll see.

REGINA: (*Preparing herself tea*) Before I came to the door, I walked once more all around the house. The old nurseries, the attic rooms, all the sites of our fantasy. I was even in the place where Johannes killed himself. (*She shrugs her shoulders with the expression: it was nothing.*) Everything was almost exactly the same as it was before. The servants were waking up behind their doors; a bit later they waited in their rooms for someone to ring. Everything was cleaned up and wound up. Ready to start purring, as on all of the fifty times three-hundred and sixty-five days that are gone. Including the days when I was not here, when I was unhappy, when, in a strange house, I bit the bedsheets and cried into them.

THOMAS: The house grows more and more empty. Anselm is gone. Maria is gone; I bet Josef will take the next train.

REGINA: Oh, I should like so much to prostrate myself one more time on the earth, between the carpet's flowers. Look at me just like that — hold me back with your evil sober eyes, so that I don't do it!

THOMAS: We used to sometimes walk on large flowers like this — following the ornaments. They were not this large, but wildly tangled together.

REGINA: The flowers grow immeasurably when one lies upon the earth. The chair legs stand stiffly, and absurdly planted in their places, like flowers without crowns. That is the world. The vast world.

THOMAS: We once sat in a closet — do you remember? — Hidden.

REGINA: (*Walking carefully along a pair of large curves of the carpet pattern, back and forth, sometimes stepping from the one to the other.*) It is so uncanny. I can move myself all around but I really can't move myself all around. At night, when I am awake, I would never have the courage to get up and walk upright through my room. Even when I take my hand out and lay it under my head, I have to quickly remove it again. It's so uncanny that it just lays there in the strange world, without my seeing it. It's no longer my hand; I have to pull it quickly back under the covers so it can heal back on to me.

THOMAS: (*Continuing his thought*) We sat in a closet and our jugulars pulsed with excitement. (*He interrupts himself.*) But nonsense, we are no longer children. (*Pointing to the patterns Regina has been walking on*) One never escapes from what has been predetermined. Sometimes I feel as though everything was already decided in childhood. Climbing, one always comes back to the same place, circling over the emptiness around a predetermined outline. It's like a spiral staircase.

REGINA: (*With half playful, half real horror, pointing at the rising staircase*) That's it! I don't want to see it! (*She takes refuge on the divan.*)

THOMAS: (*Himself frightened*) How easily you are frightened! (*He sits down with brotherly casualness next to her.*) Last night I dreamt; of you. We sat together in a closet —

REGINA: But how your heart is beating. Through your jacket.

THOMAS: But isn't this room like a closet? Isn't this whole empty house like a cleaned-out closet? Thus, we are turned back around again.

REGINA: (*Straightens up halfway, gripped by a frightening thought.*) What will we do now?!

THOMAS: Nothing, Regina. The gilded nuts never hang on the real tree. We only search for them there; which is remarkable enough. Every year, once in a while,

I may perhaps have secretly wished that Maria would leave. For a letting go, a soft wandering into the distance, a musical accompaniment for a procession that had not yet begun. The way *you* are. It probably really looks something like stars, swinging at the tips of long staffs; sleeping leaves, through which light, like hands, moves. But maybe it's lovely to think of such things.

REGINA: And isn't it jarring to walk through a night like that? Virtuous Thomas! (*She lays down again.*)

THOMAS: No, meaningless, both ways are meaningless! So aimless, so pointless, the whole thing!

REGINA: Wait. I can't even imagine how I was then. I lay under a bush and put a beetle into my mouth. It played dead. And I counted my pulse. And I said to myself that at a certain number he would emerge from my magical, illuminated mouth as a small prince. Yes, that was certainly magic. To swallow a piece of the world. Then I spit the thing out, when the number was past; but the next time I thought the same thing again; because I had a mysterious feeling about myself. That's how I lived. For a long time. Then everything got more and more common. Yes. More and more pointless. Ever more meaningless.

THOMAS: Don't you think that a smell of fish wafts in here from the surrounding fields? An indecent smell. (*He stands behind her head.*) And if I look at you, upside down like this, you are like a plastic playing card, a gruesome object, not a woman.

REGINA: But at night you dreamt we sat in a closet?

THOMAS: You were older than you are, as old as Maria, and at the same time you looked like you did 15 years ago. You were screaming, like yesterday, but it was soft and beautiful. We sat there altogether calmly. Your leg lay upon mine like a boat on a pier; then again like the sweet, coruscating back and forth streaming of the wind in the tree tops. It was happiness.

REGINA: But how is that done?

THOMAS: *Done?* I don't know. By slicing each other up in despair and rolling around in the strange innards like a dog on a carcass?

REGINA: *This* end was predetermined! We don't know what we should do! We will always stand behind this wall! I can't bear it anymore!

THOMAS: (*Holds her head firmly and kisses her*) You I can kiss, my depraved sister. Our four lips are four worms, nothing else!

REGINA: I would like to surround you with the softest parts of my body. The way it surrounds me. Because I have always loved you. Like myself. But not more. Not more.

THOMAS: Ah ... once this kiss stood far and alluring before me. Now it's just as far behind me, burning. We never emerged from it. Never. Never. You feel that!

(*Miss Mertens has entered and has seen. She wants to retreat, shocked, but the two of them notice her.*)

MISS MERTENS: Oh, Regina, you have consoled yourself quickly; I wanted to leave without saying a word. This house is ruled by a point of view that is incomprehensible to me.

(*Regina and Thomas burst into a somewhat forced laugh.*)

THOMAS: Understand, that was no love scene that you just witnessed. It was an anti-love scene. It was what one might call a despair scene.

MISS MERTENS: I do not presume to judge.

THOMAS: What were we in despair about, Regina?

REGINA: (*Still in the same tone*) We were in despair over the fact that nothing remained for us but to behave once more like school children. (*Falling out of the role*) Mertens! Listen! Don't leave me all alone! I need someone to hold my head. Thomas would sit sadly beside me when I was dying and just tell me that it was an interruption. He would demand that I, as a dying person, help him to express why this moment is nothing but a lackluster physical catastrophe, while fear and sorrow gleam so magically on either side of it.

THOMAS: But don't be silly.

MISS MERTENS: I will leave this evening. I will spend the rest of this day outside of the house. Please don't joke with me even as we part for good; you are no longer thinking of dying.

REGINA: But Mertens: Haven't I always thought about it?

MISS MERTENS: I don't know what you were thinking when you pretended to me that your faith was so splendid that it could not be satisfied within the narrow confines of reality. I suffered under an illusion. Because I, too, once lost my beloved; but I have been purely faithful to him to this day, for 21 years. (*Exits.*)

THOMAS: There you have it! Sin is filth. But virtue is also only enjoyable when fresh!

REGINA: Now she will really leave. Maria, Josef, Mertens — order recedes, like gums from teeth in a case of scurvy; soon they will fall out.

THOMAS: Why do you let yourself be oppressed! Especially by a person like that. (*They sit crouched over, far from each other, and cannot continue their endeavor.*)

REGINA: (*Defiantly*) Because I don't know what I should do. Don't you understand? I have always had something I was *supposed* to do. Now I no longer know. Come! No, stay! The mystery: I, among all of this — is at an end.

THOMAS: Nothing maintains its luminosity up close or under loveless scrutiny; a little glow worm: if you catch one, it's a lightless little gray sausage! But to know that gives one an even more bedeviled feeling than to poetically prattle: Little lantern of God!

REGINA: Thoughts hold little charm for me.

THOMAS: Perhaps you are right. There is little one can say against that... but then I can't help you.

REGINA: ... When I left you, after Johannes, I still had courage. Some sort of courage. Expectation; I called it — naturally dishonestly — mourning.

THOMAS: Naturally, it was hunger.

REGINA: Yes, courage. But what came instead was an endless swell of empty hours. I simply don't understand how other people manage to fill them so well.

THOMAS: They swindle, of course. They have a career, a goal, a character, acquaintances, manners, principles, clothes. Mutual insurance against a collapse into the million-meter depth of space.

REGINA: But everything that happens is only half serious; half game! One invokes the most horrible thing of all, and it comes quite casually into being, without terror or tension. Because there happens to be or not be a telephone nearby, out of boredom, out of the pointlessness of resisting. Because all of life just continues on by itself and without you, without guilt or innocence, once one has begun it.

THOMAS: (*Goes to her and looks at her irresolutely*) Out of a thousand causes; that all can be investigated by a detective or a connoisseur of humankind; but not out of the one, the deepest cause: out of yourself.

REGINA: (*Defensively*) We can't begin again. (*She moves farther away from him.*) People believe that they own you; your whole being offers itself up to them, while, inside of this puppet who is insanely repeating the same lines over and over, you are not even there.

At one time it was lovely: mystery, magic, a formula for insane strength. Somehow good and grand.

THOMAS: But in fact, just: the beginning of the illusion that every young person has about himself, that morning mood. One can do whatever one wants, and everything returns back to one like a boomerang thrown into the air.

REGINA: One enjoys perfuming oneself eccentrically and eating complicated delicate dishes. And one day one catches oneself, and finds that one only ever drinks tea, eats bonbons, and smokes cigarettes. One feels swept up into a plan that had been made at the very beginning, and one is locked in. The predetermined calculation takes one over, what everyone knows; sleep at specific times, meals at specific hours, the rhythm of digestion that follows the sun around the earth....

THOMAS: And in summer the fertilizations increase and in autumn, the suicides.

REGINA: It drags you in! And the men will continue to come to me like something incomprehensibly groveling; like centipedes, like worms; you don't see any difference and yet you feel as if the life in each one is different …!

THOMAS: (*As if he were seeing a vision, looks through the window into the distance*) Soon Maria will be standing far away with Anselm, in a strange landscape. The sun will shine on the grass and the bushes like it does here, the thickets will mist over, and all the flying creatures of the air will rejoice. Perhaps Anselm will lie, but in that far off landscape I cannot know what he is saying ….

REGINA: Are you unhappy?

THOMAS: Every conflict is only significant in a specific atmosphere; the way I see this one in this far off landscape, it's all over. It cannot be brought into harmony, Regina; all final things cannot be brought into harmony with ourselves. Only he who does not need that may be well.

REGINA: Help me, Thomas, advise me, if you can.

THOMAS: How should I help you? One must simply have the strength to love these contradictions.

REGINA: But what will you *do*?

THOMAS: I don't know. Now I think one thing, but perhaps later I will think something else. I would like to just go on ….

REGINA: Go away with me! Let's do something! Anything at all! Please help me! Otherwise my old will is going to turn into a pulp of disgust!

THOMAS: But Regina. The world seems almost physically wider, if one side of it has always — up to that moment — been obstructed by the proximity of another person. All of a sudden one stands there astonished in a wide half circle. Alone.

REGINA: To stay the way I am, I cannot! And to change? How then?! Like Maria?!

THOMAS: You just wander around. Everyone who goes their determined way is dangerous for you, as long as you stay on the uncertain mendicant's path through the world. Nevertheless, you belong to them in some way. Don't say too much, when they look at you sternly; silence; one hides oneself under one's skin.

REGINA: (*Suddenly turning to leave*) You have, then, left me with only one alternative! The one I did not mention to you before!

THOMAS: Exaggerations! I specifically asked you for no more of those. In these last days I sometimes thought about it. But if one could stand afterwards besides one's own corpse, one would be ashamed of such premature haste. Because the mosquitoes will sting one indiscriminately on these beautiful summer days and one will be gripped just as much by a horror at the thought of infinity as by a need to scratch oneself.

REGINA: (*Laughing*) Thomas, Thomas, you are an unfeeling man of reason.

THOMAS: No, no, Regina, if anyone is at all, then I am ... a dreamer. And you are a dreamer. People like us just appear to be unfeeling. We wander, watch what the people who feel at home in the world do. And carry something inside ourselves that we do not sense. A sinking down through everything into bottomlessness at every moment. Without going under. The condition of creation. (*Regina kisses him quickly and rushes outside, before he can grab her.*)

THOMAS: But, Regina!.... No, no, she won't do anything foolish. (*He stands up anyway and follows her.*)

CURTAIN

VINZENZ AND THE MISTRESS OF IMPORTANT MEN

A Farce in Three Acts (1924)

DRAMATIS PERSONÆ

ALPHA

BÄRLI (A rich businessman)

THE SCHOLAR

THE MUSICIAN

THE POLITICIAN

THE REFORMER

THE YOUNG FRIEND

THE GIRLFRIEND

DR. APULEJUS-HALM

VINZENZ

ACT ONE

A room at night. Partially and weakly illuminated by a streetlight. A second room, like an alcove, slightly raised and separated by a half pulled-back curtain, where a lantern burns very dimly. An ottoman and some indistinct dark objects can just be made out in the front room. About three in the morning. Alpha and Bärli enter from the side. Both in evening dress and opera cloaks. Alpha turns on the lamp of a vanity table in the foreground; with a screen standing alongside it, so that only a small surrounding area is illuminated. Bärli stands beside her.

BÄRLI: This can only have one end!

ALPHA: Tell me, why can it only have one end? Look at this brush; it has two ends. No, it has as many ends as it has hairs. Count its ends. I would like to know, once and for all, where people get such certainties!

BÄRLI: You must marry me!

ALPHA: Your mind has less fantasy in this regard than my hairbrush.

BÄRLI: My mind is completely without fantasy in this regard. But I have seen men get down on their knees before me, begging for mercy for their business and their family —

ALPHA: And — ?

BÄRLI: And I have never granted it to them.

ALPHA: I think that's something I like about you.

BÄRLI: I have had women shown out, who pleaded for their husbands —

ALPHA: Were they proud women?

BÄRLI: Yes, there may have been beautiful women among them, even crying mothers.

ALPHA: I think I really do like that about you. I'm the same way. A crying mother wouldn't move me either.

BÄRLI: I dare say, I am, with my business dealings, an economic factor in this nation. And more than once, I have wagered all of this power on one card, only to throw it into the air and win it again. In this regard, I have fantasy, Alpha, a sufficiently wild fantasy!

ALPHA: And?

BÄRLI: (*Despairingly*) But why, why do I do it?! Alpha, it has no meaning for me anymore! I have produced, just to produce. You sense that I have something more to offer than these gossiping cripples who surround you: I can do what I want. But what do I want, for God's sake? What in the world do I want?!! You have made me unsure about this; you must marry me.

ALPHA: As I have said already, my hairbrush has more fantasy.

(*Bärli makes a desperate gesture.*)

ALPHA: Well?

BÄRLI: Don't think that I will put up with such resistance from a woman.

ALPHA: But what are you going to do?

BÄRLI: I will kill you and myself!

ALPHA: Kill — ?

BÄRLI: Yes.

ALPHA: You adore me that much?

BÄRLI: I only see these two possibilities: either you marry me or I kill us.

ALPHA: Say that more beautifully.

BÄRLI: How?

ALPHA: Wouldn't you rather say: "United, either in life or in death"?

BÄRLI: Don't mock me!

ALPHA: (*Standing up*) But this is really tasteless. Your association with business and your lack of literary culture have given you the feelings of a serialized romance novel!

(*Bärli attacks her. The little lamp goes out. Brief shadowy struggle. Alpha falls. Bärli binds her hands and feet with a rope, which he pulls from his coat, and carries her to the illuminated ottoman in the alcove.*)

ALPHA: Oh! Oh! You are shameless. You are so terribly shameless! And old!

BÄRLI: Will you marry me, Madame?!

ALPHA: No!

BÄRLI: Marry me, Alpha?!

ALPHA: It's shameless of you to get so familiar, just because you are pretending to think about death. Ooooh! (*She sticks her tongue out at him.*) With this farce, you have forfeited everything! (*She turns around, with her back to him.*)

BÄRLI: I only pretended to send my car away. It is waiting downstairs. There is enough gas for three days. Write a letter to our friends, with some excuse or other, about why we have to depart to suddenly, and we will flee to my estate in the mountains.

ALPHA: (*Looking over her shoulder*) Why do I have to write a letter to do this?

BÄRLI: It's the way I thought it up.

ALPHA: And then?

BÄRLI: I have arranged for a minister, so we can get married immediately. I am abducting you. I am stealing you away for my own!

ALPHA: And then? You can't possibly abduct me all your life, or incessantly steal me away for your own: what will happen next?

(*Pause*)

BÄRLI: (*Somewhat meekly*) We will be wordlessly happy.

ALPHA: Wordlessly?

BÄRLI: Certainly! We will be wordlessly happy!

ALPHA: You have thought this out imprecisely. Again, you are at a loss for words.

BÄRLI: Yes, Alpha, I lack the words. I have always lacked the words when I wanted something. That's why I just take it for myself! That is why I don't speak like the others, but just take! I will treat you with such respect! I will remove every stone from your path. I will worship you. We will love each other. You will have all my riches at your disposal. I will not bother about them at all —

ALPHA: Now that's the first thing you've said so far that wasn't banal.

BÄRLI: To possess something, which you do not possess, no — obsess over — this is the way I am — has no meaning for me anymore —. I have accumulated a lump of clay. My possessions mock me. (*Both fists pressed against his temples*) Ever since you said I was an idiot, I have begun to think about myself for the first time. Even though you say it gently, it doesn't matter; what matters is that I have begun to think about myself. And I can't think about myself! I never learned how to. Or I have forgotten. That is why I live helplessly — like an animal.

But if I could hand the world to you, piece by piece, I think I could create the whole thing all over again!

ALPHA: You are actually quite nice when you talk like this. You seem important.

BÄRLI: Shall I untie you?

ALPHA: No, not yet. (*Pause*) Kiss me! (*Wild embracing until Alpha loses her breath.*)

ALPHA: (*Reflecting*) But you still haven't told me what will happen afterwards. I can't possibly sit in your castle forever, like a stone in a ring?

BÄRLI: I can't even live without your sharp little tongue anymore. I feel as if you were melting me like a pointing, thrusting flame melts a block of iron. You torment me. I am making myself ridiculous; I run about, bumping into things — which I only just noticed were there.

ALPHA: That is certainly true, but I wouldn't be able to look into a mirror after a while without seeing you there next to my image.

BÄRLI: I am going to carry you down now. I'll untie the rope in the car.

ALPHA: No, it won't work; don't do anything stupid, Bärli. Today is my name day, the others will be here soon.

BÄRLI: (*Wildly*) They don't deserve you!

ALPHA: Why not?

BÄRLI: I can't say exactly why not! Enough! I'm going to carry you off now.

ALPHA: (*Defending herself*) No! I don't want to go! I will scream! I will scream so loud that everyone in the house will come running! (*She knocks over a vase and water flows out. Bärli becomes momentarily sober and lets go. His voice changes.*)

BÄRLI: Okay. You disdain me. I am in no mood to humiliate myself further in front of you. So, now the other thing must happen.

ALPHA: What?

BÄRLI: Do you have any last wishes to dictate to me?

ALPHA: (*Nervously*) Why are you looking at me so earnestly?

BÄRLI: (*Pulling a pistol out of his pocket*) Because I am going to shoot you now. You can be sure that I will kill myself right after I kill you.

ALPHA: (*Trying to strike an attitude of superiority*) If you were a cavalier, you would know that you must kill yourself first. (*Then, overcome by fear*) Put it away! ....

BÄRLI: (*Laughing and shaking his head sadly*) No, Alpha, I am not joking; now I am going to take you with me. (*He looks at her and raises the pistol slowly.*)

ALPHA: (*Screaming*) Help!

BÄRLI: It's no use.

ALPHA: Vinzenz!! …. Help! …. Vinzenz! Vinzenz!!

(*The unexpected and never-before-heard name makes Bärli put the pistol down. He looks around, looks at Alpha inquisitively, and notices that someone else is in the room.*)

BÄRLI: What is the meaning of this?

(*He takes a few steps in the dark and turns on the lights. Discovered behind a distant chair, Vinzenz — tall and thin — rises. He is a man in his late 30's, not without elegance, but clothed modestly. He laughs nervously.*)

ALPHA: (*Turning toward him*) Coward! Betrayer! Coward!

BÄRLI: (*Angrily, threatening with the pistol*) What are you doing here??

VINZENZ: (*He lifts his arms, half in defense, half in a 'hands-up' gesture. Quickly*) Dear friend, dear friend! I didn't want to increase the catastrophe. You probably would have shot me right off. But I only got here an hour ago. I have nothing to do with this business.

ALPHA: He's my childhood friend.

VINZENZ: Alpha wanted to speak with me alone.

BÄRLI: (*Looking at him disdainfully*) Him?… !

ALPHA: Yes. Shoot him down! The little coward wouldn't have moved!

VINZENZ: I believe that the mood has been spoiled for the time being, or else I would gladly retreat again, if you would rather ...?

BÄRLI: (*Again*) Him! .... (*He throws the pistol onto the table.*) You have no cause to fear.

VINZENZ: (*To them both*) I was, of course, too little informed about your private affairs to have allowed myself to interrupt such a moment. — By the way, you wouldn't have anything against me loosening Alpha's shackles now, would you? (*He does it.*)

ALPHA: (*Emphasizing every word calmly and matter-of-factly, while she allows Vinzenz to massage the parts of her body that were chafed by the rope*) Coward! Betrayer! Egoist!

VINZENZ: (*Carefully massaging*) You could just as well have demanded of me that I should have jumped onto a train traveling at full speed.

ALPHA: (*Standing up and walking toward Bärli*) We are through! (*Bärli nods absentmindedly.*) I am going to rest for a while; I can no longer bear your presence; go! Go, the both of you!

BÄRLI: (*Bolting the pistol and putting it away*) Go and rest, Alpha, but allow me to sit here quietly and write a few farewell letters while you sleep next door.

ALPHA: Vinzenz! Show the gentleman out! And go with him!

VINZENZ: No, Alpha, how can I do that? I am on this gentleman's side here. You must give him time. Can't you just close the curtain while he orders his thoughts a bit?

ALPHA: (*Extending her hand to Bärli*) I liked you very much! But you will leave in an hour, and after I have awoken, I will never — see — you — again. (*She goes behind the curtain, which she pulls closed. Sticking her head out once more.*) Vinzenz! Send the guests away! (*Movements of undressing, then her head comes out once more*) No, the gentlemen can wait. But I will not be woken. (*Once more, the same*) You two gentlemen can talk without concern; it comforts me to hear your voices. (*Exits.*)

VINZENZ: Have you bolted your pistol? (*Bärli checks.*) Would you have anything against it, if I put it in this iron case here for safety's sake?

BÄRLI: (*Giving it to him*) Keep the cowardly thing. It mutinied at the shooting of an "innocent" bystander, when you unexpectedly appeared. That was weak. I will never use *this* pistol again! Something like this can only happen in one rush.

VINZENZ: I understand and honor your position.

BÄRLI: You heard everything. I have exposed myself as ridiculous in front of you! Who are you, really? (*They sit down.*)

VINZENZ: In what sense do you mean?

BÄRLI: That's not something you can answer right off? I was — before the cursed day when I met this person — a businessman; from front to back. I made my way to the top like a butcher. It was not always appetizing. I reached right in up to my shoulders and that's something at least! Then she spoke to me suddenly — but how long have you known Alpha?

VINZENZ: Maybe sixteen years.... She was seventeen then.

BÄRLI: And you still love her?

VINZENZ: God forbid!

BÄRLI: God forbid? Another point of view. — But why have you come at such an unconventional hour, if you don't love her?

VINZENZ: The hour? Unconventional?

BÄRLI: It's not uncommon? Three o' clock in the morning? A time when one sometimes works, usually sleeps, or at least roams around with someone? Hmm.... What line of work are you in?

VINZENZ: Word-maker.

BÄRLI: What — ? A writer?

VINZENZ: No; less. Word-maker, Name-maker. May we discuss this later. I hate to interrupt your story.

BÄRLI: You will not presume to think, sir — ?! Do not presume to think, because I am talking with you in this way?! I'm waiting for the train to depart! So, one talks. One is accessible. Because there is no reason not to use these last torn-out quarter hours.

VINZENZ: I am here. — One locks up — do you know how it is? — And then one turns toward the stairwell, to check if one has really locked up; and one turns once more?.... Call it pedantry, if you will. I wanted to end a conversation left unfinished ten years ago; I had to wait an hour before you came. And now I don't even know when I will get to my conversation.

BÄRLI: You will get there no more. I too had just this one hour after the ball. A visitor will soon come, and with every half hour, another. By the gray of the morning, you will see a society of five gentlemen gathered here, five choice fops, who imagine God knows what, just because they can come at this hour on Alpha's name day. If you have known Alpha so long, she will surely have said to you once, too: you are doing it all wrong.

(*Vinzenz taps him softly on the knee, laughing.*)

BÄRLI: What?

VINZENZ: Colibri!

BÄRLI: What?

VINZENZ: Later! Continue! Don't let yourself be interrupted!

BÄRLI: She will already have said it to you, then. She says it to everyone, mark me well. And so, she tells me:

you are doing it wrong. Fundamentally, neither your activities, nor your successes satisfy you. Yes, she says: that which you are proud of, that which you have given your life up for, is stupid. But I am made of a different wood than these other customers. I see through it. Yet, I notice immediately: she is right. She is right!

VINZENZ: (*To himself*) Colibri.

BÄRLI: You see, one doesn't think about it. If one isn't a common thief — but a man with something to do — he has no interest in philosophy. But one needs philosophy and all that; it can't be denied; just as one needed religion in the old days. And when Alpha says: three o'clock in the morning and not like man and wife (but, of course, a little like man and wife), you understand. When she twists life around in this way, and then you talk with her about your life —. Have you ever looked through your legs? Like this, with your head upside down? That's exactly the way it is! Everything looks totally different and like new! You realize, for the first time, that you are alive; or that you have not lived!

VINZENZ: Colibri!

BÄRLI: But what the devil do you mean with your "Colibri"?

VINZENZ: Roasted words.

BÄRLI: But sir, you are speaking nonsense!

VINZENZ: True, but life fits it all together. Alpha speaks roasted words. I must give you some advice, some advice! Colibri, they are the torrid-colored words that fly around the flaming sun of ancient forests.

BÄRLI: Wha — ?

VINZENZ: It's false, but it sounds wonderful. The literal congruity of the incongruous.

BÄRLI: Sir?!

VINZENZ: One can blend incongruent fragments together, with worlds alone, in such a way that no one notices it.

BÄRLI: (*Standing up*) I became a businessman. I don't know how. I would have had to have been especially dumb not to do good business, and I did better business than others, because I am a powerful man. Don't underestimate that: you can do more with money than you can imagine. Almost everything. Any woman would take me gladly. I won't stand for this.

VINZENZ: But sir, yes! I find you so congenial! Let me give you some advice!

BÄRLI: I don't need your advice. The idiots who are coming will laugh because Alpha will have the impudence to make me ridiculous in front of them. Me! Who has more power in one finger than they have in all their bones! I must teach them a lesson. That's it!

(The doorbell rings; they are startled.)

BÄRLI: *(Bad-tempered)* Will you have the kindness to go see who is there?

VINZENZ: But you have to talk with me more.

(While Vinzenz is in the front room, Bärli lifts the curtain, looks at Alpha thoughtfully, goes to the iron cabinet, but cannot open it.)

VINZENZ: *(Returning)* You are better acquainted with the customs of the house than I. This gentleman claims to be Alpha's husband and to be invited for this hour.

(Dr. Apulejus-Halm enters after him.)

BÄRLI: *(Haughtily)* I am shocked to see you.

HALM: *(Obligingly)* Frankly, I am shocked not to find Alpha in your company.

VINZENZ: *(Parodying the elegant tone)* Unfortunately, she felt herself somewhat put upon, and betook herself to rest. But she gave instructions to invite everyone to wait until all of the guests were assembled. *(He takes a large and beautiful bouquet from Halm and puts it in a vase.)*

HALM: She begged me urgently not to miss the celebration of her name day.

(Bärli takes the bouquet and throws it in a corner. Vinzenz picks it up, pats Bärli on the back solicitously, well-meaningly,

and puts the bouquet back in the vase. He offers chairs. He and Halm sit down. Pause.)

HALM: (*Hesitantly, to Vinzenz*) I am amazed to *see* you.

VINZENZ: Yes, it was many years ago; I didn't recognize you in the dark. You were cozier in those days; you looked fatter, so to speak. But we should make ourselves some coffee. (*He finds a samovar and lights it.*)

HALM: (*Preciously*) If the smell of sleeplessness will not wake the sleeper.

BÄRLI: Allow me to depart. I am not good company today. I am going to write my letters now. (*Exits into the adjoining room.*)

HALM: (*Changed*) Well? What happened?

VINZENZ: He wanted to shoot her dead on the spot if she wouldn't marry him; he was in such a hurry, that he didn't allow himself to sunder your marriage before cementing his.

HALM: His car has been downstairs for an hour now. Don't try to make a fool of me, my dear.

VINZENZ: I have nothing more to report. He is, by the way, a likeable man, don't you think? I don't want to have anything more to do with this business.

HALM: But the money I gave you for it, you took it without any scruples?!

VINZENZ: Shhh! Don't make a terrible pun like "unscrupulous." If you insult me again, I'll call in Mr. Bärli and he will doubtless break all your bones.

HALM: (*Hissing*) You are a scoundrel!

VINZENZ: Oh ho! If you say it just a little softer, it loses so much of its power.

HALM: Scoundrel!

VINZENZ: That time it sounded almost tender, as if you had said "Schnookums" to me. You know, of course, that lovers even whisper curses to each other while embracing; it has its own charm.

HALM: (*Meekly*) Why have you betrayed me.... ?! You could have gotten even more money from me .... (*Jealously*) Alpha gave you money, didn't she? She always had an unexplainable weakness for you.

VINZENZ: Listen, Doctor. I am about to see Alpha again after many years. You offer me money, if I use the meeting to provide you with grounds for an adultery claim, whether it be from my own activities or through observation of another's in case that honorable man brings Alpha home. You have made a mistake about me. I didn't take your money —.

HALM: But what in the world are you talking about?!

VINZENZ: I didn't take your money. I let it be given to me. That makes a huge difference. I had found, so far, no reason to return it. And one must learn, as a human, how to receive. Besides, I had the choice, up until the last moment, whether I would abuse your trust or Alpha's, and that was extremely pleasurable to me, because it assured me a certain independence; you know, of course, that I have a slight weakness for Alpha. But why are you, after so many years of marriage, behaving so wretchedly?

HALM: I must tell you; I will tell you: now that it has backfired again. I can't stand it anymore, letting it eat me up inside. I am so unhappy…! (*He is a weak man and cries, drying his little goat beard.*) I don't have much use for Alpha, as you know. I don't have much use for women altogether: they are made of too much fat and too many expectations. But Alpha was always just right for me in that regard, since she doesn't have much use for men and can't stand the great womanish brouhaha about love.

VINZENZ: Shh …! (*Warns him with a gesture not to disturb Alpha.*)

HALM: But she sleeps so soundly, once she has fallen asleep; there is something wonderfully boyish about her; we could be so very happy together. But then, as you know, I am an art critic —

VINZENZ: Didn't I advise you, in the old days, to occupy yourself more with art sales?

HALM: I can only hope that you never have so little need of advice as I had of yours. — I bought what I could critically support, and I critically supported what I bought. My riches increased in harmony with my theories. I have not become the nothing that you once were so happy to think me.

VINZENZ: God! It was probably little more than a certain rivalry. One can't help but be a little unjust toward the spouses of those one believes love one. (*He serves the coffee.*)

HALM: You see, that's it! Alpha is the vainest person in the world, and I make more of the men who love her than she does, but she must have them all. As long as she does not possess a man, she says charming things to him, because she plays like a child with the new words and distinctive perfume of his career. She has a collection of the choicest career fragrances. And these idiots are flattered! See, she speaks to the business buffoon about music, she asks the musician about the naval battle of Aboukir, and she reads the historian the stock exchange figures. She does the same with all of them; she caresses each one, on the one hand, with her thirst for knowledge, makes him feel that he is wholly unique, and, on the other hand, keeps him in bondage by condemning him for what he is not.

VINZENZ: She tells the scholars that they are not businessmen, the musicians, that they are not scholars, the businessmen that they are not musicians; in short, to all of them together and to each one, she says: you are not human? And each one suddenly realizes that his life is idiotic? Because life is idiotic.

HALM: I say deliberately: idiots! I am the only one who secretly creates this atmosphere of art, which these men of business, of facts, of science drink up like schnapps. I, the estranged art critic! I am the one who has invented all those unexpected, tender, and deep remarks about love and life, which all have something refreshingly chilly in their warmth. I provide the genuinely womanly charm of spirituality and those vague thoughts, which are so much more comprehensive than those thought by men. For years now, I have provided every innovation in exotic clothing and habit. Alpha doesn't have one thought of her own! So, I provide all the culture, all the fantasy, all the intoxicating thrills. I visit in this house, and these idiots! Do you think that one of them finds me charming? Indispensable? Important? Does one of them even recognize my merit?

With connections to these people, I could be one of the most respected men of my time; but the only thing that matters is packaging; in the world, just as in love! Do you understand now that I suffer with this woman?! I am a thinking man; I can back up what I say with the authors whom I read, but Alpha just gets it from me, chirps it back out, and the presentation, with a bosom and a broader seat, and so on, guarantees the reception.

And what's more — this is the worst part — she charms because of her masculinity, which is hidden behind her boyish womanliness; but I am, nevertheless, still a bit more masculine than she is, and I have to watch my real merit recede behind this watering-down and fatty degeneration! It makes me doubt the value of the world and it is simply unbearable to live with her!

Now do you understand that I want to get my revenge at long last? If I am the procurer, then I will sell her at least. That buffoon in there wants to marry her, like all of them. But he is the only one whom she might marry, because he has an enormous amount of money. He will pay me for her. He will restore my losses! At the least, he should recognize my achievements!

VINZENZ: And you are perhaps of the opinion that such blackmail is the easiest living in the world? You would have no more money troubles?

HALM: I don't know whether or not I think that. Perhaps I do think that, too. I am defenseless against peripheral thoughts.

VINZENZ: They are also quite immaterial compared to the deeper implications. (*The doorbell rings somewhat violently.*) That must be the suitors. You open up; you are better acquainted with the customs of the house than I. (*Halm goes to open up. In the meantime, Vinzenz goes, with a cup of coffee, to see Bärli. Halm returns with the visitors.*)

HALM: (*Walking backwards, directing the way through the dark of the front room*) Shhh...! Let's set up the party table here. (*He sets a table straight. The gentlemen turn about each other politely with "after you's."*)

THE POLITICIAN: The lock down there must be broken. I couldn't open it. But oh, my gentlemen, otherwise I would have been sitting here a long time before you, as the oldest and most trusted friend! (*He holds up a set of keys.*)

THE YOUNG MAN: What? The lock? It must be your key; mine opened without resistance. (*He shows off his key.*)

THE POLITICIAN: Wha — ? How? How did you get a key? (*He turns it, looks at it from all sides to check its authenticity.*)

THE YOUNG MAN: (*To a third person*) What, you don't have one?

THE POLITICIAN: (*To the young man*) But how do you deserve? What have you accomplished in life? Young man, what right do you have to this key?

THE YOUNG MAN: But dear sirs — I am new — I didn't realize — you all stood in front of the door — I introduced myself to you all on the stairs, didn't I — — — ? (*In the meantime, all of them have taken their keys out and are comparing them with each other's. One wears his on a chain around his neck; another one keeps his in his pants pocket; a third one in a case.*)

THE MUSICIAN: (*To The Politician*) You were already at the door when I came — I didn't know that you had a key — — —

THE SCHOLAR: (*To them both*) I saw the two gentlemen standing there — it wasn't my day — — —

THE REFORMER: Yes, if only I had known; but you all stood freezing outside the door when I arrived — — — !

THE POLITICIAN: My key didn't work just now!

ALL: And we didn't know — !

THE YOUNG MAN: And I didn't think anything of it. I was the last to arrive and I opened the door. I was given a key for this purpose the day before.

THE POLITICIAN: What? *You* unlocked it?

THE YOUNG MAN: Yes, who else?

ALL: It was just opened all of a sudden, I thought — — — . Did you think anything? — — — No, it seemed totally natural — — afterall, I didn't even think about it; I thought, after all, that I had opened it myself! (*One to the other*) But tell me, how long have you had a key?

HALM: (*Entering, protesting about the noise*) But gentlemen, you are going to wake Alpha up before we are ready! What does it matter, anyway?! Everyone likes to talk once in a while in a magical tête-à-tête, and that is why we have a key, otherwise the people in the house would talk.

THE MUSICIAN: (*To himself*) But there must be some sort of misunderstanding. (*Separates himself.*)

THE POLITICIAN: (*To Halm*) Well, at least you don't have a key?!

THE YOUNG MAN: I don't believe I know this gentleman. My name is Marek —

HALM: (*Condescendingly*) Apulejus-Halm.

THE POLITICIAN: He doesn't belong in our circle; he is the husband, ho, ho….

HALM: Shhh! Shhh! Don't make so much noise….

THE POLITICIAN: But seriously, he isn't his wife's friend. She finds it unpleasant, even just to be reminded of him. They live separately. Really, why have you come today, of all days?

HALM: It is not so bad as you make it out to be, Herr Councilman.

(*Trying to distract them*) Look! (*He points to The Musician, who has just opened up a musical score on the party table and is about to write something in it with a pencil.*)

THE POLITICIAN: I always find a musician to be somewhat ridiculous.

THE SCHOLAR: Truly, an unreal existence.

ALL: Now, really, can you understand how anyone could be a musician?

THE MUSICIAN: (*In the meantime, alone, oblivious*) Fundamentally, the world is music. It is the highest. I thank you, Lord, that the others don't know that you have given the soul of your angel, Alpha, to me alone. (*He turns back, meeting The Scholar on his way to the table.*)

THE SCHOLAR: (*In passing*) Do you earnestly believe that you will make Alpha happy with a musical score?

THE MUSICIAN: (*Near the others*) Really, can you understand how someone could be a scholar?

THE SCHOLAR: (*Alone, oblivious*) I am not so tasteless as to compare myself to Beethoven. But provided I were Beethoven, how could I prove it without being an historian at the same time?! I thank you, Lord, that you have awoken in this woman a taste for objectivity, to strengthen my faith in my profession. (*Returning to The Reformer*) Oh, it's only Eschenmeyer's philosophy, which was recognized only because Herbart quoted it with the author's name in the second edition of his *Introduction to Philosophy*, even though he calls him "the most backward of many other backward imitators of Christian Wolff" in all other editions.

THE REFORMER: And this is The New World! (*The others tap themselves on their temples behind his back.*)

THE SCHOLAR: (*To the others*) Really, can you honestly understand — — — ?

THE MUSICIAN: (*To him*) But you cannot earnestly believe — ?

THE SCHOLAR: I ask you, can one really, with music alone — ?

THE MUSICIAN: A spiritual man!

THE SCHOLAR: What do you mean spiritual? Music is purely sensual!

THE REFORMER: (*Meanwhile*) I! Perhaps she! Besides us, no one!

HALM: (*Calming them down*) Shhhh! Shhhh! Now you are really going to wake Alpha too soon!

THE POLITICIAN: (*Interrupting the objection*) It's just the official state almanac, but there is nothing more instructive; Alpha has me explain it to her for hours. Therein lies reality! It's true, even in politics, we have our spiritual foundations, but — (*He throws the thick book on the table.*)

THE YOUNG MAN: If you don't mind me saying so, I believe Alpha is more interested in contemporary issues. She asked me for the engineers' handbook, *The Lodge*. I study engineering, you know. I intend to take over father's factories.

HALM: (*Interested*) Your Herr Papa has extensive factories?

THE YOUNG MAN: Oh, very!

THE POLITICIAN: Has anyone ever directed your attentions to the fact that, aside from these intellectual attentions, there are also some little hands-on attentions, attentions, ho-ho?

THE YOUNG MAN: I have also taken the liberty of bringing this Indian weaving.... (*He spreads out a shawl.*)

HALM: (*Enraptured*) Oh, how charming! It makes me feel just like one of the twelve hundred wives of the King of Burma. (*He puts on the shawl, in feminine fashion.*)

THE MUSICIAN: (*Enviously*) I brought this charming loincloth that a student brought from the Easter Islands.

HALM: Oh! Oh! How you spoil Alpha! (*He enthusiastically puts the loincloth on, too, in front of the mirror.*)

THE POLITICIAN: Unfortunately, I had too much to do — business for Alpha —

THE SCHOLAR: This golden bonnet is a copy of the cap Queen Anne of England wore in 1312, when —

HALM: (*Practically tearing it out of his hand*) Oh! How wonderful! How I look! — — — (*He has put it all on. To all*) How wonderful you are!

(*While Halm plays dress-up in front of the mirror, enraptured, and forgets that they are supposed to remain quiet, a light turns on behind the curtain. Now Alpha enters — in charming pajamas. She is looking amiably at the company, while reserving at the same time the possibility of feigning boredom, when she notices Halm and her presents.*)

ALPHA: (*Furiously*) What do you think you are doing? Look at yourself!

HALM: Darling, your friends couldn't bear to miss celebrating your name day together — (*Avoiding her eyes*) — this invented, this artificial name day, which suits you so well.

ALPHA: Leave that be, and leave us alone!

HALM: (*With a heightened defensiveness*) I thought — because I was the only one allowed to know your real name day —

ALPHA: (*Transforming her fury into grandeur*) Dear gentlemen, I had the name of a great queen. I was 15 years old and defenseless when my mother, neglectful of her duty, married me off, despite my resistance, to this man, who made devious promises to her. Since then, I have, of course, renounced not only his name, but my own beautiful given name, which innocently had become associated with his.

HALM: (*Extremely agitated*) But gentlemen, gentlemen! If you have any sense of justice: I am the one who came up with the name Alpha. She herself begged me to do so, because before, she — — —

ALPHA: He is suffering from delusions! Look at him! He is not normal; he's like an envious hussy! (*Everyone looks at Halm, who is now cowering in the corner.*)

ALPHA: Even if I can forgive him for marrying me, it is still an outrageous abuse to take this marriage seriously. Just because some state officials — whom I don't even know — pronounced him to be my husband once, he allows himself to come to me, without being invited, whenever he wishes! Free me from him! The very existence of such a man is simply unbearable!

(*Meanwhile, Bärli has stormed from the next room, looking wild, seemingly held back by Vinzenz. He stands still, with a look of shock, and stares at Alpha.*)

ALPHA: (*Altered*) Oh! ... I had a dream, before you gentlemen arrived. I was riding on top of a car, up front. Bärli had abducted me. He had tied me to the hood. We were driving away wildly. But — (*To Bärli*) — we never arrived ....

BÄRLI: (*Handing Vinzenz a check*) Here is the money. Arrange everything necessary. (*To Alpha*) Good luck to you, Alpha! That is, you will hear from me once more. But then it will be the last time that ... that .... (*To the others*) — And this band of clowns!!!

ALL: Outrageous! What was he thinking? What! The impudence!

THE YOUNG MAN: (*Who has caught Vinzenz's eye*) I have never met this gentleman, have I? (*Goes toward him*) My name is Marek, student of engineering.

CURTAIN

ACT TWO

The same scene as in Act I. By day, the room is a precious and somewhat naive mixture of boudoir and study. Alpha in a charming house frock; girlfriend in street clothes. Both are dressed elegantly but with "spirited originality."

THE GIRLFRIEND: (*Embracing Alpha*) Oooooh!

ALPHA: What is it?

THE GIRLFRIEND: I adore you! (*Presses herself against her and kisses her.*)

ALPHA: Aaa… gh! (*Can barely defend herself.*)

THE GIRLFRIEND: Don't you love me just a little bit too?!

ALPHA: (*Acting as if she were playing with a big over-friendly dog*) Calm down, won't you!

THE GIRLFRIEND: And you say he's really a cold, evil person?

ALPHA: Vinzenz is a man who has always been considered evil and heartless by everyone, even his parents.

THE GIRLFRIEND: Marvelous! Wonderful! That suits me perfectly!

ALPHA: Such people often have very deep hearts.

THE GIRLFRIEND: Of course; terribly dark hearts.

ALPHA: That's an awful cliché.

THE GIRLFRIEND: Don't get mad at me right off. You know I can't express myself like you. Oh you! (*Squeezes her stormily again*) And they say he has God knows how many vices? How does he spend his time?

ALPHA: He works in an office.

THE GIRLFRIEND: That's strange.

ALPHA: Little dummy! As a mathematician. He's a mathematician for a large insurance company. He creates the — you know — the formulas about how people have to die, I mean, how much they have to pay. I myself don't know precisely.

THE GIRLFRIEND: That must be very difficult, no?

ALPHA: Of course, it's extremely difficult. He could certainly be a professor if he wanted.

THE GIRLFRIEND: But just the same, he's always been only a tutor or an insurance mathematician or agent, or at most a substitute teacher? That's marvelous!

ALPHA: He is a person who cannot be bound by anything. Just like myself.

THE GIRLFRIEND: Of course, the women chase after him!? They are so shameless!

ALPHA: They say he's had many wicked adventures.

THE GIRLFRIEND: Nasty adventures with women?

ALPHA: Worse. Gambling, brawls, cocaine, police trouble, I don't know.

THE GIRLFRIEND: (*At her neck*) You! You! Tell me: why does he have to belong to you, of all people! I would simply steal him away from anyone else! I would kill them! (*Desperately*) And you say for sure that love doesn't mean that much to him?

ALPHA: Does his love mean much to me? Women. Stories!

THE GIRLFRIEND: It doesn't mean anything to me either. Of course, it's *mankind* I love. It's just my misfortune that it's much quicker with men.

ALPHA: He doesn't have much time for music either.

THE GIRLFRIEND: You said that art bores him, for the most part? He's right — Oh Alpha! I think I hear him in the front room!? (*She runs off, but not before Vinzenz enters.*) I really care less for music than you think. For a real man, music is certainly nothing, and for us poor women, it's only something because there are so few real men! Sometimes I could just wring my violin's neck! (*Kisses Alpha quickly and provocatively, caresses Vinzenz with a long and ardent look, and exits.*)

ALPHA: What a pity that her breath smells so unpleasant when it's hot …. I am so very happy that you're here again. I'm so sick of it all!

VINZENZ: (*Looking at her*) You've changed very little. Your expression is a bit different now, but with you, that's artificial anyway. My God, what a girl you were!

If I close my eyes you're standing on the gangplank, the wind is ruffling your skirt, your legs are akimbo, and you are holding up your arm, which is holding up a small white handkerchief, and up it flares like an air-colored flame. It was our trust that went up in flames, our love and our dreams. You stood there like a Berserker.

ALPHA: And you were supposed to return in three weeks, and didn't come back for 15 years!

VINZENZ: Yes, that's just it. One can see it, of course, from two sides, from then and from now. Then you had grand ideas: wealth, passion, fame, all of these things were not yet there! And for reality, all you had was me. You were as unspoiled as a hungry stomach, and you had a wonderful appetite for life. But I did too. We were not really like a man and a woman at all, but like two girls who long for the same man.

ALPHA: But I liked you!

VINZENZ: Yes, that's just it: I liked you too. Back then, on the steamer, you had not yet disappeared, you still stood there, stunning and small, and I resolved then and there to — how shall I say it — to dissolve our promise. I liked you that much! I liked you so much that every shrub, every small howling dog, more or less, had a "you-accent." You understand this, because you liked me in the same way. One isn't a body anymore, but only a little cloud in a clear diaphanous element wherein other people and things are just like little clouds too.

One understands the language of the mountains and valleys, the water and the trees, because one can't speak to another with words any more, just with the happiness of existence, like two small scratched-out lines next to each other in eternity. In the end, one can't even eat a crust of bread anymore, one chews on it like a prayer wheel.

At that time, I was at the height of this happiness — then, when I left. Then I said to myself suddenly, that Kathi — in those days you weren't called Alpha yet — so I said to myself, that it was impossible to be named Kathi or Vinzenz and always find oneself in such conditions.

ALPHA: — No one here knows my name! Please don't forget! —

VINZENZ: Except for Halm, who was courting you at precisely that time. Wasn't I right? The devil knows what these conditions are. But one thing is certain: that one can capture them in stone like Bernini did with his St. Therese hit by an arrow from heaven, or in verse, but not in flesh and blood. Where does this unearthliness come from? Then suddenly it gripped me: wherever it comes from, I want to see it too. I followed my love on its journey, in advance, so to speak.

ALPHA: You must have believed. (*She pulls him next to her.*)

VINZENZ: (*Pulling away*) To just throw my cap high into the air? It might have reached the gravitational field of the moon and never come back, and I would have had to fly after it? And do you know, Alpha, *who* said that for the first time? And do you remember when? Two days before my journey? And do you remember who didn't want to throw the cap? To which moon did she soon fly after it? When I recollect, it seems to me that you must have already been wavering then between me and the honorable heavenly body of Mr. Apulejus-Halm.

ALPHA: (*Grasping his hand*) You asked for too much — for those days.

VINZENZ: (*Freeing himself again*) No, Alpha, you were right! You see, in the end, later, at one time or another, I too threw my cap, and a few weeks later a fluttering goose splattered to the ground. There must be, with these things, some obscure explanation. And I couldn't talk to anyone but you about this. Wherever I was, or whomever I was with, I always had the feeling: I must speak to you about this first — you, the one who knows how we were in those days. During my wanderings, it seemed to me: because we lost the way at the same time, we could only find it again together.

ALPHA: But now? Remember, you said that one has to look at your return from now too!

VINZENZ: (*Smiling*) What did I say? Now?.... Oh yes.

Quite right .... Tell me, Kathi, — (*Taking her hand*) — as long as one is a young girl, it must be so — life, and expectation, must be so — must be as exasperating as if one were looking at it through a window of frosted glass? I can finally understand this now, because later all of the panes have been smashed. Shards, empty frames. (*Pulling her toward him*) I'm so sick of it all. And you — are not happy either ... ? But, in front of that which was never finished between us, there is still one magical window, the last one. Let's shatter that too. (*They kiss. Embracing toward the alcove. Stopping at the ottoman on the way.*)

ALPHA: (*Concerned*) You won't imagine it's any big thing that I love you? It's completely unimportant.

VINZENZ: You love Bärli a little bit, don't you?

ALPHA: Now really, what is that?

VINZENZ: Precisely. Nothing at all. Money is nothing at all so long as it's locked up in petrified cages of stocks and ventures and such. I have a wondrous invention. No one knows about it. You're the first one I'll tell. We'll be much much richer than Bärli. Can you imagine what it means to be rich?

ALPHA: Really, what does Bärli have that's so special?

VINZENZ: God! He's a poor devil compared to us! He's like a waiter who has to carry his tray of glasses carefully; but we will throw ours away, as often as we wish, because we will get another one immediately.... You have heard that there are systems in gambling?

ALPHA: But Vinzenz, that's total nonsense!

VINZENZ: Of course, all the ones that you can have heard about are nonsense; there isn't one of these gaming systems that I couldn't undo with my little finger. I have a lot of experience with that.

They're all dilettante attempts, which contradict probability calculus. Therefore, we mathematicians say that a "system" is impossible too. But now listen to this: what I will tell you now, you certainly don't know. There are two studies by a well-known scholar concerned with this question and which prove *why* the actual recurring numbers in every experiment deviate from the calculable so-called "mathematical expectations." And they do. In roulette, for example, a long sequence is much less frequently the result, although mathematically one would expect one. Have you heard of this?

ALPHA: (*Like an arrogant child*) Of course; I only forgot it for a moment.

VINZENZ: Thus, it exists. And so, one can, on the basis of this experiment, correct the mathematical calculation, right?

ALPHA: (*As above*) Yes.

VINZENZ: But the particulars, with which that professor attempted it, were false! A lengthy technical dispute ensued, which still continues, because so far only one person has discovered the correct formula, and he has not yet announced it —

ALPHA: You?!

VINZENZ: And is not planning to disclose it!

ALPHA: (*Kissing him stormily*) Oh you! You! I have always known it! But you will explain it to me more clearly later? I think I understand it already, but if it gets even more difficult, I will simply have to study mathematics. That is really wonderful, I will know something that even my university professor doesn't have any idea of!

VINZENZ: But he's an historian!

ALPHA: Something which no man — no man, you say, besides yourself? — has any idea of!

VINZENZ: We have something much more important to do. You have influential friends. I only lack the initial capital.

ALPHA: (*Thoughtfully*) But I've never asked them for money. They'll find it strange. They might not do it at all.

VINZENZ: Well, what do you live off then?

ALPHA: They give me advice, tips, you know? Bärli, then the councilman, they know all that in advance. Then they buy and sell on my account.

VINZENZ: And when you have losses —?

ALPHA: I have never lost.

VINZENZ: Ah ha, then all is well. You see, you will simply do your business with me, just let them do the buying. I will found the "Society for the Prevention of Immoral Gambling" and you will purchase my stock. It will only be necessary for a moment; with my first operation I will break the next best casino.

ALPHA: Then you will have an insane amount of money, and then? What will we do then? What will we do with the money?

VINZENZ: We will never come to the end of *earning* money. We will buy ourselves three cars and travel. In the front, you and I. Then our personal servants. Then, if you like, two of the board of trustees of our society — as long as we are free of them. We will go to Nice, to Spa, to Monaco, to Ostend, to the United States, to South America. We'll have an ocean liner built for us, fitted out like a castle. We'll travel in our own trains. We'll scatter so much money among the masses — it will mean nothing at all to us — until the people grovel before us like reptiles. Our reputation will precede us everywhere! When we need money, we'll just suck another casino dry.

ALPHA: And if there is not one more casino left?

VINZENZ: Then we'll turn the principle around and open one ourselves. This formula works that way too, you see. An unbreakable casino. Or would you prefer that I sell my formula to an existing casino?

ALPHA: No, no!

VINZENZ: Precisely. We turn the formula around, and make a casino monopoly. We'll simply suck up all the money in the world. God knows what will come out of that? It simply can't be predicted. We could buy the central Asian desert, irrigate it, and create a garden kingdom there. We could rule it with the laws which we thought up in the old days, before I went away. You will be a queen.

ALPHA: Those are banal inventions now, Vinzenz.

VINZENZ: Yes, as ideas! Wanting to be Caesar or Goethe or Lao Tse, that is banal. But consider how it changes, if one really *is* it. With our money, we can make anything we want successful, anything in politics, art, morality, anything that is relevant to life; and we can destroy whatever does not please us. It really is inconceivable.

ALPHA: (*With wide open eyes*) No, the end is unforeseeable. And your formula is real?

VINZENZ: Here, look. (*He pulls a packet of papers out of his pocket.*)

ALPHA: Differential equations, right?

VINZENZ: You're really wonderful; everything you know! Partial and iterations. And — do you know, it's understandable that Bärli went crazy from love of you.

ALPHA: What? Bärli?

VINZENZ: (*Darkly*) A deep neural imbalance.

ALPHA: (*Totally weak, leaning upon him*) It's impossible to conceive of. My whole life long I've tried to conceive what I would do, if I could do everything I wanted. Don't underestimate me because of the people you've seen around me; I've merely experimented from different sides, but I've never taken them seriously. Do you know, I believe I am really an anarchist: they have never silenced my longing to arrive, ultimately, at my proper place! And now you put your arms around my body. And you lift me up like the great magical bird that has come again. And we fly up ever so high.

VINZENZ: Wherever we please — !

ALPHA: High up to the never-silent voice, which spoke to me. (*Springing up, wild*) I don't believe it, Vinzenz! (*Falling upon him*) Do with me what you will…!

(*Vinzenz carries the swooning, surrendering Alpha wistfully, intoxicated himself and smiling, into the alcove, and pulls the curtains closed.*)

THE GIRLFRIEND: (*After a moment of peeking and listening, sneaks in, goes to Alpha's writing desk and takes — her hat on her head — paper and writing implements. Re-reading parts aloud of what she has written.*) Forgive me, beloved, that I've listened in. I'm unhappy. No, I'm happy. Yet I'm unhappy. I admire you even more ever since he loves you. But I'm unhappy. He's the only man that I've ever seen. You know, sadly, that I've seen many. Whenever one appeared before me — with his hungry eyes, moist with sympathy… it always touched me deep down. (*She cries.*) I don't know how I'll go on anymore. I'll leave him my fortune as a contribution to your initial capital. I could also speak with Prince …. Or take me on as your female companion …. Oh, I know that one cannot share a miracle like this! Your ruined, deeply unhappy — do not be angry if I say deeply unhappy, I know that I am not worthy of either of you — —

(*Bärli enters; in contrast to his previous behavior, strangely peaceful; black from head to toe, solemnly agitated, a Browning automatic in his hand. He bumps into The Girlfriend, who has gotten up, and falls markedly out of his role.*)

BÄRLI: (*Huskily*) What are *you* doing here?

THE GIRLFRIEND: I? Mr. Bärli?

BÄRLI: Yes.

THE GIRLFRIEND: But!

BÄRLI: Go!

THE GIRLFRIEND: But?

BÄRLI: Immediately! (*He lifts the pistol toward the paralyzed Girlfriend.*) You're in my way!

(*The Girlfriend flees the room with a terrible scream. Alpha opens the curtain astonished and indignant.*)

BÄRLI: Aah! (*He hides the pistol behind his back.*)

ALPHA: Aah! You have a pistol again! Vinzenz!

VINZENZ: (*Already at the door*) I'll get help! I'll be right back! (*He makes the sign of insanity. Exits.*)

ALPHA: (*Calling after him*) Vinzenz! Vinzenz!

BÄRLI: (*Foreboding, silent, forcing Alpha slowly through the room, the pistol behind his back. Darkly*) Don't make any noise, Alpha, it won't help anymore.

(*Alpha tries to get to the door; he forces her wordlessly into the opposite corner, Alpha tries to get to the window, the same thing. Finally, Alpha stops, defeated.*)

ALPHA: Wha — What do you want?

BÄRLI: Sphinx.

ALPHA: Sphinx? Oh God, you are ill, Bärli. Let me call someone.

BÄRLI: Killed anyone who couldn't answer her questions. If you answer just fifty percent of my questions, I will just kill myself. Do you love life? Would you like to be 16 years old again?

ALPHA: Yes, you see, one would have to .... Oh God! One can't just ask such things ... !?

BÄRLI: (*Makes a sign of refusal; the question is unanswered.*) Is it all over after death, or not?

ALPHA: Well, you see, the professor ... — but the councilman says —

BÄRLI: Which of your friends do you love the most?

ALPHA: None! Really none!

BÄRLI: Whom do you treasure the most?

ALPHA: Well, every one, really, in his own way.

BÄRLI: Why do you love music?

ALPHA: But I can't possibly know that!

BÄRLI: Well then why do you make music?

ALPHA: (*Looks at him speechlessly*) You're ill, oh God, Bärli, let me get someone.

BÄRLI: Did you never regret something?

ALPHA: Re — ?

BÄRLI: Yes. Re-gret! I mean, are you sorry for all the sins of your life, from the bottom of your heart?

ALPHA: Oh certainly. For sure. Very.

BÄRLI: What then?

ALPHA: Well, I've forgotten by now.

BÄRLI: So, you're not clear about the hourly increasing mass of sins, regret, virtue, good resolutions, while you are living them?

ALPHA: (*Forcefully*) No! Never! One can't know that! No one!

BÄRLI: (*Taking another tack*) Would you kill, steal, commit adultery, forgive your offender?

ALPHA: That depends!

BÄRLI: Are you haughty, envious, revengeful, gloating?

ALPHA: That can't be answered so simply!

BÄRLI: You are answering my pistol. Answer *me*, precisely! What principles do you base your actions upon?!

ALPHA: That can't be answered so simply!!! That depends!!! It's a matter of context!!!

BÄRLI: May I withhold wages today? Not even partially? When have I taken something from others and when not? Why is truth better than lies? Cheerfulness better than sorrow? Morality better than immorality? Should one have children? —

ALPHA: Oh God! (*She hides herself, shaken by fear, in a blanket, which she pulls over her head.*)

BÄRLI: (*Unable to stop*) Should one be selfless? Should one be nationalistic or international? Why do I go to the cinema? Like to see acrobats? (*In the meantime, he has just realized what Alpha has done, lifts the pistol up slowly, weighing every word.*) You have, with your mind, deeply shaken mine, Alpha. Through your influence, my existence has lost its meaning. I wanted to look inside myself and think about myself. But what answers do you have to my questions?! I free myself from you!

ALPHA: (*Coming out from under the blanket*) But you must ask in another way! One has to have feeling for it, as in a dance! (*She sees herself faced with the pistol.*) Aaaa ... a!!!

(*Bärli takes three shots, each one quickly after the other, at Alpha. Alpha screams; she tries to flee and falls on her face. A chair falls over, and a tall upright mirror breaks.*)

BÄRLI: (*Hesitates, shakes his head*) One must ask in another way? One must understand it like a dance? — I'll be damned if this isn't something new again? This situation is just making me ridiculous; one really should be ashamed in front of the rationality of furniture while one waltzes in between its feet. But what good does it do!! (*He takes two shots at himself and falls on his back, his head turned toward the side. After the second shot, Vinzenz enters. Alpha starts to moan loudly. At these sounds of pain, Bärli lifts his head up and looks concerned in her direction. Vinzenz thumps him back down in his place roughly. He bends over Alpha and sprinkles her forehead with water. Alpha moans even more heartily.*)

VINZENZ: Alpha! Alpha! How sweet your little heart beats!

ALPHA: (*Opens her eyes in response to his attentions and caresses.*) I'm not dead?

VINZENZ: Sweet little Alpha, you are younger like this than I've ever known you to be.

ALPHA: Oh, I'm so badly wounded.

VINZENZ: No. There's nothing wrong with you. He shot to the side of you.

ALPHA: That's impossible. I felt the bullet distinctly.

VINZENZ: No. You're totally fine. I've examined you.

ALPHA: (*Standing up*) Oh, it was frightful! But — it was interesting too. Is he not dead, too?

VINZENZ: No; he is.

ALPHA: (*Approaching closer*) But I don't see any blood?

VINZENZ: Leave him be. Don't touch him. He's horribly wounded. He shot himself in the back. I saw it. Unfortunately, I returned at just that moment. (*He pulls her away.*)

ALPHA: A frightful person. But original. It was remarkably beautiful…. Do I look different?

VINZENZ: You've become more tranquil.

ALPHA: Yes, that's what it is. How do you always find the right word?! Do you know, I feel badly for him just the same. It is really something, to shoot oneself and another because of love; you, for example, couldn't do it. And I am so thankful to him; I feel so light. Just imagine: almost dead! Actually, I have always been somewhat afraid of it, but in the end, it too is frightfully overrated. One really must be thankful for an experience like this, as if he had shot through a chain which still bound me to the silly life I led before you returned. We will be wordlessly happy, Vinzenz, really wordlessly…! What moved???

VINZENZ: Nothing. He just slumped a little deeper onto his face. (*Thumps him.*) Don't look! (*The doorbell rings.*)

ALPHA: Oh no, that must be the others. Don't open up! Or send them away! Don't let them in!

VINZENZ: That won't work Alpha; we would fall under unpleasant suspicion if we were to hide now. (*It rings again.*) I'll briefly explain it to them and take them right into the other room. I have to talk to them about the casino anyway.

ALPHA: Oh yes, you must do that right away.

VINZENZ: But it would be better if you weren't there. It would look bad, if you — (*It rings again.*) were to speak calmly about business now, so soon after. But I can do it, just as soon as I explain the incident to them.

ALPHA: But I'm afraid to be alone with him.

VINZENZ: (*At the door*) But *Alpha*, how few women can understand, like you, that this is, after all, nothing more than a bourgeois episode!

ALPHA: You're wrong; he was *spiritually* shaken. But it will be better if I don't speak much. (*Vinzenz exits.*) I'll sit myself in the corner with a book. (*As soon as she sits down with her back to Bärli, she is gripped by childish fear. Restraining herself*) It must be a book whose level is above such conflicts. (*She opens a book, but turns around* *again fearfully.*) But I will not read it. I will hold it closed on my lap. It is actually more proper, in a situation such as this, if one doesn't read, but merely suggests that one really should be reading. (*She places herself in position.*)

VINZENZ: (*Ushering the friends in*) You see the situation. *Alpha* refuses to speak; she is too shocked. I beg you, let us leave her for the moment; come with me into the next room, I'll quickly explain to you what happened.

THE POLITICIAN: But we have to call the police, it can't be left like this.

VINZENZ: That has already been taken care of. And for this reason as well we should go next door.

(*The Musician, with his handkerchief to his nose, turning his back to the dead man at all angles, is the first to enter the other room. The others follow. In the doorway.*)

THE SCHOLAR: But it is really inconsiderate to perpetrate such inconveniences.

THE YOUNG MAN: Ill breeding. (*Exits.*)

(*Alpha remains motionless, staring at nothing in particular, her back to Bärli.*)

BÄRLI: (*Slowly lifting himself up carefully at first, and looking around, then quickly, pulling off his jacket.*) Please, can you lend me a clothing brush, Alpha. (*Alpha turns around with a muffled scream.*) I've had enough of this. (*He fetches a brush for himself, cleans his suit furiously* *and puts his jacket on.*) These oafs were the one thing missing. To lead me into such a ridiculous eccentricity! Don't make a fuss, I want to leave.

ALPHA: (*Livid with anger*) What? You didn't really shoot at yourself either?

BÄRLI: Blanks, fantasy shots; Colibri shots, as Vinzenz calls them.

ALPHA: What an ignoble comedy! You wanted to make a fool of me?!

BÄRLI: I believe I have acted like a fool myself. But only you are responsible for that. Otherwise I would never have allowed myself to be led astray by this scoundrel Vinzenz. Listen: I promised him another check for this comedy. I'm crossing a zero off, that's enough for you two! (*Offering it rudely*) Adieu.

ALPHA: You owe me an explanation! You dared to — I could have died of fear — and you claim that you plotted this with Vinzenz...?

BÄRLI: Adieu, adieu. I will give no explanations. I am freed, exactly as free, in fact, as you reported earlier that you were.

ALPHA: But you are, in addition to everything else, indulging in entirely disrespectful and rude behavior!!!

(*Vinzenz enters, disturbed by the loud conversation.*)

ALPHA: Vinzenz! This gentleman is trying to use you to excuse his unworthy behavior; he claims to have prepared this with you?

VINZENZ: Listen Alpha, if we scream, more people will come in; there is already decidedly one person too many in this room: let us be happy if Mr. Bärli will be that one. I will explain everything to you later, when it's quiet. (*Looking at the check*) But first let me say that there is one zero too few here.

(*Alpha rips the paper out of his hand, crunches it up and throws it at Bärli. Bärli kicks it back angrily.*)

VINZENZ: (*Lifts the paper up, smooths the check out, lays it on the table, sets up the ink well and chair, and invites Bärli to write.*) God, truly, I didn't do it for the money. But if this thing seems to you even a tenth as valuable as what you wanted to give for it before, you can prove that your liberation was worth a ten-times larger honorarium.

BÄRLI: (*Looking at him, laughing slowly*) You're not at all wrong. I wouldn't say that I have no reason to be thankful. (*He sits at the table. Alpha grabs the ink well from him and throws the quill on the floor.*)

VINZENZ: (*Calmingly to Alpha*) But I just advised him to shoot with blanks instead of committing a double murder.

ALPHA: (*Haughtily repudiating*) But whatever for?

VINZENZ: Well, he wanted to give you something to remember. One has to let uncomplicated people like him have their way; there's no other way for it. (*Since Alpha ignores him, to Bärli*) Didn't I say to you: you're a businessman, take death on credit!? Didn't I advise you: shoot blind and you won't have the need any more to really shoot? I promised you that afterwards the only thing you would take seriously would be money!

BÄRLI: And I do, you can be sure.

VINZENZ: (*To Alpha again*) He has experienced everything that one can experience in this. The sequel is not at all valuable: people shaking their heads, police commissions, coffin. It's really not worthwhile to actually live it! That's why I advised him in this way.

ALPHA: But that was outrageous!

VINZENZ: Of whom?

ALPHA: Of you!

BÄRLI: (*Who, in the meantime, has written out a new check with the fountain pen.*) I see, Alpha, that I have made myself guilty of yet another injustice where you're concerned — (*Alpha ignores him coldly. He shoves the check toward the edge of the table; to Vinzenz*) Here. (*To Alpha*) But you are safe from me at least: one doesn't do anything twice. (*Stands up.*)

ALPHA: That's wrong: one falls in love as often as one wants!

VINZENZ: (*Who was studying the check*) You made such a strong impression on him that he believed he couldn't live without soul. I told him: simply do this one single time and you will never take your passions seriously again! The realm of the soul is a business and it relies on faithfulness and belief. But in questions of money — tell me: is the check good?

BÄRLI: (*Looks at Alpha hesitantly and tears himself away.*) Yes. And God forbid that you ever fall into my hands! (*Exits immediately.*)

ALPHA: So, you're an infamous intriguer!

VINZENZ: But I saved your life by healing him of his passion.

ALPHA: My life! But what business of yours was his passion?!

(*The friends stick their heads through the door.*)

VINZENZ: Yes, what do you think, in the meantime he has gone quietly on his way.

ALL: (*At once*) How? What? Tasteless! Joke? Dumb! Tactless!

VINZENZ: Yes, really unfathomably tactless. But just for that, we will not accept him into the "Society for the Prevention of Immoral Gambling." (*To Alpha*) I have forgotten, dear friend, to impart to you, that its incorporation, in the meantime, has been definitively sealed.

CURTAIN

ACT THREE

Scene: the same as in Act Two. Alpha in a bizarre mourning dress. Vinzenz in a shabby suit. Packing paltry possessions into a questionable canvas suitcase very carefully, with an almost petty-bourgeois prudence.

VINZENZ: It was very beautiful! But it is better that I move out. Your beautiful gifts! It will all be a precious memory for me.

ALPHA: (*Walking angrily back and forth in front of him*) They say that this whole idea of the gambling formula was a shameless swindle!

VINZENZ: Forget it!

ALPHA: They have made inquiries. They claim that you simply cheated them!

VINZENZ: Well, yes; naturally.

ALPHA: That you only wanted to worm money out of them!?

VINZENZ: Not exactly that. But why work yourself up so much about trying to prove them wrong?

ALPHA: But I won't allow such a thing to be thought of me!

VINZENZ: Of you?

ALPHA: That you are nothing but a confidence man!

VINZENZ: Now see here, that is very unpleasant. These are all people with connections and influence. A councilman. A scholar. A celebrated pianist. They swear that I belong in jail. That's very unpleasant for me, as I've never known, my whole life, where I belong. I don't have the means to pay a lawyer for the sole purpose of proving once more — if he even succeeded — where I do not belong.

ALPHA: (*Forcefully*) But I won't have it! I've declared that you are far superior to them; and so it must remain!

VINZENZ: Yes Alpha, I may be far superior to them; but you see, not precisely on such points.

ALPHA: (*Stopping in front of him with a jolt*) It's true: You've actually behaved utterly ridiculously to me also.

VINZENZ: In what way, dear Alpha?

ALPHA: Well, you have, when I think about it, behaved really — oh no, I wouldn't say that you've behaved badly, that would give you too much credit, but you've conducted yourself ridiculously. You come back, driven — so *you* said! — by longing, and in — so *you* said! — the most blissful moment of your life, you think up a totally childish intrigue.

VINZENZ: But didn't I save your life with it?

ALPHA: You made yourself ridiculous!

VINZENZ: Such things are often reversed with neurotic characters; we make jokes when we are sad, or laugh at a funeral. I was afraid of such an overwhelming reunion.

ALPHA: (*More conciliatory*) And this morning you suddenly want to leave the house! You have to understand that by doing this you make yourself look like an entirely imbalanced person. Like — like a neurotic character, who could be capable of anything.

VINZENZ: Look, Alpha, I don't want to contradict you. Even back then I did not treat you well.

ALPHA: Oh, please, that was my own free will, that I didn't search out your hiding place.

VINZENZ: Right. But if I were simply a confidence man, I would not have lied about the casino to you, too ….

ALPHA: (*Repulsing him*) Oh …! Oh yes; you lied to me disgracefully! You had the impudence … you lied to me in the midst of caresses … you … but I don't care so very much about that, you know! You just believed in it yourself, at those moments, and it is clear that you are the type of the fantastical liar!

VINZENZ: Let's suppose that's true: but what does lying mean? To assert that something desirable is so, instead of that it should be so? A moral reformer does the same thing, except that one has an even firmer conviction. And what increases the uncertainty in the world more: if I maintain six different things on two different days, or if your six friends have six different philosophies at the same time?

ALPHA: It means: convincing someone of things which do not accord with the facts. (*She throws herself on the ottoman, disappointed and dejected.*)

VINZENZ: But doesn't everything accord with the facts? Look, now I have it: a fantastic liar is that liar whose lies accord with the facts! The facts themselves are fantastic. If you assert that the sun revolves around the earth, you are, according to the latest research, no less correct than if you say that the earth revolves around the sun. Mothers sacrifice themselves for their children, but they sacrifice their children too. Fire devours and fire nourishes. Man makes order because he makes messes, and he makes messes because otherwise he'd have no use for order. He is abstinent and he drinks. Punishes the thief, but also the poor.

ALPHA: (*Frustrated, despairing*) Stop it! Don't start with your lies again! You aren't capable of being earnest!

VINZENZ: (*Hands on his temples*) It's a fearful noise. A noise and a hellish jangling crashing! And in this jangling hammering, wherein one can't understand one's own thoughts, in this truly criminal disorder, I too sometimes simply start a little ball rolling; and the remarkable thing about it is: in whatever direction — no matter how off course — you, too, set an action like this going; it always succeeds in reality, as if it had been expected there all along.

ALPHA: (*In front of him*) You must tell that *to them*. You'll tell the people your opinion, my friend!

VINZENZ: I? To them? God forbid. I've always fared worse than my lies. I have to give in to them altogether. They're after me because Bärli avoids them since the incident.

ALPHA: Well? So?

VINZENZ: They've threatened my struggle for livelihood and my existence, and I — have nothing — it turns out — to defend.

ALPHA: Coward! Not I! I will marry you! (*Vinzenz fends her off.*) I will! Even though I am even more weary of being together than you are; it's not a question of that! (*She begins to pace again.*) They dare to dictate to me what I should do! They dare to forbid me you! Me, for whom you are, God knows, totally meaningless! I do still have, thank God, something to defend! Do you know what an anarchist is? Yes? Well, I am a woman anarchist. As long as I live. I didn't make the world. I would have made it much better too, if I had been asked; that is no great art. And I'm supposed to take this world, made by men, seriously? That's what they want from me; I'm supposed to respect the world! I'd sooner become a suffragette!

VINZENZ: You have it much easier, too. Yes, if I had your natural gifts. (*Referring to her body*) If I were a woman — (*The doorbell rings. Quickly packing up*) It's them!

ALPHA: (*On the way to the door*) Well, what would you do!?

VINZENZ: I? If I were a woman?! and if people, as soon as I showed myself to be interested in them? joyfully opened up to me — of their own free will — their intimate selves? I, their moony night, their nightingale, their weak hour: what I couldn't make out of the world, if I were a woman! But I'm not the one they love; I'd better hide! (*Quickly exiting into the adjoining room....*)

ALPHA: (*Calling after him*) Not I! I don't know what I'm going to do! But it will be something violent!

(*The friends enter, arrange themselves polygonally. The speakers move around Alpha, during the following, in nervous diagonals and side-long paces. Sometimes one of the group stops in front of her. The Young Man: silent synchronized signals with the others.*)

THE MUSICIAN: (*Mediating*) Dear *Alpha*, have you considered our objections?

ALPHA: I would like to know whose business that is besides mine alone?

THE MUSICIAN: We are very concerned.

THE POLITICIAN: That man is no company for you. Society has established laws. He is clearly *déclassé*.

THE SCHOLAR: Mr. Bärli would have wanted to return to us long since, had it not been for his unpleasant memory of this man.

ALPHA: Bärli? But I forbade him to enter my house.

THE MUSICIAN: Well, yes — he hopes. He has desisted from his headstrong schemes.

THE SCHOLAR: There was, it's true, something lacking in his behavior, but —

THE POLITICIAN: He is, in a word, a desirable contact.

ALPHA: (*Not unpleasantly moved*) So Bärli hopes — ? ... No.

THE MUSICIAN: (*Despairing*) But this insurance agent — (*frightened by Alpha's angry look*) yes, yes — mathematician....

THE SCHOLAR: And what a mathematician he has proven himself to be!

ALPHA: Sirs, I find you most impudent.

THE SCHOLAR: This is no pleasant task, the one we've had to take upon ourselves. But there are simply some difficult and disagreeable duties of friendship. Every one of us would have told you, but you would certainly have — have —

THE MUSICIAN: Yes, Alpha, you would certainly have not listened. You would have most certainly become indignant, none of us wanted to take that upon himself; no —

THE SCHOLAR: So, we've just decided to present it to you together.

THE POLITICIAN: Mr. Bärli knows about it too and has declared himself in agreement with this solution.

THE MUSICIAN: Yes, yes, even he. Even he disapproves of excesses of fantasy and imagination.

(All stand frozen around Alpha.)

THE SCHOLAR: And so we are informing you that we have agreed ... to trust that you will ... choose ... between Vinzenz ... an utterly vulgar confidence man, who has dared to annoy a man of Mr. Bärli's stature ... and our friendship. I was picked, by drawing lots, to inform you of this.

ALPHA: So? I think that is excellent. Of course, I can't decide on the spot. In any case, you can be sure that I will miss you more terribly than you miss me.

THE MUSICIAN: *(Softly)* Then you will miss us very terribly....

THE SCHOLAR: But it was never quite like this, never like now, when you have taken a man into your lodgings!

THE POLITICIAN: That's another thing we have agreed upon: you are too defenseless.

ALPHA: Too defenseless? What's that supposed to mean?

THE POLITICIAN: As a single woman you are too defenseless.

THE MUSICIAN: The incident with Bärli was proof of that. (*All agree.*)

ALPHA: Perhaps you would all like to live with me now?

THE POLITICIAN: We've thought it over. You need a larger, more proper home with servants. As beautiful as this romantic arrangement here was —

ALPHA: I might consider that.

THE POLITICIAN: I wanted to say: as beautiful as this romantic arrangement here is —

THE SCHOLAR: As much as we, all of us, knew how to appreciate your atmosphere —

THE MUSICIAN: And as much as we will enjoy thinking back on it —

ALPHA: (*Impatient*) Well, what? What?

THE POLITICIAN: You must get married again, Alpha. You need masculine protection and greater order. We voted upon it, and it is our unanimous decision.

ALPHA: But this is madness! Which one of you, then, according to the voting results, may I marry?

THE POLITICIAN: That would have destroyed our circle —

THE SCHOLAR: Yes, Alpha, I wouldn't have been able to witness your marriage with any one of us other than me.

ALPHA: So, whom may I marry?

THE POLITICIAN: Well, you see, Alpha, actually — you already are married.

ALPHA: What? Halm?

THE POLITICIAN: Yes, Apulejus-Halm.

ALPHA: (*Looking from one to the other*) You dare to suggest this to me? Halm, that goat, whom I drove out of my bedroom, before I had even recovered from shock, when in my innocent youth I was prostituted to him?!

THE MUSICIAN: Yes, yes; that's exactly what we prize in him.

ALPHA: What?

THE MUSICIAN: That he lets himself be driven out.

THE SCHOLAR: He has shown himself to be a really true friend, ever since the incident with Bärli; he has worked tirelessly and self-sacrificingly, to shed light on the situation and to help us make a clear judgment of this Vinzenz fellow. He is, in the main, the one to thank.

THE MUSICIAN: And then he confided something to us that is really splendid. He is, haha, no, *Alpha*, he is hoho, not at all troublesome to you or an unpleasant thought for us. He is, when it comes to women, a cherub?

THE POLITICIAN: He has assured us that the reinstatement of the marital bond would not, in any respect, lead to even the smallest encumbrances. We will come and go as we do now, without him concerning himself about these spiritual relationships. He simply finds the present situation of a so-called "wild marriagelessness" — not without justice — to be socially improper and detrimental to his professional position.

ALPHA: (*Baffled*) Well — really, that is rich...! (*She looks at her enemies one by one, like a tiger. She calls*) Vinzenz! (*In the next room it stays completely quiet.*) I'm marrying Vinzenz!

THE MUSICIAN: But he doesn't want to at all, Halm told us.

ALPHA: *I* don't want to! That is beyond your comprehension. (*She seems to search for, at all costs, a saving idea which will show her superiority.*) Didn't you notice that I am wearing a wedding dress already?! One moment! (*She runs excitedly out the door.*)

THE MUSICIAN: (*Shakes his head in pity; the others too with shaking heads pity Alpha's agitation.*) The opposite of bourgeois life; it is the opposite, never forget that, gentlemen, which does this to us, we, who are ourselves not the usual sort.

ALPHA: (*Pulling The Girlfriend inside. Pointing to her own black dress*) Is this a wedding dress?

THE GIRLFRIEND: Yes, it's a wedding dress.

ALL: But it's a mourning dress!

ALPHA: Yes, it is also a mourning dress.

THE POLITICIAN: But you're not woeful over anyone.

ALPHA: On Bärli's behalf.

THE SCHOLAR: But Bärli's not dead.

ALPHA: Therefore, woe for him.

THE MUSICIAN: You *did* want to woo him?

ALPHA: Who said that?

ALL: Oh, you're woeful over him.

ALPHA: Woe *him*.

ALL: But I don't understand — you say, that's a wedding dress? You do want him to woo you?

ALPHA: Woo without him. This would be very simple for some other people: I'm woeful on his behalf.

THE SCHOLAR: On his behalf? Just now you said: without him?

ALPHA: Well yes, of course: for him.

THE SCHOLAR: For? Not over?

ALPHA: For! that means: without him. — You still don't understand that I'm woeful for him without him?

I am as woeful for him as if he had killed himself and me from passion, because I didn't want to marry him. Because he did not do it. Without him.

THE SCHOLAR: (*For all*) But I don't understand what the point is?

ALPHA: Without h-i-i-m!!!

THE SCHOLAR: But you said, didn't you, that this was a wedding dress: who is it then that you want to woo?

ALPHA: My darling, they don't understand! They can't even understand a dress. They think so simplistically. If I say that black is white, then it is white for my soul. And Bärli is dead for my soul. And a mourning dress is a wedding dress. And you, all of you, are totally dead too! Isn't it true, darling, they would never be able to understand, how deep the delirium of your attachment is, precisely because you are not a man —

THE GIRLFRIEND: Oh *Alpha*, the haziest dreams are the most beautiful! (*Alpha throws her arms around The Girlfriend.*) Their coarse heads think that for there to be love there must be a man involved, and that a man, if he stays with me a few days, must — must! How primitive! They don't understand how immensely criminal it is that they don't understand me! But we will show them, by allowing Vinzenz to stay here with us as long as he wants to.

ALL: (*Movement.*)

THE POLITICIAN: Yes; well then — !

ALL: Then — ?

THE MUSICIAN: It's not right, Alpha, that you sacrifice your proven friends —

THE POLITICIAN: For a tramp!

ALPHA: (*On The Girlfriend's breast*) You still don't understand that you are not needed. You are insulting me with your protection. (*She signals to them angrily with her foot, that they should go, vibrating with obstinacy.*)

THE GIRLFRIEND: But Alpha! I didn't know about this? Alpha? Have you thought this over?

ALPHA: (*Angry, tearful*) What?

THE GIRLFRIEND: You really want to, because of Vinzenz — ?

ALPHA: What? What?

THE GIRLFRIEND: Nothing.

ALPHA: You know something?! (*The Girlfriend caresses her all the more tenderly.*) You know something?! (*She grabs her enquiringly by the shoulders.*)

THE GIRLFRIEND: (*Finally overcome by love, shame, regret, she throws her arms around her neck, then sinks down in front of her on her knees.*) He is unworthy of you! … He is a seducer …!

ALPHA: (*Coldly pulls away*) You? — You had — something with him?

THE GIRLFRIEND: (*On her knees*) You know, it is my weakness!... But he... he....

ALPHA: Phooey.... Oh, you're repulsive. Like a wet rag that hurls itself at every man. And here too? Here?

THE GIRLFRIEND: There was so much — there was so much love of humanity in it. It began so normally...! (*Embracing her*) Forgive me. Forgive. You know how I love you!

ALPHA: (*Suddenly grabbing her by the hair, hitting her in the face, etc.*) This is how you love me, like this!!! (*They struggle.*)

THE GIRLFRIEND: (*Whimpering*) Please, please, I love you so....

(*Everyone jumps up, tries to separate them, they are practically torn apart. It is, without a doubt, not a pretty picture. Vinzenz enters from the next room to see what the noise is. The Girlfriend is on the floor. Alpha is on her knees on the side, distressed.*)

ALPHA: I am ashamed of myself... (*Looking from one to the other*) Oh, what must you think of me — ? (*She is on the point of breaking down in desperate tears.*)

VINZENZ: Well, what *do* you think — may I say it? (*Alpha throws him a helpless look. The Girlfriend jumps up and flings herself on Vinzenz's chest. Vinzenz puts her in The Musician's arms.*) Just for a moment! (*To all*) An uncommon talent for tragedy!

(*Alpha looks at him and understands the salvation.*)

ALL: (*Disbelieving*) That was acting?

VINZENZ: But of course. (*He helps Alpha up. Then to The Girlfriend*) You must forgive us. You couldn't be warned, of course, in the interest of naturalness. (*To all*) There is nothing, as you know, for which Alpha does not have an abnormal aptitude, but we needed a test. She was asked to turn the next best insignificant occasion into a "scene." Because we only use scenes which come directly from life; only these are natural. We are even thinking of using our money to affect destinies, so that we can film them. No more professional acting! I have been, for some time now, affiliated with the cinema: "Light and Love: Society for the Production of True-to-Life Filming within the Confines of the Law." We seem to have just gained, with Alpha, a staggering performer.

ALPHA: One thing is true: our film actresses don't have enough humanity; they are banal masks.

VINZENZ: And that which normally happens in reality really belongs in the movies.

THE POLITICIAN: But Light and Love? That's some invention! Isn't that the name of a missionary organization!

VINZENZ: Is that so? Possibly. But you must admit that it's also a great name for a film company.

THE MUSICIAN: (*To Vinzenz*) And you? And we?

(*The Politician shrugs his shoulders and prepares to leave.*)

THE MUSICIAN: And the marriage? And Halm?

VINZENZ: I am hoping.

ALPHA: (*Who has, in the meantime, composed herself*) You are — all of you — immensely insignificant to me. You are all spiritually dead for me. Vinzenz too.

VINZENZ: We can hope. You all mistrust me wrongly. It will be cleared up. — But in the meantime, let's leave the two artists alone. (*He accompanies the friends out the door.*)

(*Alpha and The Girlfriend, in the meantime, have fixed their hair and faces before the mirror.*)

THE GIRLFRIEND: (*Nervously*) You were so rough…. (*Discreetly*) But you excited me so!

ALPHA: We have to talk. I acted very oddly. That was really very odd …. Of course, you wouldn't dare believe — if you want Vinzenz — ? He never meant very much to me.

(*Vinzenz returns carefully, trying to sense the mood: overcoat and hat, little suitcase in his hand.*)

THE GIRLFRIEND: Oh, you have only just now come close to me!

ALPHA: We'll speak tonight then. Here is the key. Wait —

(*She looks in vain for a key. Vinzenz silently places his in her hand. The Girlfriend takes the key and goes quickly, without looking at Vinzenz.*)

VINZENZ: Well, shall I go now, too?

ALPHA: (*Begins to walk up and down again nervously, as in the first scene*) You mustn't think that I hold a grudge against you. Shall I help you out with something? You lost your job, after all, while you were with me.

VINZENZ: Give me your hand. (*He reaches his toward her.*) It was really quite trying for me, the reunion with my soul. (*Alpha doesn't take the offered hand. Vinzenz goes to the mirror and brushes his hair thoughtfully.*) But if I may give you some parting advice: call these nice gentlemen back again.

ALPHA: This has an end! This must come to an end!

VINZENZ: Look! (*He holds up the brush by both ends, with all the bristles forward.*) So many ends! Don't you remember?

ALPHA: If everything about you were as trustworthy as your memory for others' mistakes, then it would never have come this far. (*She takes the brush out of his hand and continues to pace.*)

VINZENZ: Oh, dear Alpha, it's about something else, look! (*He shows her something, which he still holds between his hands.*)

ALPHA: What?

VINZENZ: This end is the last one: a white hair.

ALPHA: (*Taking it from his hand quickly*) That's my girlfriend's.

VINZENZ: Perhaps it is mine. The next one will be yours. One reaches a certain age; one can't play the little child forever, and say the world should have been different than it is. (*Tenderly melancholic*) Don't let me leave with an insincerity. Naturally you think that I'm a confidence man, too? But it's not at all true.

ALPHA: (*Standing still*) Why must you lie in parting too?

VINZENZ: But for God's sake, no. You also think that I've been in jail, that I knock around with murderers and loose women and gamble? I will tell you the plain truth: in truth, I live like everyone else. I get bored, spend my free hours at the movies, the music hall, or playing a modest bourgeois game of scat; go to the theater, to art exhibitions, and get bored there too; live my life, like every other upstanding person does, without the consciousness that he is its cause, and without melody, direction, intoxication, depth. The only thing that I have over other people is that I have no real profession; maybe that's why I see through things a little more easily than the others.

ALPHA: You're not a bad person?

VINZENZ: Unfortunately not. Not that I wouldn't have any talent for it —

ALPHA: Precisely. (*She continues with her pacing, but stops again.*) What doesn't one have talent for! But one can't use it for anything!

VINZENZ: That's what you think. You really revealed more talent for passion just now than I myself would have thought you capable of. But how does one get beyond talent? I'll tell you: only by lack of talent, by work, by taking things seriously, and other unpleasantness; genius can only distinguish itself as a deviation from non-genius; and talent without the necessary stupidity, lacks so-called earnestness.

It's better if one doesn't take one's talent seriously.

ALPHA: You lack earnestness about yourself! — I've already told you that you are spiritually dead for me. But why, back then, couldn't you — now I'm talking about the past — why couldn't you, back then, when *I* was sent to you, find the courage to be earnest?!

VINZENZ: The doorbell is ringing! (*He goes to open it.*)

ALPHA: Answer me! (*It rings again, very emphatically.*)

VINZENZ: But love between two important people is not just a private affair. (*He runs out. Comes back.*) — It is their total relation to the world! I can only advise you: make your peace with the world. Look, he has a bouquet of flowers.

(*Apulejus-Halm has entered, meticulously dressed, with a bouquet of flowers in his hand. his entrance is very controlled and confident.*)

ALPHA: Wait! (*To Vinzenz*) You are a defective Genius! Not I!!!

VINZENZ: If only I had the tiniest defect! I would be irresistible! — Then I would have a mania, a hobby horse, a secret perversion, a calling; I would be an artist, a lover, scoundrel, miser, bureaucrat, in a word, any old important man at all, and I would have earnestness for life. But I am fatally healthy. (*He looks at Halm unselfconsciously.*) I see everything around me so clearly: here is a multi-colored goldfinch of earnestness. Yet I am a comprehensive person, this is my misfortune; while everyone else is painted in one color, I am speckled in different colors. And naturally, all I have to do is let myself be seen a little under the feathers, and every person believes that I am painted like him.

HALM: (*Formally, from an unapproachable height*) You are a confidence man. That has been established.

VINZENZ: At most, if I feel lonely, from fellow feeling, so to speak, I might make use of my multi-coloring, and act, for a while, as if I were a confidence man. (*To Alpha*) My only con-artistry consists in the fact that I'm not one. (*He stretches his hand toward Alpha.*) Don't be angry at me. — And don't make him wait so long.

ALPHA: (*Shrugs her shoulders in disappointment. She has decided on something.*) What are the flowers for?

HALM: (*Holding up the bouquet*) Our friends have surely already spoken to you. I have reason to hope, that after — after this recklessness, you have learned to value the true faithfulness of a spouse.

ALPHA: (*Taking the flowers*) Dear Halm, I value your achievements. And I will answer you too, in a moment. But please, you must connect me with someone first. I will give you the number. (*She looks in the telephone book.*)

HALM: (*In the meantime to Vinzenz*) You're done for. But can I help you perhaps in any way?

VINZENZ: I would like to become a servant: perhaps you have a recommendation?

HALM: A servant? Delicious.

VINZENZ: I would like best of all to work for you; I'm already acquainted, more or less, with the circumstances.

HALM: You would like to keep making jokes. But the circumstances have changed!

ALPHA: Here, Halm dear; please call this number for me.

HALM: (*While making the connection*) This is a very important man, this Baron Ur of Usedom.

VINZENZ: (*Suspicious, to Alpha*) He's the one, isn't he, who sat next to us in the theater box once, that little chimpanzee?

HALM: An immensely rich and culturally engaged man.

VINZENZ: The one with the disgusting rash on his head?

HALM: It's in the process of healing. — Yes, Halm here, Doctor Halm, spouse of Alpha, yes, my wife is coming herself.

ALPHA: Thank you, Halm. It's Alpha... Oh?.... (*She listens, without answering. The men stand silently. Alpha interrupts the conversation, covers the mouthpiece with her hand and turns to Vinzenz.*) So you really want to go?

HALM: Of course, he must go!

ALPHA: (*Picks the telephone up again.*) All right, you can come in half an hour. Don't tire yourself out before you get here. (*She hangs up.*) Do you know what this means?

HALM: No?

ALPHA: Three weeks ago, he made a proposal of marriage to me.

HALM: (*Shaking his head admiringly*) Dear me!

ALPHA: Which I turned down. But I had to assure him of one thing: if I ever regretted my decision, I would inform him of it by the shortest route. (*She lets herself fall exhausted into a chair, simulating nonchalance with difficulty.*)

HALM: But Alpha, we are actually married; we have never been properly divorced!?

ALPHA: So? (*Tired*) Then please run to a lawyer and fix the situation. I won't have anything more to do with such nonsense. (*To Vinzenz*) And you?

VINZENZ: You are amazing. I admire nothing so much in you as your vanity; I lack that; it is your strongest characteristic.

ALPHA: But it will be hard for you now?

VINZENZ: Since Halm has rejected me, I'll start as a servant for a demi-mondaine, or a businessman.

ALPHA: But you can't be serious? We haven't much time, Vinzenz.

VINZENZ: I am serious in my own way. If one can't find one's own life, one has to submit to a stranger's. And in that case, it is best not to do it out of enthusiasm, but for money, straight out. There are only two possibilities for an ambitious man: to create a great work or to be a servant. For the first I am too honest; for the second I am just honest enough. Maybe, if you ever wanted to — it's just that I'm afraid that your overhasty step may make you unhappy —

ALPHA: Shall I work in the same house, perhaps? You could get me a job, where you are, as a servant girl?

VINZENZ: No, I wanted to ask you to go to another house; we are, perhaps, too much alike after all.

THE END

PLAY FRAGMENTS

PRELUDE TO THE ZODIAC, A MELODRAMA (1922)⁶⁰

Country road. Snowstorm. Dark evening. Man, Woman come along, struggling grievously, remain standing, exhausted.

MAN: Need, Death! (*He lets a heavy peddler bag glide from his shoulders and leans wearily against it.*)

WOMAN: What are you doing?! For an hour now, you've said nothing but this nonsense.

MAN: It's only been a half hour; there must be a cause. I should have left the damned rucksack. I've left behind every other possession, but I've had to schlepp these last dregs with me through the weather! Need, Death! Ha-ha, "No," I thought, "I must save it!"

WOMAN: We will die if we stand still. Help me forward instead. (*She can barely stay in place against the storm.*)

---

60. This is the only dramatic piece besides Musil's two plays, *The Utopians* and *Vinzenz and the Mistress of Important Men*, published during Musil's lifetime. The rest of the play was never written and his intentions for what we have here are disputed by scholars. Christian Rogowski disagrees with Egon Nagonowski's interpretation that Musil intended to write an Expressionist drama, influenced by Wedekind, Reinhardt, and Kaiser, concluding that it is more likely that the playlet might rather "have been conceived as a parody of Expressionism, especially of the pathos associated with the Expressionistic episodic passion play" (Rogowski, *op. cit.*, 64–5).

MAN: Yes, surely we will die.

WOMAN: Come, come! No house for four hours now, must be one soon!

MAN: (*Leaning on a tree*) I can't. I have gone too far already.

WOMAN: But what should I do then? Shall I just croak here on the street — like a horse?!

MAN: Onwards!

WOMAN: Onwards!

MAN: No, you! Go alone.

WOMAN: Oh, God, I should just leave everything here behind?!

MAN: Onward, onward! You will find a house soon. Onwards, I say!

WOMAN: But I'm afraid of the storm.

MAN: Onwards, I say. Else you shall perish. (*He hits her with his stick.*)

WOMAN: Ow! You animal!

MAN: Else you shall perish!

WOMAN: God will punish you for hounding me into the night alone! (*Departs, howling*)… hounding me into the night alone….

MAN: (*Screaming after her*) Else you will perish, for sure….

(The woman fights her way with difficulty through the storm. Exits.)

MAN: I will die alone! .... You die fifty feet further. *(Leans against his tree again. Pulls a half-empty bottle of schnapps out of his breast pocket, holds it up against the last shimmer of light.)* Yes, yes, still a bit, still a little bit. *(Throws the bottle, without drinking, into the snow.)* Need, Death, I am free of the woman, don't need the schnapps; drinking only comes from language.

(A wanly-spreading shimmer of light pours out of the bottle and suddenly the two Words stand in it. Medium-height forms in dark, hooded coats, merging together at first into one outline.)

MAN: Since when do I know you? You weren't sung to me in my cradle! Damned words! You were the worm in the apple of my life! But, oh, the apple was still so sweet!

NEED: Didn't you laugh, when old people trembled?

MAN: *(Cheered up by the thought)* Yes, yes.

NEED: When you saw a face that was distorted by misery and illness?

MAN: Yes, yes. And I still laugh when I think of it. It's a stupid bluster to pull faces at suffering the same way you pull off your hat.

NEED: I love you! I have always loved anyone who can speak like you can!

MAN: By God, you didn't start loving me until I was 30 years old. And how modestly you orchestrated it. First a fleeting visit just once, twice every few months — that keeps things warm without becoming tiring. Then a few hours of company every day. And all of a sudden you were lying beside me every night and couldn't be pushed out of bed any more.

NEED: When I threw one arm around your chest and one around your belly, how you would turn yourself toward me and hold on. How your groans cut through me when I rode upon your neck!

MAN: You sold off my pillow and pulled off my sheets. I even had to sleep without straw!

NEED: And no more night shirt and soon only one shirt at all. And no bath and no warm water and almost no soap either. How you stunk toward the end, my boy, in your still-living body; like wild game. And you had gone to grass long before.

MAN: When I ate the dog's leftover food from his bowl, that brought me to my senses. What a genius is man, even at the bottom! Others can wear my silk shirts with pleasure.

NEED: Enough. My dear; you are already boring me with all this. I was true to you because of your philosophical fancies. I have company.

MAN: It's Mr. Procurer, isn't it?

NEED: Yes; he will beat you now. I don't have any more time to deal with you.

MAN: Oh, my little bat, do I deserve this?

NEED: Have you ever deserved anything?

MAN: But in that case, certainly not a Death as stately and clever as your Mr. Procurer?

NEED: As long as things went well for you, you spit into the hand that reached out to you and when you yourself had to hold out the beggar's cap, you would quickly put it back on whenever a rich man came by. Don't dawdle on that account. No one will help you.

(*In a flutter of light, it looks for a moment as if The Procurer and his Girlfriend were standing in front of the collapsed Man. Then the picture vanishes.*)

(*The light is lit again and a beautiful woman stands next to a wayside cross as if she had emerged from it. Blue-white, silken baroque gown, gold crown upon her hair. The Man has propped himself up on his stick, as if he wanted to go further.*)

THE HEAVENLY ONE: Wait, my child, where are you going? Don't you know that I am your mother?

MAN: What trunk did you creep out of? Won't you tell me? An aroma from that place flows from you.... And look at that splendid silk you're wearing; it glistens like little electrical sparks. Like the logs in the stove when the boy fell asleep. You electrify me. You torment me. The stove smelled like the night. The sleds jingled past along the courtyard's wall. The little girl sat in the hollow of my bright ear, the flakes that powdered her hair flew around the lanterns of my eyes, the horses sniffed in my nose, oh! And whenever I cracked the whip, the little girl sprang through a hoop, threw her little apple-blossom-red skirts up into the air and the silver stars on her bloomers exploded. But soon the night began to thaw, large drops, then mirror-black platelets — .

THE HEAVENLY ONE: Wait, my child. Where are you going?

MAN: Oh, you are right. It wasn't even winter. The winter was terrible, with brutal adults in a room. It was a longing for winter. Autumn. Mother opened the trunk, the sisters crowded vainly around. Oh, now I remember everything. How sweetly it smelled, like fur and camphor. I have loved you, I have, forever! Fragments of silk came out of it. Petticoats. Sweat shields. Winter stockings. Feathers. Melting prongs. Butterflies. Green birds. Moons ... the woman rose magically from the trunk.

Where were you when I was grown up and could have embraced you?! Must I see you again now for the first time?! How gruesome the women were! My sisters like naked cake dough. And, after the second child came out from her thighs, the Eve that was officially assigned to me looked like the backside of a goat. False? Why?

It's always the same soft soul-dumpling you jab with your fork, after all is said and done.

THE HEAVENLY ONE: Wait, my dearest one.

MAN: Yes, just shine on, why don't you. (*The light beam becomes brighter. The background becomes clear. On the other side of the falling snow a blooming landscape appears, as if visible from its high ledge.*) What are you doing?

> What are you conjuring there?
> From out of an evening like a burst-open shrine.
> Thing after thing floats through the night, softly, fine.

THE HEAVENLY ONE:

> Beloved, this world is yours and mine!
> Like a dance through a gentle sloping meadow,
> That glides away from us, in softly twisted green,
> leading the enchanted foot still further downstream —

MAN: You and I feel our way, already too hedged in,
While space spreads all around like a sailor's dream!

THE HEAVENLY ONE: And now the dance separates us, it seems, now weaves us drunkenly close in many places. While turning —

MAN: — That something broad and ghostly paces

> You feel; I too; it makes us tremble to our core
> The earth descends, lifts us entwined from off the floor!

(*The Man has performed a ghostly, lonesome dance. Suddenly he sinks down and, when he falls, the vision is extinguished. When he gets up again, his old Mother is standing in the pool of light before him.*)

MAN: Wait, my child! We already know this! Old devil, do you see, do you see, where you have brought me?

MOTHER: (*Holding out her hands*) My child! My child!

MAN: Right-oh: Your child. Your little suck-mouth, your little sugar tush, your little dolly! Your hope! Your will! Your love! Your, your, your, your!!!! Blasted umbilical chord, you would have loved to play ponies with it and with us all your life long! Did you give me money, when I read and read and bought books?!

MOTHER: But I did give it to you, didn't I?

MAN: Yes, but then when I married my wench, this Satan, like you, whom you immediately threw out in the cold, then you gave me none.

MOTHER: No, then it was she who brought you bad luck!

MAN: Yes, she brought me bad luck!

MOTHER: (*Spreading her arms out toward him as if in pain*) My child! My child!

MAN: It's a bit of luck that you don't even budge an inch. And when I was ostracized and thrown out, did you give me money then, to restore my reputation?

MOTHER: But I had no more. You know that your debts had already swallowed everything.

MAN: And you dare to say this?! A mother, who has no money, a mother, who can't sweep stones out of the way, lets it snow feathers, fetches down stars, is a swindle! Off with you!

MOTHER: Oh, you have an evil heart!

MAN: — is a base flop! (*He cries.*)

(*The apparition disappears.*)

(*A pretty, lively young girl in a costume from fifty or sixty years ago appears to him.*)

MAN: Thank God, a pleasant diversion; what are you up to, child?

GIRL: I'm climbing trees.

MAN: Naturally. But beware of the storm.

GIRL: It took my hoop away.

MAN: Your contrivance is not particularly sharp, but, oh, how charming your legs are! Climb! No storm can hurt you; no, a storm could hardly touch your skirt. You see, I am an old uncle; laugh at me a little. Let me see your teeth, so glimmering, and your breasts must be just as shimmering. I will crack jokes for you. Will pose you riddles.

What is most beautiful in all the land?
A pi-i-ink hair band.
And next? And next?
A sweet, obedient Jumping Jack man,
A Jumping Jack man, a peddlar man,
A Jumping Jack, peddlar man is next,
To pull, to pull
For girls —

So you must come rhyming next: Marie? Stephanie? Melanie? Rose-Marie? My mother's name is Rosemarie too. Well, What's your name?

GIRL: Guess!

MAN: Guess, guess! I'll bet you are looking for a pretty man in that tree!

GIRL: A good man and a little boy, a golden little boy that he will make for me.

MAN: And what will become of the little boy? Something great? Yes, something gratifying and liberating. How you remind me; if only I knew of what?

> Like dead grandfather's coat,
> A quiet room, mysteriously wide afloat,
> You hung in the fragrant wardrobe of the world.
> Oh childhood glowing, from the dark unfurled,
> Oh loneliness, under the lady's silken suit,
> Brightened by the beloved's golden date fruit!

I must have seen you somewhere in a picture, from the time of my grandparents; who are you? Who so sweetly reminds me?

GIRL: (*In the same accents as in the earlier scene*) Don't you know that I am your mother?

MAN: Which?...!

(*The apparition disappears.*)

(*All of the fiends, one after another, become visible against the trees on either side of the road. All in city furs. The Judge in his cap, The Professor with his skull covered, The Profiteer with a top hat, The Servant in a stiff round hat, The General with a general's hat, The Politician with a black floppy hat.*)

MAN: You're here too?

THE PROFITEER: I wanted to get a look at you.

MAN: Yes, freeze to death, while you're at it.

THE PROFITEER: Don't worry; I'm warm.

MAN: If I had a fur like yours on, I would come up with something better than to just think about being warm while others are freezing.

THE PROFITEER: That's precisely why you don't have a fur; don't you know that yet, you idiot!?

MAN: Ah, Judge! If I get it, you get it. Tie him up, twist his blood-money arms from his torso, brand his fur with justice! The way you were able to do it to me!

THE JUDGE: Nothing doing, my dear. The legal noose had already been prepared for you; when society can't fit someone into any other box, it eventually detains him in a courtroom's box. But being good at earning money and stability is nothing but an over-eager exaggeration of the fundamentally necessary basis of order.

MAN: *Ach?* And the way you seized upon me because of minor offenses! Shook me back and forth between the bars because of obscene, because of revolutionary, because of subversive, because of my malcontent attitude!

THE JUDGE: Stop your carrying-on, you grouser! Being a martyr is not a bad racket. But one has to earn a right to be a reformer!

THE PROFITEER: Earn money!

THE PROFESSOR: Earn a right! This scalawag was talented. He could even have been a professor by now. But he lacked the scholarly sense of honor.

MAN: To be the custodian of a corner of a corner, the lighthouse for navigation upon a drop of water, to spend decades trying to loosen one tiny knot on the belt of life, while others are dragging her, with all her clothes, into bed: a paragon of human ambition!

THE PROFESSOR: You were not pure enough for the world-abnegating efforts of the spirit: one must have a sense of right! Have a right!

THE JUDGE: (*Chiming in like a carillon*) Have a right!

THE PROFITEER: (*In musical call and response*) Have money!

THE SERVANT: (*In discant*) Saved! Saved!

MAN: What? You too? You thief! Didn't you steal my money right from out of my pockets?!

THE SERVANT: Saved! Saved! You left it lying around; I started my business with it, let it flow into the general circulation of goods, for the well-being of the people! Gentlemen, I call you as witnesses!

MAN: Wretch! Villain! Pawing like a mole in broad daylight and mistaking the moon for a gold coin! You quarter-otter, you dime-louse!

You pouch kangeroo, you goldfinch, you penny-pinch, you — blindworm! (*Laughs.*)

THE SERVANT: (*Forgivingly*) Saved!

THE PROFITEER: (*Heartier*) Have money!

THE JUDGE AND THE PROFESSOR: (*Growling*) Have a right!

THE SERVANT: Saved! Saved!

THE GENERAL: Shaved! Shaved!

MAN: You?

THE GENERAL: I am commanding.

THE PROFITEER: (*Waving away The General*) He has no money.

THE PROFESSOR AND THE JUDGE: (*Adding*) He does not respect what is right.

MAN: (*Gently*) We went to school together.

THE GENERAL: (*Snubbing him*) Look alive! Stand at attention! I am Power.

THE PROFESSOR, PROFITEER, AND JUDGE: I! I! I!

MAN: Slash and burn: an honorable burial, indeed! Where is The Politician?

THE POLITICIAN: *L'état c'est moi.*

MAN: Very simple! And — we will really indulge you in this!

THE GENERAL: None of you know this man. If he is not constantly forced to wash himself, to keep orderly, to eat with a knife and fork, he will go right back to walking on all fours.

MAN: You are quite right, at least by half: on twos. But you are right altogether. Oh, there was only one time I should have had the power! Listen, listen:

ALL: We have no time.

THE SERVANT: You always talked; and never worked!

THE PROFITEER: One must act!

THE GENERAL: That is how it is.

THE SERVANT: It is high time that people like you disappeared.

ALL: That is how it is.

MAN: I will live longer than all of you! I!!

ALL: It is high time that you perished!

MAN: You all!

ALL: You! You! You!

MAN: You all! You all! You all!

THE WIND: (*Howls hilariously-frightening hu-hu sounds all the while.*)

ALL: (*Like an increasingly louder, swelling carillon. Their hair standing up on end under their hats; they rage like angry dogs on chains from their trees and point their fingers at the man, which he does back.*) He should lay himself down and die already!

MAN: (*Jubilantly*) I am immortal!

(*He breaks down. The picture dissolves.*)

(*The Man crouches, broken down, at the foot of a tree. The Snowflakes arrive. A Boy and a Girl as their representatives. Fantastic costumes. They disperse light.*)

BOY SNOWFLAKE: There he kneels, cover him.

GIRL SNOWFLAKE: Disgusting! He smells of schnapps.

BOY SNOWFLAKE: Do it; we have orders!

GIRL SNOWFLAKE: I would like any animal more. They make such pretty, clean shapes with their feet.

BOY SNOWFLAKE: Do you want to become an ice crystal!? The master has given his order.

GIRL SNOWFLAKE: Be nice, won't you? Do it quickly. Then we can melt together. Please, dear Snowflake!

(*Ballet.*)

(*Storm and Cold appear on stage: a shaggy old man in the costume of a machinist and an ugly old hag.*)

STORM: (*Sitting himself down on a heap of gravel and happily lighting his pipe*) Thank God, resting .... The Master pinched all my limbs again to make me howl and blow everything around properly.

COLD: You really aren't even a storm at all, just a wind.[61]

STORM: Quite right. In a civilized area, nobody just dies on a country road. Except because of a car. But sometimes the master has violent ideas. Thank God that we were able to fulful his commands afterall, and blow out the tenacious fellow's life light. What's that, old dame?

(*He claps his hands cheerily. The ballet whirls around tiredly.*)

BOY SNOWFLAKE: Come on! Gliding flight!

GIRL SNOWFLAKE: I don't want to any more.

BOY SNOWFLAKE: *Ach*, you two had better make cold and storm, or else we will melt.

STORM: I'd much rather play around a little with some warm smoke.

---

61. Continuing his interpretation of this playlet as a parody of Expressionism, Rogowski suggests that this line, "sounds more like a satirical allusion to the famous Expressionist journal, *Der Sturm* [the storm] than a quasi-tragic death scene" (*ibid.*, 64).

COLD: I want to rest for once, too.

GIRL SNOWFLAKE: Sloth! *Ach*, you are letting it get so warm, I am dying.

COLD: People claim that dying together is the highest thing that can be experienced.

BOY SNOWFLAKE: But we have a man to kill!

STORM: Already done.

(*All of them move toward the sunken figure, who has been covered by snow. The two Snowflakes melt together on his grave, exhausted. All of the characters of the play become visible again against the trees.*)

MOTHER: (*Reaching out her arms*) My child! My child!

PROFITEER: Gentlemen, I believe I speak for everyone from my heart, when I say: not one ill word more about the dead!

MOTHER: (*Stretches one arm painfully out, raising the other slowly in front of her eyes.*)

ALL: (*Their hats ceremoniously over their breasts*) Oh God, oh God, oh God, already another is dead![62]

CURTAIN

62. Piling on more evidence for his reading of this playlet as a parody, Rogowski cites Nagonowski's note explaining that this rhyme (*Gott* rhymes with *tot* in German) was sung in Vienna as a well-known parody of a beloved funeral march song (*ibid.*, 65).

THE DOUBLE-I OR THE LOSS OF PERSONALITY OR THE CIGAR SALESMAN AND GOD [63]

Prelude: The Main Character and the Industrialist (Demiurgos) step in front of the curtains. Behind them two stage hands with armchairs. Or the Main Character and the Industrialist are conjured from out of the prompt box, amid thunder and lightning. He is thick-necked, fat, elegant, Jewish with pince nez and a short, black full beard.

MAIN CHARACTER: A flea stung me. *(Looking at his hand)* How is that possible in a century of almost complete mastery over nature? We don't live in the Romantic Era anymore, do we? I feel insulted for civilization. So I became thoughtful and all morning I observed fleas

---

63. This text was transcribed from 20 numbered, hand-written, 2-sided pages inserted in Musil's Notebook 10 (1918–1921), which includes sentences and phrases written diagonally and vertically, with notations indicating where they should be inserted. The transcription, in the appendix to Notebook 10 in *TB II*, 1121–1129, has been modified slightly here for greater legibility. Orthography has been regularized and abbreviations spelled out. The order of some of the material is also uncertain. The title given here is a combination of all of the titles suggested within the draft. "Bios" appears to be a possible name for the man with the double I, otherwise referred to throughout as the

in my room. They could not be chased away. They considered my room their own; they circled around the lamp and broke up into groups for their amusements. I said to my wife ... that one is ashamed to reach out one's hand to someone who doesn't belong in good intellectual society, but is not even in a position to ....

And more: I was overpowered by the memory that I had only just recovered from the sniffles a few days earlier. It suddenly came alive to me that this constituted an invasion of alien beings into my body, a battle ....

I realized that I nourish myself with the help of intestinal bacteria, etc.

And that ultimately, each one of us is a commonwealth made up of cells.

At the same time, I was reading these old farces.

And, finally, these psychological studies (Marbe, etc.).[64]

↵ "Main Character." The theme of de-personalization or loss of self was familiar to Musil from his doctoral dissertation on Ernst Mach, who famously declared that the self was nothing but a bundle of nerves. Hermann Bahr's essay, titled after Mach's phrase "The Unsalveagable I," would also have been familiar to Musil from his reading of Bahr's 1904–5 essay collection, *Dialogue On the Tragic*, wherein Bahr writes of Mach's "horrifying book." "People," Bahr continues, "are depicted who suddenly lose their self and begin new existences as new beings, but then just as suddenly and mysteriously are hurtled back into their old ones" (See *TB II* fn 3, 288–9).

64. Reference to Karl Marbe, German cognitive psychologist.

The manufacturer: I only make things in series.
Battle for survival, a Jewish principle.

The main character has himself declared dead, returns, is loved by his wife as another person, with different qualities. The wife: all culture, modern.

Bios, factory, organic products.

(Main Character enters, behind him two stage hands with 2 club chairs. He tells them where to place them, sits in one, picks up a book and says into the prompt box: It can begin. Then: lightning and thunder and Bios climbs out of the prompt box and onto the stage.)

THE 2ND HUSBAND
THE OTHER SIDE OF THE TRAGEDY

MAIN CHARACTER: (*Is melancholy*) I can't bear it that you loved him before me.

THE WIFE: But look here, that was nothing.

(The curtains part; The Wife sits arranging papers, addressing death announcements. The Painter helps her.)

THE WIFE: It's tormenting that I don't have a single photograph of him, only paintings.

THE PAINTER: You possess him in a much more subtle way like that.

(*Letter from Demiurgos as witness of his last hours: he has even designated The Painter as the executor of his papers and as support for his wife.*)

THE PAINTER: A good fellow, our .... But it is antiquated to give oneself over to pain like this over a rotting cadaver.

(*Then the Main Character really succumbs to a condition of split personality. He could be declared ill by a doctor whom he befriends. In Act I, Bios, as funeral agent, is always around to inform the Main Character.*)

THE WIFE: (*To the Main Character*) Today I saw someone on the street who was the spitting image of my deceased husband.

(*The Main Character pretends he was a friend of the deceased.*)

Didn't he look like me?
But no.
Because it would be terrible if you had felt any of the feelings you feel for me for anyone else before.

(*She confesses to him, under pressure, all of the wrongs she had done to her former husband. He slips her a card that he had written previously to another woman.*)

THE DOUBLE I OR THE LOSS OF PERSONALITY OR THE EXPERIENCE OF THE CIGAR SALESMAN

Act I. Berlin. Cigar shop. Christmas Eve. Foul weather. The Merchant sits around and talks with his usual round of friends about the bad business, about how the Merchant is really the pioneer and the backbone of Germany (after the officer came, and did not revolt, he straightened up unconsciously), about how they would beat the Frenchies to a pulp again, if necessary, that the Austrians were dishrags, the Jews, well, better not to say anything there — and the like. Lamps are lit. A few customers come in. A nephew, who writes for *Der Anfang* [the beginning] and *Die Aktion* [the action], is mocked, with good reasons, since some people contribute something to Germany and others (which he himself senses with compunction) can't afford to. His wife brings coffee through the back door. A customer comes. Do you know who that was? The one ... who ... has that villa on ... Street. Tea room cartel or something (or he prints the backside of streetcar permits), is treated with respect, but also with the feeling: I could possibly achieve that too. A constable comes and complains about a poster. The Merchant cringes. —

God enters (beforehand, the Merchant elaborates on his psychology of customers' appearances). D'ya know? Fine, fine; ya don't notice right off. The eyes are part of it.

Just a soft hat, no top hat. But the way it's indented in the front, concave … the prince … wears his like that now. It's finer now than in the days of the Kaiser. (*And the like.*)

God, with a great, long beard tucked into his coat, open lapels, soft hat. He slips a bit because of the wet floor. The merchant smiles at his friend. He doesn't deserve it, but we'll invite him in politely. God greets him. The Merchant, embarassed, says G'evening. (*That's not something fine.*) God speaks politely and softly. —The Merchant: Wha? Huh? Don't understand. God says: I am looking for a cigarette. The Merchant: Christmas specials. Spreads out Manoli, Waldorf Astoria … 15, 12, 10, 8. More or less in a mood of patronage, to do the customer honor.

God says: I am looking for a specific cigarette. Perhaps you have it: Novelta.

Which?

Novelta.

Nah, we don't carry that one.

I smoked some in Munich by chance, and I was told they came from Berlin. I have asked already in 25 shops, and no one knows of them.

What are they called?

Novelta.

Nah.

At the least, I'd like to know where I can get them.

What do they cost?

100 for 90.

Nah, dear sir, such a penny cigarette can't be found here in all of the west. No such thing here. We wouldn't have customers here in the fine west side for something so cheap.

But couldn't I at least ask at the factory?

You couldn't ask the factory (*Smiles at his friend*). It'd be a little hole in the wall somewhere in the East or the North. No one knows it. That's where they'd be made. We sell Russian ones — see, from 3 pennies and up. Tosses him a few opened cartons and serves a lieutenant, with opened red lapels, who has just entered.

Good Evening.

How may I help you? What would you like?

Give me — nah — 5 cigars — what do you have?

(*Flattered, protesting*) Ah — import? Henry Clay, the finest brand, from 50 cents to 2 marks?

Nah.

Bock? Juhl? Christmas pleasure at 25 cents — an excellent kind, favorite of many? Juhl: General Major at 20, 15, 10, 8 pennies? Carsten & Co.? Tropical Planter at 20 and 35? Hamburg Assortment from 7 to 22 cents a piece?

Which would be an ideal sale for him.

Give me 5 General Majors for 10 pennies a piece.

Yes, indeed. (*Packs them up.*) Any other desires? — Cigarettes? Tip-Top, with gold mouthpiece? A favorite of the officers?

Nah. (*The salesman hands him the bag, comes out from behind the counter, and accompanies him to the door.*)

Can you tell me how I get to the Memorial Church from here?

A right over there and then straight ahead. Straight ahead. Can't miss it; you're welcome. (*He opens the door for him. Returns. Puts the money away. Irritated that his soul forced him to make such a big deal out of such a small sale. Looks at God. Makes a remark to his friend.*)

Well, have you decided?

No, I really don't want these Russians; only this one kind pleases me. Can you order them?

Nah.

Can't you at least tell me where I can find them?

No, sir.

It is really not about the price, but about the excellence of the wares; when something so good can be made for such a very little, I admire that.

So that's it.

I would be interested in that.

Not me.

Tell me, are you really just here to sell stupid things that are provided for you once and for all at a set price? Or rather ... (*God tries to awaken his soul, in hopes that it could be expanded from the job of a cigar Merchant, and then into the wider world. But the Merchant, annoyed about his bad business, has sat down by the oven, and utters coarse answers.*)

Are you an agent from this hole-in-the wall factory? What do you really want? Stand there and tell me things and no one asked you to?

Oh, nonsense.

Sir, better you should leave and buy your wife something warm to wear under her nose. Or, if you don't have any money, go and steal someone else's time and buy her some quiet with it. Sir, leave me in peace. Leave me in peace, do you hear? Get on out of here. To the Devil! If you don't go, I'll call the constable! Do you know what a royal Prussian constable is?

God grows afraid, and slams the door closed with a clang. Thunder. Dazzling lightning. The other one had fallen into a doze and wakes up with a start. Bios is there.

Lightning continues. Flashes of light and dark for a few seconds.

Bios disappears through the wall. Have him write a note: that he is going to kill himself; farewell.

Left alone, he looks at the note. The whole thing could have been like a dream, but the note is the epiphany. It has some sort of suggestive effect. Since it is here, after all?! He follows the note's command. One sees him closing the blinds through the glass door. Then with his collar opened through the display windows.

Later: Happiness in loss of personality (*last act*).

The Wife, when she comes: *Auah!* Now he's gone. Now he's dead. Without saying a word. (*She cries.*) And Woldemar won't want to either (*grows frightened*) now that I'm a widow.

Later, when he returns, another cigar merchant is there. As her husband.

As his double self he leads the life of a reckless loan shark. One can achieve anything of this kind here. He has a romantic weakness for the life of a modest cigar merchant.

In the second act, his new existence. Hall of a grand, luxury hotel. He lives there with his secretary, mistress, and grand suite. Daily, he invites all manner of aristocrats. Everything without money, on credit. In a short time, he is in so much debt that his associates have to stop him.

He waits in the hall. Discussion with his secretary about the dangers of the situation, since there is no more than 200 marks in his business's holdings. The hotel manager pressures him about payment. His car waits. An enormous bouquet arrives. He has it paid for by the till. The chairman of the board of one of the largest banks is also staying at the hotel for a few days — while his apartment is being renovated. Connections are somehow orchestrated. Before leaving, the director speaks with him. He could have simply asked the hotel personnel about him, but he is too proud to do so, trusts his knowledge of men too much. The de-personalized man tells the director about his enormous cigar scheme. Claims he has come from Russia, has great estates and resources there, etc. The other one grows suspicious, because he seems to be lying outrageously. He only needs to check, but why bother: the man can lie a bit, even if it isn't true, if he pleases me; it's his nose, that's it, his nose.

A general comes who is treated with respect.

Do you know how much he earns? — 15,000 marks. That's something, eh?

The scheme is already in motion, but a little shaky; still needs to be financed in higher style.

Intuition in big business. See Notebook...[65]

Before that a man of letters (friend of his nephew), hesitates for a moment, summons the courage because of the likeness. You remind me so agreeably of an old — that is, of the uncle of an old friend of mine. — Of course, not really, just a modest cigar merchant.

---

65. A note in *TB II* directs us to Musil's Notebook 7 (*TB I*, 295), wherein he discusses intuition in reference to the industrialist, writer, and politician Walter Rathenau, one of his main models for Arnheim in *The Man Without Qualities*: "Only those who have intuition are able to triumph over others in business" and again the appendix to Notebook 8 (*TB II*, 1095): "later this feeling of the impossibility of failure develops [with old Rathenau's father, Emil]. That is where R[athenau] junior got his concept of intuition, that is not only relevant for mystical life" (*TB II*, fn d, 1127).

Disappeared, by the way, without a trace. — Strange case. Don't you think that other worlds slide into the palpable world? This culture of scholarship, enslavement to facts ... etc.

In the meantime, an elevator boy or someone like that, shamelessly against writers.

At the mention of the cigar merchant, the Main Character becomes conspicuously friendly and smooth, but at the literary exegesis, he hardens himself proudly, ready for business. Okay. What was it you wanted? Project: hotel magazine. Advertisements that make the publication of poems possible.

That's nothing. I don't understand anything about art, but if there were something to the man, he wouldn't be so modest.

The Main Character interrupts him in the middle and makes him wait when the Director comes. Pleased with the lucky conclusion. The man of power had reached him his hand in a sudden impulse, but then corrected it with a tip of his hat — Says to the Writer: doesn't sound like much. But we'll see. You know what? I like you. I'll think it over a bit. But naturally without the poems; just the advertisements.

ACT 3. CIGAR SHOP.

Long late-spring evening. Before Pentacost. The stores are open longer. The Woman is alone. The Main Character enters. The Woman is shocked. But then quickly notices the lack of similarity. The Main Character lives in an other, new, elegant area. Says: but he has a strange preference for this one. He gets hazy, woozy, almost lyrical when he walks slowly like this through these streets. And especially this shop. He left home. It suddenly was too much for him. He doesn't know why. That is, he thinks: stress, he just wants to have a few hours alone for once. In the evening there will be grand company. He needs the finest cigars, for two thousand marks. Wanted to take a car at Nollendorf Place and drive in the city. When he saw the shop, he couldn't go any further. He felt tired. The Woman can order him one by telephone. She is a little mistrustful because of the large order, which she could be left in the lurch with, but she is relieved that he explains that he wants to stay there. He has her order his car for later. Asks about the business and seems to be well-versed. He asks after her husband. He has gone around the corner, to take a little break. A good businessman shouldn't do that at this time of day. God, men. The blissful one—that is, oh, God, who even knows?—the Main Character says that he was there in the past, but doesn't remember him clearly. Yeah, a man about so high, a little worn out. And now they start talking about infidelity, love, the miseries of marriage, etc. The Main Character courts her a little.

In between, the Nephew comes with his friend. Again, surprise, then quickly relaxing. The Main Character says: I have thought it over. Let's do it. But naturally you can't be the editor. That won't work. — What are you earning now? Hesitantly: sometimes this much, sometimes that much. — Fine. I'll take you into my firm for 200 marks. I spoke with … about the new hotel magazine — he'll be the editor — an important writer. The man has a name, has already achieved something, etc. The young man protests — oh, yeah? Who is an important writer, then, to you? — Heinrich Mann, Wedekind … and, and ….

ACT 4.

Private office of the Main Character. The instances of recrudescence of his former life increase to crisis level. He remembers. He opens up. The chairman of the board doesn't believe him. He produces documents. My dear man, I believe you are experiencing a little delusion. After it fades again, you should take three weeks in the mountains. — Later: I will commit you to a mental hospital if you publicly utter one word. The corporation is on the verge of an important transaction.

In the meantime, he has become the son-in-law of the big financier. The doctor is his constant companion, explains his symptoms to him, and tries to talk him out of them.

The Wife comes with her husband. She, too, naturally defends against this reincarnation and instinctively rallies the most convincing arguments against the idea. But he knows about a birthmark or something similar. Nevertheless. The new husband gets jealous.

He calls a doctor. He declares it a mild case of depersonalization as a result of exhaustion. Advises rest. Once, during this discussion, the Main Character rushes to the window. Someone is passing by — God himself, he thought. Was just a delusion. Finally, happiness of depersonalization.

A STYLITE [66]

A STYLITE: In the old days, pairs of lovers used to meet near me. People rushing by felt a trembling in their breasts! Now only dogs care about pillars.

THE YOUNG WOMAN: Here old man (*Throws something in his rice bowl.*)

(*A month later.*)

THE YOUNG WOMAN / YOUNG MAN: Excuse us, dear Stylite! We have so much to do! Here.

(*A month later.*)

THE YOUNG WOMAN: Excuse me, dear Stylite! I am in a hurry now. I will come by again the day after tomorrow.

(*After eight instead of two days.*)

THE YOUNG WOMAN: Here, old man! Don't think I am bad or forgetful! I know everything, but sometimes I can't do it any differently.

A STYLITE: Of course, of course! I wouldn't even say that you have any obligation!

(*After six weeks instead of one.*)

---

66. A hand-written text, dated between 1918–1919. From the *Klagenfurter Ausgabe. Band 15: Dramen-Fragmente.*

THE YOUNG WOMAN: Oh! I know very well! I will come find you this time in just a few days! Let me be precise: in three days at the most! Don't hurt me and don't retaliate!

(*This time, a long period has passed.*)

THE STYLITE: What shall I say to her? The days have already turned into weeks, and now the weeks will give birth to an eternity. The young man acts as if he knows nothing, and the young woman forgets everything. But my earthly podium must be freshly white-washed from time to time, among other things. (*Considers.*) What should I do? Awaken religiosity in the breasts of these people whose heads are filled with distractions and don't notice anything besides my height? Chattering and uttering humbug, providing the ridiculous spectacle of a stone saint who gets down from his pinnacle and runs after them? (*Irritated*) It is not very tactful to put me in the position of having to decide like this!

(*Finally, the Stylite writes a letter. It is a somewhat shameful spectacle. The creator in heaven laughs about his exquisite world.*)

GOD: Aren't you ashamed of yourself, old Stylite?

STYLITE: Of course I am. But why don't you nourish your saints yourself?

(*God shrugs his shoulders and laughs. And the Stylite would like to laugh at God, too, if he were not afraid.*)

This play dedicated, with best regards, to ….

TEMPORA MAIER [67]

Dramatis Personæ

TEMPORA MAIER, Time. *(Loves boxers — not without a bad conscience — engineers, enterprising merchants, the Clemenceaus and [Romain] Rollands,*[68] *etc. When it comes to writers, with condescension, the type of [Kasimir] Edschmid.*[69] *— Loves health.)*

TRUSTY MAIER, Wholesale Merchant

---

67. Draft from Musil's Notebook, volume 19 (1919–1921). Written above the title, in pencil, presumably by Martha Musil, are the words: "Draft for a satirical drama." See *TB II*, fn 142, 368. Although the passages are reproduced here as if they came one after the other, in the original hand-written text some of them have been inserted to the side of and parallel to the main text. I have also made some minor orthographical changes for consistency's sake. While the German version in *TB I* includes words that have been crossed out by Musil, they have not been included here.
68. Romain Rolland, who was an outspoken pacifist during and after WWI, is compared here with the exemplary nationalist, anti-pacifist Clemenceau. See *TB II*, fn 143, 368.
69. Edschmid was a German writer, who initially allied himself with the Expressionists, but who took a turn back toward Realism in the mid-1920's. At the time of this writing, Musil would probably have associated him with Expressionism.

FAUST BELLYPUNCH, World Master of Boxing[70]

FOUNTAINMOUTH, Writer (possibly a second writer named **TINCLANK**)

DUMBEST and **PARROT**, National Assemblymen

FIEND and **THINK**, Satyrs[71]

PASTOR OBSTIPATIUS SEIGERT

FAITHLEIN SEIGERT, His Daughter

EUGENIE BELLYPUNCH, Faust's Grandmother

EGYDIUS GANTER, University Professor of Feuilletonistics

(An idea that is held onto for longer than five minutes is already a compulsion. Except in economics.)

---

70. The word "Faust" in German does not only suggest the famous Dr. Faustus, but is also the word for "fist."
71. On a loose sheet of paper, inserted into Notebook 19, Musil has written, under the title, "Satyrs": "A socially-minded collective that is rich in models worthy of imitation and praise, that is rife with the spirit of harmony and spiritual sympathy, that is enlivened by intellectual interests and ruled by a spirit of justice and a love of beauty that provides from the outset every normal personality with a psychophysical attitude, etc.

    The stimulation and the inspiration, the appreciation and the sympathy, the presentation of opportunities must always be accompanied by deliberate repression of misleading seductions, by conscientious warnings, by vivid antipathy for the unethical, the immoral, and the ugly..." (Appendix to Notebook 19, *TB II*, 1135).

A love story, on the second level. On the first, a satire [satyr play] about conditions that will come.

The butt of the satire is not Eugenics, but that which wants to be made eternal with the help of eugenics.

Journalistic writing: Perutz, Höllriegel,[72] etc. has already created a dry, exact narrative style that has replaced the family magazine novel in the newspapers, for which they may, indeed, congratulate themselves. But they would say: we influence the people through the newspapers; more than can be said for you Ethico-Æsthetes. We have created the novelistic style of the times, which is precisely the newspaper style: intelligent, curious, chopped up into bits, etc.

One compares it to Dostoevsky, etc.

ACT I

Nature preserve near to a futuristic metropolis. View of a vast, delightful field, surrounded by trees. To the right and the left of the stage, the forest crowds in. On the right side, upfront, stands a single old tree; under it, a bench.

TEMPORA MAIER: Well, this could be the place. I must admit that I feel a bit frightened. One hears such incredible stories about these satyrs.

---

72. Reference to Leo Perutz (1882–1957), playwright, short story writer, adventure fantasy novelist; Arnold Höllriegl (1883–1938) was a Berlin journalist and sometime editor of the Viennese newspaper, *Der Tag*, travel writer, and short story writer.

FAUST: You couldn't have chosen a better companion, Tempora. My right hand can knock down a two-year old bull. I can also dispatch a three-year old bull with five blows to his skull. (*They make themselves comfortable.*) It only took me 23 minutes to win the world championship and I can calculate that my hand (*wooing*) is worth 25,000 marks a minute.

TEMPORA MAIER: (*Changing the subject*) I am indescribably excited to find out who will win the Schiller Prize tomorrow for the best feuilleton of the last two years.

FAUST: Pschaw! Two thousand marks!

TEMPORA MAIER: That is only symbolic. You must know that spirit cannot be compensated with money. The choice is between Fountainmouth and Tinclank.

FAUST: On the occasion of my world championship fight, Tinclank wrote that my blows revealed more intuition than Goethe's poems. — By the way, who was Goethe? — I think Tinclank is the better of the two. He has the modern spirit. But basically, all of them are merely imitative people, who only write words about other people's actions.

TEMPORA MAIER: I must repeat to you again that you lack the proper understanding of spirit. I could never do without ingenious men like Fountainmouth and Tinclank. Only just consider, what it meant to all of us, when Fountainmouth, in the Whitsuntide edition of *The Steelyard*, established how much our contemporary spirit, under the tutelage of the feuilleton, has become so much sharper and sprightlier than the ponderous breadth of former times.

FAUST: That's why we have a Professor of Feuilletonistics at the university. That's more than enough.

TEMPORA MAIER: You are a despiser of spirit, Faust Bellyblow.

FAUST: Tempora, if I say university professor, I mean it in earnest. That is where these things belong. That is where they are put in order. It is calming to know they are there. But they have as little to do with me as a corpse in the anatomy department: excepting, of course, if I had hit him myself. The only thing that is alive is action; without thoughts!

Moreover, you interest yourself more than I like for this professor, Egydius Ganter. I assure you, when I see this man's chest, I have to hold my nose. (*They both are silent; enraged.*)

TEMPORA MAIER: (*After a while, sheepishly*) I am afraid, Faust Bellyblow. I have heard that these satyrs defile virgins.

FAUST: In truth. But you are insulting me again! I have promised you that I would catch one of them live. Then *you* can defile *him*, or do whatever you want with him.

TEMPORA MAIER: You are crude, Faust!

FAUST: Forgive me. I was careless, and something that I read in the morning paper just flew into my mouth.

TEMPORA MAIER: Is it true then, that people want to apprehend these creatures, if they really exist, before the eugenic medicinal court?

FAUST: Of course, this is true. There is even supposed to be an expedition going out soon. And I think that they definitely should go before the eugenic medical tribunal.

TEMPORA MAIER: You are an expert on the higher Health Court?

FAUST: Precisely. There are few people among us who would be more competent to rule on questions of our healthy progeny.

TEMPORA MAIER: And what is really known about these satyrs?

FAUST: I must admit that I have never interested myself too much in the question. It is said that they once were important for poets. I mean, for people who, themselves, were like them. They are indecent.

TEMPORA MAIER: Oh! Horrors! Indecent!

FAUST: I must admit, I never was too interested in them. A relict of the bygone life of the mind.

(Some writers even today. They go searching in the woods. Blei and ... fall from a branch. The girl pleases him. Nostalgia. The party comes. Exits.)

(Faust and Tempora turn back. Engagement to be married. In fury, he catches one from a tree.)

FAUST: They are unhealthy.

TEMPORA MAIER: Pfui! Unhealthy?

FAUST: Yes, they are a repulsive remnant of an uncivilized past. *(He takes his jump rope out of his bag and begins to jump over it like a child at play, swinging it from behind over his head and jumping over it with his feet.)*

TEMPORA MAIER: What are you doing, Faust?

FAUST: I am training the flexors and the extensor muscles of my legs.

TEMPORA MAIER: I mean, why are you doing it so savagely, without culture? *(Faust stops, questioningly.)* You must practice body-spirit: in between every jump, one must raise one's eyes to the sky, while thinking deep thoughts about Hellenic culture. This is the Greek form of pilgrimage. Soul and physical strength grow at the same rate.

FAUST: That bores me. *(Weighs the rope in his hand before packing it away.)* With this rope, I will catch one of the satyrs for you.

TEMPORA MAIER: You know, I passionately adore decency and health. But tell me: what actually does unhealthy and indecent mean?

FAUST: (*After reflecting a while over this new question*) I should think: whatever is neither decent nor healthy.

TEMPORA MAIER: That's circular logic, Faust. Our strict, logical education does not allow for that.

FAUST: Perhaps you are right. But what counts as healthy is decided every year by our parliament, no? And what is decent simply need not be questioned by any healthy person.

TEMPORA MAIER: Yes, but what do these satyrs do?

(*The whole society arrives. Egydius Ganter also, etc. Trusty Maier — pokes at Faust's muscles: You are so enchantingly healthy, whole, etc. — Milrath from the* World Evening Post. *Socialistic wait-and-see battle plan. Capitalism gets increasingly stronger. But Socialism has become an institution of the Capitalistic world. The poor man lives badly and expensively — the rich man well and cheaply. The poor man gives evidence of great bravery, but does not have the civilian courage for a revolution. Thus, the rich man believes that the organization is good, because it makes the poor man manly.*)

FAUST: Tempora, I must admit that I really have no idea about what they do. I simply do not know. One has never crossed my path nor insulted me, so that I might take notice of him. But we shall go into the woods and I will catch one for you. Then you can ask him about anything you wish to know. I give you my word that the fellow will deliver his last truth to you. May I take your arm?

TEMPORA MAIER: It is too early. It is disobedient to go on, before the elders arrive.

FAUST: We will just go a little bit ahead; in fifteen minutes we will be back. (*Tempora lays her arm upon his. Enamored, Faust continues*) If a man hits me in the arm with a sledge hammer, its shaft will fly out of his hand, but if your arm lays upon it like a down feather, it trembles: I am neither a politician nor a scholar, but I am willing to bet that decent and healthy mean nothing more than this. (*Both exit in the direction of the woods.*)

(—? *Men and women. Offspring of Harlequins and Columbines? Come out of the woods; not from the trees. Even libertinage is dull without resistance from society.* —)

(*Think and Fiend climb down from an old tree. Dark, strange, somewhat worn clothing. Fiend, the older one, looks like a gaunt man-about-town; Think, lyrical, spiritually passionate, young. They sit down, emotionally and physically exhausted, upon the grass.*)

(*Also: one of the satyrs is caught, the other one sneaks in disguised, and learns thus about this whole world. Fantastically checked clothing, tight trousers, a sort of waistcoat.*

Fiend very tall and lean. Think: a childish face with a little pointy nose …. Have you ever heard of such roguery? They are murdering spirit!)

FIEND: They will only stop spirit from being bred. Pitiful....

THINK: They want to send out an expedition against us. Did you hear?

FIEND: Yes, my dear Think, they want to nip it in the bud. Poor boy — you haven't even had much chance to make use of it yet.

THINK: Pathetic! This health sniveling! They want to treat the writers and intellectuals like robbers, alcoholics, and the terminally ill, to keep them from reproducing!

FIEND: The operation is not at all brutal and doesn't hurt. — The operation doesn't hurt and is spiritually very liberating. —

THINK: But consider the infamy!

FIEND: My dear young friend, I would not see it so terribly. Just think how far we have fallen in general, even without this. We had to remove ourselves into the woods and had to publish the newspapers, *The Tree-Monastery* and the *Treetop* from here. Well and good. We debate fiercely in these two newspapers about the meaning of the world. But we are not allowed to show ourselves in the world, beyond the woods or beyond these two newspapers. The university and the daily papers are there for the intellectual. In school, one learns how to make verses. Morality is firmly established, and any ambiguities are handled by the Health Court. We have no social function. We also have no income. And for the last hundred years we are treated like a vacuum on all official public occasions. So that we did not starve, we have become accustomed to this animalistic life in the trees. But I admit to you that I am sick of living off the gifts of crazy women, who read our books because they have not found the right man. Am utterly sick of it. I couldn't care less if they castrate me. On the contrary, that would free me from these women readers and it would all be a part of the world order. Did you, by the way, see the beautiful lady who was sitting here?

THINK: A giant calf with an even more gigantic butcher!

FIEND: *Ach*, I miss the world. It is what it is, but in any case, it is steady, warm, and eventful material. I am going to give up writing and become the manager of this boxer.

THINK: We're too passive. We are the exceptions, the unique cases, etc.

FIEND: We have already let it go too far. In the law there is no exception, only a monstrosity.

THINK: We will finally make the people think about their private affairs, etc., just as I always vainly hoped to do.

(He wants to unify the intellectuals before the Expedition and instigate an intellectual invasion — overthrow — in the city, rushing through the streets like the suffragettes — first Christians — and suchlike. Fiend remains skeptical, but they both agree to go into the woods. The search party comes and they retreat to their trees.)

TEMPORA MAIER AND HER CONTEMPORARIES
A PICTURE OF THE FUTURE

We get a description of this future world.

There are only free thinkers and Church devotees; every intellectual expression is measured by one of these two positions.

They want to go into the woods to warn their fellows, but the party comes and they have to hide in the trees.

Central points: Trusty Maier and Faithlein Seigert. Around the former, people who are bidding, more or less, for the hand of his daughter. From the realms of politics, business, literature, and science. Around the latter, there is one person who lays more emphasis on "depth."

They go toward the woods also. Tempora Maier and Faust return. Faust delivers his offer of marriage, wherein he proves that the boxer is the epitome of contemporary virtues.

While Tempora Maier stalls and rejects him, he becomes furious and discovers Think's leg and pulls him down. Fiend leaps, clamoring from the tree and is caught by Faust's other hand. Faust ties them both up and encourages Tempora to begin her questioning.

But then the search party, alerted by the cries, comes back. Each person asks a characteristic question, which Fiend and Think answer only by sticking out their tongues. It is decided that it would be better to turn them over to the Psychotechnical Institute, so they are left tied up.

— Only the weary, skeptical satyr is caught; the other escapes to the woods. And then one knows that this will lead to revolution.

His wife brings him breakfast. That means: we were married in the bad old days —

I am one of the most important people in the history of human evolution —

Recently, someone was castrated due to an error in the apparatus and then it turned out that he was one of the Virtuous Superiors, or such like. There have been cases in which the wrong people were married to each other and such like.

1: Institute's servant smears the tachistoscope. Asks assistant: what do we have for our daily program today?

2: A commission of foreign nations is there for research purposes.

3: Simultaneously other investigations: a bride and groom, a politician, a deracinated person.

National Psychotechnical Institute

ACT II

Institute and takeover. Think and Fiend are interrogated. The day's agenda is prepared. Marriages, professional examinations, moral investigations, castrations, etc.

While Think and Fiend are interrogated, the intelligentsia attacks the city. In the form of an epidemic-scare. They flag down the people, throw themselves in front of buses, speak at concerts, etc. Since they enter one by one, they cannot be caught. They preach to the people: Your life is not a life.

Of course, the Psychotechnical Institute is in the government building. Also, the main headquarters of the police defense squad. On account of the increasing dramatic reports of assailants, one finds out what is happening outside (also persiflage of these reports. Something is missing for an important national examination — extreme agitation about this. Relieved by the revolutionary outbreak. For example, the messenger must burst in like a marathon runner. — This is a long-established rule. Specific gestures are employed to result in specific feelings). Order is threatened. Delegations from political parties appear, repeating slogans such as: What? The life that we have preached is not a life?

Saving idea of the Police President: to sic the writers on the intruders. These windbags confuse their listeners, the attacking intelligentsia is not organized enough, and so the assault crumbles and the satyrs are captured.

During the attacks, the imprisoned Fiend becomes the spokesperson of the assailants. They negotiate with him about what should be done with the intelligentsia. (He continues in this role after the failure.)

The director of the Psychotechnical Institute turns to him with the suggestion that scientific methods could also be useful to the new intellect; science is value-free; the significance of health must be introduced from outside.

At the same time, the Professor of Feuilletonistics approaches.

A priest comes too, to save religion; it persists in those institutions that are psychotechnically virulent and is indifferent to varieties of religious content. (Existence of the church is merely a button on the pocket handkerchief of humanity, to remind it of the transcendental.)

ACT III

Must be a satire of the society, without the writers on the stage. The people from the first act have become uncertain. But the ideals are re-stabilized.

A weedy Major for the war.

Politicians for politics.

The Parliament establishes what is healthy.

Lies. Quickly: a spoonful of hormones.

Wholesale Merchant Maier is chosen as president. Rebellious wretches are made reasonable.

It is proposed that money should be made holy, to anchor it even more deeply among the people. Maier demurs. It is better if God remains the club president and money the General Secretary.

Form of government: the representatives are chosen by the scholars after an "aptitude test" and then elected according to various programs, which they must learn in dead languages.

(The political exam.)

Size of oral cavity.

Elasticity of vocal cords.

Faithfulness to creed. Good memory, slowness of conceptualization, rigid emotional life, economic sense, partial colorblindness — only able to see primary colors. Strong will. Abstract emotions. No pre-reactions. The main thing is a sense of community, conformity with the others.

Principles are scientifically simplified and officially approved. All parties share the same ones. The classical program will contain pronouncements about culture.

— Tempora visits Fiend. Eugenie visits Fiend. —

Scholars examine the life principles.

Parliamentary resolutions are only valid for a few years. Until definitive probe is completed. Power of the Parliament rests on material privilege.

The people have sports sensations and novelties; the technological novelty is developed to an extreme.

After fierce debates about the elimination of money, it is reintroduced again, but its "value" is regulated. (President's speech.)

In the hour of need, they had turned to Paul Ernst,[73] but now distance themselves from him in favor of something more in keeping with the times. Satire on idealists.

(Instead of acts, scenes.)

The question is raised: punishment of the intelligentsia or rendering them harmless. The ruling is drafted and pronounced. But interrupted and overturned by Tempora's and Eugenie's declarations of love. With this the act is ended.

[ALTERNATE ACT II][74]

Act II: Love scene of a fifty-year old woman.

— In addition: Act II — some kind of war instigated by the other satyrs. Technical. But it is met with fascistic-heroic gestures.

---

73. Paul Ernst (1866–1933), German writer of prose fiction, plays, and journalism. Initially a member of the labor party and a proponent of Naturalism, later a founder of Neo-Classicism and one of the replacements for the many Jewish authors expelled by the Nazis from the Prussian Academy of the Arts in 1933.
74. I have moved this scene, which in the manuscript is below Act IV, before it, in response to Musil's note: "Perhaps: Merge Acts II and III, which both really contain the same thing, into one (III)."

A FIFTY-YEAR OLD WOMAN *in front of her mirror. Open peignoir, busty; strong, healthy, unbeautiful legs. She does her hair, powders, looks at herself.*

LADIES' MAID

GRANDMOTHER: Doubtless, beauty is something extraordinarily relative. The plum-smooth skin of a seventeen-year-old is beautiful, no? Your plum-smooth skin is beautiful.

MAID: I don't know.

GRANDMOTHER: You don't even know it! These concepts are that uncertain. One even finds the crevices of a glacier worthy of admiration. Human beings don't take enough trouble understanding the beautiful. (*She looks at her leg.*) Doesn't this leg still express passion?

MAID: It is a leg as beautiful as any other.

GRANDMOTHER: In the last twenty, in the last ten, in the last five years, I am supposed to have become someone different? I wish I knew! Every morning I saw the same face in the mirror that I saw the night before. I will not deny that I may have looked somewhat different twenty years ago; but how shall I express this to you: the change did not take place with antipathy at all! The change happened under amicable arrangements, so to speak, with myself! With my agreement! As I already said to you, every morning and evening.

MAID: (*Shyly*) But it isn't possible, I just mean, if I take one step, I am still standing near you, and then if I take one more step, I am still standing near you; but now I am standing far away from you.

GRANDMOTHER: But I am standing just as close to myself as I was 25 years ago. And when you have too many children, and when your husband dies in good time, as long as you don't give up on your soul when you are still living, you will also be standing right where you are now, from your own perspective.

MAID: Your hair is starting to go white again, a finger-width from the roots; shouldn't I engage the hair-colorer in the next few days?

GRANDMOTHER: Engage her, my dear. But my digestion is better than my granddaughter's. A plate of crayfish with a glass of ... wine still pleases me so much that I can hardly express it to you. Everything gives me pleasure. And you see that from my breasts: there are certainly peoples who prefer a heavy, pendulous womanly breast over those ridiculous pointy caps.

Love scene with sympathy for Potiphar:

(She sympathizes with the revolutionaries, like all erotic people; but in the end, they only allow her to get married one more time. Only in this form is the libido of an old woman tolerated.) (Ganter, who does not want to marry her, battles against this standpoint.)

(*Satyr I is brought to her tied up. Grandmother looks at him with sympathy. Satyr I understands and is shocked. Vision of the maid gives him some assurance.*)

MAID: So that is one of the satyrs?

GRANDMOTHER: It's not so bad. They make them sound much worse than they probably are. I will determine right away whether or not he is a cultured gentleman. You are imprisoned and face a terrible lot.

SATYR I: So it seems.

GRANDMOTHER: A pure woman's soul can save you. — Now it must seem like a fairy tale to him.

SATYR I: Could anything worse happen to me?

GRANDMOTHER: I don't know where I'm getting these ideas; but it is a matter of my faith in God. As a little girl I was taught to commend my soul to Him, and He really never did anything to make it more independent. It is still just as tender as a little girl's who has been promised that instead of the stepmother, her good mother would come; she never came. Along the way, I have become a grandmother, over the course of 25 years, and was never married. That sounds so ridiculous, that from a certain age on, one hides it from people, but I expect that you, as a man of intellect, will understand it. You will feel that here a creature calls upon God and that human life would be incomprehensible unless you returned my love.

SATYR I: Potiphar's wife has not yet been released. She haunts through the mockery of the centuries. But I am no Joseph; you must excuse me for lacking the requisite naiveté. I am a man on the edge of departing. I succumb to the banal charms of a young bosom. I love foolishness. But my friend Satyr II, who is still young, will love you with the necessary passion. You must help us to overcome this society.

(She reaches for him. He attaches himself to the young woman.)

ACT IV

Everyone gets married; satire of this. The intelligentsia are pardoned and the two writers who share the Schiller Prize are crowned. The intellectuals are not castrated. Instead, they build a large stone court for them, a kind of reservation.

Faust fears cows, but not bulls. Scientific boxing; but the main thing is one's ability to make money. Marries Faithlein.

Tempora marries a salesman, as is fitting for the daughter of the president, but only after she swings back and forth between Faust and Ganter. (Heart-to-heart scene with her father.)

Ganter marries Eugenie, only after scientifically ascertaining that her libido is not libido, but originary force.

Finally, they give up on the idea of the reservation, when the intellectuals promise not to make any demands on society.

INDEX OF PERSONS & WORKS

A

ADORNO, Theodor, xxv
ALBACH-RETTY, Rosa, 146
ANDREYEV, Leonid, works by: *The Life of Humans*, 90
ANSELM of Canterbury, xxxvi
AQUINAS, Thomas, xxxvi, 80
ARTAUD, Antonin, xxv
ASLAN, Raoul, 209

B

BACH, Ernst, 36
BAHR, Hermann, 42, 512
    works by: *Dialogue on the Tragic*, 512
BARUFFI, Ferruccio, 125
BEARDSLEY, Aubrey, 90
BEER, Rudolf, 36
BEETHOVEN, Ludwig von, 13, 438
BERGSON, Henri, 169
BERNAU, Alfred, 35
BLEI, Franz, xi
BONN, Ferdinand, 21, 121
BONSELS, Waldemar, 184
BRECHT, Bertolt, xxv, xxvi
BRIEUX, Eugène, works by: *Red Dress*, 161
BROCINER, Marco, works by: *Behind the Curtain*, 96
BROOKE, Arthur, 116
BRUANT, Aristide, 185
BÜCHNER, Georg, xvii, xviii, 21, 98–106, 118, 123, 154, 194, 209
    works by: *The Death of Danton*, xviii, 21, 98–106, 123; *Woyzeck*, 99, 123, 154
BUDDEN, Julian, works by: "The Two Toscas," 3
BYRON, George Gordon (Lord), 11

C

CALDÉRON, Pedro (de la Barca), works by: *Lady Goblin*, 175
CARPENTIER, Georges, 36
CHEKHOV, Anton, 89, 158
    works by: *The Three Sisters*, 87; *Uncle Vanya*, 86
CHIARO di Luna, 124
CLAUDEL, Paul, 81, 82, 195, 201–202
    works by: *Break of Noon*, 201–202; *The Exchange*, 81–82
COURTHS-MAHLER, Hedwig, 5, 116
CRAIG, Gordon, 90
CSOKOR, Franz Theodor, 167

D

DANTE, 24
DÄUBLER, Theodor works by: translation of *Le Paquebot Tenacity*, 158–160

DEFREGGER, Franz, 193
DENIKIN, Anton Ivanovich, 86
DEUTSCH, Isaak, 163, 178
DIETERLE, William, 173
DILTHEY, Wilhelm, 8
DOSTOEVSKY, Fyodor, 89, 184, 530
    works by: adaptation of
    The Brothers Karamazov, 87
DUHAMEL, Georges, 168, 169, 195
    works by: *The Light*,
    168–170
DURIEUX, Tilla, 161, 164
DUSE, Eleonora, 180
DYMOV, Ossip, 162, 178
    works by: *Der zinger fun
    zayn troyer*, 162

E

EDSCHMID, Kasimir, 528
EDTHOFER, Anton, 215
ERNST, Paul, 544
    Fanta, Walter, works by:
    Klagenfurter Ausgabe,
    xxxviii; Robert Musil
    Gesamtausgabe, xii, xiii, 13,
    35, 96, 189

F

FLAUBERT, Gustave, 120
FONTANE, Theodor, 11, 127, 151
    works by: *Awakening*, 151
FOREST, Karl, 130
FRISCH, Ephraim, xiv
FRONDAIE, Pierre, 43

G

GARDEN, Magda, 149
GAUGUIN, Paul, 162
GEYER, Siegfried, works by:
    Mary, 200
GLANZ, Egon, 83
GOETHE, Johann Wolfgang
    von, xxix, 11, 55, 57, 87, 91, 133,
    171, 172, 176, 453, 531
    works by: *Clavigo*, 171, 172,
    175; *Stella*, 175–177; *The
    Sorrows of Young Werther*,
    172
GORKY, Maxim, works by:
    The Night Asylum, 87–89
GREGOR, Nore, 168
GRILLPARZER, Franz, 121
GRÜNBAUM, Fritz, 184
GRÜNEWALD, Matthias, 143
GUILBERT, Yvette, 185–188
GÜNTHER, Carl, 209

H

HAGENBUND, Der, 124, 125
HARDT, Ludwig, 162
HAUPTMANN, Gerhart, 4, 13,
    99, 101, 138, 151, 152, 194
    works by: *Florian Geyer*,
    121; *Schluck and Jau*, 151
HEBBEL, Friedrich, III, 133, 205
HEINE, Heinrich, 162
HEINE, Thomas Theodor, 17
HERDER, Johann Gottfried, 57,
    58, 63

works by: *On the True Meaning of the Liberal Arts and Primary School Education*, 58
HERTERICH, Franz, 36, 43, 44
HEYSE, Paul, 4
HOFFMAN, E.T.A., 123
HOFMANNSTHAL, Hugo von, 43, 44, 175
works by: puppet adaptation of Caldéron's *Lady Goblin*, 175
HÖLLRIEGEL, Arnold, 530
HORKHEIMER, Max, xxv

I

IBSEN, Henrik, 6, 11, 81, 138, 139, 140, 141, 164, 206
works by: *Brand*, 138–145; *Hedda Gabler*, 5, 164; *The Master Builder*, 6

J

JESSNER, Leopold, iv, xvii, 138, 142–145

K

KAFKA, Franz, iii, 127
KAISER, Ernst, works by: translation (with Eithne Wilkins) of *The Man Without Qualities*, xxxi
KAISER, Georg, 7, 11, 127, 130, 165, 166, 213, 494
works by: *David and Goliath*, 130; *Court Clerk Krehler*, 11
KANT, Immanuel, 57, 59
KERR, Alfred, xi, xiv, 98
KIERKEGAARD, Søren, 139
KLITSCH, Wilhelm, 141
KOKOSCHKA, Oskar, 124
KORFF, Arnold, 210
KORTNER, Fritz, 142, 144
KRAUS, Karl, xii, 202
works by: *Dream Game*, 202; *Dream Theater*, 202

L

LAUBE, Heinrich Rudolf Konstanz, 20
LAUTENSACK, Heinrich, 109
LAZAR, Maria, works by: *The Hangman*, 78; *The Poisoning*, 79
LHERMAN, Jo, xvi, 218
LEIVIK, H., works by: *Schmattes*, 165–166
LESSING, Gotthold Ephraim, 147
LILIENCRON, Detlev von, 162
LION, Ferdinand, 195
LOSSEN, Lina, xvii, 173, 176
LÖWY, Siegfried, 214

M

Mach, Ernst, 512
Maeterlinck, Maurice, 11, 23, 90, 151, 169
 works by: *L'Intruse*, 151; *Wisdom and Fate*, 23
Makart, Hans, 183
Mann, Heinrich, 128, 524
Mann, Thomas, xi, xii
Marco Polo, 222
Marinetti, Filippo Tommaso, 84
Marlitt, E., 77, 149
Martin, Karlheinz, 215
Meister, Monika, works by: "Theater" in *Robert Musil Handbuch*, xxv
Mercier, Cardinal, 188
Mirsky, Mark, xxxviii
 works by: editor of *Fiction Magazine*
Moissi, Alexander, xvii, 21, 111–114, 115–122, 123, 162, 173
Molière, 27–129, 197
 works by: *Le Malade imaginaire*, 197; *The Miser*, 127–129
Molnár, Franz (Ferenc), 43, 76–78
 works by: *The Swan*, 76–78
Moscow Art Theater (MAT), iv, xvii, xxvii, xxxii, 86–93, 98, 106, 131–137, 145, 163, 178, 182
Müller, Hans, 23, 94

N

Nachbusch, Noe, 179
Nagonowski, Egon, 494, 510
Nestroy, Johann, works by: *Love Affairs and Wedding Bells*, 161
Nietzsche, Friedrich, xxiii, xxxvi, 34, 120, 139, 148, 151
Nemirovitsch-Dantschenko, Vladimir, 86, 90
Nübel, Birgit, xii, xxxviii
 works by: editor (with Norbert Christian Wolf) of *Robert Musil Handbuch*, xii, xxiii, xxv
Novalis, xxxvi

O

Offenbach, Jacques, 206
Orleska, Miriam, 180

P

Pabst, G.W., 78
Pallenberg, Max, 129
Pater, Walter, works by: *Studies in the History of the Renaissance*, xxxvi

PAULSEN, Friedrich, 59
PERUTZ, Leo, 530
PFOHLMANN, Oliver, works by: "Literatur und Theaterkritik" in *Robert Musil Handbuch*, xii, xiv
PIKE, Burton, xxxviii
works by: *Robert Musil: An Introduction*, xxi, xxxiv, xxxv; translation of *The Man Without Qualities*, xxxi
PIRANDELLO, Luigi, works by: *Six Characters in Search of an Author*, 203
PIRCHAN, Emil, 143
PITAVAL, François Gayot de, 97
POLGAR, Alfred, xi

R

RATHENAU, Walter, 521
REINHARDT, Max, xvii, 111, 171–174, 175–177, 494
REUMANN, Jakob, 83
REY, Étienne, works by: *Beautiful Women*, 177
RHODE, Alice, 210
RIGOLETTO, 128
ROGOWSKI, Christian, works by: *Implied Dramaturgy*, xxi, xxii, xxvi, xxxvi, 41, 494
ROLLAND, Romain, 158, 528
ROMAINS, Jules, works by: *Doctor Knock*, 195–199

ROTH, Marie-Louise, works by: *Gedanken und Dichtung*, "Musil als Kritiker," xi, xiv
RUSSIAN Cabaret, The, 181–184, 187

S

SARDOU, Victorien, 3, 220
works by: *La Tosca*, 3
SCHAUKAL, Richard, 119
SCHIELE, Egon, 124
SCHILLER, Friedrich, xxix, 2, 39, 55, 124, 531, 548
works by: *Letters Upon the Æsthetic Education of Mankind*, xxix, 55; *Wilhelm Tell*, 124
SCHMITZ, Siegfried, 162
SCHNITZLER, Arthur, 43, 44, 83, 84, 109, 119, 204–210, 218
works by: *Anatol*, 209; *Comedy of Seduction*, 204–210; *Comedy of Words*, 210; *Green Cockatoo*, 119; *La Ronde*, iv, 82, 83, 109
SCHOBER, Johannes, 83, 109
SCHÖNE, Albrecht, works by: "Über den Gebrauch des Konjunktivs bei Robert Musil"
SCHÖNHERR, Karl, 43, 156
SECOND School of Nancy, 197
SHAKESPEARE, William, xviii, xxix, 10, 40, 98, 99, 115–117, 120–121, 133, 142–145, 151, 152

works by: *Hamlet*, 28, 90, 113, 115; *Othello*, 21, 28, 120–121; *Richard III*, 142–145; *Romeo and Juliet*, 115–117

Shaw, George Bernard, xvii, xx, 3, 107–110, 111, 197, 211–215, 218, 219

works by: *Arms and the Man*, 107–110; *Major Barbara*, 211; *Saint Joan*, xx, 211–215

Sokel, Walter H., works by: *Anthology of German Expressionist Drama*, xviii–xix, xxvi

Stahl, E.L., works by: *Das englische Theater im 19. Jahrhundert*, 57

Stanislavski, Konstantin, iv, xvii, xxxii, 33, 86, 87, 90, 136, 144, 182, 183

Steinsieck, Annemarie, 215

Sternheim, Carl, 109, 127–130, 213

Streitler, Nicole, works by: *Musil als Kritiker*, 13

Strich, Walter, works by: "The Curse of the Objective Mind," 78

Strindberg, August, 146–148

works by: *The Father*, 146; *Miss Julie*, 146

Suarès, André, 195

Sudermann, Hermann, 2, 4, 5, 23, 26, 28, 29, 148

works by: *Morituri*, 3; *The Raschoffs*, 26, 28, 148–149

Surguchev, Ilya, works by: *Autumn Violins*, 136

T

Toller, Ernst, xxxiv, 189–194

works by: *Lame Man*, xxxiv, 189–194

Tolstoy, Leo, 111–112, 122

works by: *It's All His Fault*, 122; *The Light Shines in Darkness*, 111–112

U

Unruh, Fritz von, 4

V

Vanity Fair, 198

Viertel, Berthold, 202

Vildrac, Charles, 158–160, 195

works by: *Le Paquebot Tenacity*, 158–160

Vilna Troupe, 178–180

Voltaire, 153

W

Walser, Robert, iii

Wedekind, Franz, 109, 194, 200–201, 213, 218, 219, 494, 524

works by: *Solar Spectrum*, 200–201

WEDDERKOP, H., works by: "Expressionist Stage," 10

WEGENER, Paul, 26, 28, 147, 149

WERFEL, Franz, 11–12, 150–157
    works by: *Goat Song*, 11–12, 150–157; *The Mirror Man*, 11–12

WERNER-KAHLE, Hugo, 194

WIESE, L.V., works by: *Sociology of the School System*, 57

WILDE, Oscar, 189

WILDGANS, Anton, 13, 14, 17–19, 23, 156, 251, 253
    works by: *Cain*, 13; *Dies irae*, 18–19; "Harlequinade," 19; *Love*, 251; *Mid-Day*, 13

WILKINS, Eithne, works by: translation (with Ernst Kaiser) of *The Man Without Qualities*, xxxi

WOLF, Norbert Christian, works by: "Die Schwärmer (1921)," xxiii; editor (with Birgit Nübel) of *Robert Musil Handbuch*, xii, xiv, xxiii, xxv, xxxviii, xxxviii

Z

ZIEHRER, Karl Michael, works by: *Der Landstreicher*, 27

ZOLA, Emil, 148

COLOPHON

THEATER SYMPTOMS
was handset in InDesign CC.

The text & page numbers are set in *Adobe Jenson*.
The titles are set in *Arpona* by Felix Braden.

Book design & typesetting: Alessandro Segalini
Cover design: Genese Grill & Alessandro Segalini

Cover image: Robert Musil, Ea Allesch, Martha Musil, Franz Blei (kneeling), and unidentified Pierrot at Viennese Fasching Ball, from the Sammlung Corino (Bad Vilbel).

THEATER SYMPTOMS
is published by Contra Mundum Press.

Contra Mundum Press   New York · London · Melbourne

CONTRA MUNDUM PRESS

Dedicated to the value & the indispensable importance of the individual voice, to works that test the boundaries of thought & experience.

The primary aim of Contra Mundum is to publish translations of writers who in their use of form and style are *à rebours*, or who deviate significantly from more programmatic & spurious forms of experimentation. Such writing attests to the volatile nature of modernism. Our preference is for works that have not yet been translated into English, are out of print, or are poorly translated, for writers whose thinking & æsthetics are in opposition to timely or mainstream currents of thought, value systems, or moralities. We also reprint obscure and out-of-print works we consider significant but which have been forgotten, neglected, or overshadowed.

There are many works of fundamental significance to *Weltliteratur* (& *Weltkultur*) that still remain in relative oblivion, works that alter and disrupt standard circuits of thought — these warrant being encountered by the world at large. It is our aim to render them more visible.

For the complete list of forthcoming publications, please visit our website. To be added to our mailing list, send your name and email address to: info@contramundum.net

Contra Mundum Press
P.O. Box 1326
New York, NY 10276
USA

OTHER CONTRA MUNDUM PRESS TITLES

2012 *Gilgamesh*
      Ghérasim Luca, *Self-Shadowing Prey*
      Rainer J. Hanshe, *The Abdication*
      Walter Jackson Bate, *Negative Capability*
      Miklós Szentkuthy, *Marginalia on Casanova*
      Fernando Pessoa, *Philosophical Essays*
2013 Elio Petri, *Writings on Cinema & Life*
      Friedrich Nietzsche, *The Greek Music Drama*
      Richard Foreman, *Plays with Films*
      Louis-Auguste Blanqui, *Eternity by the Stars*
      Miklós Szentkuthy, *Towards the One & Only Metaphor*
      Josef Winkler, *When the Time Comes*
2014 William Wordsworth, *Fragments*
      Josef Winkler, *Natura Morta*
      Fernando Pessoa, *The Transformation Book*
      Emilio Villa, *The Selected Poetry of Emilio Villa*
      Robert Kelly, *A Voice Full of Cities*
      Pier Paolo Pasolini, *The Divine Mimesis*
      Miklós Szentkuthy, *Prae, Vol. 1*
2015 Federico Fellini, *Making a Film*
      Robert Musil, *Thought Flights*
      Sándor Tar, *Our Street*
      Lorand Gaspar, *Earth Absolute*
      Josef Winkler, *The Graveyard of Bitter Oranges*
      Ferit Edgü, *Noone*
      Jean-Jacques Rousseau, *Narcissus*
      Ahmad Shamlu, *Born Upon the Dark Spear*

2016	Jean-Luc Godard, *Phrases*
	Otto Dix, *Letters, Vol. 1*
	Maura Del Serra, *Ladder of Oaths*
	Pierre Senges, *The Major Refutation*
	Charles Baudelaire, *My Heart Laid Bare & Other Texts*
2017	Joseph Kessel, *Army of Shadows*
	Rainer J. Hanshe & Federico Gori, *Shattering the Muses*
	Gérard Depardieu, *Innocent*
	Claude Mouchard, *Entangled — Papers! — Notes*
2018	Miklós Szentkuthy, *Black Renaissance*
	Adonis & Pierre Joris, *Conversations in the Pyrenees*
2019	Charles Baudelaire, *Belgium Stripped Bare*
	Robert Musil, *Unions*
	Iceberg Slim, *Night Train to Sugar Hill*
	Marquis de Sade, *Aline & Valcour*
2020	*A City Full of Voices: Essays on the Work of Robert Kelly*
	Rédoine Faïd, *Outlaw*
	Zsuzsa Selyem, *It's Raining in Moscow*
	Carmelo Bene, *I Appeared to the Madonna*
	Dejan Lukić, *The Oyster*
	Paul Celan, *Microliths They Are, Little Stones*

SOME FORTHCOMING TITLES

Marguerite Duras, *The Truck*
Oğuz Atay, *While Waiting for Fear*

THE FUTURE OF KULCHUR
A PATRONAGE PROJECT

LEND CONTRA MUNDUM PRESS (CMP) YOUR SUPPORT

With bookstores and presses around the world struggling to survive, and many actually closing, we are forming this patronage project as a means for establishing a continuous & stable foundation to safeguard our longevity. Through this patronage project we would be able to remain free of having to rely upon government support &/or other official funding bodies, not to speak of their timelines & impositions. It would also free CMP from suffering the vagaries of the publishing industry, as well as the risk of submitting to commercial pressures in order to persist, thereby potentially compromising the integrity of our catalog.

CAN YOU SACRIFICE $10 A WEEK FOR KULCHUR?

For the equivalent of merely 2–3 coffees a week, you can help sustain CMP and contribute to the future of kulchur. To participate in our patronage program we are asking individuals to donate $500 per year, which amounts to $42/month, or $10/week. Larger donations are of course welcome and beneficial. All donations are tax-deductible through our fiscal sponsor Fractured Atlas. If preferred, donations can be made in two installments. We are seeking a minimum of 300 patrons per year and would like for them to commit to giving the above amount for a period of three years.

WHAT WE OFFER

Part tax-deductible donation, part exchange, for your contribution you will receive every CMP book published during the patronage period as well as 20 books from our back catalog. When possible, signed or limited editions of books will be offered as well.

WHAT WILL CMP DO WITH YOUR CONTRIBUTIONS?

Your contribution will help with basic general operating expenses, yearly production expenses (book printing, warehouse & catalog fees, etc.), advertising & outreach, and editorial, proofreading, translation, typography, design and copyright fees. Funds may also be used for participating in book fairs and staging events. Additionally, we hope to rebuild the *Hyperion* section of the website in order to modernize it.

From Pericles to Mæcenas & the Renaissance patrons, it is the magnanimity of such individuals that have helped the arts to flourish. Be a part of helping your kulchur flourish; be a part of history.

HOW

To lend your support & become a patron, please visit the subscription page of our website: contramundum.net/subscription

For any questions, write us at: info@contramundum.net

www.ingramcontent.com/pod-product-compliance
Lightning Source LLC
Chambersburg PA
CBHW031842220426
43663CB00006B/466